CZECHOSLOVAKIA BEFORE MUNICH

CZECHOSLOVAKIA BEFORE MUNICH

The German minority problem and British appeasement policy

J. W. BRUEGEL

CAMBRIDGE
AT THE UNIVERSITY PRESS · 1973

Published by the Syndics of the Cambridge University Press
Bentley House, 200 Euston Road, London NW1 2DB
American Branch: 32 East 57th Street, New York, N.Y.10022

Library of Congress Catalogue Card Number: 72-80589

ISBN: 0 521 08687 6

Printed in Great Britain
by Alden & Mowbray Ltd
at the Alden Press, Oxford

To the memory of

ELIZABETH WISKEMANN (1900–1971)

without whose encouragement,
advice and active help this book
could not have been written

CONTENTS

PREFACE

The purpose of this book is to tell the truth about a complicated problem. Having studied the English and French literature of the last decades on the problems of Central Europe, I managed to find among the large numbers of books devoted to that area only a single one dealing in a fundamental way with the question of Czechs and Germans living together in one country. The exception is Elizabeth Wiskemann's book *Czechs and Germans* (first published in 1938, reissued in 1967) which tries to analyse the complexities of that situation and the efforts of the German democratic parties in Czechoslovakia – until 1935 backed by the vast majority of the German electorate – to integrate the Germans fully into Czechoslovak democracy. Her book, however, ends some time before the disastrous developments of the summer and autumn of 1938 and obviously could not take into account the contents of the relevant diplomatic and other documents which became available only many years after the Second World War. Consequently, it was my aim to fill this gap and describe the attempts which were made to create a Czechoslovak State which would at one and the same time have fulfilled the Czechs' and Slovaks' desire for independence and have been a modern democracy in the Western style, treating all its citizens – among them more than three million Germans – with the same degree of justice.

To begin with I had to investigate whether in 1918 it would have been feasible and desirable to retain old Austria-Hungary as a territorial unit, but transforming it into a modern state by granting equal rights to Germans and Czechs, Hungarians and Poles alike, and therefore abolishing the previous German and Hungarian hegemony. I concluded that the question of desirability did not arise, because the preconditions for the unavoidable process of transformation simply did not exist. On the other hand, the Czechs and Slovaks could not in 1918 set up a viable independent state without the inclusion of the districts of Bohemia, Moravia and Silesia, at the time inhabited predominantly by Germans and one of the most highly industrialized regions of Europe. It was likewise in the interest of those Germans to remain linked with the Czechs in a state forming a reasonable economic unity. By embarking on a truly European policy, T. G. Masaryk, Czechoslovakia's first President, tried to overcome the contradiction between the desire of the Czechs and Slovaks to be undisputed masters in their own house and the necessity of conceding full ethnic justice to its German and other minorities.

Early hopes that he might succeed were later jeopardized by the results of the world economic crisis coupled with threatening signs of the seeming 'invincibility' of German National Socialism. Hitler was allowed to march from one success to another; he first solved the problem of mass unemployment and then implemented un-hampered his first bids for world domination. It is not surprising that the masses of the Sudeten Germans were enormously impressed and even mesmerized by the overwhelming achievements of a régime which for them was characterized not by arbitrary lawless-ness and dictatorship, but by the re-employment of millions of workers. Measured by this yardstick, the efforts of a small neigh-bouring state to come to grips with mass unemployment were bound to look pitiful. In spite of overwhelming odds, however, large numbers of Czechoslovak Germans did not despair of demo-cracy and demonstratively showed they preferred a modest existence in free and democratic Czechoslovakia to better living conditions in the Third Reich where freedom was suppressed. This book is meant as a tribute to those forgotten heroes of democracy's struggle against authoritarianism.

The book was first published in German in 1967 under the title *Tschechen und Deutsche 1918–1938* (Nymphenburger Verlagshand-lung, München) and was intended to acquaint the Germans with a period which had previously been presented to them almost entirely in distorted propaganda versions. In my forthcoming German book I also deal with the subsequent period 1939–45. The present English edition is by no means a literal translation of the German original. About half of the German text has been eliminated alto-gether, as it would have been of lesser interest to English readers.

But weighty additions give the English text quite a different emphasis. Since the publication of the original German edition the British 'fifty years' rule' has been replaced by one withholding Cabinet and other public papers from the eyes of the historians for a mere thirty years. This has enabled me to study and make use of Foreign Office and Cabinet papers for the crucial period during the 1930s when British policy aimed to avoid, or at least postpone, a second World War by appeasing the dictators. It has thus, for example, become possible to tell for the first time the amazing story of how a comparatively primitive political confidence-trickster like Konrad Henlein was for many years able to mislead and take advantage of one of the shrewdest British diplomats. I hope that this book, the first fully documented description of British appeasement policy in respect of Czechoslovakia will be regarded as contributing to a not inconsiderable extent to knowledge of contemporary history.

London   J.W.B.
January 1973

Place-names in Czech and German

Note: Czech names are used in the text, except in quotations from German diplomatic and similar documents

Aš	Asch
Brno	Brünn
Česká Lípa	Böhmisch-Leipa
České Budějovice	Budweis
Český Krumlov	Krummau
Cheb	Eger
Chomutov	Komotau
Děčín	Tetschen
Domažlice	Taus
Františkové Lázně	Franzensbad
Hlučín	Hultschin
Horní Litvinov	Oberleutensdorf
Jihlava	Iglau
Jirkov	Görkau
Kadaň	Kaaden
Karlovy Vary	Karlsbad
Krnov	Jägerndorf
Kroměříž	Kremsier
Lednice	Eisgrub
Liberec	Reichenberg
Litoměřice	Leitmeritz
Mariánské Lázně	Marienbad
Mikulov	Nikolsburg
Nová Bystřice	Neubistritz
Olomouc	Olmütz
Opava	Troppau
Ostrava, Moravská Ostrava	Ostrau, Mährisch-Ostrau
Podmokly	Bodenbach
Šternberk	Sternberg
Teplice-Šanov	Teplitz-Schönau
Ústí nad Labem	Aussig
Žatec	Saaz
Znojmo	Znaim

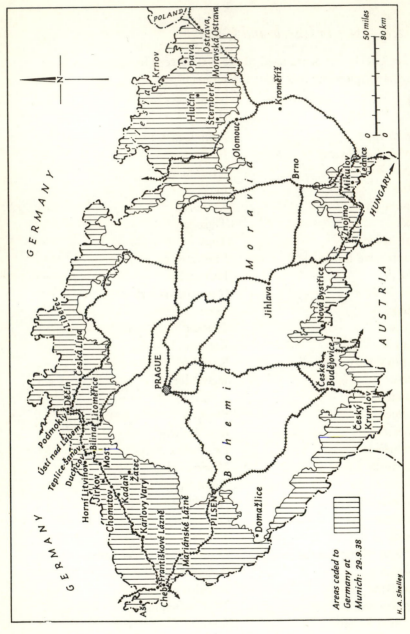

POLAND

GERMANY

Silesia

Krnov

Opava

Ostrava, Moravská Ostrava

Hlučín

Šternberk

Kroměříž

Olomouc

GERMANY

Liberec

Česká Lípa

Děčín

Podmokly

Ústí nad Labem

Teplice-Šanov

Duchcov

Litoměřice

Bílina

Horní Litvínov

Most

Jirkov

PRAGUE

Brno

Moravia

Znojmo

Mikulov

Lednice

HUNGARY

Chomutov

Kadaň

Žatec

Karlovy Vary

Jihlava

Nová Bystřice

Aš

Cheb

Františkové Lázně

Mariánské Lázně

PILSEN

Bohemia

Domažlice

České Budějovice

Český Krumlov

AUSTRIA

Areas ceded to
Germany at
Munich: 29.9.38

H. A. Shelley

50 miles
80 km
0

Western Czechoslovakia from 1918 to the Munich Agreement (September 1938)

1 COULD AUSTRIA-HUNGARY HAVE BEEN MADE VIABLE?

Any discussion of the German–Czech problem of the past, present or future must begin by considering whether the dissolution of Austria-Hungary could have been avoided and if so, whether it would have been desirable to avoid it. Was the multinational state stretching from Podmokly (Bodenbach) in the north to Kotor (Cattaro) in the south, from Feldkirch in the west to Cernauti (Czernowitz) in the east a suitable base for the erection of a democratic union of the peoples by which it was inhabited? Or was its fate to be 'the prison of the nationalities', the destruction of which was devoutly to be wished for so that its people could live in freedom?

Those who, as victims or at least as spectators, experienced the horrors first of the Nazi and then of the Communist dictatorship will perhaps feel amused when confronted by attempts to describe the Austro-Hungarian monarchy as 'the prison of the nationalities'. The *mot* ascribed to Jan Masaryk in the Second World War – 'What do we Czechs want? To be oppressed by the Habsburgs!' – does illustrate the difference between the active brutality of German Nazism and the, in general, merely passive and obstructive policy of the Habsburg monarchy. At the same time, however, it demonstrates only a preference for the lesser evil because the ideal was not attainable: after all, to quote Campbell-Bannerman, even 'good government is no substitute for self-government' and no nation wants to be oppressed, however benignly. And anyway, it was not really quite so benign.

To the Czechs, Slovaks, Slovenes, Croats, Poles, Italians and Romanians living in the Austro-Hungarian monarchy before 1914 no choice between lesser and greater evil presented itself. They considered themselves confronted by a system which appeared to them to be the greatest evil imaginable and the sole obstacle to the achievement of their happiness.

1

Czechoslovakia before Munich

The position of the Czechs

The Czechs, who formed a two-thirds majority in Bohemia and Moravia and a considerable minority in Austrian Silesia, did not merely feel averse to the régime; they also suffered from the non-existence of another State which could have fulfilled their aspirations. To achieve independence in defiance of Austria was beyond their wildest dreams and even if this dream had been realized, it would have remained incomplete because the Hungarian régime would never have allowed the kindred Slovaks to secede. The fate of the Slovaks, i.e. their complete national extinction through Magyarization, was very much more unfavourable than that of the Czechs who to some extent had long been able to fight back. However, the general hopelessness of the situation led to two contrasting reactions on their part. While the majority of Czechs veered more and more towards outright rejection of the existing State without as yet any concrete alternative, the politicians, with the tacit support of the electorate, tried to continue a more positive approach by exploiting all the possibilities still remaining open to them. These plans centred round the attempt, after Francis Joseph had broken his promise to follow up his coronation in Budapest as king of Hungary by one in Prague as king of Bohemia, to obtain recognition for the so-called 'Bohemian States Right' (*Staatsrecht*) which would have given the 'Czech Lands' – Bohemia, Moravia and Silesia – a special position within Austria and the Czechs the leadership in these areas.

There had of course been a great variety of proposals for constitutional reform within Austria or Austria-Hungary with the aim of transforming a country generally suffering under injustice into one with at least ethnic justice.[1] They all had one thing in common: none could be based on the Austrian Constitution of 1867 which had assured all nationalities inhabiting Austria of their equal status when in fact no attempt was ever made to translate this praiseworthy precept into practice. It is quite true that old Austria did not know the legal concept of a 'state language', but in actual fact German, which was spoken at home by at most a third of the total

[1] A well-documented summary of the so-called 'Compromise negotiations' can be found in the essay by Suzanne Konirsh, 'Constitutional Aspects of the Struggle between Germans and Czechs in the Austro-Hungarian Monarchy', in *Journal of Modern History* (Chicago), September 1955, pp. 231–62.

population, was the only generally accepted medium of communication. In the Vienna *Reichsrat* (Parliament) every deputy was allowed to speak in his own tongue but only speeches made in German were recorded. Such restrictions were perhaps not considered too irksome in the nineteenth century when virtually all Czech deputies came from the educated and literate classes and spoke German, but when, around the turn of the century, workers and artisans started to be elected, many of these new national representatives were thus deprived even of the chance of having their speeches taken down. The most impassioned indictments of Austrian semi-absolutism, even the final renunciation of allegiance to the State in 1918, had to be uttered in German if they were to make any impact.

The Brno Nationalities' Programme

To the rising Socialist movement belongs the credit of having first tried to eliminate the national squabbles which obstructed all progress. The driving motive was not merely the inherent wish to have justice done and the despair about the petty quarrels which prevented reform, but perhaps even more the fear lest the 'Austrian International', represented in the trade union movement and the Austrian Social-Democratic Party, should collapse unless a solution of the national question acceptable to all the nationalities could be found.

The deeply felt Social-Democratic desire to overcome the difficulties resulting from the multinational character of the State found its most concrete expression in the Programme of Nationalities accepted by the joint party conference at Brno (Brünn) in 1899 after a speech by the German–Bohemian workers' leader Josef Seliger.[1] It called for the reconstruction of Austria as a democratic federation of nations, the break-up of the existing provinces and the creation as far as possible of homogeneous, autonomous areas with

[1] Ludwig Brügel, *Geschichte der österreichischen Sozialdemokratie* (Vienna 1923), IV, 339. Otto Bauer, *Die Nationalitätenfrage und die Sozialdemokratie* (Vienna 1907), p. 527. An excellent modern account of the background and scope of the Brno programme is given by Hans Mommsen in his work *Die Sozialdemokratie und die Nationalitätenfrage im Habsburgischen Vielvölkerstaat* (Vienna 1963). Mommsen rightly attributes more importance to the programme as 'an important means for the internal integration of the party rather than as a weapon against bourgeois nationalist agitation' (p. 8).

suitable protection for the minorities left within them. It also rejected the German Nationalists' demand for a 'state language' by which they of course meant the legalization and perpetuation of the existing ascendancy of German.

This was no doubt a far-sighted concept of an ethnically equitable basis about which German and Czech Social Democrats could, perhaps for the last time, agree. Yet the authors of this plan did not abandon themselves to any illusion of an early fulfilment. At that time social democracy was of far greater interest to the secret police than to politicians, and so the contents of the Brno programme were scarcely noticed outside the narrow circle of those who helped to design it. For the Social Democrats themselves it had anyway been rather a question of defining the problem for their own ranks and above all of maintaining at least the outward appearance of a unified stand by Socialists of all Austrian nationalities. And here the main defect of this and similar programmes becomes obvious: it could never be anything more than the 'Austrian nationalities', for Hungary could not be included. Given the absolute constitutional supremacy of Hungary over its own 'subject' peoples within the Austro-Hungarian monarchy, this defect was irremediable, but it sapped the vitality of the Brno Nationalities' Programme and all similar projects. Could the Czechs seriously be expected to contemplate a solution which did not allow the cognate Slovaks to join them but left them to the fate of the other non-Hungarian people within the confines of Hungary, i.e. deprivation of their ethnic character?

Independently of the Brno programme the Austrian Socialist Karl Renner had skilfully elaborated a similar plan for rebuilding Austria as a democratic and ethnically equitable state with a system of national self-government, joining for the first time the idea of territorial autonomy to the principle of personal autonomy vested in the members of national minorities. Even Renner, however, did not dare advance the suggestion of extending his system to Hungary where Slovaks, Ruthenians, Germans, Romanians, Serbs, Croats and – in Fiume (Rijeka) – Italians lived with practically no redress against the despotism of their Hungarian overlords.

Renner's reputation as the Socialists' main spokesman for the nationality question was soon to be contested by Otto Bauer, his junior by eleven years. Until the latter's death, the two were to remain involved in ideological combat conducted both in public and in private. For a 25-year-old, Bauer's first publication, *Die National-itätenfrage und die Sozialdemokratie* (The problems of the Nationalities and Social Democracy), showed astonishing maturity and boldness of conception. He avoided coming to grips with the Brno programme (which he later dismissed with the terse comment 'It was an illusion'),[1] neither did he attack Renner openly, but many of his ideas were utterly novel, even revolutionary. Thus he rejected the concept of a union of nations – Renner's favourite idea – and proclaimed that the end of national strife would be brought about by proletarian socialism 'which unites every nation in an autonomous State'.[2]

Other authors, too, tried to find a solution. In 1904 Richard Charmatz expressed his belief that 'Austria's future must be as a federal State of democratic nationalities, joined to Hungary under one monarch'.[3] He was in favour of the autonomous territorial division of Austria as in the Brno programme.

A Romanian from Transylvania who at the turn of the century lived in Germany proposed a solution which in certain respects was based on Renner's ideas, but, unlike Charmatz, tacitly ignored Renner's decisive avowal of democracy as the essential prerequisite of all reforms: Aurel Popovici, whose book *Die Vereinigten Staaten von Grossösterreich* (The United States of Greater Austria) was but a naive and reactionary appeal[4] to the Habsburg dynasty to split Austria-Hungary – Hungary was to be included – into fifteen regions by way of a *coup d'état*. It appears that Popovici was mainly concerned to see Hungary limited to the territory predominantly inhabited by Hungarians, but Francis Joseph lacked both the energy and the power to put such a programme into practice.

Serious consideration was not given to any of these plans. Francis Joseph and the ruling classes realized, perhaps more clearly than

[1] *Victor Adlers Aufsätze, Reden und Briefe*, vol. 6 (Vienna 1929) (preface by Otto Bauer). See also Bauer's *Nationalitätenfrage*, p. 355.
[2] Bauer, ibid. p. 526.
[3] Richard Charmatz, *Der demokratisch-nationale Bundesstaat Österreich* (Frankfurt 1904), pp. 6, 46.
[4] In his heavily anti-semitic book Popovici acknowledges himself to be an admirer of Houston Stewart Chamberlain's racial theories.

they would have been willing to admit, that any fundamental attempt to reorganize the state could only end in its destruction and that the only chance of continued existence for the unwanted multinational community lay in 'muddling through', by making minor and unavoidable makeshift concessions to the spirit of the times. In the struggle for universal suffrage in the early years of this century the non-German nationalities of Austria fought side by side with the Social Democrats, the only party in the German camp unreservedly in favour of reform. Helped by the mood created by the Russian rising of 1905, Austrian Social Democracy succeeded in forcing the Emperor to concede universal suffrage, which did not, however, make Austria a democratic country.[1]

German fears of democracy

Predominantly Czech towns such as Budějovice (Budweis), Olomouc (Olmütz) and Moravská Ostrava (Mährisch-Ostrau) were administered wholly by Germans, and despite all constitutional promises, in Brno which was at least half Czech there was until 1918 not a single Czech local councillor. In Moravia, with its large Czech majority, the Germans were ready to come to an agreement with the Czechs only on condition[2] that 'what is German today, remains German'. The injustice perpetrated in Brno, Olomouc and Ostrava and even more so in those provincial towns which were almost entirely Czech and all of which were exclusively under German administration, was thus to be rendered permanent.

The nationalist squabbles had, of course, their root in social questions. It was a sort of class struggle – not between exploiters and exploited, but still between a privileged caste and those, who, by destroying these privileges, wanted to obtain justice. Simply by having the 'right' native language, the Germans had an important advantage, primarily of course in selection for public jobs. To learn

---

[1] After the electoral reform of 1907 one deputy was allotted to every 38,000 Italians, 40,000 Germans, 50,000 Slovenes, 52,000 Poles, 55,000 Croats and 55,000 Czechs and only one to 210,000 Ruthenians. (Cf. Karl Braunias, *Die Fortentwicklung des altösterreichischen Nationalitätenrechts nach dem Kriege*, Vienna 1938, p. 11.)

[2] Josef Kolejka, 'Moravský Pakt z roku 1905' (The Moravian Pact of 1905), *Československý časopis historický* (Czechoslovak Historical Journal) (Prague), 1956, p. 598.

Czech was a demand utterly irreconcilable with the national dignity of the German overlord. Zealously the Germans defended their time-honoured prerogative not to have to learn the despised vernacular, simply by forbidding any attempt to introduce procedural Czech. They gave no thought to the fact that their intransigence was destroying the possibility of peaceful co-existence within the state.

Czech politics in old Austria

The ordinary Czech people had by that time abandoned any hope of coming into their own in Austria; wherever possible they simply ignored the state. This negative attitude was not shared by the politicians, among whom the sagacious T. G. Masaryk, who practically formed a one-man party and was therefore under no tactical obligations, still expressed the hope in 1909 that it might yet be possible to arrive at a satisfactory solution within the confines of the Austrian empire.[1] And Edvard Beneš' doctoral thesis, which he wrote in Paris at the age of 24, rested on a similar premise.[2] His next work, a propaganda pamphlet which also appeared eight years later in Paris, already showed in its title – 'Détruisez l'Autriche-Hongrie!' – the change of heart which had taken place in the meantime.

František Palacký, the nineteenth-century Czech historian and politician, is famous for his often-quoted statement that Austria would have had to be invented had it not already existed. What is generally overlooked is that this was not meant as a defence of the existing state of affairs but rather as an expression of the hope that the Habsburg monarchy, detached from the German Bund (the mid-nineteenth-century precursor of the Reich), would create a just order for its non-German majority too. At the Kroměříž (Kremsier) diet of 1848 Palacký had submitted a proposal[3] to split up Austria, which at that time still included Hungary, into eight regions, one of which would have contained the Czechs and

[1] Victor S. Mamatey, *The United States and East Central Europe 1914–18. A Study in Wilsonian Diplomacy and Propaganda* (Princeton 1957), p. 18.

[2] Edvard Beneš, *Le problème Autrichien et la Question Tchèque. Études sur les luttes politiques des nationalités slaves en Autriche* (Paris 1908).

[3] A. J. P. Taylor, *The Habsburg Monarchy 1809–1918* (London 1948), p. 67.

7

Slovaks: the constitutional union of these two peoples was thus not an invention of 1918. Palacký's comforting valediction to his nation, uttered in 1867 when he had become disillusioned and resigned, is far less frequently remembered: 'We existed before Austria, and we shall continue to exist after Austria.'

Even Masaryk, a declared opponent of romantic Slav nationalism, had to reconsider his views in the light of experience (Beneš was at that time not yet engaged in active politics). It was above all moral indignation which made him despair of a future within Austria: his indignation at the Austrian annexation of Bosnia and Hercegovina (1908) and at the obdurately anti-Slav policy which the Vienna government pursued during the Balkan wars (1912/13).

The Moravian Compromise

All negotiations aiming at a modicum of ethnic justice were condemned to failure through the purblind refusal of the German ruling parties to abandon something they had come to regard as their 'German heritage' (*Deutscher Besitzstand*). While it is true that Austrian governments repeatedly included Czech ministers who helped to spread Czech influence within their sphere of authority, it is equally a fact that in Bohemia and Moravia the most elementary Czech political grievances could often not be aired: a *rapprochement* between the two nationalities remained as far away as ever. Because of continual obstruction the Bohemian diet – a thoroughly undemocratic body anyway, in which the Germans insisted on a majority quite out of proportion to their numerical strength in the country – was replaced by an even less democratic appointed administrative committee. It was only in Moravia that a ray of hope appeared when, after many fruitless discussions, the so-called Moravian Compromise (*Ausgleich*) was reached in 1905. While it did not open an era of joint reconstruction work, as had been hoped, it did at least blunt the edge of the bitterness. It was adopted in a similar form in 1910 in the eastern province of Bukovina, but the Moravian arrangement could not really form the prototype for the solution of all nationality problems, for, in the words of A. J. P. Taylor:[1] 'the Moravian compromise certainly showed how two peoples of different nationality could live together in the same

[1] Ibid. p. 200.

8

province; it did not show how two nations could settle their conflicting *historical* claims'.

Until 1905 there had been a German majority in the Moravian
diet although in the province as a whole the Czechs formed nearly
70 per cent of the population. In the course of their efforts to stave
off the inroads of universal suffrage the German and Czech right-
wing parties came to an agreement by which the Czechs were to
be guaranteed 73 seats to the Germans' 40 – still a disproportionately
high number of the latter. Moreover, since important changes were
dependent on a two-thirds majority in the diet, the Germans
retained an effective veto. The diet was based on national constitu-
encies but their *raison d'être* was a purely electoral one and there
was in no sense an element of national autonomy. The electorate
was restricted in its choice of representatives to those of their
registered nationality, so that for instance Czechs had to vote for a
Czech candidate.

This system of registration by nationality might have represented
a form of real progress if the electors had indeed been free to choose
the nationality in which they wished to be included. In practice,
however, this was done 'from above', and many Czechs found
themselves included in the German registers. One must therefore
be wary of overrating the Moravian Compromise. In Bohemia,
where the Germans were comparatively stronger and therefore
less anxious to have their influence constitutionally safeguarded,
all attempts to alleviate the bitterness between the nationalities
by adopting the Moravian procedure failed. Still, this compromise
remained, as it were, an oasis in the desert of nationalist squabbles
which for example effectively prevented the Czechs from obtaining
a second university, thanks to the resistance of the municipal
authorities of Brno, even after the Vienna government had conceded this demand. Until 1918 therefore, six million Czechs had
to remain content with one university while slightly over nine
million Germans in Austria had five. Each of the German colleges
of higher technology in Prague and Brno had only one Czech
equivalent, although there were four times as many Czech students
as German ones (8,000 compared with 2,000). Up to 1918 there
had been in Bohemia 81 German grammar schools compared with
90 Czech ones, and 35 German technical colleges in Bohemia with

12 in Moravia, as against 26 Czech ones in Bohemia and only 6 in Moravia.[1] It is significant that one of the critics – albeit a belated one – of the German policy of 'what we have, we hold' was a historian who later acquired renown as a prominent Nazi official: Professor Josef Pfitzner[2] admitted that

Germans in many cases refused to understand that all these national transfers favouring the Czechs were simply expressions of a natural and organic development which might be delayed but not stopped...The majority of Sudeten Germans defended to the bitter end their claim to leadership and to German supremacy in Austria.

The outbreak of the First World War

As long as there was peace the Czechs contented themselves with by-passing as far as possible the existence of the Austrian State and demonstrating their solidarity with the anti-Austrian Serbs. The outbreak of the war in 1914 inevitably led to more active manifestations of hostility, though equally inevitably Czech anti-Habsburg resistance had its ups and downs according to the progress of the war. It gained strength as long as the threat of a Russian invasion hung over Austria, when hopes were set upon the Czar's liberating mission – a hope not shared by Masaryk or the Czech left wing. It flagged after the Russians had been driven out of Galicia in May 1915 and large areas of pre-war Russia came under German and Austro-Hungarian occupation. Masaryk and Beneš had gone abroad to stimulate the interest, particularly of France, Britain and America, in the Czech question, of which little enough was known in the West. In Austria a state of emergency had been proclaimed, civil liberties suspended and Parliament prorogued.

Whole Czech army units, such as Prague's own No. 28 Infantry Regiment, had gone over to the Russians. The German Nationalists, pleased to see Austria at long last playing the rôle they had always wanted her to play, a helpless adjunct of the German Reich, dependent upon 'big brother's' military aid, were only too eager to pour oil on the flames. Friedrich Naumann's book *Mitteleuropa*, in which the author envisaged Central Europe under German military

---

[1] Speech by Otakar Srdinko in Prague Parliament, 10 July 1920, *Stenographic minutes of the sessions of the National Assembly of the Czechoslovak Republic* (hereafter *Parliamentary Minutes*), p. 197.
[2] Josef Pfitzner, *Sudetendeutsche Geschichte* (Liberec 1935), p. 54.

hegemony, threw light onto the dark background where the schemes were hatched for a *coup d'état* to ensure that the Germans remained supreme in Austria.

The fate which the extreme German nationalists planned for the non-Germans in a victorious post-war Austria can be seen in a memorandum called 'Easter Demands' (*Osterbegehrschrift*)[1] published in March 1916. Slav numerical predominance was to be further curtailed by cutting away not only Galicia, but Bukovina and Dalmatia as well, from central parliamentary representation. German was to be the official language throughout: even in Prague Czech could only be used in the lower courts and no longer in appeals to the higher ones. 'Wherever there now exist more favourable provisions for the use of the German language, these will remain in force.' Bohemia was to be split up: not however into a German and a Czech half but into 'a German and a bi-lingual administrative area'. In the German-speaking part of Bohemia 'only German officials may be employed': there was no question, naturally, of an analogous provision for the Czech parts. In the field of education the 'Easter Demands' stipulated that 'the State will have to build German elementary schools in multi-lingual districts wherever actual necessity or the public interest call for them. The number of non-German grammar schools in the multi-lingual areas is to be kept to a minimum and no new non-German universities are to be created.'

But all these proud nationalist pipe-dreams evaporated as the war situation became gloomier for the Central Powers. Francis Joseph had died in November 1916 and his well-meaning but feeble successor Charles panicked, hesitating between extremes of policy as it became increasingly obvious that the tide was turning against him. In order to appease the Czechs he released their leaders Karel Kramář and Alois Rašín who had been sentenced to death and subsequently reprieved to serve long sentences. The Germans, angered by this 'weakness', were to be mollified by the creation of a separate province of 'German-Bohemia'. To obtain peace he started

---

[1] *Osterbegehrschrift* (Easter Demands), *Forderungen der Deutschen Österreichs zur Neuordnung nach dem Kriege* (Basel 1916). (Extracts printed by Josef Redlich, *Oesterreichische Politik und Verwaltung im Weltkrieg* (Vienna 1925), pp. 254–5.)

secret negotiations with France behind the back of his German ally by acknowledging the justice of the French claim to Alsace-Lorraine. He denied his moves when they became known and finally had to suffer the word 'liar' thrown at his foreign minister by Clemenceau. In August 1918 when everything was crumbling away, Charles decided to throw in his lot unreservedly with the Germans in Germany and in his empire by trying to implement the plans for splitting up Bohemia into two parts – without consulting the Czechs. Needless to say, all these gyrations helped neither to calm the Germans nor to win over the Czechs.

For a long time the elected representatives of the Czech people had to tread warily. While the outcome of the war remained in doubt they tried to stave off persecution and above all reprisals for the activities of the Czech leaders abroad by presenting declarations of loyalty to the Habsburg monarchy. This, however, could not go on after the Vienna Parliament was at long last recalled in May 1917; neither did they need to, for a public forum was now available to the Czechs again. A joint statement by the Czech parties called for a Czechoslovak State, although with the face-saving proviso that this should still be within the Austrian Empire.[1] By January 1918, in the 'Epiphany Declaration',[2] it was no longer considered necessary to keep up this pious pretence. And in the Vienna Parliament on 2 October 1918, in the name of all Czech parties, František Staněk renounced his nation's allegiance to Austria: henceforth only orders issued by the Government in Exile recognized by the Entente would be obeyed.[3]

What was the attitude of the German ruling classes in those critical months? With very few exceptions, its blind downhill rush would have done credit to the Gadarene swine. Almost to the very end it kept up its clamour for the 'German state language', a demand which, since German was practically the official language anyway, could only mean that they were determined to stamp supremacy on to the country by law. The German Nationalists were unable to see the

[1] Emil Strauss, *Die Entstehung der Tschechoslowakischen Republik* (Prague 1935), p. 189.
[2] Bauer, *Die Österreichische Revolution* (Vienna 1923) (new edition 1965), p. 30. Text printed in Strauss, *Entstehung*, pp. 197–200.
[3] Strauss, ibid. pp. 250–1.

writing on the wall, however gigantic the letters, even as late as September 1918, only a few days before even Ludendorff insisted on an immediate armistice. Rudolf Heine, one of their members of Parliament, cheerfully announced to a meeting in Northern Bohemia[1] that 'assurances of the continuation of the German policy had been demanded from, and obtained by, the Austrian Minister–President Hussarek', and Heine's Styrian colleague Raimund Neunteufel was to press similar untimely demands upon Hussarek even later:[2] 'On 17 September we called on Hussarek, whom we particularly reproached with regard to the Slovenes...We demanded the strictest prohibition of meetings...Above all he was enjoined not to make concessions of any kind to the Slovenes.'

The blindness of the German nationalistic parties, against which the more reasonable Christian-Social and Agrarian parties could not prevail, did not of course mean that Czech policy on the other hand invariably represented the acme of wisdom. But there is all the difference in the world between the attitude of those who obstruct the rise of an emergent nation and the struggle of the latter for its rights. In the wake of this process there were occurrences in Europe in 1918, and there are such occurrences now in Asia and Africa, which do not always appear reasonable. They are, however, the inevitable concomitants of an historical development which it would be senseless to oppose.

Understandably enough, the German Social Democrats in Bohemia, Moravia and Silesia became more worried about their own prospects as the war drew towards its close. The German Socialists in Bohemia convened a conference in Prague at which Karl Renner was asked to speak.[3] A resolution was carried calling for the autonomy of all the Austrian nationalities in the form of a 'free community of nations having equal rights which is the only guarantee for their own security as for that of the existence of the State as a whole'. Even more outspoken in their anxiety were the speakers at the first joint meeting of the German Social Democrats of Bohemia, Moravia and Silesia on 16 September 1917 at Brno.

[1] *Prager Tagblatt*, Evening edition, 4 September 1918.
[2] Paul Molisch (ed.), *Briefe zur deutschen Politik in Oesterreich von 1848–1918* (Vienna 1934), p. 394.
[3] *Bohemia* (Prague), 11 June 1918.

Here a last attempt was made to save what remained by reviving the principles of the Nationalities' Programme, first enunciated in that city eighteen years earlier. In the meantime it had become a dead letter for the Czech Social Democrats. On the basis of the old programme the German Social Democrats hoped to arrive at a compromise, giving freedom to the Czechs without compelling purely German districts to come under Czech control. The voice of reason speaks from the resolution carried at the 1917 conference, the last paragraph of which at least deserves to be retrieved from oblivion:[1]

The German workers of Bohemia, Moravia and Silesia believe that no other policy is worthy of the German nation or would in the long run serve its interests but one of equal rights, of democracy, of the autonomy of all nations of the Monarchy and of proportional participation in the rights and duties which are the responsibility of all.

But even the German Social-democrats of the monarchy soon ceased to believe that somehow the programme of 1899 could regain its magic in 1917. When he returned from his Russian prisoner-of-war camp Otto Bauer considered:[2]

If we wanted...to prepare the Party spiritually for its task in the approaching revolution, we would have to eliminate the effect of Renner's theory of the necessary superiority of the 'supra-national state', to educate the masses in the belief in the unconditional recognition of the right to self-determination, to overcome the influence of the Brno nationalities programme of 1899 and to go back to the old tradition of republican democracy: The task of the Austrian revolution was the dissolution of the Austrian State itself and the erection of free national States on its ashes.

Emperor Charles's Manifesto of 16 October 1918 'To my loyal Austrian peoples', in which he promised a reconstruction of Austria (Hungary was still expressly excluded) as a community of free self-governing nations fifteen or even ten years earlier would have been heralded as a momentous event: now it fizzled out without any impact at all, hardly even noticed by those to whom it was addressed. It was far too late: the military defeat had by now set its seal on the fate of the Habsburg Empire. But the military collapse was only the last link in the long chain leading to, and not the cause of, the

---

[1] *Arbeiter-Zeitung* (Vienna), 17 and 19 September 1917, *Parteikonferenz der Sudetenländer, abgehalten am 16 September 1917 in Brünn* (Brno 1917).

[2] Bauer, *Österreichische Revolution*, p. 62.

dissolution of the monarchy. Victor Adler, the Social-Democrat leader, pointed this out in the Vienna Reichsrat on 3 October 1918.[1]

Even if there were a change in the fortunes of war, old Austria could not be saved. The disintegration of Austria or the realization of its disintegration goes back much further than the reverses which have hit the Central Powers...The disintegration has long been latent and the war has only brought to the surface what was already in existence.

Reading the war memoirs of Masaryk or Beneš,[2] one would come away with the impression that the break-up of the Austro-Hungarian monarchy was almost entirely due to the influence of the émigré politicians on the Entente, after the latter had buried its hopes of detaching the 'lesser evil', Austria-Hungary, from Germany, and adopted the views of the exiles. It is understandable that Masaryk and Beneš, in their accounts to their nation, should have reported their activities abroad with some pride. But when Wilson, Clemenceau and Lloyd George, after much deliberation, made the war aims of the émigrés their own, it was not so much because of the émigrés' advice but because the historical development, which had by-passed the Habsburg State, had been recognized.

[1] *Victor Adlers Aufsätze, Reden und Briefe*, vol. 9 (Vienna 1929), p. 253.
[2] T. G. Masaryk *The Making of a State, Memoirs and Observations 1914–18* (London 1927), Edvard Beneš, *My War Memoirs* (London 1928).

2 THE END OF THE OLD ERA – 1918–19

On 28 October 1918 the representatives of the Czech political parties, united from right to left in the *Národní Výbor* (National Committee), took over power in Prague in a bloodless revolution. The Czechoslovak Republic was born. It claimed sovereignty over the whole territory of Bohemia, Moravia and Silesia, where, mostly in the border regions, more than three million Germans lived. How did the Czechs justify this claim and how did the Germans react to it?

From the very beginning the new Czechoslovak Government regarded two things as indispensable: the maintenance of the unity of the 'Czech lands' and the addition of the Slovaks. As early as October 1914, in a discussion at Rotterdam with Professor Seton-Watson, about which the latter reported to London, Masaryk had declared his aim to be the unification of Bohemia, Moravia and Silesia with Slovakia. In Silesia, Masaryk was willing to make territorial concessions, but Northern Bohemia was indispensable for the new State. Masaryk afterwards returned to Prague which he was to leave for the duration of the war in December 1914. In a memorandum prepared for the British Foreign Secretary, Sir Edward Grey,[1] Masaryk refers to the apparent contradiction between the ideal of self-determination to which his people aspired and the desire to incorporate large numbers of non-Czechs:

First, though we advocate the principle of nationality, we wish to retain our German minority. It seems to be a paradox, but it is on the principle of nationality that we retain our German minority. Bohemia is a quite unique example of a mixed country; in no country are two nationalities so intermixed and interwoven, so to say, as in Bohemia. Between the Germans and Italians, for instance, the ethnographical frontier is simple, sharply cut; it is not so in Bohemia – in a great many places and in almost all the cities we have Bohemian [i.e. Czech], or German minorities.

[1] R. W. Seton-Watson, *Masaryk in England* (Cambridge 1943), p. 128.

16

The end of the old era – 1918–19

Masaryk's book *The New Europe*, written in 1916 without the aid of source material, was intended to serve his propaganda campaign. It hence betrays a certain superficiality of reasoning unusual in so penetrating an author. He resolves the complex problem into the simple question: What would be fairer[1] – to keep over nine million Czechs and Slovaks under German rule or three million Germans under Czechoslovak rule? The answer to this question, as posed, is obvious enough, but Masaryk's ideal, which he so often propounded, was after all that no people should rule over another.

At any rate, it is possible to deduce from these statements the thesis, however vaguely formulated, that self-determination can only be meaningful if the State which is based upon it is economically viable. Setting aside conditions in Moravia and Silesia, where there was hardly a homogeneous German settlement of any size, Bohemia, with its predominantly Czech agricultural centre and mainly German industrial periphery, was an economic unit which could only be split up for reason of nationalist obstinacy on one side or on the other at the cost of great and useless sacrifices.

While on 28 October 1918 some Czech politicians in Prague took over authority from the agents of the dying Habsburg monarchy, others in Geneva were meeting their émigré colleagues for the first time. The most prominent of these was the new Foreign Minister Edvard Beneš. Karel Kramář, who had been sentenced to death in 1916 on a trumped-up charge of high treason and later reprieved, was hurriedly provided with a passport by the Vienna authorities so that he could take part in the meeting. In his memoirs Beneš describes these negotiations as follows:[2]

The Prague delegates also laid emphasis on the question of the Germans in Bohemia. It was recognised that in this respect we must proceed cautiously so as not to create any prejudice for ourselves when vindicating the historical frontiers of the Czech territories. We therefore unanimously passed a resolution that the definitive government should include one German as a regional Minister without Portfolio.

[1] T. G. Masaryk, *The New Europe (The Slav Standpoint)* (London 1918), p. 53. In his memoirs Masaryk has repeated this view in a much less objectionable form: 'The question arises whether it is fairer that a fragment of the German people should remain in a non-German State or that the whole Czechoslovak people should live in a German State?' (Masaryk, *Making of a State*, p. 386.)
[2] Beneš, *My War Memoirs*, p. 445.

17

Masaryk comments in his memoirs[1] on this decision: 'In a democracy it is obviously the right of every party to share in the administration of the State as soon as it has recognised the policy of the State and the State itself.'

The Geneva resolution, which incidentally was never implemented, may not even remotely have met the exigencies of the situation, but it shows that there was no intention of disfranchising or otherwise oppressing the German population.

The first session of the provisional Parliament, composed of nominated Czech and Slovak members, took place on 14 November 1918 in Prague. In his opening speech the president of the assembly, the Czech Social Democrat František Tomášek, said[2]

When I greet these brothers of ours (the Slovaks)...I cannot fail to note that the representatives of our German fellow-citizens are still absent from our midst. It would be pointless to invite or lure them here. Not our words, but our actions will persuade them that they have no cause to fear the future. Let us complete the great work of democracy by constructing our political life on the basis of true liberty, let our laws and our whole system be imbued with the spirit of progress and let us thus build up our country as the model home for all. I am convinced that the time is not far distant when they too will find the way to join us in the common task.

In the same session Karel Kramář, the first Premier, introduced his Government. Understandably, he discussed the German problem at some length in his speech. To the Germans, who so far had not been able to make up their minds to join the Czechoslovak representatives but who, he had no doubt, would eventually find their way to them, he promised equality of rights and he expressed the hope that they would soon realize the need for co-operation. But at the same time have gave a warning that he was determined not to permit any dismemberment of the country:

In the name of the first Government of the free Czechoslovak Republic I am able to declare here that the German people living within the borders of our State need not harbour the least fear for their national development. Faithful to our own past and our democratic traditions we shall put no obstacle in our fellow-citizens' path towards the fulfilment of their cultural and linguistic aspirations, provided they loyally recognise the State. It is true that our State will be a Czech one, because we have achieved our aim by our blood and suffering. But it would be our wish and pride to know that nobody here, who is not a Czech, need feel oppressed.

[1] Masaryk, *Making of a State*, p. 389.
[2] *Parliamentary Minutes*, vol. 1 (Prague 1918), p. 8.

Masaryk's home-coming

Elected President by the Provisional National Assembly on 14 November, Thomas Garrigue Masaryk returned to Czechoslovakia in December and arrived in Prague on 21 December 1918. On the following day he delivered his first political message, from which the reference to 'immigrants and colonists', meaning the Germans in contrast to the 'indigenous' Czechs, is often quoted. This was no doubt a *faux pas* which, coming from a man of Masaryk's calibre, sounded unconvincing enough. When the Germans had been in the country for several hundred years, to call them 'immigrants' in comparison with the rest of the population could not form the basis for a political argument. Anti-Czech propaganda took up his words with alacrity, concealing the entirely conciliatory spirit in which they had been uttered and also the not entirely insignificant fact that Masaryk himself retracted them later to some extent, a thing not usually done by prestige-conscious politicians. In his memoirs Masaryk said[1]

Our Germans, as I pointed out in my first Message, originally came to us as colonists; and the significance of this German colonisation would not be lessened even if it were true that a few Germans were already living in the country. Yet this does not mean that, as colonists, our Germans are second-class citizens. They were invited to come by our kings who guaranteed them the right to live their own lives in full measure...I for my part acknowledge and deliberately adopt the policy of our Přemyslid Kings who protected the Germans as a race.

Here are the relevant passages in Masaryk's inaugural address of 22 December 1918[2]

First, as far as the Germans in our lands are concerned, our programme has been known for a long time: the territory on which they have settled is our territory and will remain so. We have created our State, we have preserved it and we are re-building it: I should like to see the Germans helping us; that would be a more sensible line to take than their present doubtful efforts...

I repeat: *we* have created this State and this determines the constitutional position of our Germans who originally entered the country as immigrants[3] and colonists. We are fully entitled to the wealth of our land which is necessary to our and the Germans' industry. We will not and cannot sacrifice the large Czech minorities in the so-called German area. Moreover, we are convinced

[1] Masaryk, *Making of a State*, p. 387.
[2] T. G. Masaryk, *Cesta demokracie* (The Path of Democracy), 1 (Prague 1933), 19–22.
[3] The official report says 'emigrants', although Masaryk of course meant 'immigrants'.

that considerations of their own economic advantage will draw the Germans over to us. It will be up to them to adapt themselves...I sincerely hope that we shall come to terms as soon as possible...No one will be able to blame us if, after so many bitter experiences, we have become cautious, but I assure our minorities that in our State they will be able to enjoy full national rights. The American republic suffered the carnage of a civil war rather than permit its Southern territories to secede; we shall never permit our ethnically mixed Northern areas to break away. By building up a really democratic system of self-government we shall have the best means for a solution of the problem of nationalities. A clear-cut frontier is not feasible because of the widespread intermingling.

The splendour of his welcome did not dazzle Masaryk. On the following day he uttered this warning in the Council of Ministers:[1]

We shall have to come to an understanding with the Germans; force won't lead us anywhere. Consideration for the Germans in Bohemia calls for friendly relations with Germany. Our geographical position as well as our historic background in the heart of Europe both call for an agreement with Germany.

Finally, on the evening of 23 December 1918 – following immediately upon a four years' stay among the enemies of Germany and before he had entered a Czech theatre – Masaryk and the whole of the Government attended a gala performance of *Fidelio* in the German Theatre in Prague.[2]

Masaryk's view on the German problem, as expressed in his New Year's message of 1919,[3] was conciliatory, yet firm:

Democracy is also my guide-line in the question of nationalities. I recognise the national principle and the right to self-determination but in the given administrative circumstances there are boundaries which are the result of national interrelationships and which make any straight frontier demarcation impracticable. A union of the German minorities is geographically not feasible, just as it is not feasible to unite all Czech minorities geographically. There is no other way for them, but to remain together...There is moreover an obvious difference in the application of the right to self-determination. With the exception of a few small frontier minorities we Czechs and Slovaks are a homogeneous nation; our Germans on the other hand do not represent their whole nation but only its colonising avant-garde...

Above all we note here the argument that a clear frontier cannot be drawn through ethnically mixed areas. Masaryk also stated his conviction, later to be frequently repeated, that Czechoslovakia was after all the only practicable political structure available to Czechs

[1] Masaryk, *Cesta demokracie*, I, 48.
[2] Harry Klepetar, *Seit 1918...*(Ostrava 1937), p. 26.
[3] Masaryk, *Cesta demokracie*, vol. I, p. 50.

and Slovaks, while the Germans could look to other States too. The claim by the Czechs and Slovaks to independence, in a form which would make their State politically and economically viable, can however be maintained without the additional argument that there was 'ample national scope' for the Germans elsewhere. The goal of human endeavour appears not so much to find 'ample national scope', whatever that means, but to lead, as far as possible to a decent life in a congenial atmosphere. The reference to a 'colonising avant-garde' was likewise out of place. It would have been sufficient to say that the realization of the right to self-determination by the Czechs and Slovaks inevitably involved restricting the claim to an analogous right by the relatively small part of the German nation living in Bohemia, Moravia and Silesia.

To the German leaders everything which might appear as a 'surrender to the Czechs' was abhorrent and a leap in the dark. They neither could, nor would see, that *any* step they might take was one into uncertainty. They did not fully understand – it was not entirely their fault – the prevailing political reality, and clung instead to the absurd hope of being able to play off one ally against the other, and to Wilson's *dicta* on the right to self-determination, which would surely apply to them too. Only a short while before, President Wilson had been abused as a pharisee, hypocrite, and notorious German-hater. Now he was being overwhelmed by tele-grams from all over German-Bohemia and Southern Moravia, in which local administrations rendered fulsome praise to his ideals and invoked his help against all sort of injustices. They did not appreciate that the man whom the Czechs honoured as their liberator could not at the same time also become the liberator of the Germans from Czech rule. It was, of course, much easier to send a telegram to Wilson than to take a practical step which might lead to a *rapprochement* between the nations.

Until 1918 the German Social Democrats had strongly opposed the German Nationalists in all respects and particularly on the ethnic question. Now, for the first time, all German political parties had formed a temporary coalition with the aim of achieving the right to self-determination for the Germans too. They had, however, no very clear or common idea how this right would be used.

Czechoslovakia before Munich

Establishment of the Province of German-Bohemia

On 21 October 1918 the German deputies elected in Austria in 1911 proclaimed the 'independent German-Austrian State' with 'jurisdiction over the whole German ethnic area, particularly the Sudeten territories'. (The Germans in old Austria used to call Bohemia, Moravia and Silesia *die Sudetenländer*, i.e. the Sudeten territories. Hence the expression 'Sudeten Germans' which was later used first for the Germans living in the border-regions and then for all Germans in Bohemia, Moravia and Silesia.) Neither this resolution[1] nor the statements made during the ensuing meeting mentioned an Austrian Republic or an *Anschluss* to Germany. It is clear that the possibility of some sort of common framework within Austria–Hungary was still envisaged for the resolution set itself the task of initiating 'negotiations with the other nationalities regarding the transfer of the administration to the new national States and the re-organisation of the relations between the nationalities'. Following the Prague events of 28 October a meeting was hurriedly convened in Vienna for the 29th. Here the Bohemian Germans, elected to the Vienna *Reichsrat* in the halcyon days of 1911, declared themselves to be the 'Provisional Provincial Diet' of German Bohemia, and this area, although not clearly defined, was proclaimed 'an autonomous province of the German-Austrian State'. So a new province was born – on paper. But it did not include the German districts of Southern Bohemia, which at the beginning of November set themselves up as the 'Böhmerwaldgau' (Bohemian Forest District) and expressed their intention of joining Upper Austria.

A far more difficult task awaited the Moravian and Silesian delegates. A province of 'German-Moravia' would have been a caricature of an administrative organization; Silesia had considerable Czech and Polish minorities and the whole country around its capital Opava (Troppau) was Czech. If German-Bohemia, in the form proclaimed in Vienna, had no geographical links with unambiguously Austrian territory, this applied even more to the decision taken on 30 October 1918 to form a province constituted by the

---

[1] Text printed in *Studienausgabe der Verfassungsgesetze der Tschechoslovakischen Republik* (Study Edition of the Constitutional Laws of the Czechoslovak Republic) ed. Leo Epstein (Liberec 1923), p. 53.

German districts of Northern Moravia and Silesia, with Opava as capital. It was even difficult to think of a name for this province: eventually 'Sudetenland' was chosen (after the mountain range straddling across Northern Moravia and Silesia). The 'Sudetenland' of 1918 is thus by no means identical with the far bigger area attached to Germany after the Munich Agreement of 1938 and administered until 1945 under the name of 'Sudetenland'.

Finally, on 3 November, the district of 'German Southern-Moravia' was established, to be attached to Lower Austria. Thus there were now four new administrative areas, lacking any kind of co-ordination or political co-operation. Only German-Bohemia had an administration in reasonable working order and even there it lasted only a few weeks. Its Provincial Governor (*Landeshauptmann*) was to be the German Nationalist leader Rafael Pacher, but he never took up his duties and formally resigned on 5 November. His successor was another German Nationalist, Rudolf Lodgman-Auen, with the Social Democrat Josef Seliger as Deputy-Governor; Governor and Deputy-Governor, respectively, in Opava were Robert Freissler, a moderate Nationalist, and Hans Jokl, a Social Democrat.

Only two meetings of the German-Bohemian provincial diet could be held at Liberec (Reichenberg), the proposed capital. Conscious of the difficulties created by the bilingual character of many of the districts in the province, the diet at its opening on 29 October, 'anxious to preserve the right of German-Bohemia to self-determination without rejecting any justified Czech demands', instructed the Governor[1] 'to take up contacts with the representatives of the Czech people with a view to creating a special provisional administration in those communities which are clearly of a mixed national character until such time as conditions are finally settled'. The resolution could not be carried out, but it proves that there was no intention of any wholesale burning of boats. A similar wish not to sever all ties was shown in the decision creating the province of 'Sudetenland'.[2]

The gravest problem facing the German-Bohemian provincial government was the fight against the terrible malnutrition and even

[1] Ibid. p. 56.
[2] *Prager Tagblatt*, 31 October 1918.

outright starvation inherited from the war. But nothing could be done unless a *modus vivendi* with Prague was reached.

Warnings against military adventures

In those troubled days there were two groups which planned to push the war-weary German army into new adventures and to embroil Germany, just beginning to work its way towards democracy, in a war with the new Czechoslovak State. These two groups were on the one hand the German generals and on the other certain German Nationalists from Austria. Serious consideration was given to the plan to occupy German-Austria or German-Bohemia, or both, with troops sent from the Reich, purely of course in order to maintain 'law and order'. Ludendorff, the Chief of the German General Staff, was evidently not content with having lost *one* war. On the contrary, in his chagrin he actually hoped to find consolation in facile new conquests. In a memorandum addressed to the Foreign Minister Solf towards the middle of October,[1] Ludendorff railed against the unreliable Austrian Emperor Charles, who was bound to give in to the covetous Slavs; it was therefore essential for the Germans to annex at once the Austrian territory inhabited by Germans: 'For the disappointments which the war has brought us in other fields, this development [the *Anschluss*] would at any rate be a valuable compensation. We ought not to ignore it.' In Vienna the German Nationalists were importuning the local representatives of the German High Command with requests for a German occupation, and German officers, infuriated by the lack of stamina shown by the Austrians, were only too ready to lend their ear to such foolhardy advice. Fortunately the German diplomatic service, while still under the Kaiser's authority, adopted a more responsible attitude. On 11 October 1918 the Saxon Minister in Vienna (certain

---

[1] Ludendorff to Solf, 14 October 1918, *German Foreign Ministry* (from now on abbreviated *G.F.M.*; these references are to the photostat copies made of the files), serial 7479, frames 187450-2, quoted by J. Hannak, *Karl Renner und seine Zeit* (Vienna 1965), p. 325. Some of the documents printed here have previously been summarized by Arthur G. Kogan in 'Germany and the Germans of the Hapsburg Monarchy on the Eve of the Armistice 1918: Genesis of the Anschluss problem', *Journal of Central European Affairs* (Boulder, U.S.A.), April 1960, pp. 24–50.

German States such as Saxony and Bavaria still had their own legations in Vienna) had warned his Government in Dresden:[1]

The military gentlemen are always ready for 'marching orders'. In my opinion it would be very desirable if nothing came of it because it would not only jeopardise our chances at the peace negotiations but also permanently poison our relations with our Czech neighbours.

As early as 22 October a three-man delegation from Vienna had been negotiating in Berlin for military assistance 'in case of a Czech invasion'[2] – not a very promising enterprise for Germany to undertake at a time when she was on the verge of collapse. The authorities in Berlin, however, could not make up their minds, until 'all the plans discussed had to be abandoned'. Nevertheless at German headquarters, the hare-brained idea of sending as a 'compromise solution' German infantry units and 'some cavalry' into Bohemia, not as combat troops but for police purposes, was seriously entertained.[3] The German Nationalists afterwards reported to Vienna all sorts of atrocity tales about looting and called for immediate aid from German troops. This kind of propaganda petered out when Victor Adler, who had taken over the Foreign Office in Vienna on 30 October, brushed the stories aside and objected to any intervention by the Reich.[4]

No matter how much they were cajoled, even the Kaiser's diplomats realized quite clearly that there was no enthusiasm among the Germans in Bohemia for secession from the predominantly Czech heart of the country. Count Botho von Wedel, the German Ambassador in Vienna, had informed Berlin towards the middle of October that the Bohemian Germans were not unanimous: they were 'not irredentists'.[5] It is worth quoting his report, corroborated by countless similar ones:

Economic interests, particularly the industrialists' fear of competition from the

[1] Nostitz (Vienna) to Vitzthum (Dresden), 11 October 1918, *G.F.M.* serial 7479, frames 187497-9.
[2] Molisch, *Briefe*, p. 29; Strauss, *Entstehung*, p. 293.
[3] Hintze (Representative of the G.F.M. at the High Command) to G.F.M. 29 October 1918; Hindenburg to Hintze, 2 November 1918, *G.F.M.* serial K1151, frames 294638 and 294659.
[4] Wedel to G.F.M. 3 November 1918, *Akten betreffend Boehmen*, oe/no. 101, fascicle 1236/2 (these and similar references are to the original files of the G.F.M.).
[5] Wedel to G.F.M. 14 October 1918, *G.F.M.* serial K1151, frames 294630-2.

superior German industry, are of great importance in this respect...Objections, if only isolated ones, are raised in the purely German town of Reichenberg: *it was not reasonable to abandon all these important interests in Bohemia, one would just have to make the best of things, get on with the Czechs and learn Czech...* It seems that the Socialists will carry most weight in the future development of the German character of the region. *Irredentists tendencies have so far not appeared among them* [i.e. the Socialists].

A remarkably sensible attitude was shown by the German Consul-General in Prague, Friedrich von Gebsattel, who had occupied this post since 1913. On 25 October 1918 he warned Berlin of the intentions of the German Nationalist hotheads, thereby opening the long series of German diplomatic statements which between 1918 and 1938 compared the unreasonable outlook of the Sudeten German Nationalists with the existing chances for democratic co-operation with the Czechs. Gebsattel thought it unwise for the Germans in Bohemia to take a hostile attitude to-wards the new Czechoslovak State:[1]

The prospects for the Germans in Bohemia would be altogether different if they now voluntarily agreed to remain within the Czech State. Even though they could not expect all their national aspirations to be fulfilled, the Germans would still find that the Czechs were willing to meet them more than half-way. There has been no lack of friendly, promising offers by the Czechs in the last few weeks and there have been broad hints that they would be ready for immediate negotiations. *I have no doubt about the sincerity of the Czechs' promises.* Should, therefore, the Germans be prepared to sit down at the conference table with the Czechs now, it would be the most auspicious time for them to obtain far-reaching concessions. It must be clearly understood, however, that the Germans would have to grasp the hand extended to them at once, before the peace negotiations begin. The Czechs can await the outcome with equanimity...but the Germans would then be in a much less favourable position and in particular could not expect consideration for their national interests to anything like the present extent...It would therefore appear to be in the interests of the Germans in Bohemia to use the present favourable opportunity to achieve the best possible position in the Czechoslovak State by direct negotiations.

The day after, Gebsattel pleaded afresh for good relations with the Czechs[2] by pointing out that 'any support by Germany for the separation of German-Bohemia from Czechoslovakia would hit the latter at her most vulnerable spot'.

The transfer of authority from old Austria to Czechoslovakia,

[1] Gebsattel to G.F.M. 25 October 1918, *Akten*, 1236/2.
[2] Gebsattel to G.F.M. 30 October 1918, *Akten*, 1236/2; also Kogan, 'Germany and the Germans', pp. 44–5.

Gebsattel reported two days later,[1] proceeded in an orderly manner without any serious incidents; the citizens of the Reich in Prague 'were treated with special consideration'. Neither did any harm befall the German population of Bohemia:

Some officials employed by the Austrian Governor and other authorities to whom the Czechs objected, were sent on leave; all other officials of German extraction, even those in senior positions, remain at their jobs for the time being.

In Litoměřice (Leitmeritz) and Chomutov (Komotau) there had been 'riots' but the German mayors of these, almost entirely German towns, like the mayor of Ústí (Aussig) before them had turned to the Czechs for help. It 'was immediately forthcoming'.[2] Gebsattel continued:

During the many discussions I had in the course of the past week with the Národní Výbor it struck me how obstinately the Czechs defended their view that German-Bohemia was an inseparable and indivisible part of their State... They would feel extremely provoked if Germany were to send troops or even police units into Bohemia...The good relations which have begun to develop would immediately give way to bitter enmity...In our own interest it seems to me imperative not to heed such calls for help and to refer those who issue them to the Národní Výbor, even if the calls should come from places on the frontier of Germany and Bohemia, such as Bodenbach, Tetschen or Reichenberg. If German towns such as Komotau and Leitmeritz can turn to the Národní Výbor, there is no reason why other places should not do so too.

In accordance with these recommendations, Saxony refused to accede to calls for succour.[3] The German delegates from Bohemia found a 'complete absence of sympathetic response to their requests when they tried to persuade the Saxon Government at the beginning of November to send armed assistance'.

Austria on the other hand could not brush off such appeals for help quite so easily; they came after all from territories over which it had claimed sovereignty. But when the Czechoslovak troops began to occupy the disputed areas, the Austrian Government rejected any form of military action. The attempt to recruit military units in Bohemia from German soldiers returning from the front failed because of their war-weariness.[4]

[1] Gebsattel to German Chancellor (Akten, loc. cit.).
[2] Gebsattel to G.F.M. 4 November 1918, serial K1151/2, frames 294393-4.
[3] Molisch, Briefe, p. 30.
[4] Rudolf Lodgman, 'Meine Verhandlungen mit dem Národní Výbor' (My negotiations with the Národní Výbor), in Teplitz-Schoenauer Anzeiger, 25 November 1923, quoted by Strauss, Entstehung, p. 303.

The military occupation of the areas under dispute (leaving aside those where local German administrations had called for Czech aid anyway) took place in consequence of the Armistice agreement and with the Allies' express consent. France had guaranteed the new state its historic frontiers from the very beginning. Great Britain, Italy and the United States later agreed to the occupation of the border regions,[1] thereby implying that in the peace negotiations they would at best be prepared to consider minor frontier rectifications, but no separation of the border areas inhabited by Germans. On the whole the military occupation did not meet with any sort of resistance.

As the Czechoslovak troops were approaching Liberec the German-Bohemian provincial government withdrew *via* Saxony to Vienna. No such heroic gestures were made at Opava, where Freissler, in agreement with Vienna, formally ended his activities as soon as the Czechs were ready to occupy the town.[2]

No contacts with the Czechs?

Were there, then, no contacts between the Germans in Bohemia and the victorious Czechs? There were only two attempts to make any, and both failed. Lodgman appeared in Prague as early as 30 October to start negotiations with the *Národní Výbor* on his own responsibility. According to the Czech historian Ferdinand Peroutka:[3]

Lodgman had been invited by the Czechs whose intention it was to get the Germans to co-operate. This was bound to fail at the time because the Czechs insisted on negotiating on the basis of the German area being united to them,

---

[1] In a note dated 7 January 1919 the British Government rejected Austrian protests and expressed the opinion that 'until the decision by the Peace Conference the frontiers of the Czechoslovak State should coincide with those of the historic frontiers of the provinces Bohemia, Moravia and Silesia'. France had already taken a similar stand before, on 20 December 1918, and Italy followed one day later. See Beneš, *Der Aufstand der Nationen* (Berlin 1928), p. 686; *Bericht ueber die Taetigkeit der deutschoesterreichischen Friedensdelegation in St Germain-en-Laye* (Vienna 1919), II, 70–1; Epstein, *Studienausgebe*, (Liberec 1923), p. 70. Only Beneš reports the American declaration of agreement (Beneš, ibid. p. 687).

[2] Robert Freissler, *Vom Zerfall Österreichs bis zum tschechoslowakischen Staat* (Zoppot–Berlin 1921), p. 159.

[3] Ferdinand Peroutka, *Budování státu* (Building the State) (Prague 1933–6), I, 185.

while Lodgman assumed that this would not happen. Neither part was prepared to give way.

Antonín Švehla, a leading member of the *Národní Výbor*, said to Lodgman: The Czechoslovak nation has carried through a revolution. The matter is now closed. We invite you to work with us. The discussions went on for several hours without Lodgman conceding for a moment that the matter had indeed been settled in the Czech sense: he maintained that this was for the Peace Conference to decide and that in the meantime the Germans had the same right to their own government as the Czechs. The offer to the Germans to send delegates to join the *Národní Výbor* and subsequently to the Revolutionary National Assembly was rejected by Lodgman on principle. He demanded that the government of German-Bohemia be recognised and treated as an equal.

It was different in Moravia. On 29 October, Moravian delegates of the *Národní Výbor* called on the Austrian Governor of the province and demanded from him the formal surrender of his authority, as in Prague the day before. He consulted Vienna and was authorized to submit but enjoined to insist that the body which was to take over the administration of the province should include representatives of the Germans in Moravia. It was agreed that executive power was to be vested in a six-member committee in which the Czechs were to have four seats and the Germans two.[1] Comprising a minority of only 25 per cent in the province, to have obtained a one-third representation on this body would undoubtedly have been advantageous to the Germans – the only condition being that they recognize the constitutional union of Bohemia, Moravia and Silesia. This they refused to do, however, and they were consequently not included in the provincial administration. Perhaps even their agreement would not have made much difference in the long run: it might be that this experiment would soon have proved a failure. But the fact remains that the Czechs in Moravia had shown an unusual measure of goodwill towards the Germans.

On 4 November the Deputy-Governor of German-Bohemia, Seliger, went to Prague in order to take up the question of food supplies for his province with the members of the *Národní Výbor*, almost all of whom he knew from his days in the Austrian Parliament in Vienna. He was cordially received and treated like an old colleague in the discussions.[2] He was assured that there was to be no discrimination between German and Czech districts in the provision

[1] *Tagesbote* (Brno), of 30 October 1918.
[2] Strauss, *Entstehung*, pp. 297–8.

of food. Formal negotiations between the *Národní Výbor* and the German-Bohemian provincial government on these matters were however rejected, since this could have been construed as a degree of recognition for the Germans. In the subsequent talks, Alois Rašín remarked that the right to self-determination was all very well, but now when the Entente had won it was a case of *force majeure*. Even more ominous was the aside made by him a short while later, however dispassionate and casual it is said to have been: 'We do not negotiate with rebels.' This phrase was not Rašín's: he was repeating an expression originally used by the Austrian General Windisch-graetz to the Czechs after the Prague Revolution of 1848 had been crushed. It was thus a typical case of getting one's own back, seventy years later, particularly when one realizes that Rašín, who had been sentenced to death in 1916, may well have been longing for such an opportunity. But if this was indeed in his mind then Seliger, a Social Democrat who had fought for the rights of the Czechs in old Austria, was a singularly inappropriate person against whom to exact revenge.

Professor Franz Spina, whom we shall meet again as protagonist of German co-operation with the Czechs but who at that time did not yet play any part, later found that *all* the German parties during this period had been wrong:[1]

I am convinced [he wrote] that the Germans could have gained considerable political advantages if, during the revolution of 1918–19, in correct appreciation of the temporary political helplessness of the German people, they had promptly started negotiations with the Czechs about their collaboration in the affairs of State.

Austrian territorial claims

Not unnaturally, the newly formed Vienna Government of 'German Austria' tried to create a favourable bargaining position for itself at the Peace Conference. The first resolution of its 'Provisional National Assembly' on 21 October 1918 – in other words of the Parliament elected in 1911 reduced to its German members – claimed 'sovereignty over the whole German ethnic territory of old Austria'.[2] A note sent to Wilson by the same body on 30 October

[1] Franz Spina, 'Die Politik der deutschen Parteien in der Tschechoslowakei', *Süddeutsche Monatshefte* (Munich), November 1928.
[2] Epstein, *Studienausgabe*, p. 53.

reduced the demand for thr right to self-determination to 'the continuous areas of (German) settlement'.[1] When the so-called 'Territorial Law'[2] was given a reading in the Assembly on 22 November 1918, the provisional government wanted to incorporate the sensible provision that

subject to the final demarcation of the state frontiers after negotiations with the other national states newly established on the territory of the Austro-Hungarian Monarchy (and) subject to the demarcation decided on at the Peace Conference ...the newly created provinces of German–Bohemia and Sudetenland belong to German–Austria.

But subsequently a concession was made to the extremists which gravely jeopardized the claims of the new State to be taken seriously. The final version of that law simply enumerated

the lands of Lower Austria including the district of Southern Moravia and the German area around Nová Bystřice (Neubistritz): Upper Austria including the district of German Southern-Bohemia...German Bohemia and Sudetenland *as well as the German ethnic areas of Brno, Jihlava (Iglau) and Olomouc*

as parts of the new State. The 'German area round Nová Bystřice (in Southern Bohemia) had no connection at all with the remaining German ethnic territory. The same applies to the large chunks claimed around Brno, Jihlava, and Olomouc. Freissler later condemned[3] this legislative action as 'political dilettantism', carried through against the determined opposition of the Premier (State Chancellor), the Social Democrat Karl Renner.

The still-born province 'Sudetenland' was written off by the Vienna Government at the earliest possible moment. The demands for parts of Brno etc. were never repeated. Other territorial claims were maintained. The demand for self-determination united the German political representatives from Bohemia for a short time, but by 'self-determination' some understood a free decision about which State to join, others the maintenance of the relationship with truncated Austria, others again the extension of this adherence to Austria to the incorporation of German–Bohemia with Austria in the Reich, while a fourth group advocated the direct attachment

[1] Freissler, *Zerfall*, p. 93.
[2] Epstein, *Studienausgabe*, p. 62; Kurt Trampler, *Deutschösterreich 1918/19* (Berlin 1931), p. 80.
[3] Freissler, *Zerfall*, pp. 115–16.

of the German-inhabited border areas to the Reich, irrespective of the ultimate fate of Austria. Thus, even if all these groups did want the, or at any rate *a*, right to self-determination, the practical implications were not quite so simple. The existing confusion was reflected in the indignant description of events later given by the German nationalist historian Paul Molisch:[1]

Among the population only those groups stood aside which feared national independence might be detrimental to their real or supposed interests...The relationship between German-Bohemian industry and the Sudeten-German liberation movement was by no means free from internal contradictions. There were individual industrialists who took part in the movement and supported it privately. On the whole, however, the industrialists were torn between two conflicting sentiments. On the one hand the two German-Bohemian Chambers of Commerce of Cheb (Eger) and Liberec staunchly supported the German-Bohemian movement, while on the other hand industry generally looked on these aspirations with a good deal of scepticism, going so far as to ask itself whether economic considerations did not call for agreement with the Czechs. The provinicial government looked on the wavering attitude of so important an economic group with displeasure...After the Czech occupation of German-Bohemia the great majority of industrialists never seriously opposed incorporation in the Czech state.

Things were no better at Opava, and according to the same source:

In several cases German industrialists appealed to the Czechoslovak authorities, who told them that the inadequacy of coal supplies was entirely due to the Opava provincial government (of the 'Sudetenland'). These industrialists then said that the prospects for this government were hopeless. Naturally this detracted from its standing and made its position even more difficult, but that did not unduly concern German industry in Silesia: with very few exceptions its leaders were inclined to keep on good terms with the Czechs whilst cold-shouldering the Sudeten-German liberation movement...The plan to install a railway administration authority at Krnov (Jägerndorf) found no great welcome, mainly because of the negative attitude of the Silesian manufacturers towards the liberation movement...It must be admitted that a considerable part of the population at Opava looked at the whole concept of a separate government there sceptically, even ironically...It was above all economic objections which were raised against the liberation movement, and not only by the larger industrialists but by small merchants and tradesmen.

No better news was forthcoming from South Bohemia, which bordered directly upon Upper Austria:

On 17 November 1918 a meeting took place at Krumlov (Krummau)...which enthusiastically welcomed the incorporation of the area into German-Austria as

---

[1] Paul Molisch, *Die sudetendeutsche Freiheitsbewegung in den Jahren 1919–1920* (Vienna 1932), pp. 31, 35, 54, 56, 60, 106, 111, 142, 148, 172.

part of Upper-Austria. Despite this, a rather ominous observation could be made: no industrialists or farmers spoke at the meeting. Industry, fearful for its supply of coal, was not anxious to see the province attached to German-Austria and certainly did not support the liberation struggle, while the farmers disliked the more stringent food supply regulations in force in Upper Austria.

All these matters had already been reported to Berlin by the German Ambassador in Vienna, Count Wedel, in a secret minute dated 29 April 1919:[1]

German Bohemia (*Deutschböhmen*) is lost to us, according to the news I have received. The inhabitants increasingly accept Czech rule. The industrialists make a pretence of German national feeling but in their hearts they tend – with few exceptions – to stay in Bohemia (*Tschechien*) as this brings them more advantages.

One of the most interesting admissions in this respect is contained in a secret letter written by the Austrian Chancellor Karl Renner to Otto Bauer, the Foreign Minister in his Government, in December 1918, after having spoken to Hans Jokl, a German Social-Democratic deputy from Austrian Silesia[2]

Jokl thinks that if the Czechs offered autonomy to the Germans, 99% of them including the workers would opt for Czechoslovakia. Since similar views reach us from German-Bohemia in large numbers, I am anyway worried that we may suffer shipwreck.

All this disposes of the convenient theory that the Sudeten Germans would never have joined Czechoslovakia if they had been consulted. No doubt the Czech leadership committed the error of not converting by a generous offer the basic willingness of the ordinary Germans to co-exist peacefully with the Czechs in a common State into a positive acknowledgment of the Czechoslovak Republic. This does not alter the fact, however, that until 1935 no parliamentary elections in Czechoslovakia ever showed less than two-thirds and sometimes as much as four-fifths of the German voters adhering to parties with a positive approach to the State. The German nationalistic irreconcilables who persisted in stubborn opposition remained a

---

[1] Wedel to Langwerth (G.F.M.), 29 April 1919, *G.F.M.* serial 4662/1, frames 21175-7.
[2] State Chancellor Karl Renner to State Secretary Otto Bauer, 12 December 1918, *Oesterreichisches Staatsarchiv*, Vienna, New Political Archive. Personal files of State Secretary Dr O. Bauer, vol. VIII, 'Czechoslovakia'.

small though vociferous minority until the world economic crisis and Hitler's achievements set them on the path to success.

Growing realism in the country was not even halted by a tragic event which burdened German–Czech relations with the responsibility for spilt blood. On 4 March 1919 the newly elected Austrian Parliament was to meet in Vienna. Since no elections could take place in the areas claimed both by Austria and Czechoslovakia no delegates could be sent from there. To avoid individual protests the Social-Democratic Party called for a general cessation of work and for a peaceful demonstration for the right to self-determination on that day. The other political parties perforce followed suit. Most of the demonstrations appeared to have been peaceful: in Teplice (Teplitz) Josef Seliger actually spoke under the protection of the Czechoslovak authorities.

Unfortunately there were exceptions. In several towns Czech soldiers suddenly began to fire on the unarmed and unprotected crowds. Some local commanders lost control over the situation, either because their new power had gone to their heads or simply because they were terrified of the demonstrations. The result was fifty-four deaths. The question of guilt is not in all cases easy to settle. The largest number of dead, twenty-five, was in the West Bohemian town of Kadaň (Kaaden). The (purely German) town administration issued declarations, conceding that 'the disastrous affray was begun by a young demonstrator who threw a stone at the soldiers. One soldier immediately began to fire, without waiting for the command of a superior officer.'[1] The next place on the list was the North Moravian town of Šternberk (Sternberg) with sixteen dead. Who started the shooting was never established, but two Czech soldiers were among the victims. However tragic were the results of the whole affair, its impact on political relations was relatively slight. The bulk of the Germans did not become more intransigent afterwards, indeed rather less. At a meeting at Česká Lípa (Böhmisch-Leipa) attended by representatives of all parties, according to Molisch,[2]

above all economic considerations made themselves felt. The spokesman of the

---

[1] *Prager Tagblatt*, 20 and 23 March 1919.
[2] Molisch, *Sudetendeutsche*, p. 137.

Agrarian Party declared that his Party reserved complete freedom of action for itself... The Christian-Social delegate... demanded a change in the stubbornly oppositional tactics so far adhered to by the German-Bohemians. On this discordant note the meeting dissolved.

Towards the end of May a conference of the German Agrarian Party took place at Litoměřice which was resolved to 'take up contacts with the peasantry of the other nation'.[1] It was the first expression of what was later to be called 'activism', i.e. active German co-operation in the State. On the Czech side, too, the conciliatory attitude did not change after 4 March. At the beginning of May the Minister for Defence, Václav Klofáč, welcomed a group of returning soldiers of German origin who, as prisoners-of-war in Italy had volunteered to join the Czechoslovak fighting forces, established in Italy from Austrian prisoners-of-war. Speaking in German,[2] he told them the new State would do justice to its German citizens.

The attitude of the Weimar Republic
The position adopted by Germany in response to the developments in the neighbouring State remains to be discussed. On the day after the Prague events of 28 October, the German Consul Gebsattel, still speaking for the Kaiser's Government, had been the first foreign representative to call on the *Národní Výbor* with an expression of goodwill. By 5 December 1918, *Prager Tagblatt* (a liberal German paper) was already able to publish an interview with an anonymous official of the Berlin Foreign Office who declared that the Reich would not feel entitled to protest in Prague against the Czechoslovak occupation of German-Bohemian towns: 'We recognise the Czechoslovak State and are ready at any time to receive its diplomatic mission.' At Dresden a few days later the first German–Czechoslovak trade agreement was signed: Germany undertook to send coal to Czechoslovakia.[3]

It has already been pointed out that attempts to obtain armed help from Germany against the Czechs remained fruitless. While not openly discouraging the Austrian desire for incorporation into the

[1] *Documents on British Foreign Policy 1919–39* (*DBFP*), First Series, VI:4 (London 1956), p. 15.
[2] *České Slovo* (Prague), 10 May 1919.
[3] *Bohemia*, 12 December 1918.

35

Reich, the Weimar Republic took a much more detached view with regard to the Germans in Bohemia, Moravia and Silesia. The statements made by Foreign Minister Brockdorff-Rantzau in the Weimar National Assembly on 14 February 1919 clearly show that the German Government did not intend to go beyond an unavoidable minimum in the case of the Germans in the new Czechoslovak State. It is perhaps even more remarkable that not a single Nationalist member of the Weimar Assembly complained that these official statements did not go far enough; in fact neither in this or in any later debate were the Germans in Bohemia, Moravia and Silesia even mentioned by anyone. Brockdorff-Rantzau based his policy in this respect on the report he had from his confidential envoy in Prague, Professor Samuel Saenger, later German Minister in Prague. 'Repeated and detailed as well as private discussions with President Masaryk, relations with whom had lost nothing of their former cordiality,' wrote Saenger,[1] had made it clear that Czechoslovakia demanded the whole of Bohemia, Moravia and Silesia,

because the historic sense of justice had never become extinguished among the people and because the character of these settlements demanded it...The President...conceded that a satisfactory development of the new republic could only be expected on the basis of complete agreement with the German-Bohemians. This could best be achieved on the model of something like English local government...In passing was mentioned the well-known fact that the German-Bohemian manufacturers and merchants were for economic reasons averse to annexation to Austria or even directly to Germany. The President is, moreover, convinced that Czechoslovak could not be viable without the territories inhabited by the Germans...We should not render any assistance to a German-Bohemian irredentist movement, once the Peace Conference has given its decision on the frontier demarcation of the Czechoslovak Republic. More than that: we should then try to persuade the Germans in Bohemia to take a politically active part in the new State.

Later, as German Minister in Prague, Saenger maintained these views. When Wedel, the German Ambassador in Vienna, reported to Berlin rumours about a mass exodus of Bohemian Germans to Germany, where they were to enrol in German 'fighting organizations', the German Foreign Office issued a circular emphasizing that this 'could in no circumstances be considered since it would

[1] Saenger to Brockdorff-Rantzau, 6 February 1919, *G.F.M.* serial 4665, frames 219580-6. Extracts in Dagmar Perman, *The Shaping of the Czechoslovak State* (Leiden 1962), p. 177.

endanger our international position'. Everything would have to be avoided '*which might be construed as partisanship in the conflict between Germans and Czechs in Bohemia*'.[1]

A fresh disappointment was in store for the German Nationalists, when Lodgman in February 1919 again turned to Dresden for armed intervention. The Social Democrat Richard Lipinski, then Minister of the Interior of Saxony, entreated Lodgman to 'abandon the movement, because it would compromise the German revolution abroad by making it appear to be striving after annexations'.[2]

Certain German politicians from Bohemia tried their luck in Berlin as late as May 1919 without being any more successful. Any hopes for armed adventures were finally quenched when the German Foreign Office explained to them the 'difficult situation of the Reich' and advised them 'to remain content with autonomy within the Czech State'. Consequently they were told on 17 May 1919 in the name of the Foreign Minister, then at Versailles, that 'nothing should be done now which might make the peace negotiations more difficult for the Reich'.[3]

Clearly Germany had to concentrate her efforts on ensuring that too much of Reich territory proper would not be lost. Anything which in the circumstances would create the impression of an annexationist enterprise had to be eschewed. Moreover, it was obvious that the fate of the Germans in the Czechoslovak Republic was going to be incomparably better than that of the Reich citizens whose homes were successfully claimed by Poland.

[1] Telegram for circulation by Langwerth, 9 June 1919, *G.F.M.* serial 4662, frames 214494-5. Extracts in Perman, ibid. p. 179.
[2] Molisch, *Sudetendeutsche*, p. 143.
[3] Ibid. p. 165–7.

3 VERSAILLES AND ST GERMAIN

German right-wing propaganda blames the peace settlements of 1919 for having deprived certain sections of the German people of the right to self-determination. The boot was, however, on the other foot: by means of these settlements the right to self-determination of many nations which until then had been under alien rule was realized.[1]

Neither was the fate of countries and nations decided in 1919 by statesmen who allegedly had no knowledge of the problems they were called upon to tackle – even if Lloyd George, the leader of the British delegation, was said to have boasted in the middle of the peace negotiations that 'he had never heard of Teschen'.[2] A whole array of experts was at work at the time, travelling the length and breadth of the disputed areas, and this applies with particular force to the American delegation which tried to make up by intensive study for its lack of familiarity with European affairs. All the decisions of the Peace Conference, even the most controversial ones like the award of South Tyrol to Italy were taken only after the relevant facts had been examined. All counter-arguments provided by the German or Austrian delegations were carefully considered.

As far as Czechoslovak territorial claims at the Paris Peace Conference were concerned, the Allies were unanimous in not permitting an Austrian *Anschluss* to Germany since they were determined to prevent a vanquished Germany from increasing territory. By implication this principle excluded the possibility, never in fact contemplated, of giving the German-inhabited districts of Bohemia, Moravia and Silesia which were adjacent to Germany to that country. The right to self-determination has never been

---

[1] This was correctly stated by Lloyd George in *The Truth about the Peace Treaties* (London 1938), II, 751: 'The treaties of Paris constitute the greatest measure of unconditional liberation of subject nations ever achieved by any war settlement on record.'

[2] Harold Nicolson, *Peace Making 1919* (London 1945), p. 14.

regarded as the fulfilment of national desires without consideration of the conflicting rights of others. Under the existing circumstances the Germans in Bohemia, Moravia and Silesia could either be included in Czechoslovakia or their territory given to post-war Austria. No one, however, could, and in fact no one did, expect the incorporation into Austria of areas such as Northern Bohemia or Silesia which had no territorial links with it.

At no stage during the Paris negotiations was the question of maintaining the unity of the 'Czech lands' (Bohemia, Moravia and Silesia) a subject for discussion. The only point at issue – which will be dealt with later – was whether certain fringes of territory could be ceded to Germany; Beneš, the Czechoslovak Foreign Minister, was inclined to think they could.

The Czechoslovak memoranda

The Czechoslovak delegation at the Peace Conference submitted its territorial claims at the beginning of 1919, in a total of eleven memoranda. They were in no sense masterpieces of diplomatic finesse but rather hurriedly concocted propaganda, full of the exaggerations inevitable in such documents and not quite innocent of internal contradictions. Yet they hardly influenced the proceedings in Paris one way or the other.

The Czechoslovak *aide-mémoires* contained certain maximum demands: the unrealistic desire (not expressed very forcibly) for a corridor joining the country to Yugoslavia, the intention of extending the Slovak borders at the expense of Hungary and any number of frontier rectifications to the disadvantage of Germany. None of these were ever considered by the Peace Conference. Leaving aside these extremes, what the Czechoslovak delegation seriously had set its mind on, namely the maintenance of the territorial unit formed by Bohemia, Moravia and Silesia, was reasonable enough. But when in 1937 Beneš came to discuss the matter retrospectively[1] he could,

[1] In two series of articles, under the pseudonym 'XY': 'Germany and Czechoslovakia' (*Prager Presse* of 15, 18, 20, 22, 25, 27 and 29 August and 1 and 3 September 1937) and 'Czechoslovakia at the Peace Conference and our Minorities' (in the same newspaper of 6, 8, 9, 10, 12 and 14 October 1937). The series has appeared in part in an English version: see 'An Active and Responsible Czechoslovak Statesman' [pseudonym for Beneš], *Germany and Czechoslovakia* (Prague 1937).

with some justification, point out that Czechoslovakia had been the only country actually ready to cede territories to defeated Germany, if only by way of compensatory exchange. He wrote:[1]

While claiming at the Conference a small strip at Hlučín (Hultschin) which had a Czech majority, the Czechoslovak delegation also submitted a proposal for territorial exchange and frontier rectifications... with the intention of more than compensating Germany by ceding to her an area which had belonged to the Czech crown for centuries!...Considerable opposition was raised in Prague at the time by the extremist defenders of the historic frontiers...Nevertheless the members of the delegation thought it right to maintain a moderate attitude even towards a weakened Germany.

The Germans immediately affected by the proposed cession of their territory to Germany were, however, by no means entirely in favour of the idea. Count Wedel, the German Ambassador, reported from Vienna to the Foreign Office in Berlin on 3 June 1919:[2]

The Czechs seem to have planned to cede to the Reich Eger and Asch, as well as the two North-Bohemian districts of Rumburg-Schluckenau and Friedland which project into Saxony and Silesia, but they have abandoned the idea because of the importance of Eger as a railway junction...But they are said to be still in favour of surrendering the small district of Rumburg which juts deeply into Saxony...with its 100,000 inhabitants. In the district...there is no unequivocal joy at the prospect of being separated from the rest of German-Bohemia, nor is there any special predilection for Saxony. In general the annexation idea is subject to ups and downs among the Germans...even if they prefer not to admit it.

Whatever one's views about the Czechoslovak territorial proposals of 1919, they certainly did not arise from the arrogance of a victory over a vanquished foe.

The Aide-Mémoire III

Some of the steps taken by Czechoslovakia between 1918 and 1938 were essentially the realization of the 'Easter Demands'[3] of the German Nationalists in reverse. Nothing of this kind can be detected in the *Aide-Mémoire* III, entitled 'The Problem of the Germans in Bohemia', even though it was compiled in the first flush of victory and independence immediately after the war. This most important and most controversial of the Czechoslovak memoranda promised the Allies a liberal policy towards those citizens of the new State

---

[1] *Prager Presse*, 14 October 1937.
[2] *G.F.M.* serial 4662/1, frames 214485-6. See also p. 33.
[3] See p. 77.

who were not of Czech or Slovak origin. The language of the minorities would be generally recognized: the régime would be similar to that of Switzerland. This last point will be dealt with separately.

The *Aide-Mémoire* III grossly overestimated the strength of the Czech minorities living in the German areas of Bohemia. Nevertheless, Western Bohemia apart, there were Czech minorities all over the German ethnic area. With the Czechs' distrust for anything connected with Vienna the *Aide-Mémoire* III maintained that in the census of 1910 the number of Germans in Bohemia was overestimated by something like 800,000 to 1,000,000. In fact, the Czechoslovak census of 1921 which gave, together with 150,000 Germans in the former Hungarian areas (Slovakia and Ruthenia), a total of 3,100,000 Germans proved that the number of people incorrectly classified as German in the 1910 census was at most of the order of half-a-million. Although the exaggeration may have been tendentious no one was deceived. The Peace Conference based its decisions on the Austrian census of 1910, assuming that within the frontiers provided for her at St Germain, Czechoslovakia had 3,747,000 German inhabitants.[1]

Not in the *aide-mémoire* but in the oral *exposé* given by Beneš to the Council of Ten (the premiers and foreign ministers of the five Great Powers, France, Great Britain, the United States, Italy and Japan) on 5 February 1919 it was claimed that the Germans in Bohemia knew[2] that their separation from the rest of the country was impossible but that they were intimidated by 'a small number of pan-German agitators from Vienna'.[3] If by 'Vienna' Beneš implied that the Austrian Government was the culprit, the suggestion was quite unjustified. The Austrian Chancellor and leader of the delegation for the Peace Conference was a realist. After his

[1] H. W. V. Temperley, *A History of the Peace Conference at Paris* (London 1925), v, 155. The report about Czechoslovakia by the Commission for the New States reports that the Germans 'number about 3,000,000' (David Hunter Miller, *My Diary at the Conference in Paris* (New York 1926), XIII, 79).
[2] Since Clemenceau habitually used the expression 'La Bohême' when he meant Czechoslovakia, it is possible that Beneš used this term too when he referred to Bohemia, Moravia and Silesia.
[3] Hunter Miller, *My Diary*, XIV, 211ff. *Papers relating to the Foreign Relations of the United States. The Paris Peace Conference 1919* (Washington 1942–7), III, 880.

arrival at St Germain he lost no time in quietly throwing overboard all the unreasonable ballast with which he had been burdened before he left Vienna.[1] He merely asked for the unconditional inclusion of Southern Bohemia and Southern Moravia into Upper and Lower Austria respectively. In the main he demanded the realization of the principle of self-determination by means of plebiscites.[2] In order to avoid any later accusation of 'betrayal' he took with him to St Germain delegates from the parts of Bohemia, Moravia and Silesia claimed by Austria, one of whom, the expert for Southern Moravia, Oldofredi, later recounted a discussion he had had with Renner on the journey to Paris[3]

To Lodgman, Seliger and Freissler he (Renner) has not got much to say. Their Provinces – German-Bohemia and Sudetenland – are bound in his opinion to Czechoslovakia. He was not quite so pessimistic about Southern Bohemia and Southern Moravia but warned his colleagues not to hope too much.

The British and American points of view

The critics of the – certainly not ideal – peace settlement of 1919 like to point on the one hand to the negative attitude allegedly taken by the British Prime Minister David Lloyd George towards the Czechoslovak territorial claims, and on the other, to the refusal by the U.S. Secretary of State Robert Lansing to accept strategic considerations as criteria for the demarcation of frontiers. Both Lloyd George and Lansing[4] were indeed plagued by doubts, which shows that there was no lightheartedness about the decisions made:

[1] See Renner's letter to Bauer, dated 12 December 1918, where it is predicted that given the promise of autonomy, 99 per cent of the Germans in Bohemia, Moravia and Silesia would vote for incorporation into Czechoslovakia (see p. 33).

[2] See the notes by Renner who led the Austrian delegation, of 15, 16 and 25 June as well as 10 July 1919 in *Bericht*, 1, 88ff. and 324ff.; also Nina Almond and Ralph Haswell Lutz (eds.) *The Treaty of St Germain* (Stanford, U.S.A. 1935), pp. 276, 448, 297ff.

[3] Hieronymus Oldofredi, *Zwischen Krieg und Frieden* (Vienna 1925), pp. 70–1, 75.

[4] The French chairman of the Special Committee for Czechoslovakia, Jules Cambon, later related an altercation he had with Lansing about the problem of strategic frontiers in the Council of Foreign Ministers on 1 April 1919: 'I could not refrain from retorting – and my colleagues smiled at it – that the Americans were too little concerned in European security; that when one is near a fire, one has a certain preference for the fire brigade' (Geneviève Tabouis, *The Life of Jules Cambon* (London 1938), p. 332).

Renner's objections, for instance, to the first draft of the Austrian peace treaty led to not inconsiderable concessions to Austria at the expense of Czechoslovakia.

As far as the British point of view is concerned, the Foreign Office had drawn up a directive, first published by Lloyd George in 1938,[1] for dealing with the Czechoslovak frontiers, in which the Czechoslovak claim to the undivided 'historic lands' of Bohemia, Moravia and Silesia is supported. The Prime Minister himself was of course not bound by this directive. In his rather belated *The Truth about the Peace Treaties* (1938) Lloyd George asserts that he had been opposed to the Czechoslovak demands and that only Balfour, the Foreign Secretary, but not he himself, had finally agreed to them. The facts, however, were against him.

The Americans, just about to make their appearance in world politics, were in a different position from Lloyd George. Today no American politician, whether Republican or Democrat, could seriously advance the thesis that strategic considerations are not sometimes of overriding importance. But this was exactly what Lansing did, at any rate during the initial stages of the proceedings. He received the answer that one had got to create viable States, and the French diplomat Pichon retorted that 'a country composed according to Lansing's ... would on the map look as spotted as a panther'.[2]

This may have been the reason why in the first session of the 'Czechoslovak Commission' of the Peace Conference on 27 February 1919 it was agreed to maintain the historic frontiers, subject only to possible minor modifications,[3] and it explains why a plebiscite in the areas disputed between Austria and Czechoslovakia was never even considered.

Before this stage was reached, the Americans had sent several experts to Central Europe in order to gain first-hand experience there. The opinion of one of them, Professor Archibald Coolidge, is notable as a model of objectivity and justice.[4] He suggested the

[1] Lloyd George, *Truth about the Peace Treaties*, II, 927ff.
[2] Hunter Miller, *My Diary*, XVI, 13; *FRUS*, IV, 544.
[3] Hunter Miller, *My Diary*, XVII, 88–9.
[4] See vols. I and II of the *FRUS* Collection Papers. (See further A. C. Coolidge, *Ten Years of War and Peace* (Cambridge, U.S.A. 1927).)

possible cession of some South Moravian and South Bohemian areas to Austria and of the Cheb (Eger) area to Germany. He also envisaged the possibility of yielding parts of North Moravia and Silesia to Germany, but he insisted that the German-inhabited industrial region of West and North Bohemia should remain within Czechoslovakia. The American delegation in Paris, however, did not follow Coolidge's proposals. With the exception of the Cheb area they put forward different suggestions for frontier modifications.

Allen Dulles, the chief American delegate in the Czechoslovak Commission, was an advocate of the unity of the Czech lands: it was he who was responsible for the draft of the final resolution which considered that the separation of the German districts involved a danger to the new State.[1] In the course of the Peace Conference Lansing himself underwent a change of mind. In his Versailles memoirs he rejected the claim that the principle of self-determination should be the guiding light for peace settlements with a decisiveness which is bound to appear as overemphatic even to those who do not regard it as a general panacea.[2] He pointed out that as early as December 1918 he had indicated in a memorandum his misgivings lest the right to self-determination become the fulcrum with which to launch 'impossible demands' at the Peace Conference: 'The phrase is simply loaded with dynamite. It will raise hopes which can never be fulfilled. In the end it is bound to be discredited. What a calamity that the phrase was ever uttered! What misery it will bring to mankind!' Experience, he later declared, had amply shown that the principle was 'practically inapplicable'; success had proved how futile it was to put the word into general circulation. National safety was the chief object in the life of a nation, 'as self-preservation is in the life of an individual'.

The decision against frontier rectifications

When Lloyd George tried to place the responsibility for the decision of 1919 about the Czechoslovak frontiers on the shoulders of the Foreign Ministers, he seems to have overlooked what passed during the meeting on 4 April 1919 between himself, Clemenceau, Orlando

[1] *FRUS*, VII, 96.
[2] Robert Lansing, *The Peace Negotiations, A Personal Narrative* (New York 1921), pp. 87–91.

and Wilson's representative, Colonel House. It was at this meeting that the real decision was taken. Those present had before them the report of the Czechoslovak Commission of 26 March,[1] which suggested the maintenance of the existing frontiers between Bohemia, Moravia and Silesia on the one hand, and Germany and Austria on the other. Certain rectifications of a strategic nature in favour of Czechoslovakia were to be compensated by territorial cessions of border areas to Germany (Aš, Rumburk, Frýdlant). The Czechoslovak delegation had agreed to this proposal. Only the Americans wanted to give Cheb, too, to Germany.

Regarding the inclusion of millions of Germans into Czechoslovakia, the Commission issued a declaration, saying that the recommendation for maintaining the unity of the 'Czech lands' had been unanimous, and continuing:

The Commission fully acknowledged the fact that the incorporation of so large a number of Germans into Czechoslovakia may involve certain disadvantages for the future of the new state.

The Commission was at the same time unanimous in its recommendation that the separation of all areas inhabited by German-Bohemians would not only expose Czechoslovakia to great dangers but equally create great difficulties for the Germans themselves. The *only practicable solution was to incorporate these Germans into Czechoslovakia.*

In the elaboration of its recommendations the Commission was guided by the following considerations:

(*a*) Economically: The whole Bohemian territory inhabited by Germans is industrially and economically much more dependent on Bohemia than on Germany. The Bohemian Germans cannot exist without Czech economic co-operation, neither can the Czechs exist economically without the Germans. In this respect there is complete mutual dependence.

(*b*) Geographically: Bohemia, surrounded by its mountains, forms a natural geographical unit. The mere fact that the German population had in the fairly recent past settled in the border regions of this area does not appear to the Commission an adequate cause for depriving Bohemia of its natural frontiers.

(*c*) Political reasons: Politically the German-Bohemians had always belonged to Bohemia.

(*d*) Reasons of national security: These result from geographical considerations. The mountain chain which surrounds Bohemia forms the country's defensive wall. To withdraw this defensive system behind the line created by the mountains would mean the surrender of the country to Germany.

The United States delegation wishes at the same time to state clearly that it was guided in its decision fundamentally by geographical, economic and political reasons.

[1] *La Paix de Versailles* (Paris 1939), IX, 142–52; Hunter Miller, *My Diary*, XVI, 11–16.

Czechoslovakia before Munich

According to the notes made by the Commission's Secretary,[1] Clemenceau, the chief French delegate, added the following comment:

I am now reading the report of the Commission responsible for the frontier between Bohemia and Germany. The (proposed) solution is very complicated and envisages all sorts of modifications, many of which really amount to territorial concessions to the Germans. This seems to me quite useless. The simplest thing would be to keep the frontier as it existed before the war and to leave it to Bohemia and Germany to arrange for individual transfer agreements if they consider this course of action right. As far as the German Bohemians are concerned, this question has nothing to do with the peace preliminaries between us and Germany.

The notes (which are not in shorthand) continue:

LLOYD GEORGE: This is indeed a question which is connected with the partition of the old Austrian Empire. I agree with you to respect the old frontier between Bohemia and Germany.
HOUSE (U.S.A.): That seems to me to be the best solution.
CLEMENCEAU: We are therefore agreed, subject to President Wilson's approval, simply to maintain the old frontier between Bohemia and Germany.

Wilson, who was prevented by an attack of influenza from taking part in the meeting of 4 April 1919, did not raise any objection. Thus the question of Cheb had been quietly dropped. Sometimes it is said that in reality Wilson did not agree to the frontiers of Czechoslovakia as fixed in 1919, and that he did not even know of the existence of millions of Germans in the new state. There is no truth in this, as can be seen from a message found much later in Wilson's papers and dated 2 July 1919, when he was already on board ship.[2] In this message Wilson warned Lansing that the 'greatest caution should be exercised' in any attempts to readjust the frontier of Czechoslovakia according to ethnographic principles. He pointed out that 'there is a certain district in Bohemia, for example, which is undoubtedly German in population but which lies within the undoubted historic boundaries of Bohemia and constitutes an integral part of her industrial life. In such circumstances

[1] Paul Mantoux (ed.), *Les délibérations du Conseil des Quatre* (Paris 1955), I, 148. A rather less precise rendering of this text had been known since the publication of André Tardieu's essay 'Les Allemands de Bohême et les Traités de la Paix' in the Paris weekly, *Gringoire*, of 23 September 1938.
[2] Perman, *Shaping of the Czechoslovak State*, pp. 206–7.

ethnographical lines cannot be drawn without the greatest injustice and injury.'

In conformity with this directive the final reply of the Allies to the Austrian delegation, drafted on 25 August 1919, declared:[1]

The Allied and Associated Powers...believe that the German-speaking people living on the borders of these provinces (Bohemia, Moravia, Silesia) ought to remain connected with the Czech people in order to co-operate with them in the development of that national unity in which history has associated them.

A 'second Switzerland'?

It is often stated that the Czechoslovak delegation in Paris obtained approval for her frontiers including more than three million Germans only in return for the promise that Czechoslovakia would be a 'second Switzerland' – a promise which was not kept. The *Aide-Mémoire* III declared in general terms that as far as the internal structure of the country was concerned, the Czechoslovak régime would resemble that of Switzerland. It is most unlikely that the promise of a liberal policy towards the minorities or the *aide-mémoire* as a whole had any influence on the decision of the 'Big Four' of 4 April 1919. It has been shown that this decision was based on other grounds although this does not exclude the possibility that it was facilitated by Beneš' assurances about the minorities. But neither then, nor later, when Beneš, in May 1919 (at a time when the decision about the frontiers had already been taken), referred to it again in the negotiations about the Minorities' Treaty, was the desirability of following the Swiss model mentioned by the Principal Allies.

The fact that new frontiers put millions of people whose native language was not Polish, Czech or Romanian under the sovereignty of new States strengthened the conviction among the Major Allies that something would have to be done to protect the rights of these minorities. It was decided to place the new or completely reconstructed states (such as Yugoslavia and Romania), whose democratic institutions were not yet fully trusted, under some sort of treaty obligation. Not surprisingly the initiative came from the American-Jewish organizations who wanted to protect the large Jewish communities in Eastern Europe against discrimination. The

[1] *FRUS*, VII 865; Almond–Lutz, *Treaty of St Germain*, p. 470.

United States Government took up this suggestion and a treaty was first concluded with Poland which was to serve as a model for similar ones with the other states concerned.[1] In the case of Poland, but especially Romania, the great powers encountered great difficulties before they were able to persuade the new governments to agree to treaties which were looked at askance as a limitation of sovereignty. Not so in the case of Czechoslovakia. Beneš readily agreed to sign a Minorities Treaty on the Polish pattern with the sole stipulation that it should not contain anything singling out the Jews as needing special protection, as this would have been considered offensive by his Government.[2] His condition was accepted by the Allies.

Apart from this omission and a special provision relating to Ruthenia, the agreement signed with Czechoslovakia was identical with that concluded with Poland[3] and, like all similar agreements, contained a clause authorizing the new state to declare one language to be an 'official' one. This privilege, which in Czechoslovakia was enjoyed by the Czech (and Slovak) languages, was thus entirely within the framework of the minorities' protection system and not peculiar to Czechoslovakia alone.

The legend of the promised and unrealized Swiss solution derives from an informal note which Beneš wrote down on 20 May 1919 at the request of the French diplomat Berthelot who was the chairman of the Commission for the New States. It begins with the general declaration:[4]

> 1. It is the intention of the Czechoslovak Government to create the organisation of the State by accepting as a basis of national rights the principles applied in the constitution of the Swiss Republic, that is, to make the Czechoslovak Republic a sort of Switzerland (*une sorte de Suisse*), taking into consideration, of course, the special conditions in Bohemia.

So nothing definite was promised, for any concrete interpretation which one might attach to the phrase '*une sorte de Suisse*' is immediately put in doubt by the reservation about Bohemian con-

---

[1] Temperley, *Peace Conference in Paris*, v, 125. For details see Erwin Viefhaus, *Die Minderheitenfrage und die Entstehung der Minderheitenschutzverträge auf der Pariser Friedenskonferenz von 1919* (Würzburg 1960), p. 163.

[2] *Prager Presse*, 9 October 1937.

[3] Text printed by Viefhaus in English, *Die Minderheitenfrage*, pp. 231-5.

[4] Hunter Miller, *My Diary*, xiii, 69-70; *La Paix de Versailles*, v, 53-4.

ditions. In fact Beneš declared later[1] that what he had in mind was not at all the

creation of a new Switzerland with identical institutions but on the contrary a state with institutions...related to the special conditions in Bohemia and which adopt certain of the principles of the enlightened Swiss régime.

Switzerland, in other words, was nothing but a synonym for liberal treatment and the reference to it only a more impressive-sounding paraphrase of the old promise of a liberal attitude towards the minorities. After the general preamble Beneš gave a long and detailed explanation of how he proposed to create 'a sort of Switzerland', subject to 'the special conditions in Bohemia'. It was to be constructed as follows (it might be mentioned that up to 1938 Czechoslovakia did broadly conform to the pattern laid down in this note by Beneš):

2. There will be universal suffrage under the proportional system which will assure to the various nationalities of the Republic proportional representation in all elective bodies.
3. The schools will be maintained by the State, throughout its territory, from the public funds, and schools will be established for the various nationalities in all the communes where the number of children, legally ascertained, proves the necessity of establishing such schools.

Not even Nazi propaganda was able to deny that these promises had been put into practice.

4. All public offices (professions) will be open to the various nationalities inhabiting the Republic.

This principle was embodied in the Czechoslovak constitution.

5. The courts will be mixed, and Germans will have the right to plead before the highest courts in their own language.

One cannot claim that *all* the courts were in fact bilingual but in the Supreme Court of Appeal and the Administrative High Court cases were dealt with in German, if a German litigant was involved coming from a district where at least a fifth of the inhabitants were German-speaking. Such a concession never was, and is not now, granted in any other country which provides protection for its minorities. In the circumstances it would have been difficult to keep

[1] *Prager Presse*, 10 October 1937, quoted by Viefhaus, *Die Minderheitenfrage*, p. 183.

German altogether out of the ministries and the courts, but the same benefit accrued to the much smaller Hungarian, Polish and Ruthenian minorities.

> 6. The local administration (of communes and districts) will be carried out in the language of the majority of the population.

This has never been the subject of any complaint. Point seven concerns religious freedom. Here likewise no promise was made that was not kept. The next paragraph, on the other hand, is fraught with much greater difficulties: it concerns language policy.

It is clear that even at that early stage it was planned to give the Czech language a certain position of prominence (which incidentally does not run counter to the Minorities' Treaty signed later). 'In ordinary practice' it would no doubt have been possible to satisfy the population linguistically even more than turned out to be the case; German was not used officially '*à titre égal*'. But it *was* used, as will be shown later.[1]

> 8. The official language will be Czech and the State will be known abroad as the Czechoslovak State; but in practice the German language shall be the second language of the country and shall be employed currently in administration, before the courts and in the central Parliament on equal footing (*à titre égal*) with Czech. It is the intention of the Czechoslovak Government to satisfy the population in practice and in daily use, but reserving a certain special position for the Czechoslovak language and element.

The memorandum ended with this declaration:

> 9. To express this in a different way we may say: the present state in which the Germans had an overwhelming preponderance will remain; only the privileges that the Germans enjoyed will be reduced to their just proportion (for example the German schools will be reduced in number because they will be superfluous).
> It will be an extremely liberal régime which will very much resemble that of Switzerland.

Paris, May 20, 1919

Switzerland is invoked afresh but again in such general terms that no concrete promise can be inferred from it. In Beneš' note it was stated clearly how far the 'resemblance' to the Swiss régime was to go: it was simply a question of moderation and tolerance between

[1] See p. 60.

the language groups, just as many years later in a speech at Bratislava[1] President Masaryk was to claim that 'national tolerance was the mark of the Republic'.

While no one can say that before 1938 Czechoslovakia was a paradise on earth, no promise to copy Switzerland completely was ever given and later betrayed.

The response to the Czechoslovak promises

After studying the Beneš memorandum of 20 May 1919 the 'Commission for the New States' came to the conclusion that these promises went far beyond the minimum requirements of the minorities' treaties but that it was neither practicable nor even necessary to put them into legal form. With undisguised relief at having got rid of one of the many troubles besetting the Peace Conference it was declared:[2]

The position of the Germans in Bohemia is of course completely different [i.e. from the situation of the Hungarians and the Ruthenians]; they had until recent years been the dominating influence in the State, they form a highly developed, very capable element and, in the past, have been a very aggressive population. It is clear that the prospects and perhaps almost the existence of the New State will depend on the success with which it incorporates the Germans as willing citizens. The very magnitude of this task makes it one quite different in character from the mere protection of the other minorities with which the Committee has had to deal; it is one which goes so deeply into the heart of all the institutions that the solution of it is probably best left to the Czechs themselves.

The Committee has received a communication from Dr. Beneš...in which he has informed them that it is the intention of the present government to treat the Germans with the greatest liberality, and the proposals go far beyond anything which the Committee would have felt justified in putting forward. Under the circumstances therefore they consider that it would be wiser not to make any specific reference to the Germans.

After the decision of the Peace Conference had been announced, the representatives of the Germans inside Czechoslovakia maintained their defiance in their outward attitude and there was an orgy of pathetic vows 'never' to surrender their demand for self-determination; these oaths, however solemn, were soon forgotten

[1] Consul Schellert to G.F.M. 15 October 1930, *G.F.M.* serial L439/III, frames 132573-7.
[2] Hunter Miller, *My Diary*, XIII, 78–80, also 162–3, *La Paix de Versailles*, X, 61–2, also 122.

because even if there could not be much enthusiasm for being included in a predominantly non-German State, they found no response among the population at large. To crown it all, many of those who had sworn 'Never!' had meanwhile, on 15 June 1919, exercised their right to vote as Czechoslovak citizens in the Czechoslovak local elections.

No single group or party was at that time rash enough to abstain from the chance of taking part. After all, this was the very first free election which the Germans had experienced, based on the system of proportional representation which ensured that the true ethnic structure was faithfully mirrored in local administration. The result of the borough elections was a resounding victory for the German Social Democrats, who with 44 per cent of all German votes in Bohemia became by far the strongest German party. Having previously been part of the Austrian Social-Democratic Party, they constituted themselves at Teplice at the end of August 1919 as the German Social-Democratic Workers' Party of Czechoslovakia.[1] In a long speech Josef Seliger declared the party's readiness to work actively in the new State. But the Czechs were not satisfied with this avowal of willingness to co-operate, being irritated by Seliger's insistence on territorial autonomy for the German-inhabited areas, indications of which Seliger had skilfully interwoven with his phrases of goodwill.

In a posthumous book Karl Renner, whose task in 1919 as head of Austria's Government had been to oppose the territorial demands of Czechoslovakia at St Germain, explained the motives for his actions. This was his epitaph on the old altercations at St Germain:[2]

When the territorial legislation [with claims against Czechoslovakia] was settled (in Vienna), it was above all considered to be the basis for future negotiations, especially with the Czechs. Hardly anybody expected that the newly constituted provinces of German-Bohemia and Sudetenland, which were so far removed from the Alpine lands of Austria, could in the long run remain politically joined to them. It was intended, with the assistance of local representatives, to ensure that these areas received a measure of autonomy acceptable to both sides...Consolation for the loss of three and a half million Sudeten-Germans could be found in the fact that their numerical strength and their tradition of fighting for their national existence would make them able to defend themselves

[1] Josef Hofbauer and Emil Strauss, *Josef Seliger* (Prague 1930), pp. 167ff.
[2] Karl Renner, *Österreich von der ersten zur zweiten Republik* (Vienna 1953), pp. 24, 30, 34, 211–12.

in a democratic State and with the help of the Minorities Treaty...With the exception of the German Nationalists, comprising one-fifth of the population, the Austrians tended to accept as a matter of course that the Czechs had at last achieved their Statehood...As soon as the State was established the majority of the Sudeten-Germans had accepted its existence, respected it as one of the bastions of European democracy and sincerely collaborated not only in its economic development but in the central and local government...A strong group in German-Bohemia opposed Hitler: it only collapsed when the Western Powers had clearly abandoned Czechoslovakia.

This does not answer the question whether Renner's aims could not have been better served by the opposite policy, namely by giving up those claims which he had raised purely in order to exert pressure in the conference debates. All indications suggest that this was indeed the case.

4 THE 1920 CZECHOSLOVAK CONSTITUTION

The first legislative organ of the State to be created on 28 October 1918 was the five-member *Národní Výbor* (National Committee). The function of this body concluded after two weeks with the issue of a provisional constitution dealing only with the most urgent matters and transferred all future legislative powers to the Revolutionary National Assembly, which was in effect the National Committee extended to include 270 members, of which 54 were Slovaks and the rest Czechs.

Though on the day the Republic was proclaimed in Prague the decision had been taken at Geneva to accept a German representative as Minister without Portfolio[1] in the new government, it seems that German co-operation in the Revolutionary National Assembly, at any rate at the beginning, was not envisaged. There is little doubt that under the conditions prevailing at the time when the German members of the Austrian Parliament elected in Bohemia, Moravia and Silesia in 1911 had opted for Austria, a Czech invitation to the Germans would have met with scant success.

The provisional constitution had entrusted legislative authority including the making of the constitution to the Revolutionary National Assembly, which clearly implied that its construction was to be part of the 1918 Revolution. But there does not seem to have been any firm decision to exclude the Germans (or Hungarians) from contributing to the work on the constitution, since otherwise Masaryk could hardly have referred to the possibility of their being consulted as late as July 1919. In an interview at that time he said that the Germans had opposed the revolution but that it would depend upon them 'whether they work with us on the constitution'.[2] Masaryk was never the mouthpiece of the government of the day:

---

[1] See p. 17.
[2] *Die Zeit* (Vienna), 1 August 1919; Masaryk, *Cesta demokracie*, I, 169.

even as President he reserved an unusual degree of independence to himself. Quite frequently he used the medium of newspaper interviews to exert indirect pressure on the government, especially when justice between the nationalities was at stake. It is unlikely, however, that he would have envisaged German participation in the constitutional task if in fact it had already been definitely decided to exclude it.

On the part of the Germans, a concrete proposal in this direction had already been made by the Christian-Social Professor Robert Mayr-Harting[1] who was later to be a minister in the Czechoslovak government. His idea of co-opting Germans into the National Assembly on the basis of the returns in the local elections of 15 June 1919 was not taken up. These elections had resulted in a resounding defeat for the intransigent German Nationalists and a strong upsurge of those German forces ready to come to an understanding with the Czechs. Thus the Czech contention that an invitation to the Germans to participate in the affairs of the state would mean opening the door to outspoken traitors could not really be sustained.

The position of the Social-Democrat Premier Vlastimil Tusar in this matter was, however, not an easy one. He had replaced the first Premier, Kramář, whose party had been crushed in the local elections but who continued to bask in national glory because he had undergone the martyrdom of an Austrian death-sentence. Tusar was considered to be lax in national matters, if not actually pro-German, and Kramář fought a bitter struggle for his own return to power, on the pretext that the internationally minded Social Democrats were cheating the Czech people of the fruits of their national revolution by shady deals with their German comrades. In the difficult position of having simultaneously to fight the Bolshevik wing of his own party which was a year later to divide it, Tusar had to tread carefully in order not to increase Kramář's chances. Thus, when on the first anniversary of the foundation of the State Masaryk read a presidential address in the National Assembly, the question of German participation in framing the constitution was no longer mentioned, even though the President continued to preach the gospel of national conciliation.[2]

[1] *Prager Tagblatt*, 25 June 1919.
[2] *Message by President T. G. Masaryk*, delivered at the ceremonial session of the

In an interview given at Christmas to *Prager Tagblatt*[1] Masaryk was quite outspoken in this respect. If the Czechs were blamed for not inviting the Germans to help build up the State, then he must point out that until the Peace Treaty was signed the majority of the Germans in the country had regarded themselves as citizens of Austria!

As long as this attitude continued, it was not formally possible to offer membership of the National Assembly to the Germans. This would have created a conflict of conscience for them and we would have risked our advances being rebuffed. But even if they had accepted, what use would their presence there have been, considering their attitude at that time?...Unfortunately the peace negotiations have been more protracted than I had hoped they would be and therefore the state of uncertainty for us and the Germans has lasted for a long time. Now, however, the situation has become clear and I have only one desire: to see that our own political conditions, too, become clarified as soon as possible. It is my unshakeable conviction that every national minority must be recognized. This principle has already been realized in the local electoral system and it will be similarly applied for all other purposes. For me the language question is not one of party politics but fundamental to good government. A suitable solution of this problem will eliminate many of the German complaints.

On the initiative of the German Social Democrats the first discussion took place on 20 December 1919 between representatives of this party and of the Government. The German delegation's main demand was for the full representation of all nationalities in the Constituent Assembly, but Tusar ruled this out on the grounds that the Germans had, until recently, formed 'governments of defiance'. During the interregnum between the collapse of the old order and the birth of the new the Revolutionary National Assembly had been an absolute necessity and its activities had also benefited the Germans. The constitution and the electoral system were going to be determined by the existing National Assembly, but the Germans could rest assured that, just as in the case of the local elections, justice would be the guiding principle.[2] A similar reply was given two days later to the other German parties under the leadership of Lodgman: Tusar made no bones about what he called 'revolutionary law', by force of which the National Assembly was in office.[3]

National Assembly on 28 October 1919 (Prague 1919), pp. 15–16. Masaryk, *Cesta demokracie*, I, 202.

[1] *Prager Tagblatt*, 25 December 1919.
[2] Klepetar, *Seit 1918*, p. 101.
[3] Ibid. pp. 101–2; Peroutka, *Budování státu*, II, 1306–7.

This reference to revolutionary law to defend the fact that the constitutional foundations of the State were to be laid by a nominated body consisting exclusively of Czechs and Slovaks was little more than an excuse, possibly valid if the constitution had been promulgated immediately after the end of the war. In fact, it was not accepted until 29 February 1920 and then only after heated discussions and long after the Peace Treaties had been signed. It may well be that an agreement between Czechs and Germans on the constitutional issue was not possible, however desirable it may have been particularly in this case, to achieve unanimity for reasons of prestige. But lack of unanimity would surely have been no obstacle to a sensible compromise, reached on a democratic basis. It seems much more likely that Tusar's real fears were of a tactical, not fundamental nature. The German Socialists wanted to raise in this connection the problem of national autonomy for the German-inhabited areas. This was not really essential from the constitutional point of view and could have been solved at a more propitious time. In Tusar's view any discussion of the autonomy question in connection with the constitution would only have intensified Czech national passions, exacerbating the right-wing oppositional agitation with dire results for the Government just at a time when there were Communist uprisings in neighbouring countries and a Communist régime in Hungary. Hence what appeared to be the line of least resistance was chosen and all plans for co-operation between the various nationalities dropped.

A liberal constitution

When German Nationalists describe the Czechoslovak Constitution of 1920 as 'an arbitrary act', one might be led to assume that it had a pronounced anti-German bias. In fact, even a most searching examination would fail to elicit anything designed to deprive the Germans (or any other nationality) of their rights. It was a characteristically 'Western' or 'liberal' constitution, based on the principle of civic equality 'without consideration of race, language or religion' and guaranteeing to all citizens the usual rights of political freedom. Parliament was to be elected on the system of proportional representation and the vote was to be universal, equal, direct and secret so that no population group could be disenfranchised. One section of the Constitution, dealing with the 'Protection of racial, religious and linguistic Minorities' incorporated the obligations assumed under the minorities' treaty. It guaranteed the free use of their national language to everyone, schools for national minorities with instruction given in their own language and appropriate subsidies from public funds for cultural and other purposes. A general constitutional provision, although never followed up by legislation, forbade 'every kind of forcible denationalization'. The most important constitutional safeguard, however, was embodied in the Constitution in the form of a declaration that

Differences of religion or language do not form an obstacle to any citizen of the Czechoslovak Republic within the general body of the law and in particular do not debar him from admission to the public service, or from the practice of any trade or profession.

Though the Constitution guaranteed to 'racial, religious and linguistic minorities' certain rights 'wherever a considerable proportion of Czechoslovak citizens of other than Czech language lives' many people objected to the fact that the Germans, who were so numerous and economically as well as culturally disproportionately important, were 'only' given minority status in Czechoslovakia. After all, the Paris Peace Conference had said that the problems of the Germans in Czechoslovakia were 'quite different from the mere protection of other minorities'.

But the idea of the political isolation of a national minority, a 'state within a state' as it were, would appear to be feasible, though probably not desirable, only where this minority is numerically too small to count compared with the main population. A separate existence for the Sudeten Germans inside Czechoslovakia, but ignoring the political reality of that state, would not only have sapped the vitality of the latter but would have reacted unfavourably on the economic structure of the German-inhabited parts. On the other hand, Czechoslovakia should have set out to try to remove the stigma of political inferiority from the minority concept, leaving it with its mathematical significance.

Even before the Constitution was promulgated the National Assembly had passed a series of laws which contrasted strikingly with what one would have expected as the logical consequence of a collapse of historic proportions, namely the elimination of German influence. Instead the local government electoral system (to which reference has been made) attached so much importance to mathematical justice that it was made possible for the Germans of Prague to participate in municipal administration for the first time. Poorly attended German grammar schools which had existed in entirely Czech towns disappeared. On the other hand a law passed by the Revolutionary National Assembly in April 1919 assured the Germans that the basis of their educational system would remain intact: elementary schools with instruction given in German were to be built or maintained wherever there were at least 40 pupils over a triennial average (for the secondary schools this number was 400).

The law of July 1919 (relating to local public libraries) provided that all towns and boroughs with more than 400 inhabitants declaring themselves to belong to a national minority would have to build special minority libraries from public funds; their administration was to be entrusted to a committee of members of the minority concerned.

The language law

Together with the Constitution itself a special language law was enacted. The principle of civic equality which the former guaranteed was infringed here on one important point, for the Czech and Slovak languages and all those who used them were given a privileged position. The language law was, more than anything else, an act of revenge for the discrimination the Czechs in Austria, and the Slovaks in Hungary, had had to bear and, vicariously, for the even worse fate that would have been in store for the Slav nations had the Germans won the war. However, Masaryk again did not hesitate to show how little he liked the turn events were taking. In 1892, speaking in the Austrian Parliament, he had criticized the Germans for treating the language' 'as a kind of fetish'[1] and his attitude had not changed when after 1918 some Czechs developed the same tendency in favour of the Czech language. On 29 October 1918 he had already written to Beneš from America: 'We shall have to negotiate with our Germans so that they will accept our State, which is not going to have a nationalist structure but will be genu-

[1] Quoted by Josef Hofbauer, *Der grosse alte Mann* (Prague 1938), p. 119.

inely a modern democracy.'[1] In May 1919 he expressed the view,[2] that the Germans were to be given everything they had a right to, for the Austrian practice of making concessions only under pressure should not be followed. When, in summer 1919, the draft of what was to become the language law was submitted to him, he returned it with lengthy comments which illustrated his critical attitude and his honest desire to see justice done both to Czechs and Germans.[3]

According to the language law, courts and other authorities were obliged to accept written or oral submissions in the minority language, wherever, in the smallest administrative unit (the local juridical district) more than 20 per cent of the population were of German (or Hungarian or Polish) origin. Judgments or other official responses had to be given bilingually, in Czech and the minority language concerned. In 1926 the position of the minorities was improved to the extent that in court districts with more than a two-third German majority German cases were dealt with entirely in German, thereby excluding the 'State' language completely. The practical implications of these provisions can best be illustrated by figures[4] which show that of 3,321,688 Czechoslovak citizens speaking German 299,728, that is 9.5 per cent, had no 'language right': these Germans, living in predominantly Czech surroundings, had to use Czech (or Slovak) in their dealings with authority. Over 90 per cent of the Germans did not suffer from any restriction in the use of their native language when dealing with officials or the courts, and in a large part of the German area, actually in 105 court districts, cases were dealt with entirely in German.

A certain degree of discrimination, however, did exist: Czechs and Slovaks could always use their language, even where hopelessly outnumbered; not so the Germans (or Hungarians). But the really decisive argument against Czechoslovak language practice was that it had not, after all, shed its 'old Austrian' features as Masaryk had wished, was not flexible and it often ran counter to plain common-sense without producing any benefit for the State.

[1] Peroutka, *Budování státu*, I, 187.
[2] Masaryk, *Cesta demokracie*, I, 128.
[3] Peroutka, *Budování státu*, II, 1561–2.
[4] Werner Glück, *Sprachenrecht und Sprachenpraxis in der Tschechoslowakischen Republik* (Halle 1939), pp. 53–62.

Was Czechoslovakia a 'National State' until October 1938 or a 'State of Nationalities'? To the chagrin of Kramář and other Czech nationalists the constitution nowhere proclaimed Czechoslovakia a 'National State' nor did it concede any special privileges to the Czechs and Slovaks or Czechoslovaks (as Czechs and Slovaks were regarded as two branches of one nation). Beneš as Foreign Minister was opposed to this idea as its implementation would have created difficulties for him when assuring the League of Nations of the equality of all Czechoslovakia's citizens. After his return from the Peace Conference he addressed Parliament for the first time on 30 September 1919, giving a lengthy report on the Paris proceedings.[1] The Conference, he explained regarded the successor States of Austria-Hungary to be 'National States', as they represented the fulfilment of national aspirations; nevertheless the Conference realized that

from the international point of view these national States could not be formed as if they really were national States; it was not possible to draw the frontiers so that there would be no separate minorities.

Nineteen years later – on 17 August 1938 – Beneš explained to Henlein's delegates[2] that

the expression *les États nationaux* was used during the peace negotiations, not is the sense of National States, but merely to contrast them with Austria-Hungary.

Not content with correcting a factual misunderstanding, Beneš went further in 1938 by pointing out that

during the parliamentary negotiations over the Constitution (he) sounded a warning note against designating Czechoslovakia as a National State...He (Beneš) considered the theory of the National State to be mistaken.

In a discussion which took place a few days later on 25 August 1938, Beneš related, according to the notes made by his interlocutors,[3] that Kramář had opposed him, because 'he (Beneš) had already in the Revolutionary National Assembly stood against the idea of a State language and the plan to designate Czechoslovakia in the Constitution as a National State'.

[1] Peroutka, *Budování státu*, II, 1293.
[2] *Documents on German Foreign Policy* (*DGFP*), Series D, vol. II (Washington 1949), no. 378.
[3] *DGFP*, D/II, no. 398.

Czechoslovakia before Munich

Before 1938 there was only one consistent advocate of the theory of the 'National State' in Czechoslovakia, namely Kramář and his ever-diminishing party. None of the other Czech parties used the term. The bureaucracy, however, did frequently behave as if the State had been created for the *Staatsvolk* only and that the others were to get what was left over. It would, however, be rash to condemn Czechoslovakia on this count alone: to reconcile the needs of the Czechs and Slovaks who felt responsible for the State with the basic rights of the other nationalities was no simple matter.

The second nation in the State

With the consolidation of the State, Czech attempts to put the German problem in a different category from that of simply protecting a minority became more auspicious. The first step on the road to a reappraisal was taken by Rudolf Bechyně, leader of the Czechoslovak Social Democrats and at that time Deputy-Premier. At a meeting in Prague in 1934 he said:[1]

I trust the democratic part of the German population, but especially the German Social-Democratic workers. A new state nation has been born and a great section of the Germans is ready to stand by the Republic in all dangers.

Later on, the slogan was taken up by Kamil Krofta, the Foreign Minister.

When on 28 January 1937 the leader of the German Social Democrats and Minister of Health, Ludwig Czech, began negotiations with Milan Hodža, the Prime Minister, on behalf of the German parties represented in the Government, he could claim[2]

We take up negotiations on the assumption that the Germans here are a *Staatsvolk*. This will provide their legal equality. We wish to reconcile the ethnic groups on a democratic basis, with democratic methods and in a democratic spirit.

Though the creation of the constitutional foundations of the State by an unrepresentative body without the participation of the minorities was not only a grave but an avoidable error, all election results before 1935 show that the great majority of the German population did in fact accept the constitution they had not been

[1] Klepetar, *Seit 1918*, p. 370, *Prager Tagblatt*, 22 May 1926.
[2] J. W. Brügel, *Ludwig Czech* (Vienna 1960), p. 145.

consulted about. In 1920, 1925 and 1929 the 'Activist' parties (i.e. the German Social Democrats, the Agrarian Party and the German Christian Social, besides a few smaller groups) who, although by no means blindly uncritical, were prepared to co-operate with the Czechs on the basis of the existing constitution, received between 74 and 83 per cent of the German vote, leaving the German Nationalists and the National Socialists far behind, as the following voting figures show.[1]

	1920	1925	1929
German Activists	1,249,341	1,297,568	1,252,281
Nationalists and Nazis	328,351	409,272	393,393

In the first election results the votes of what were to be the German Communists were still included in the Social Democratic returns, which blurs the picture. The results of 1925 and 1929, however, were already fully representative, especially since that period saw the entry of two German parties into the government. In the following election, that of 1929, the total votes cast for the Nationalist opposition again fell, an indication of the basic readiness of the Germans to come to terms with the Czechoslovak State: otherwise all the German parties which had a policy of co-operation and which were prepared to air potential grievances in a democratic manner, would have lost support.

Between 1916 and 1922, by a series of acts of sabotage and risings, the Southern Irish managed to shake off British rule. There was no lack of attempts to 'suggest' a similar course of action to the Germans in Czechoslovakia who did, however, not take such advice seriously; the German Minister in Prague, Koch, was right to tell Berlin that 'the Germans of this country...are certainly not Irishmen!'[2] A few years later, in the face of the attempts of the Sudeten German Nationalists to persuade the Reich authorities that all Sudeten Germans, including those represented in the Czechoslovak government, had no more ardent desire than to obtain the right to self-determination, Koch put the record straight with his ironical comment:[3]

[1] *Statistisches Jahrbuch der Tschechoslowakei, 1920, 1925 und 1929* (Prague 1921, 1926 and 1930).
[2] Koch to G.F.M. 8 January 1923, *G.F.M.* serial L417/I, frames 19948-51.
[3] Koch to G.F.M. 7 July 1926, *G.F.M.* serial K91, frames 9189-92.

Czechoslovakia before Munich

Every Sudeten-German answers the question whether he desires the somewhat nebulous right to self-determination with the same enthusiastic Yes! he would give if asked whether he would like a villa in the Riesengebirge [a range of mountains in Northern Bohemia].

Equally realistic was the assessment of the situation given by another observer, who looked at things from a different angle. The Austrian Minister in Berlin, Felix Frank, who was at the same time leader of the pro-Anschluss party in his own country and kept in close touch with his party colleagues in Czechoslovakia, had a discussion on May 1928 with the German Under-Secretary for Foreign Affairs, Carl von Schubert, about which the latter minuted.[1]

Herr Frank then started to discuss relations between Austria and Czechoslovakia and said that in reality there were no conflicts between the two countries. Regarding the Sudeten Germans, they were unique (*ein Kapitel für sich*). He could tell me in confidence – it could not be said publicly, or the Sudeten Germans would kill him – *that any ambitions to alter the frontier would be entirely crazy*. Answering a question of mine, he admitted that such far-reaching plans were still ventilated only by a tiny proportion of the Sudeten Germans.

There was no need to say 'in confidence' what everybody knew: that the majority of Germans in Czechoslovakia, even though they did not accept it uncritically, did not reject the state, and this despite the fact that Masaryk's exhortations to the Czechs to win over the minorities had not met with anything like the success they deserved.

[1] Minutes by Secretary of State Schubert, *G.F.M.* serial 4577, frames 174285-6.

5 THE FIRST YEARS

With the increasing consolidation of constitutional life in Czechoslovakia her basic dilemma became apparent: the conflict between
the ideal of building up a State on a modern, democratic basis such
as Masaryk had envisaged, dispensing justice to all its citizens without discrimination, and the psychologically comprehensible but in
practice self-destructive tendency to transform that State into an
instrument of Czech and Slovak nationalism. If the country had
been granted a few decades of peaceful development, this dilemma
might well have been largely overcome; hopeful signs of such a
trend had already appeared in the years after 1933.

The conflict between Czechs and Germans was naturally sharpest
in the early years of the new State, when the Czechs crowded into
those positions from which they felt they had previously been
excluded in their own country. Though the political left grouped
around T. G. Masaryk and later Edvard Beneš was always more
attached to the ideal of ethnic justice than the right represented by
Kramář, even the cosmopolitan Masaryk, who wished to educate his
people to become true Europeans, had in his first address to the
nation referred to the Germans as 'immigrants and colonists',
expressions which he later regretted and withdrew.[1]

What happened in Czechoslovakia in the years before 1926 –
the progressive elimination of German and the extension of Czech
influence to sectors partly or wholly closed to it before – was only
the historical process of the displacement of one ruling class by
another. There has never been an instance when a long overdue
removal of old privileges has been immediately followed by an era
of law and justice for all alike: on the contrary, the general rule has
been for the nation which, before the revolution that brought it
victory, had been the underdog to assert itself more violently than
the Czechoslovaks did after the First World War. This is not to

[1] See p. 19.

deny that with the abolition of old privileges some new privileges were created, the moral justification for which was not entirely due to the fact that they benefited a nation previously oppressed.

During the early years there were only a few isolated acts of violence against the Germans in Czechoslovakia; of course this does not mean that all harshness was avoided. Even if comparatively few changes were made in the bureaucratic apparatus at the end of 1918,[1] it could not be expected that the régime should establish its new State in order to keep in their jobs people whose hostility was notorious; these were gradually pensioned off. As, in the beginning, even the German political parties prepared to collaborate with the Prague Government showed hardly any interest in having German officials in the newly created ministries, they employed few non-Czechs.

The Germans' chief complaint in the early years concerned the closing of their schools. In reality this only affected schools suffering from such poor attendance under the new conditions that their existence could no longer be justified. A further wave of school closures began in 1925, after the low birth rate of the war years had drastically reduced the number of children of school age. In Slovakia on the other hand there was no German school system in existence before 1918; under Czechoslovak rule German educational institutions – primary and grammar schools – were created for the first time. In general it will be found that in this important respect the Germans in Czechoslovakia did not do badly compared with the Czechs or even the Germans in Germany.

Naturally there were repeated attempts to eliminate or at least reduce the quite disproportionate economic influence of the Germans. The only notable result was the agrarian reform, long overdue, which parcelled out large landed estates. No doubt Czech applications for shares in the apportioned land received preferential treatment, but even in this sector, where justice was least regarded, the result was not nearly as catastrophic to the Germans as is often maintained.

Apart from a certain pressure, there was hardly any official encroachment on the rest of the economy; a German Foreign

---

[1] Gebsattel to Reich Chancellor, 1 November 1918, *G.F.M. Akten betreffend Boehmen*, vol. 44, no. 1236/3. See p. 26.

Ministry summary of October 1925 could rightly state:[1] 'The Czechoslovak endeavour to bring Sudeten-German enterprises into economic, and especially financial, dependence on the economy of the State has so far produced no results worth mentioning.' That this did not change to any material extent later is shown in a report by Koch, the German Minister in Prague, to Berlin at the end of 1934:[2]

If the average of the figures specified in the preliminary reports is taken, it will be found that during the boom years the Germans enjoyed economic powers in Czechoslovakia on a scale which was two or three times as great as that to which they would be entitled on a strictly proportional basis.

The question is then: Were the Germans deliberately excluded from playing their part during these first years or did they exclude themselves? German participation in the government had been under discussion from the very first. The decision taken by Beneš and Kramář at Geneva to include a German in the government, the perhaps half-hearted invitation to Lodgman to join the *Národní Výbor*, the willingness to give two of the six seats in the Moravian National Committee to the Germans – none of these were part of a carefully concerted plan nor were they intended to encourage German aspirations for full autonomy. There never was in fact between 1918 and 1938 any carefully concerted Government plan to settle the country's most important problem – that might be called the chief weakness of Czechoslovak policy in the field of ethnic justice. But nothing ever done or suggested revealed any tendency to oppress or even to slight the Germans or any other minority.

After the first parliamentary elections of April 1920 Premier Tusar adhered to the policy of extending a welcoming hand to the Germans. Indeed he thought of broadening the bases of his government by including German Social Democrats and Agrarians. The President, too, tried by other methods to persuade the Germans or at any rate the more co-operative ones among them to take an active part in political life. During the summer of 1919 and again later Masaryk wanted Professor Josef Redlich, an old parliamentary colleague from Vienna, to settle in Prague and become Minister of

[1] Memorandum by Köpke, 5 October 1925, *G.F.M.* serial K91, frames 008975-9.
[2] Koch to G.F.M. 6 December 1934, *G.F.M.* serial 9135, frames 642442-9.

Commerce.[1] Subsequently Masaryk offered the Ministry of Education, a key position in a multinational state, to the editor of the *Prager Tagblatt*, Rudolf Keller.[2] Keller, greatly surprised by this unexpected offer, declined the invitation because he thought, reasonably enough, that the man who was to be responsible not only for the German but above all for the Czech schools must know more Czech than he did.

Tusar's negotiations with the German Social Democrats in the spring of 1920 about their entry into the government broke down because the Germans insisted on political concessions which Tusar felt he could not grant.[3] The internal crisis of his party forced Tusar to resign in September 1920: a nationally mixed government under Social-Democratic leadership would thus not have survived for long. In the years following, the public debate about German participation in the government never completely subsided, although the Czechs did not go beyond vague expressions of willingness to consider the possibility. This was matched by indecision on the German side. As early as 1921 Haniel, Under-Secretary of State in the German Foreign Office, considered the entry of Germans into the Czechoslovak Government as within reach:[4]

Considering the close economic interests which exist between the Czechoslovak Republic and the German Reich, our policy in Prague will be one of 'wait and see', leaving the Czechoslovak Government to make any approach. This will be all the more successful...if internal conditions in Czechoslovakia lead to Sudeten-German participation in the government.

When, at the end of May 1920, the newly elected Parliament assembled in Prague, Lodgman read a solemn declaration in the name of the German non-Socialist parties.[5] This had been the method adopted by the Czechs in the old Austrian *Reichsrat* after 1879, when they had decided to abandon their policy of non-co-operation, though not their protest against the Austrian system.

[1] Josef Redlich, *Schicksalsjahre Österreichs 1908–1919* (Austria's Fateful Years) (Graz–Cologne 1954), II, 345–6.
[2] Information kindly supplied to the author by Dr Alfred M. Mayer, New York (son-in-law of Dr Keller), on 7 December 1962.
[3] Peroutka, *Budování státu*, III (Prague 1936), 1745; Klepetar, *Seit 1918*, p. 210.
[4] German Foreign Ministry Circular of 7 January 1921, *G.F.M.* serial K1173, frames 301878–84.
[5] *Parliamentary Minutes*, 1 June 1920, pp. 28–9. Reprinted in *Rudolf Lodgman von Auen, Reden und Aufsätze*, ed. A. K. Simon (Munich 1954), pp. 63–5.

After each election, therefore, they had repeated their legal reservations, subsequently trying to extract as much as possible for their nation. The Germans now tried to imitate this procedure and Lodgman waxed full of democratic indignation about the injustice done to the Germans. The next day Josef Seliger spoke for the German Social Democrats. His speech[1] did not lack strong criticism, but a different spirit pervaded his approach, and the following excerpt from his speech shows how well he understood the position of the other side:

> I know the history of your people. For ten years I sat next to you in the old Austrian parliament and worked with my Czech party colleagues. I know that the majority of your nation is democratic, freedom-loving and progressive...Among your people, too, the elections have produced a majority which professes its faith in freedom, progress and democracy.

On the one hand Seliger protested against the right of self-determination being withheld and confirmed his belief in it; on the other, he expressed his willingness 'to work on the basis of this State and this Parliament for the benefit of the German working class'.

Masaryk's admonitions

On countless public occasions Masaryk warned his own people to come to grips with the problem of the co-existence of several nationalities in their State. In July 1919, for instance, when the Agrarian Antonín Švehla was appointed Minister of the Interior (in 1922 Švehla became Premier and in 1926 headed the first Czech–German Cabinet)[2] Masaryk declared that governments everywhere have to take the initiative in settling the problem of minorities.

Could Masaryk have done more to bring the nationalities together? There is no doubt that he used the extraordinary esteem in which his people held him to insist fearlessly upon unpalatable truths which the government of the day would have found too controversial to touch. He was only too justified in sharply reproving both Czech and German nationalists. Where he failed in these

---

[1] *Parliamentary Minutes*, 2 June 1920, pp. 61–75. Also see Hofbauer–Strauss, *Josef Seliger*, pp. 193–5.
[2] Masaryk, *Cesta demokracie*, I, 158.

formative years was in direct contact with those Germans who were willing to co-operate and needed his encouragement.

Significant for Masaryk's views on the German question was his New Year's message of 1922, in which he first referred to Germany itself[1] and underlined the necessity for his country to live in friendly relations with the Weimar Republic. Then he turned to the German problem in Czechoslovakia:

In my opinion the *Czech–German question is the most important one, in fact the only one*...In the question of the national minorities we shall have to proceed according to their size: a generally applicable solution is not possible...

Our State – particularly the Czech lands – has developed in historic uniformity and it will therefore remain as it is. Territorial autonomy for the minorities cannot and will not be a matter for negotiation: the unfavourable geographical distribution of the minorities would anyway not permit it.

Our German fellow-countrymen have a right to share in the administration: in a democracy this is a matter of course. This participation, however, depends on their loyal recognition of the State, without mental reservation. I do not underrate the linguistic difficulties, but they can be overcome if both sides recognise the need for co-operation. Our State, like any other, has and must have its own language in the interest of good administration. With good will, political experience will decide when the use of the State language is unnecessary. Multi-lingual States – and there are really no others – derive their stability from the contentment of their citizens, not from their language...

Koch and the nationalist problem

In October 1921 Professor Saenger, the first German representative in Prague, was succeeded by Walter Koch who was an outstanding expert on Czechoslovak affairs. His reports, during the unusually long period of fourteen years he spent as German Minister and doyen of the Prague diplomatic corps, provide invaluable historical material. The four German heads of mission in Prague between 1918 and 1938 were men of very different outlook. Only one of them, Saenger, who had socialist leanings, felt a certain sympathy for the Czechs. This, however, did not deter him from criticizing the teething troubles of the young State. But there was one thing all four of them – the Consul General Fritz von Gebsattel (until 1919), appointed by the Imperial German régime and representing its spirit, Samuel Saenger, the Saxon Liberal, Walter Koch, and finally the professional diplomat Ernst Eisenlohr under Hitler – had in common: *they all*

[1] Hans Singule, *Der Staat Masaryks* (Berlin 1937), p. 40; Masaryk, *Cesta demokracie* II, 206–9.

tended to support the Czechs rather than the Germans in the country.
Koch quite certainly did not go out of his way to ingratiate himself
with the Czechs; for him they were simply 'an intelligent, hard-
working, nationally very conscious people of 6, 7 Millions, enclosed
on three sides by about 70 Million Germans'.[1] Precisely because
Koch looked on Czechoslovak internal policy with a very critical
eye, his criticism of the German attitude merits special attention.
Masaryk's rejection (which he modified quite considerably in 1928)
of the idea of territorial autonomy found unexpected support from
Koch[2]

The rejection of any sort of territorial autonomy is a sharp rebuff to the German
extremists, who had been campaigning under this flag...Nobody is able to
say what, in view of the geographical configuration of the area inhabited by the
Germans (*bei der Zertragenheit der deutschen Randbesiedlung*) and the mixture with
Czech boroughs, autonomy should look like, while it cannot be doubted that
the granting of autonomy to the purely German areas would be the first step
to their loss 'later on'. Masaryk's view-point is therefore understandable.

In reality, autonomy in whatever form was not the aim of the German extremists, who had no practical programme at all. The
Nationalists apart, all German parties set themselves the goal of an
undefined autonomy. Whether Koch was right or not it is interesting
that the German Minister in Prague considered justified Czech
fears that their State might be dismembered. It will be seen later
that Koch's successor Eisenlohr warned Berlin as late as 1937
against the use of the 'autonomy' slogan which the Czechs found
irritating.

It took a long time before any sense of political realism could come
to the surface and the moderate elements – these were, apart from
the Social Democrats, who always denounced German nationalism,
the Agrarians, the Catholics (Christian Socials), and the Liberals –
had the courage to stand up to Lodgman's 'negativist' policy of
nationalism *à outrance*. Franz Spina, of the Agrarian Federation,
proclaimed at a party meeting: 'It is now a question of fighting,
realistically and shrewdly, not against the State but for our rights in
the State.' Some quarters, he said, were actually afraid of a compromise because this might bring the Germans closer to the State.[3]

[1] Memorandum Koch, 7 May 1925, *G.F.M.* serial L416, frames 119123-6.
[2] Koch to G.F.M. 5 January 1922, *G.F.M.* serial L437/1, frames 126083-6.
[3] *Prager Presse*, 17 November 1922.

A year before Spina had boldly declared in Parliament that one ought not to overlook the 'thousand-year union of the two nations, full of reciprocation'.[1] Spina now moved into the front rank of those who advocated conciliation on the basis of the existing State.

At the elections of 1925 both Czechoslovak and German Social Democrats lost ground, mainly because the Communists were now standing as an independent party, but the overall strength of the German parties in favour of coming to an understanding with the Czechs remained roughly the same. Lodgman even lost his seat and he left politics with the resentful valediction (uncannily anticipating Hitler) that the people had shown itself unworthy of so excellent a leader.[2]

The year 1923 had seen an extremely illuminating exchange of views on the position of the Germans in Czechoslovakia between the Berlin Foreign Ministry and its Envoy in Prague. The Under-Secretary at the German Foreign Office, Ago von Maltzan, wrote to Koch:[3]

On the basis of your reports and of general political considerations the point of view is accepted here that the tactics and the attitude of the German-Nationalist party...are neither in line with the interests of the Reich nor with interests of the Sudeten Germans. On the contrary, it would seem to conform with the principle of a reasonable German policy if the Germans in the Czechoslovak Republic recognize its existence as a real factor and aim at a just compromise between Czech and German interests.

Asked to give his own impressions of Czechoslovakia's minorities policy, Koch expressed, in his answer,[4] opposition to any inter-ference on the part of the Reich: 'One ought not to get involved in their (the Sudeten Germans') policy, even if its folly sometimes makes one despair.' He rejected the policy of the German National-ists which consisted of loud words without deeds:

As a consequence of this sterile policy the German cause has lost more and more ground. If one wanted to achieve small successes to be followed later by bigger ones, quite different tactics would be necessary. This would involve the recognition of Czechoslovakia within her present frontiers as a reality, the accep-tance of the existing constitution, steady pressure by legal means for rights as a

[1] *Parliamentary Minutes*, 19 October 1921, pp. 314–15.
[2] *Sudetendeutschland* (monthly), Vienna 1925, no. 11.
[3] Maltzan (G.F.M.) to Koch, 30 June 1923, *G.F.M.* serial L437/II, frames 126542-3.
[4] Koch to G.F.M. 16 July 1923, *G.F.M.* serial L437/II, frames 126614-21.

strong minority, negotiations with the Czechs case by case, exchanging concessions for concessions, with the ultimate possibility, not to be rejected on principle, of collaboration within the Government...The German Nationalist party under its leader Lodgman...remains obstinately opposed to any concession to a...policy of realism. His party colleagues stigmatize any negotiation with the Czechs as treason to the German cause...

It is obvious that the sympathies of the Reich are with a reasonable *Realpolitik*. Whether they like it or not, the Germans in this country are in the same boat as the Czechs. If they succeed, without sacrificing their national dignity, in arriving somehow at a policy of peaceful co-operation with the Czechs, they will eventually gain influence in the apparatus of the State and disarm extreme Czech nationalism. This will be the best for them and for Germany.

Later Koch had this to say about Sudeten-German complaints:[1]

Every fourth person in Czechoslovakia, and in Bohemia – the essential part of it – every third one, is a German. An ethnic group which numbers 3½ Millions in a population totalling 14 Millions, lives in compact ethnic areas, is culturally superior to the majority nation, produces the highest taxable incomes, and owns the greater part of industrial wealth, is really not a minority in need of protection, but an essential part of the State. If it is united and can make its impact felt on the basis of the Constitution, no one will be able to prevent it from obtaining its rights in the long run.

After the Locarno Conference of October 1925 a discussion took place in Geneva between Stresemann, the German Foreign Minister, and his Czechoslovak colleague Beneš. A German Foreign Office minute[2] records that

During the German delegation's stay in Geneva the Reich Foreign Minister had a lengthy discussion with Beneš, the Czechoslovak Foreign Minister. In the course of this the latter broached, of his own accord, the Sudeten German problem. He began by affirming that he opposed the pan-Slav trend in Czechoslovakia with all the means at his disposal, for, in his view, the future of Czechoslovakia depends on friendly relations with Austria and Germany. Despite all obstacles he was determined not to lose sight of this aim. On the other hand he would have to take account of the strong opposition put up by the Sudeten Germans. Internal peace could only be achieved if the Germans could be persuaded to participate in the Government.

A few weeks later two German parties entered the Czechoslovak Government.

---

[1] Koch to G.F.M. 29 October 1925, *G.F.M.* serial L439/I, frames 131727-30.
[2] G.F.M. to Koch, 1 April 1926, *G.F.M.* serial K91, frames 009137-8.

6 GERMAN PARTICIPATION IN THE CZECHOSLOVAK GOVERNMENT

After the conclusion of the Locarno Pact in October 1925, which reconciled Germany with the West and included an Arbitration Treaty between Germany and Czechoslovakia, Prague foreign policy was concerned to follow this up with an 'internal Locarno'. In a speech before the 1925 parliamentary elections Beneš advocated the entry of the Germans into the Government.[1] He had gone to Locarno, he explained, in order to conclude an agreement that there should never be a war between Germany and Czechoslovakia. There was little better he could offer to the Germans in Czechoslovakia than the assurance never to bring them into war with Germany.

We wish the Germans to render unto the state what is the state's, and we gladly render unto the Germans what is just to them. We would like other countries to realise, once and for all, that we have in our midst three million Germans who are struggling to achieve what any opposition expects, namely, to participate in the government; they are not struggling for the aims of the minorities in most other countries, i.e. their national and cultural survival, which in Czechoslovakia is not endangered.

But even after the elections of 1925 in which the German extremists who opposed any co-operation with the Czechs were decisively defeated, the Activists, led at that time by the Agrarian Franz Spina and the Christian-Social Robert Mayr-Harting, dare not declare themselves unconditionally in favour of participation in the government, without prior backing from Berlin.

Towards the end of February 1926, Spina and Mayr-Harting went to see Koch, the German Minister in Prague. The Activists, they declared, had decided to let deeds follow words. They were sure of the support of broad sections of the people, who had become tired of nationalistic slogans. However, in order to counter the

[1] *Prager Presse*, 4 November 1925.

charge of 'betrayal', they needed to be able to point out to the German electorate that the Reich Government approved of their views and intentions. They wanted to make sure of this by a direct approach to the Reich Foreign Minister, Gustav Stresemann.[1]

Shortly afterwards the German Nationalists and National Socialists also called on Koch.[2] They too wished to be received by Stresemann, but did not ask for an official declaration of the Reich's intention (knowing that it would only be unfavourable to their cause) – they merely wanted to be heard. They began by asking for a Reich subsidy to the tune of 100,000 to 200,000 marks, allegedly for the purpose of 'enlightening the public', but they soon floundered in embarrassment when Koch guilelessly asked them 'why the rich Sudeten Germans did not defray the cost of their own propaganda'.

Koch subsequently set down his views in a ten-page report for the Foreign Office in Berlin.[3] He suggested that the Activists' demand for political support ought to be rejected: 'Sudeten German policies are not formed in Berlin'. He considered that the participation of the Germans in the Czechoslovak Government would spell an enormous advance:

I am convinced that henceforth, in any Cabinet reconstruction, the German group can never again be ignored. Finally, although it is true that in future the Sudeten-German question will primarily be an internal matter it remains to be seen whether this will be a disadvantage... The struggle for the constitutional position of the Sudeten-Germans will have to be fought out, not before an international forum, but within the confines of this State.

Shortly afterwards, Stresemann telegraphed to Koch[4] that he could not receive representatives of the German parties in the Czechoslovak Republic to discuss the policy to be pursued by the Sudeten-Germans within Czechoslovakia. Nor did Stresemann think it advisable to try to teach the German Nationalists in Czechoslovakia to be reasonable. Later he said in a telegram to

[1] Koch to Foreign Ministry, 27 February 1926, *G.F.M.* serial L437/4, frame 128385.
[2] Koch to Foreign Ministry, 18 March 1926, *G.F.M.* serial L437/4, frames 128386-91.
[3] Koch to Foreign Ministry, 20 March 1926, *G.F.M.* serial L437/4 frames 128392-402.
[4] Stresemann to Koch, 4 May 1926, *G.F.M.* serial 4582, frames 175913-1.

75

Koch:[1] 'I have always made it clear that I would welcome an attempt to bring about the collaboration of the Germans in Czechoslovakia.'

Two German Ministers in the Czechoslovak Government

The formation of a Czech–Slovak–German parliamentary majority was not accompanied by any pomp and circumstance, but rather by modest economic achievements. The Czech Agrarians could not obtain parliamentary approval for a protective tariff in the face of opposition from the Left. This brought to an end the Coalition Government, in power since 1922, which was replaced by a 'Government of Civil Servants' from March to October 1926. The German Agrarians presented themselves as obvious allies. Thus, the 'Customs majority' took shape first in Parliament in spring 1926. The Christian parties (Czechs, Slovaks, and Germans) were won over by the promise to raise the state stipends of the priests (the *Congrua*). Clearly no question relating to the ethnic demands of the German parties had been discussed beforehand: it seems to have been this coalition's primary concern to get the country accustomed to parliamentary voting based on social rather than ethnic groups. The Communists had emerged in the elections of 1925 as a strong party, but they were not prepared to enter a coalition of the Left nor were they acceptable to the other parties. With the Left thus weakened the right-wing parties of the various nationalities achieved a small majority.

At the beginning of October 1926, the 'Government of Civil Servants' was replaced by a parliamentary Government under Švehla's leadership, in which two German parties – the Agrarians (*Bund der Landwirte*) and the Christian Social People's Party were each represented by a Minister. It was a decidedly right-wing government, which was soon joined by the Slovak People's Party under Andrej Hlinka and the National Democrats under Karel Kramář. The Ministries held by Germans were by no means insignificant, but they did not offer much scope for concessions to German demands on the administrative level. Franz Spina became Minister for Public Works and Robert Mayr-Harting, who was Professor of Civil Law at the German University in Prague, became Minister of Justice. The government programme contained no

[1] Stresemann to Koch, 16 October 1926, *G.F.M.* serial L437/5, frame 128721.

concrete promises to the non-Slav population, but it did contain the often-quoted slogan of 'Equals among Equals'[1] – evidently designed to dispel any suspicion that the Germans were considered second-class citizens. The German parties in the coalition had accepted Masaryk's views, which he had outlined in the previous June in the following terms:[2]

I repeat what I have said before: the problem of our German minority is the most important political problem confronting us. It is the duty of those at the helm in this country to solve this problem. As soon as the Germans abandon their negative attitude towards our state and inform us of their willingness to co-operate, as soon, in other words, as they become potential government partners, they will have the same standing as all other government parties. That is so simple and obvious that it needs no pro-German sentiment to come to this conclusion, only political common sense.

'The Germans have not only the right, but also the duty, to participate in the government', Masaryk said shortly afterwards in a German newspaper.[3]

The first attempts by the Activists to exert influence on the Government in support of their aspirations were not outstandingly successful. Mayr-Harting explained[4] that it was first of all a question of safeguarding the *status quo* (*Besitzstand*) before going further. In fact, the Activists did persuade the Czechs to call off their national offensive. The Slovak Agrarian Milan Hodža, who was Minister of Education, announced that he was going to introduce legislation to bring about some measure of cultural autonomy for the minorities by strengthening the existing district and provincial educational authorities, which were already split up into Czech and German groups. But unanimity could not be reached in the Cabinet, and when in 1929 Hodža left the Government the matter was shelved.

Even if the Activists in this first period did not achieve a great deal in the way of concessions, their German Nationalist opponents' agitation was an absolute failure. The idea of collaboration in the Government retained its attractiveness and refuted the theory that

[1] Klepetar, *Seit 1918*, p. 250.
[2] Interview with President Masaryk in *Národní osvobození*, 27 June 1927, German text in *Prager Tagblatt* and *Prager Presse* of same day.
[3] *Prager Tagblatt*, 7 September 1926.
[4] *Prager Presse*, 23 December 1926.

the mass of Sudeten-Germans would always, and under any circumstances, react in a narrowly nationalist manner.

The Reich's representatives in Prague welcomed the new phase of Czechoslovak internal policy. The German Chargé d'Affaires in Prague, Viktor von Heeren, said in one of his reports:[1]

The entry of German parties into the government will be a valuable precedent for the future of the Germans...The old theory of Czechoslovakia being a national state is decisively refuted. And even if no concrete concessions to the Germans have been agreed on as the price of their co-operation, the advantages outlined above which derive from this co-operation would seem to be of great importance.

The first major law passed by the Švehla Government was an administrative reform, putting an end to a law of 1920 which had divided the country into regions. Such administrative units had, however, only been introduced in Slovakia. The implementation of the law in Bohemia would have meant the creation of two over-whelmingly German administrative units. This plan was now scrapped in favour of the old provincial organization. Most re-grettable from the German point of view, though not unjustified as a matter of practical politics, was the abolition of the province of Silesia (the only one where the German minority reached 40 per cent), on the grounds that it was too small to be independently viable (Silesia was now merged with Moravia). On this occasion some German Nationalists did somehow manage to contact Strese-mann and complain to him about the Activists' alleged betrayal of German interests. Stresemann asked the German Legation in Prague[2] whether it was true

the German members of the Czechoslovak cabinet have betrayed German inter-ests and helped Czech influence to gain the upper hand without attempting to obtain compensatory advantages and if, in consequence, the German Ministers will become so unpopular that they are forced to resign?

Heeren replied[3] that the accusation that the German Ministers had betrayed their co-nationals' interests and had helped to subject them to forced Czech assimilation is, in my view, baseless'.

[1] Heeren to Foreign Ministry, 13 October 1926, *G.F.M.* serial L448, frames 135435-8.
[2] Stresemann to German Legation in Prague, 5 July 1927, *G.F.M.* serial 4582, frame E195913.
[3] Heeren to Foreign Ministry, 6 July 1927, *G.F.M.* serial 4571, frames E 176460-1.

He considered it most unlikely that Spina and Mayr-Harting would resign to allay the alleged indignation of the German population. As it turned out, this was a remarkably shrewd prophecy. In the municipal elections of 1927, the provincial elections of 1928, and the parliamentary elections a year later, the Activist camp held its own against the Nationalist Right. Meanwhile even within the ranks of the German Nationalists those who had the last word, i.e. the German industrialists, had revolted against their party's more extremist tendencies. The moderates had seceded from their ranks and had formed their own group, which in the provincial elections of 1928 and the parliamentary elections of 1929 achieved, relatively speaking, quite considerable success, thanks to the dissatisfaction of the traditional German Nationalist voters with their party's sterile policy.

Diametrically opposed to the obdurate attitude of the German Nationalists were the tenets which guided the Activists in the Government. Spina, especially, never tired of pointing out in innumerable public speeches at that time that collaboration in the affairs of the state was the only way of serving the Germans' true interests. He also coined the phrase 'Czech–German symbiosis', which he elucidated in a press interview:[1]

We have lived with the Czechs for a thousand years, and through economic, social, cultural, and even racial ties, we are so closely connected with them that we really form one people. To use a homely metaphor: we form different strands in the same carpet. Of course, it is possible to cut a carpet into pieces, but one cannot remove the flowers woven into the pattern. We lived with the Czechs in a form of symbiosis: we have entered into a marriage of convenience with them and nothing can separate us.

But the strongest impetus towards a genuine Czech–German union came from Masaryk, who did not now hesitate to throw overboard many of his more negative post-war concepts (e.g. 'There will be no discussion about territorial autonomy'). In an interview which he gave to one of the German newspapers supporting the Activists,[2] he elaborated his old thesis that the German problem was the most pressing one in the State, maintaining that German participation in the Government was only the beginning of what he had always desired:

[1] *Le Matin* (Paris), 26 December 1926.
[2] *Deutsche Presse* (Prague), 1 December 1926.

Speaking as a democrat [said Masaryk], I am in principle in favour of autonomy, side by side with the centralist trend inherent in the modern state...I do not need to point out that I see no fundamental antithesis to the concept of the central state in the desire for regional autonomy.

No Czech politician before him had been so accommodating to the desire of the German non-nationalistic parties for more regional, especially cultural, autonomy.

Masaryk's message on the occasion of the tenth anniversary of the State (1928) rejected the idea that Czechoslovakia was a 'National State' bestowing special privileges upon Czechs and Slovaks and emphasized the necessity of self-government within the State:[1]

in a democracy...the desire for local self-government is natural: if the population of a country is such that, although numerous, its natural and cultural development is not uniform, and yet the whole people is to co-operate in the administration, then political power must also be divided according to the natural differences among the population...I am not unaware of the fact that a State, and particularly a modern state, cannot do without a centralized organisation, but it is the task of a modern democratic state to harmonize central and local government.

These words were clearly designed to dispel any Czech fears that to concede a degree of self-government to the national minorities might weaken or even destroy the foundations of the State. Less outspoken, but equally ready for concessions, was the Foreign Minister, Beneš, who when speaking a year later during the election campaign, said:[2]

We certainly wish to extend equality and justice to the Germans, but they will have to identify themselves completely with our state...The country will gladly accept their co-operation and will solve the German problem with dignity, honesty, and justice...We have now progressed so far that a final settlement of the minority question can no longer affect the basis of our national revolution...The question of the minorities will cease to be a political problem and become merely one of administration.

The German Social Democrats join the Government

The swing to the right which had taken place in 1925 was reversed by the result of the parliamentary elections of October 1929. The three democratic and socialist parties, the Czechoslovak and German Social Democrats and the Czechoslovak National-Socialists,[3] were

[1] *Prager Tagblatt*, 30 October 1928.
[2] *Vossische Zeitung* (Berlin), 21 October 1929.
[3] The (Czech) National-Socialist Party was formed around the turn of the century as nationalist counterpoise to the internationally minded Social

returned with an increased number of seats and the non-socialist majority of 1926 now became a parliamentary minority, so that a new coalition had to be formed. However, despite a setback suffered by the German Christian Socials, who consequently left the Government, the idea of German participation in the Government, to which the German Social Democrats had in principle always subscribed, had been vindicated. On the far right the German Nazi Party did achieve some success at the expense of the German Nationalists, but on the whole the right-wing opposition, which had tried unsuccessfully to rouse the electorate against German participation in the Government lost ground. In the atmosphere of political and economic consolidation nationalistic slogans about the Activists' alleged betrayal of German interests to the Czech hereditary 'arch-enemy' did not find an echo among the Sudeten Germans. This again gave the lie to those Czech nationalists who had become accustomed to brushing off the German problem with the simple argument that the majority of the Sudeten Germans would always be hostile to their State.

When František Udržal, the outgoing Prime Minister and leader of the Agrarian Party, began negotiations to form a coalition with the Czechoslovak Social Democrats, as the second strongest party, their leader Antonín Hampl explained that they could only enter the Government in alliance with their German comrades. The ties between the two Social-Democratic parties had in fact become closer until in 1928 the Social Democrats of all the nationalities in Czechoslovakia met at a joint congress in Prague and agreed on a common programme of action. In his speech to the congress the Czech Social Democrat Rudolf Bechyně showed great understanding for the ethnic puzzle of Czechoslovakia when he pointed out that it was the task of the nation 'which calls itself the Nation of the State to bring all strata of the population into the State; not by force, or threats, but through policy'.[1] One of the main

Democracy. During the 1920s it developed into something comparable to the French Radical Socialists, namely into a rallying organization for very different groups – socialist-orientated workers, nationalist petty bourgeois and democratically inclined intellectuals. In the Prague parliament the party proved its worth as a socially and politically progressive Leftist force. (It had of course nothing in common with the German National-Socialists or Nazis.)

[1] *Sozialdemokrat* (Prague), 31 January 1928.

reasons for the *rapprochement* between the two Socialist parties was the fact that the Czechoslovak Social Democrats, the first Czech party to do so, had incorporated the demand for cultural autonomy for the minorities into their new party programme.[1] It stated

> We demand a settlement of the conditions of the national minorities under legal provisions which prevent any kind of national oppression and make possible the development of all cultural requirements. The principle of cultural autonomy should be realised in such a manner that certain bodies elected by the members of each minority are given power to administer and possibly to control its cultural and social institutions.

The German Social Democrats chose their leader, Ludwig Czech, to represent them in the Government in which Spina remained as Minister of Health. Dr Czech received the important Ministry of Social Welfare and thus a Portfolio which in the later years of crisis was to become one of cardinal importance in inter-ethnic politics. The establishment by Dr Czech of strict ethnic justice in social policy and in particular in care for the victims of the economic slump, was probably the most important German achievement in government: thanks to it hundreds of thousands of Germans were saved from starvation.

The world economic crisis can be dated from 'Black Friday' on Wall Street (4 October 1929); in the long run no country remained immune. In Czechoslovakia the downward trend set in a little later than in Germany where unemployment very soon went into seven figures, thus helping to create fertile soil for the growth of National Socialism. Foundations for improvement in welfare services for unemployed, which in the lean years ahead was to become of crucial importance, had already been laid during the period of relative prosperity. At that time the existing system – which guaranteed to unemployed trades union members a state-paid addition to their union unemployment benefit – had been adequate. When the figures of those out of work began to mount, Dr Czech carried through a government proposal to multiply the assistance period by three and the state subsidy by four. Since, however, nowhere near all the workers were members of a trade union, many unemployed were left without a claim to any sort of unemployment

---

[1] *Programme of the Czechoslovak Social Democratic Workers' Party*, carried at the party congress, 27–29 September 1930 (Prague 1930).

relief. For them the Minister of Social Welfare was able to arrange special schemes of state aid which was allocated strictly in accordance with the numbers of unemployed registered locally – inevitably higher in the German industrial areas. But industrialization itself was not the only reason why unemployment was higher in the areas inhabited by Germans than in the rest of Czechoslovakia. Apart from mining, industry in the German-speaking territory was mainly concentrated on the production of export consumer goods such as textiles and glass, while the country's heavy industry was mainly concentrated in the Czech-inhabited areas. These were less susceptible at that time to fluctuations in foreign demand. During the years 1930 to 1935 704 million Czech crowns were paid by the State to German trade unions for unemployment relief, compared with 958 million crowns to Czech trade unions and 135 million crowns to 'mixed' (i.e. Communist) trade unions (at that time approx. 140 crowns = £1).[1] The greatly disproportionate amount paid out to the Germans (22 per cent of the population) was a highly undesirable privilege and resulted from the special social structure of the German area. Equally meticulous attention was paid to the equitable alleviation of distress by means of the various extra-statutory aid actions for those out of work. Between 1930 and 1935 576 million crowns were spent on relief in kind to predominantly German areas and 567 million crowns to mainly Czech ones.

The importance of German participation in the Czechoslovak Government during this time of economic and social crisis was especially emphasized by Walter Koch, the German Envoy in Prague. If the German parties were to leave the Government coalition now, he wrote,[2] 'this, in view of the depression in the Sudeten areas which have been badly hit by unemployment, would be very damaging, since the German Social-Democratic Minister for Welfare, Dr Czech, can scarcely at this moment hand over responsibility for the Sudeten-German unemployed to a Czech'. As a matter of fact, the two Czech Social Democrats who followed him in this office, Alfred Meissner (1934–5) and Jaromír Nečas

---

[1] *Czechoslovak Cabinet Ministers on the complaints of the Sudeten German Party* (Prague 1937), pp. 67–70; Antoine Karlgren, *Henlein, Hitler et les Tchèques, La question allemande des Sudètes* (Paris 1939), pp. 83–4.

[2] Koch to G.F.M. 25 February 1933, *G.F.M.* serial L465, frames 140416-18.

(1935–8) did not deviate from their predecessor's policy of absolute ethnic justice.

Cultural autonomy

It almost looked as if the time had come for the realization of a desire common to all the German parties – except for the intransigents. The Sudeten Germans had always wanted to run their own schools, extending the considerable independence they enjoyed. The attempt by Hodža, then Minister of Education, to introduce a sort of cultural autonomy has already been mentioned.[1] The question again became topical when the Czechoslovak Social Democrats included cultural autonomy for minorities in their party programme. By the end of 1932 the Slovak Social Democrat Ivan Dérer as Minister for Education was able to submit a draft law[2] to provide linguistically separate groups in local district and provincial education councils. In practice this would have meant a Hungarian educational authority in Slovakia in addition to the Czech and German ones which already existed in Bohemia and Moravia. Appropriate representation had also been envisaged for the Poles in Moravia–Silesia and the Germans in Slovakia. Two-thirds of the councils would have been lay members of the public and one-third teachers, 'so that within the frame-work of the law each nation administered its own schools'. In recommending the proposal in a parliamentary committee Dérer said:[3] 'On the question of minorities we must start from a point of mutual confidence. We (the Czechoslovaks) as the national majority, primarily entrusted with the task of preserving the State which we have founded, will have to show a certain amount of confidence in the minorities.' However good might have been Dérer's intentions, a few days after his statement Hitler came to power in Germany and the repercussions of this tragic event were immediately felt in Czechoslovakia. Any hopes for a national reconciliation along this road were dashed for the moment and in fact buried for good.

The Germans and the State

From the time of the Peace Treaty, the German parties which were

---

[1] See p. 77. [2] *Prager Tagblatt*, 14 December 1932.
[3] *Sozialdemokrat*, 26 January 1933.

later to be classified as 'Activist' – the Social Democrats, the Agrarians and the Catholic Party (Christian Socials) – had rejected all irredentist ideas by undertaking to be involved in the administration of the State on the basis of the existing constitution. With a few insignificant exceptions, even the Nationalists fulfilled civic obligations such as serving in the armed forces. Yet for some time the Activists' attitude towards the State was cool; a change in their approach could not be expected as long as the President alone systematically tried to establish better relations with the Sudeten Germans. Still, even before the mounting reign of terror in Hitler's Germany made many of them appreciate the positive features of Czechoslovak democracy, progress had been made in encouraging the activists in a more positive attitude towards the State. As early as 1928 Mayr-Harting, the Minister for Justice, had made it clear that the successful assertion of German wishes would be the easier 'the more precisely they were submitted within the framework of the State.'[1] 'This State is our State too', added Spina a year later.[2]

A statement in 1930 from the German Agrarian deputy Franz Windirsch was more striking still. Koch reported on this speech and the remarkable fact that it was not at once branded as black treason in the extreme nationalist camp:[3]

In the budget debate...Windirsch stated that the Germans regarded Czechoslovakia as their home which could in an emergency count on them just as surely as on the Czechs...My experience leads me to believe that the declaration expresses the attitude of some of the Sudeten Germans. At any rate there has been no adverse criticism from the Sudeten-German public or press.

Among the German Social Democrats it was Wenzel Jaksch, in 1938 the leader of his party, who at the beginning of 1932 recognized the importance of Czechoslovak democracy in the international balance of power:[4]

The fact that co-operation between the two great national groups – Czechoslovaks and Germans – in the State remained unbroken even at a time of severe economic stresses undoubtedly increased the prestige of Czechoslovakia in the near and more distant neighbourhood. A Czechoslovak Republic, internally and externally strengthened by ethnic harmony, would in future, too, be a reliable guarantor of peaceful co-operation in the Danube valley and a firm pillar of economic reconstruction in Central Europe.

[1] *Prager Tagblatt*, 9 October 1928.   [2] *Prager Tagblatt*, 16 January 1930.
[3] Koch to G.F.M. 11 January 1933, *G.F.M.* serial L437/6, frames 130695-6.
[4] *Sozialdemokrat*, 9 February 1932.

7 GERMANY AND CZECHOSLOVAKIA – 1918–33

It has been seen that diplomatic relations between Germany and Czechoslovakia began at the earliest possible moment – the day after the *Národní Výbor* assumed power in Prague on 28 October 1918 and therefore even before the German Republic was proclaimed in Berlin.

It was an irony of fate that the last Imperial German Consul-General in Prague, Friedrich Freiherr von Gebsattel, was to be the first advocate of the new régime in Berlin.[1] Deciding not to wait for orders from Berlin because he considered it more urgent to obtain assurances on behalf of Reich citizens living in Bohemia, Gebsattel called on the *Národní Výbor* on 29 October to offer his congratulations and was received in very friendly fashion. He informed Berlin that he had formed the impression that the new masters seemed 'sincerely to be trying to establish friendly relations with the resident Imperial representative and presumably also with our Government ... The National Committee evidently intends to recognise me as German representative. Up to now there has been no news of any disorders.' He told Berlin[2] that common sense demanded the establishment of good relations with the new State which would be disturbed if Germany were to support any attempts by Bohemian Germans to attach themselves to the Reich. The fact that he had been the first foreign representative to call had made a good impression. He had not been treated as an enemy. 'I am convinced that the Czechs do not contemplate open hostility towards us and I am indeed under the impression that they are willing to enter into good relations with us.'

On 2 November Gebsattel went a step further, in telling the

[1] See p. 26.
[2] Gebsattel to G.F.M. 30 October 1918, *G.F.M. Akten betreffend Boehmen*, vol. 43, no. 1236/2. (See above, p. 27 n. 1.)

Národní Výbor 'off his own bat', as he wrote, that Germany was prepared to accept a diplomatic representative from Prague in Berlin. 'To this information I added – on my own responsibility – that this meant the recognition of the Czechoslovak State by my Government'.[1] The next day he suggested that 'a few friendly words of welcome for the newly-created Czechoslovak State in the *Norddeutsche Allgemeine Zeitung* would in my opinion be very help-ful'.[2] His telegram to the German Foreign Office has a handwritten note in the margin: – 'We are prepared to establish good relations if the Czechoslovaks request them.'

Day after day optimistic reports from Gebsattel arrived in Berlin. Close contacts, he said, had already been established between him and the *Národní Výbor*, all his actions were meeting with sympathetic response;[3] the new Premier Kramář had received him after his return from Geneva with much civility and he had gained the impression that 'he was not at all ill-disposed towards us'.

Beneš enters the scene

These initial contacts took place without the intervention of the man who was to be responsible for Czechoslovak foreign policy between 1918 and 1935: Edvard Beneš. Until 1915 he had taught at a commercial high school and had been practically unknown even to the Czech public. It was only his war-time activities abroad as Secretary of the Czechoslovak National Council which drew his fellow-countrymen's attention to him. After the war he stayed in Paris until September 1919 in order to represent the new State at the Peace Conference. Nominally the leader of the Czechoslovak delegation was Kramář who remained as such even after the fall in July 1919 of the Government over which he had presided. But it was Beneš who was the real representative of his country in all important negotiations. This not unnaturally resulted in a sharp conflict between the two men, still unresolved at the time of Kramář's death in 1937. For years Kramář campaigned against Beneš whom he accused among other things of being 'Germano-phile'. However little justification there was for this reproach, it

---

[1] Gebsattel to G.F.M. 2 November 1918, *Akten*, no. 1236/2.
[2] Gebsattel to G.F.M. 3 November 1918, *G.F.M.* series L513, frame 151281.
[3] Gebsattel to Reich Chancellor, 7 November 1918, *Akten*, no. 1236/3.

raised an issue about which every Czech politician had to be careful. In one of his reports[1] Koch very accurately diagnosed fear as 'the strongest motive force in this people'. He meant of course fear of the Germans, and he expressed this even more succinctly in one of his first memoranda to Berlin.[2]

The struggle against German influence, encirclement, and economic and cultural penetration is after all, half consciously, half unconsciously, the core of Czech internal and external policy. As a leading politician said to me recently: What can you do? If the Czechs had not defended themselves fiercely for centuries against everything German, they would long ago have been swallowed up by the German world.

Although Kramář's line of attack was thus judiciously chosen, it failed because Beneš' meteoric rise from obscurity to being in the front rank of international statesmen in Europe flattered Czech national pride; it endowed Beneš with a seductive aura of infallibility. Since the Czechs lacked any tradition of diplomacy it was felt all the more that there could be no substitute for him.

In his memoirs Beneš defined his attitude towards Germany and the German nation thus:[3]

During the war I used to take a firm and dispassionate view of the Germans... I was not blind to the magnificent things they managed to do before and during the war. I respected their achievements. I never felt for them what one might call hatred for a nation. It was clear to me that during the war one could not minutely balance out right against wrong, guilt against innocence, and that after the war many a judgment would have to be revised. During the war one had to make every effort to win it, in the interest of peace and justice. After the war one would have to come to an understanding about reasonable and loyal peaceful co-operation...What I said against Bismarck's pre-war Germany was not meant against the Germans as a whole. There is not only a Germany of Bismarck and Kaiser Wilhelm, but also one of Herder, Lessing, Goethe, Schiller, Beethoven, Mozart, Kant and the Humboldts. There were two sorts of Germany before the war, just as there are two sorts now...A nation which has given so many great things to mankind...is a great nation.

Beneš' attitude was unknown when he rose to his feet for the first time in Parliament on 30 September 1919 and spoke of conciliation both with the indigenous Germans (who ought to be treated 'loyally and correctly') and with Germany itself.[4] Later rumours

[1] Koch to G.F.M. 23 June 1933, *G.F.M.* serial L465, frames 140454-60.
[2] Koch to G.F.M. 17 December 1921, *G.F.M.* serial 1099, frames 283271-6.
[3] Beneš, *Der Aufstand der Nationen*, pp. 661-2, 702.
[4] Printed in Beneš, *Problémy nové Evropy* (Prague 1924), pp. 7-32.

of a military treaty between Czechoslovakia and France were denied by the German Minister in Prague, Saenger. Beneš, Saenger reported, had told him that friendship with France rested on tradition and war experience. But he reserved his freedom of action even *vis-à-vis* his best friends.[1] A few days later Beneš remarked to Saenger that he was firmly convinced of the need to maintain the alliance between Britain and France 'so that Britain prevents the latter from indulging in nationalist excesses and military adventures.[2]'

Koch, who succeeded Saenger in October 1921 as German Minister in Prague, not only spent the unusually long time of fourteen years there: he also dealt for the whole of this time with the same Foreign Minister. In the innumerable reports which he sent to Berlin during these years, there is hardly ever a friendly word about Beneš or even an appreciative one. His estimate of Beneš is therefore all the more interesting. As far as internal relations were concerned, Koch recognized him as an advocate of reconciliation between Czechs and Germans;[3] in Beneš' foreign policy, however, he saw an orientation towards France which at that time of course implied an anti-German bias.

During the Weimar period Koch's opinion carried great weight in Berlin, but his evaluation of Beneš as the vassal of France was not accepted. On the other hand there is no doubt that Koch was right in his laconic description of Beneš, who, he said,[4] 'was a cool realist whose only serious consideration was what was good for his country'. At one of their first meetings Beneš assured Koch that he was particularly anxious 'to play his part in the establishment of a better temperature between Germany and France'.[5] On the other side of the frontier the German Foreign Minister Rathenau in a discussion with Tusar, then Czechoslovak Minister in Berlin, recognized Beneš endeavours towards improving relations. This he interpreted as readiness to mediate:[6]

(I said) I was glad that Beneš, whose mediation had already been helpful, should now be prepared to offer his services in the cause of Franco-German

[1] Saenger to G.F.M. 19 June 1921, *G.F.M.* serial L416, frame 118893.
[2] Saenger to G.F.M. 25 July 1921, *G.F.M.* serial L416, frames 118894-7.
[3] Koch to G.F.M. 18 November 1921, *G.F.M.* serial L417, frames 119820-2.
[4] Koch to G.F.M. 5 March 1923, *G.F.M.* serial 3086/6, frame 717616.
[5] Koch to G.F.M. 8 November 1921, *G.F.M.* serial L416, frame 118925.
[6] Note by Rathenau, 13 March 1922, *G.F.M.* serial 6143, frames 459357-9.

relations. It is true that this could best be achieved if in the course of one of his many journeys he would discuss the question with us directly. Tusar said that Beneš would welcome this.

German views were expressed even more strongly in a circular which Edgar Haniel, then the Under-Secretary of State in the Foreign Office, issued in connection with the rumour of a secret agreement between Paris and Prague. Very correctly he considered this improbable.[1]

In actual fact Beneš had so far tried to avoid tying his policy too much to any existing power constellation...Beneš, who thinks very systematically...apparently envisages the re-establishment of the European balance of power in which he attempts to increase the weak political impact of his small country by extending the Little Entente [with Yugoslavia and Romania] under his leadership.

Neutrality during the Ruhr troubles

When, at the beginning of 1923, France occupied the Ruhr in order to force Germany to pay reparations, a difficult situation arose for Czechoslovak foreign policy. Koch reported[2] that Beneš had emphasized to him the 'continuing good relations between Czechoslovakia and Germany and his great interest in a Franco-German understanding which he considered essential for the recovery of Central Europe'. 'Generally speaking', Koch added, 'I am not inclined to take his word at its face value, but on this occasion Beneš seemed to speak with a certain amount of sincerity.' In Parliament Beneš declared that relations with France as well as Germany remained unchanged.[3] To Koch he explained afterwards that he had to tread warily:[4]

He certainly had neither calling nor inclination to be the arbiter between Germans and Frenchmen and real objectivity in these questions is granted to no one today. I should rest assured that what he had to say to the French about their actions he had said in the right place; in Parliament he obviously could not do so...In conclusion Dr Beneš asked me to believe that the Czechoslovak Government did not wish to have anything to do with the Ruhr conflict.

[1] Circular by Haniel, 4 July 1922, *G.F.M.* serial L417, frames 119933-6.
[2] Koch to G.F.M. 16 January 1923, *G.F.M.* serial L416, frames 118970-2.
[3] *Prager Presse* of 30 January (Evening edition) and 31 January 1923.
[4] Koch to G.F.M. 3 February 1923, *G.F.M.* serial L417, frames 120033-4. Further material about Czechoslovak foreign policy during this period, especially about Masaryk's strictures on Poincaré's German policy, chiefly based on unpublished reports by U.S. diplomats, can be found in Pyotr S. Wandycz, *France and her Eastern Allies 1919–25* (Minneapolis 1962), pp. 281, 297–306.

Later Koch reacted with quite unusual warmth to a speech in which, a few days before Hitler's abortive Munich *putsch* of November 1923, Beneš had recommended that Parliament consider aid for Germany, then at the height of inflation:[1]

While at other times Beneš showed himself the master of indeterminate, ambiguous and philosophically embellished expressions, on this occasion he was more definite, concrete and clear. It would appear that this politician, not yet 40 years old, is gaining in stature through his contacts with the statesmen of the Little Entente and the West...As far as Beneš has discussed the German crisis in various political centres I am sure he has not done so in any way which is detrimental to Germany; not so much from any motive of sympathy with Germany in her plight but because as time goes on – I have observed this development from close quarters – he realised more and more that the ruin of Germany jeopardises the growth of his country.

The conclusion of an alliance, expressed in very general terms, between Paris and Prague at the beginning of 1924 did not unduly disturb German diplomacy.

The opinion of the German Embassy in Paris, that even now Beneš 'had not signed himself away in bondage to the rulers of France', was endorsed in Berlin.[2] Beneš had told Koch what he thought about the Weimar Republic:[3]

There was no need for him to tell me that he preferred a democratic and republican Germany as his neighbour...I (Koch) reminded him that in order to strengthen the republican régime in Germany, he must wish her success in her foreign policy; to this he eagerly agreed; 'The French,' he explained to me, 'always speak of "sécurité".' I have pointed out to them more than once that the greatest 'sécurité' for them, much greater than the occupation of the Ruhr and the Rhineland, would lie in strengthening the democratic Republic in Germany.

Geneva and Locarno

The year 1924 saw a fundamental improvement in the European situation: in France two statesmen, Aristide Briand and Edouard Herriot, came to the fore who were in favour of reconciliation with Germany. In Great Britain Labour had come to power for the first time under Ramsay MacDonald's leadership: although it was a minority government whose life was to be limited to a few months,

[1] Koch to G.F.M. 3 November 1923, *G.F.M.* serial 426, frames 122546–50.
[2] Circular by Köpke, 15 January 1924, *G.F.M.* serial L423, frames 122281–92.
[3] Koch to G.F.M. 16 February 1924, *G.F.M.* serial L417/II, frames 120518–20.

it did develop a fruitful initiative in foreign affairs. Beneš, in co-operation with MacDonald and Herriot, now tried to push the 'Geneva Protocol' through the League of Nations. This was a boldly conceived attempt to secure international peace and justice by submitting all disputes to arbitration.[1] Beneš acted as *rapporteur* to the Assembly of the League of Nations, which accepted the Protocol, but in the event the only State which ratified it was Czechoslovakia.[2] In the meantime the British Labour Government had been ousted by the Conservatives who refused to be bound by the commitments of their predecessors. A new start had to be made under less favourable auspices.

After the failure of the Geneva Protocol the deadlock was broken in February 1925 by a declaration by the German Foreign Minister Stresemann that Germany was prepared to guarantee, in the form of a Rhine pact, the inviolability of her western frontiers and to conclude treaties or arbitration with her other neighbours.[3] This gave a fresh impetus to negotiations. A German Foreign Office memorandum[4] explained that Beneš' idea of incorporating a frontier guarantee in an arbitration treaty with Germany was designed not so much to protect the 'German–Czech frontier which hardly anybody in Czechoslovakia considered seriously threatened by Germany', but rather to increase protection against Hungary.

Stresemann, however, refused to sign a frontier guarantee with Czechoslovakia. Were there any long-term annexationist plans behind this? A secret memorandum designed to keep the German diplomatic missions informed explained that Berlin had decided to limit guarantees to the western frontiers for the time being, but 'in order to prove our goodwill, at the same time to make a gesture to our Eastern neighbours'. Stresemann found it impossible to guarantee the German–Polish frontier yet to treat Czechoslovakia so obviously differently and give her an isolated guarantee would

---

[1] For Beneš' share in the drawing up of the Protocol see Emil Strauss, *Tschechoslowakische Außenpolitik* (Prague 1936), p. 81.

[2] Felix John Vondraček, *The Foreign Policy of Czechoslovakia 1918–35* (New York 1937), p. 228.

[3] Text of the German memorandum of 9 February 1925 in Herbert Michaelis and Ernst Schraepke (eds.), *Ursachen und Folgen*, VI (Berlin 1961), 334–5.

[4] Memorandum by Köpke of 20 April 1925, *G.F.M.* serial L 427, frames 122871–2.

draw undesirable attention to German intentions towards Poland.[1] Any immediate desire for frontier rectification was thus directed solely against Poland.

Much later, two years after Stresemann's death, when nationalistic tendencies in Germany had already become more pronounced, Bernhard von Bülow, then the Permanent Secretary of State in the Foreign Office, formulated German revisionist wishes as 'a return to Wilson's Fourteen Points'.[2] He enumerated what appeared to him to be violations of these points: the prohibition of the Austrian *Anschluss*, the surrender of the small district of Hultschin to Czechoslovakia, cessions to Poland, the loss of Memel and the colonies. The maintenance of the unity of the provinces of Bohemia, Moravia and Silesia in 1919 was not included in this list of grievances.

At the end of March 1925 Koch was able to inform Berlin[3] that Beneš had declared himself favourably impressed by the German initiative and had recommended Germany's early admission to the League of Nations. However the negotiations which had begun at Stresemann's instigation dragged on for a considerable time before the Locarno Conference could open on 5 October 1925. Unlike German–Polish relations, the German–Czechoslovak problem played no part in the delay. Beneš did pay a visit to Warsaw in April 1925 but resisted attempts to entangle him in an anti-German front, planned by the Poles in answer to Stresemann's hostility to them.

It was at Locarno that Stresemann and Beneš met for the first time. When, after the Western Pact had been concluded, the Polish and Czechoslovak Foreign Ministers were invited to attend the deliberations, Beneš informed the conference that fundamental agreement with the German Chancellor Luther and Stresemann about contractual settlement between Berlin and Prague had already been reached. The German–Czechoslovak Treaty,[4] signed

---

[1] Circular by Schubert, 10 March 1925, *G.F.M.* serial 3123, frames 642569–75. ('From the German point of view the idea of including Czechoslovakia in the guarantee proper can however not be entertained for the obvious reason that our position *vis-à-vis* Poland would then become quite untenable.')

[2] Note by Bülow of 15 September 1931, 'Political observations on German–French relations', *G.F.M.* serial 4620, frames 200007–15.

[3] Koch to G.F.M. 23 March 1925, *G.F.M.* serial L416, frames 119072–5.

[4] Text in Michaelis–Schraepke, *Ursachen und Folgen*, VI, 384ff.

on 16 October 1925 as part of the Locarno Pact, submits 'dispute of any kind to arbitration'. As it happened, the permanent Conciliation Commission provided for in the treaty never went into action; until 1933 there were no quarrels between the two countries, and afterwards an apostle of force like Hitler would never have bothered to make use of an arbitration procedure to gain his aims. Only by trampling on this international obligation could Hitler clear his path to the rape of Czechoslovakia in 1938.

After Locarno great difficulties stood in the way of Germany's admission to the League of Nations. Germany's demand for a permanent seat on the Council of the League of Nations would have been met without demur if certain other States had not simultaneously put in similar claims. In order to save the situation and to enable Germany to join without delay, Undén, the Swedish Foreign Minister, and Beneš together declared their willingness at a special League session in February 1926 to relinquish their temporary seats on the Council in favour of Germany. The session adjourned, however, without coming to any conclusion. Beneš then doubled his efforts behind the scenes to ensure a speedy admission of Germany to the League on acceptable conditions.[1]

By September 1926 the time had at last come. The League Assembly opened on 6 September with Beneš as chairman; he expressed the hope that they would shortly be able to welcome a new member into their community.[2] A few days later Germany was accepted as a member and given a permanent seat on the Council.

Beneš' efforts to lead Germany back into the comity of nations were not due to any 'pro-German' sentiment or an insatiable desire to see justice done. They resulted from enlightened national self-interest, but they also show that Beneš was not biased against Germany.

Beneš in Berlin and German–Czech relations to 1932
German–Czechoslovak relations were, as Beneš repeatedly said, 'correct' or 'friendly' – but not more. At any rate, a stir was caused

---

[1] 'On principle he (Beneš) would in any case vote for Germany so that she could be admitted to the Council at once' (Koch to G.F.M. 11 April 1926, *G.F.M.* serial 7415, frames 175875-9).

[2] Report on the Opening Session of the Seventh League of Nations Assembly, 6 September 1926, *G.F.M.* serial 4587/1, frames 182798-830.

in Berlin when in May 1928, Beneš accepted the invitation extended to him six years earlier by Walter Rathenau, to visit the German capital.[1] The time chosen could not have been less propitious. A few days before Beneš' arrival the German Government under Wilhelm Marx had lost its parliamentary majority and Stresemann, who had conveyed to Beneš his pleasure in expecting him in Berlin,[2] fell dangerously ill and had to abandon all activity for a long period. Beneš did, however, have a series of lengthy discussions with Carl von Schubert, then the leading official of the German Foreign Office on which the latter left very illuminating notes.[3] The fact that a notable part of the population of Czechoslovakia was German was scarcely mentioned:

After I had spoken to Beneš about some specifically German–Czechoslovak matters at a dinner...I mentioned to him that in view of the frank discussions which we had had during his visit I should like to say a word about the German minorities...in Czechoslovakia. I hoped, also from the point of view of the development of German–Czechoslovak relations, that the situation of the Bohemian Germans would continue to improve.

Beneš replied that in the talks which he had had so far with us it had always been understood that this internal Czechoslovak problem could not well be discussed. Consequently he would if necessary state after his return to Prague that we had not mentioned these matters.

As far as the matter itself was concerned, he considered it closed. The Germans were now in the Government and would always remain there; it was a completely natural development.

An attempt was made, however, to get Beneš to accept a proposal for bringing his country into a closer association with Germany. This could only have led to a Central Europe under German hegemony and the suggestion put forward by Schubert with much astuteness showed to what extent, barely ten years after the war, the old Imperial German tendencies had revived. It was skilfully rebuffed by Beneš. Schubert began his exposé by explaining to Beneš that his aim was a United States of Europe:

I said that in this context I had been thinking about economic relations in our corner of Europe. Considering our frank exchange of opinion I had no hesitation in informing him of my ideas...One might well think that large-scale economic

[1] See p. 89.
[2] Köpke to Koch, 5 March 1928, *G.F.M.* serial 6143, frames 459445-7.
[3] The following quotations are based on Schubert's notes about his talks with Beneš on 21, 22 and 23 May 1928, *G.F.M.* serial 4577, frames 174220-48, 174241-73.

co-operation between Germany, Czechoslovakia and Austria was not only possible but very promising...I did not think it an exaggeration to say that such a union was completely logical...A new customs barrier was not in my mind, this union should be regarded as the seed of further unions...

Beneš replied that Schubert's 'train of thought interested him greatly'. He then developed his own ideas of closer economic collaboration between the countries of the Little Entente, Austria, Hungary, Bulgaria and Greece, in the form of customs preferences, although he made no concrete suggestions. He countered Schubert's proposals with the warning that the Germans should not expose themselves to the suspicion of harbouring imperialist aims:

As far as my (Schubert's) idea was concerned one should be clear (said Beneš) that the union envisaged by me had political implications of the highest order. It was to be feared that such an association would encounter strong resistance in France and Britain...The other side might say that Germany was trying in this fashion to realise her plans for a Greater Germany.

Schubert tried to dispel Beneš' distrust by emphasizing the economic advantages of his plan without dwelling on its political meaning. But Beneš was not so easily hoodwinked. 'The political arguments against such an association', he said, 'were very strong all the same.' Schubert retorted that this applied with even greater force to his (Beneš') proposal: 'I must tell him quite frankly that such an association would not be acceptable to us...The position would of course be altogether different if there were any intention to let us participate in such a structure.' Schubert had been too outspoken: the cat – German hegemony down to the Aegean sea – was now out of the bag. Beneš was immediately on his guard:

Beneš replied that this involved a new difficulty. He did not think it feasible for a Great Power to join an association of the type envisaged to him. This would at once be construed as the assumption of leadership in the union by this Great Power in order to force its will on the smaller ones. An invitation to a Great Power, including Germany, would not therefore be practicable.

Beneš' only concession was that Schubert's proposals would find more fertile ground if there were wide-ranging reconciliation between Germany and France; in such circumstances he could imagine their realization.

Three German Foreign Office memoranda of the period 1927–32 show the friendly feeling for Czechoslovakia in Berlin. In 1927

President Hindenburg was informed[1] by the Foreign Office that 'relations have continuously improved over the last years'. Three years later a Foreign Office note for internal circulation stated:[2] 'With the post-Locarno *détente* between France and Germany, a considerable improvement in relations between Czechoslovakia and Germany took place. At the moment they are correct and on the Czech side positively friendly.' In September 1932, when Papen's authoritarian régime was in power, the Foreign Office had to brief Hindenburg for a discussion with the Czechoslovak Minister, Vojtěch Mastný. Hindenburg was told:[3]

Our political relations with Czechoslovakia can be regarded as correct. What prevents them from being as friendly as the close economic and cultural ties between the two countries would lead one to expect is, first, the anti-German tendency of the Czechs' minority policy, but above all the fact that whenever important questions arise on which Germany's resurgence depends, Czechoslovakia is invariably found in our opponents' camp. This trend in Czechoslovak foreign policy is inevitable in view of its preoccupation with the problem of maintaining the independence of the Czech island in the German ocean and its financial and military dependence on France. If Beneš...has within these limits repeatedly shown a sincere desire to mediate in cases of acute Franco-German tension, he did so to avoid a European conflict which could only bring dangers to his country, politically saturated as it is.

Between these three testimonials there was one rather petulant complaint by Koch which put Beneš' reputation for 'hostility towards Germany' in a somewhat different light. At the beginning of 1930 Koch revealed the real reason for the resentment towards Beneš harboured by some German diplomats:[4]

Germany cannot so easily forget that during all the incidents which have caused difficulties to the Reich over the last eleven years Beneš had faithfully backed France and that he is and always has been the main obstacle, not only for the *Anschluss* [of Austria to Germany] but also to a Central European economic alliance under the leadership of Germany.

The German generals on the other hand, by nature inclined towards distrust of anything non-German, certainly did not consider Beneš hostile. Bülow, the State Secretary in the German Foreign Office,

[1] Foreign Ministry note of 29 January 1927, *G.F.M.* serial L450, frames 136216-19.
[2] F.M. note of 5 January 1930, *G.F.M.* serial L416, frame 119322.
[3] F.M. note of 5 September 1932, *G.F.M.* serial L450, frames 136385-6.
[4] Koch to G.F.M. 17 March 1930, *G.F.M.* serial L417, frames 121458-61.

instructed the German Ambassador in Paris at the beginning of 1931 as follows:[1]

> According to our generals, one way to a military understanding with France lies in the preliminary negotiations for the general Disarmament Conference and in the person of Beneš. They would like to see the latter as Chairman and feel that he would be glad to act as intermediary between Paris and Berlin.

In fact Arthur Henderson became chairman while Beneš acted as general *rapporteur* to the conference.

One of the events which cast a shadow over German–Czech relations at the beginning of the 1930s was the project for a customs union between Germany and Austria suggested in March 1931. Julius Curtius, who took over the German Foreign Office after Stresemann's death, looked at the question purely from an economic point of view and had little understanding of the wider political implications. His Austrian counterpart Johann Schober similarly lacked the political finesse to see that his country, severely hit by the economic crisis and dependent on foreign aid, could not afford to affront world opinion. But that was precisely what a customs union project, of dubious legality and unexpectedly presented to Europe, was bound to do. Eventually the Permanent International Court at The Hague decided, if only by eight votes to seven, that a customs union between Germany and Austria would be an infringement of the latter's independence and therefore contrary to the ban on the *Anschluss* laid down in the Peace Treaty. More important, however, than a purely juridical interpretation was the fact, easily ascertainable, that the signatory powers of the so-called Geneva Protocol of 4 October 1922 (Great Britain, France, Italy and Czechoslovakia) which gave financial aid to Austria, had been of this opinion. Even Arthur Henderson, the Foreign Secretary in the second Labour Government, open-minded though he was, opposed the project.[2]

German and Austrian official sources never tired of explaining that the whole plan was harmless, indeed praiseworthy: after all, the pan-European idea would have to start somewhere and this was the realization of the plan for Europe proposed by Briand in 1930. The abolition of customs barriers was in any case desirable.

Even after the Second World War Curtius used this version in

[1] Bülow to Hoesch, 23 January 1931, *G.F.M.* serial 4620, frames 199035-9.
[2] *DBFP*, 2/II (London 1947), p. 13.

two books he wrote.[1] Proof that the worst contemporary suspicions had indeed been justified became known in 1961.[2] What German foreign policy really had in mind was nothing but the realization of the 'personal ideas' Schubert had expressed in 1928. How much value one could attach to such 'pan-European' professions is shown by a letter written by Bülow to the German Ambassador in Washington:[3]

There is, however, a plan, which can perhaps be implemented, to enter into an economic union with Austria, which would probably very speedily lead to the accession to it of Czechoslovakia and Hungary...It is quite possible that it may lead to political conflicts, although we will dress the matter up in a Pan-European cloak ('*obwohl wir der Angelegenheit ein paneuropäisches Mäntelchen umhängen werden*').

There were however people with other views in the German diplomatic service. Gerhard Köpke was one of them; he was responsible for an internal memorandum which makes different reading from Bülow's note:[4]

As far as Czechoslovakia is concerned it is a principle of Czech policy under Beneš that the formation of any such economic union, whether or not Czechoslovakia joins it, would spell the end of Czechoslovak independence, first economically and then politically. Up to the present Czechoslovak policy has been exclusively concerned with maintaining the political independence of the Czech people, achieved at last after a struggle lasting for centuries. Any threat to this independence would therefore meet with the absolute resistance of Czechoslovakia. The conviction held by leading Czech politicians that the creation of an united German–Austrian economic area would involve a direct threat to Czechoslovak independence is all the more unshakeable as it does not appear to be entirely groundless...It need not be emphasised that the loss of more than one third of her total exports would have disastrous results for a country like Czechoslovakia which relies on its foreign trade. Whether or not therefore Czechoslovakia decides to join the Customs Union, its economic and consequently also its political freedom of action would be severely restricted.

Köpke ended by declaring that Czechoslovakia must be invited from the very beginning to be an economic partner; only under such

[1] Julius Curtius, *Bemühung um Österreich* (Heidelberg 1947), p. 84; *Sechs Jahre Minister der Deutschen Republik* (Heidelberg 1948), p. 209.
[2] F. G. Stambrook, 'The German–Austrian Customs Unions Project of 1931: A Study of German Methods and Motives', *Journal of Central European Affairs*, Boulder (U.S.A.), April 1961, pp. 15–44.
[3] Bülow to Prittwitz, 20 January 1931, *G.F.M.* serial 4620, frames 199138–40.
[4] Notes by Department II on the question of a Customs Union with Austria, 21 February 1931, *G.F.M.* serial K49, frames 005116–21.

conditions would the German procedure rest on a moral basis. Almost exactly the same objections were raised by Beneš when, after the Curtius–Schober plan became known, he addressed Parliament in Prague.

Berlin's true intentions were again revealed in a private letter written by Bülow to Koch.[1]

The inclusion of Czechoslovakia in our economic system is entirely in line with the long-term foreign policy of the Reich as I visualize it. Once the German–Austrian customs union has become a reality, I calculate that the pressure of economic necessity will compel Czechoslovakia within a few years to adhere to it in one way or another. I would see in this the beginning of a development which would be likely to lead to the satisfaction of vital German interests difficult to satisfy in other ways. I am thinking of German–Polish frontier problems. If we should succeed in incorporating Czechoslovakia in our economic bloc, and if meanwhile we should also have established closer economic relations with the Baltic States, then Poland with her unstable economic structure would be surrounded and exposed to all kinds of dangers: we should have her in a vice which would perhaps in the short or long run make her willing to consider the idea of exchanging political concessions for tangible economic advantages.

He considered Beneš 'too clever not to realize that opposition based on political objections to a natural economic development cannot be kept up'. Koch's reply could not have given much comfort to Bülow:[2]

At present I still find it hard to believe that economic difficulties would coerce Czechoslovakia to make common cause with us. When they consider their political liberty in danger, the Czechs are indifferent to economic hardship. . . In the many discussions I have had about the matter I have been struck by the fact that neither Czech politicians nor foreign diplomats, even those representing neutral countries, can be deflected from the view that the Treaty with Austria was an overwhelmingly political affair and a deliberate step towards the *Anschluss*.

Bülow's lofty optimism was soon belied by events. Germany and Austria saw themselves forced to liquidate the whole experiment even before the Hague Court had given its verdict. This retreat, however, was preceded by an interesting little episode; a German financier had tried to mediate between Berlin and Prague, whence he actually brought a positive proposal. This was ignored by German foreign policy as it could not be brought in line with Bülow's avowed plans.

[1] Bülow to Koch, 15 April 1931, *G.F.M.* serial 4620, frames 199512-15.
[2] Koch to Bülow, 22 April 1931, *G.F.M.* serial 4620, frames 199520-1.

The intermediary was a remarkable character. Wilhelm Regendanz was at first engaged in the Imperial German Ministry for Colonies and later in banking; in the inter-war years his efforts were concentrated on the purchase of land in Africa for Germany as a substitute for the lost colonies.[1] After Hitler's seizure of power General Schleicher used to meet the French Ambassador François-Poncet in Regendanz's house in the Berlin suburb of Dahlem,[2] one of the pretexts for Schleicher's murder on 30 June 1934. Regendanz then left Germany for England: he became a naturalized British subject before the war broke out and died in London.[3]

It is unlikely that Regendanz went to Prague on his own initiative: it is more likely that he was sent there by the German Foreign Office in order to sound out Beneš. At any rate he kept both the Foreign Office and Brüning, the Reich Chancellor, informed of all the steps he took. At the first meeting between Beneš and Regendanz at the end of March 1931 Beneš explained his reason for opposing the customs union project. Czechoslovakia could only accede if France also collaborated, but French adherence to an agreement concluded first between Berlin and Vienna would be impossible for reasons of prestige.[4]

On 27 April Regendanz had another long discussion with Beneš 'of whose complete sincerity I am more and more convinced'.[5] Beneš told him that he was now in a position to submit proposals 'with which Briand had agreed in principle'. Their purport was that a pact in favour of 'regional free trade' between Germany, France, Czechoslovakia and Austria, if possible including Italy, should be concluded without delay. Such a structure would hardly differ in any way from a customs union, a term which 'Briand would find unacceptable, for it would savour of capitulation to Germany'. Beneš, Regendanz informed Berlin, would like to know the views of the German government as soon as possible.

Not without justification Regendanz felt some pride in the results of his mediation which were being discussed in a 'small

[1] F. W. Pick, *Searchlight on German Africa* (London 1939).
[2] *DGFP*, C/iii (London 1959), no. 64 and 129.
[3] Information by Mrs E. Regendanz, London, to the author, London, 30 March 1963.
[4] Regendanz to Bülow, 4 April 1931, *G.F.M.* serial K 50, frames 005749-61.
[5] Regendanz to Bülow, 28 April 1931, *G.F.M.* serial K 50, frames 005770-4.

circle' of the Reich Chancellery.[1] However serious the proposal by Beneš may have been – and without the approval of Paris it could never have been made – at least it merited consideration. The German Foreign Office officials were, however, not interested, and Regendanz must have been very put out when all he got for his efforts was a chilly letter of appreciation,[2] while the Czechoslovaks waited in vain for an official German reaction.

Even this strange interlude, an opportunity deliberately missed, did not permanently darken German–Czechoslovak relations.

[1] Pünder to Bülow, 4 May 1931, *Akten der Reichskanzlei*, serial K 1063, frame 272120.

[2] Bülow to Regendanz, 1 May 1931, *G.F.M.* serial K 50, frames 005782/3.

8 IN THE SHADOW OF THE THIRD REICH

Hitler's seizure of power fundamentally affected relations between Germany and Czechoslovakia as well as relations between Czechs and Germans within Czechoslovakia. The official attitude in Prague was of course to make *bonne mine à mauvais jeu* and pretend that nothing or very little had changed. This was clearly shown in the Czechoslovak Foreign Minister's parliamentary report one month after that fateful 30 January 1933:[1]

> For the whole of these fourteen years Czechoslovakia has had no serious conflict, no frontier difficulties with Germany, and would like to continue the same cordial relations with present-day Germany that she had with the Germany of Stresemann.

At Geneva shortly afterwards Beneš told Ramsay MacDonald and Sir John Simon that at a meeting with Beck, the Polish Foreign Minister, he had spoken against an alliance with Poland 'because he thought it would be very dangerous to give Germany a clear cause for fearing encirclement'.[2] In further talks with the British statesmen he repeated that he had no serious fears as regards Germany; there was no issue or dispute between the two countries.[3] Even as late as November 1933, after Germany had demonstratively left the League of Nations, Koch could report to Berlin[4] that Beneš had emphasized to him 'almost cordially' that 'he for his part would do everything to clear away any difficulty with Germany, to avoid all conflicts and to ensure the peaceful coexistence of both States'.

One of the immediate consequences of the Nazi reign of terror

---

[1] Speech in Parliament, 1 March 1933, *Schulthess' Europäischer Geschichtskalender 1933* (Munich 1934), p. 281.
[2] Record of a Conversation at Geneva between Mr MacDonald, Sir John Simon and M. Beneš, 13 March 1933, *DBFP*, 2/IV (London 1950), no. 298.
[3] United Kingdom delegate (Geneva) to Foreign Office, 18 March 1933, *DBFP*, 2/V (London 1956), no. 43.
[4] Koch to G.F.M. 9 November 1933, *G.F.M.* serial 9151, frames 684887-91.

was a flood of emigrants. Many democratic German politicians, such as the spokesmen of the Social-Democratic Party of Germany and their political sympathizers among artists, writers and journalists, succeeded in finding refuge in Czechoslovakia whence they of course did their utmost to tell the world (which was still unaware of it) the truth about the Third Reich. Although only the Czech and German Socialist papers declared their full solidarity with the political émigrés whose mouthpiece they tried to be, Koch's main occupation as German representative in Prague now was to lodge notes of protest with the Czechoslovak Foreign Ministry against the toleration of what were called 'atrocity stories'. The invariable reply to those notes was that freedom of the press precluded censorship of news.

The Reich Foreign Ministry tried to counteract the devastating effects abroad of Nazi anti-Jewish measures by collecting information on the treatment of Jews elsewhere. Was it harsh in other countries too? Koch's reply,[1] anyway, was cold comfort to their propagandists:

In Czechoslovakia there is no discrimination of any sort against Jews, neither in their administrative careers, nor in social, economic or other respects, or in the field of sport. Any such measures would be contrary to President Masaryk's principles...Jews in Czechoslovakia are not only on the teaching staff of Czech and German Universities, but also in many cases high civil servants, head masters and teachers in grammar schools etc....In view of these circumstances I do not think it possible to parry attacks on German measures by drawing attention to any similar features in force in Czechoslovakia.

Among the German Nationalists in Czechoslovakia the centre of gravity had shifted further towards the National Socialists whose demagogy appealed more to susceptible young people than to the more old-fashioned German Nationalists. But quite apart from its attraction, the impressive electoral ascendancy of National Socialism in Germany, which had increased its number of Reichstag seats from 12 to 107 in September 1930 and to 230 in July 1932, could not fail to have deep psychological repercussions in a country like Czechoslovakia, suffering from the miseries of mass unemployment. In order to understand that the German-speaking part of Czechoslovakia could not remain unaffected by these developments, one

[1] Koch to G.F.M. 3 May 1933, *G.F.M.* serial 9470, frames 667960-1.

need only recall that in neighbouring Austria, also severely hit by the crisis, the election of 1932 resulted in sensational Nazi successes. Even though largely due to natural economic factors, the higher level of unemployment in the German part of the country than in the Czech inevitably undermined faith in the working of democracy. The attraction of National Socialism was not even diminished by the fact that the Nazis' very first economic measures, above all their desperate efforts to make the Reich self-supporting as quickly as possible, harmed just those industries in the German area of Czechoslovakia which were most adversely affected by the slump anyway. Koch's report about the effect of these measures taken immediately after Hitler's seizure of power remained unnoticed:[1]

Today the Secretary of the Federation of German Industries, Dr Kislinger, with the approval of the President of the Federation, called on me to express concern that the brunt of the German payments embargo was almost entirely borne by the population of the Sudeten German industrial area which was already close to despair. He again entreated me to make this quite clear in Berlin and I could not very well reject his request. The impact of the blow which Germany directed against Czechoslovakia...was in fact felt in full force only by the Sudeten Germans.

The dissolution of the Nazi Party

Despite the harrowing news coming from Germany observers all agreed that during the first decisive months of Hitler's terror the attractive force of the Sudeten German Nazis was even greater both on those who had until then been sympathizers of the German Nationalist Party, and on former supporters of the Agrarians (*Landbund*). Leaving aside the German Social Democrats who, by pursuing a policy of active resistance to the Nazis in their country, tried to make amends for what they considered had been the fundamental failure of their comrades in the Reich, the Catholics (Christian Socials) were the only German group which still showed a certain degree of immunity to the nationalist virus.

In Czechoslovakia, however, the question of whether a Nazi organization could and should still be tolerated in a democratic republic soon arose. The problem became acute when, after the Nazi Party had been banned in Austria in June 1933, Czechoslovakia, ironically enough remained the only country with an officially

[1] Koch to G.F.M. 20 March 1933, *G.F.M.* serial 9149, frames 643568-9.

sanctioned branch of the Berlin régime. Confronted by the risk of having their party dissolved in Czechoslovakia too, Jung and Krebs, the leaders of the German National Socialists, took care not to declare their allegiance to Hitler openly and to protest that their policy 'had never been directed towards any other goal but the most harmonious possible coexistence of Germans and Czechs'.[1] Small wonder that they, who had actually held Nazi tenets even longer than Hitler, found little credence. On 4 October 1933 the German National Socialist Party was dissolved and at the same time the German Nationalist Party was also banned in order to deprive the Nazis of the opportunity of a shelter which they would quite certainly have used. In an attempt to forestall government action the Nazis had even tried to stage a sort of 'self-immolation' by pretending to dissolve the party themselves. They did of course immediately set up an illegal party leadership consisting of lesser-known people.[2] As an organized force the Nazis, who had always boasted of the 'indestructibility' of their movement, now disappeared from the scene, only to reappear in a much more dangerous form, camouflaged as Konrad Henlein's '*Sudetendeutsche Heimatfront*' (Sudeten German Home Front).

The brutality of the new régime in Germany, with its annihilation of anything that stood in its way, attracted those Germans in Czechoslovakia who saw in it a system worth emulating and repelled all those to whom human rights and human dignity were not merely catch-phrases. Between these two groups there was, at first, a third one whose supporters while not actually approving the unbridled barbarism, managed to salve their consciences by explaining it away as a temporary phenomenon. The contrast between lawlessness across the border and the protection of the rule of law within the State, enjoyed by German citizens too, could not fail to strengthen the feeling of gratitude among democratic Germans in the country for being fortunate enough to live in Czechoslovakia – by then (apart from Switzerland) the only democracy surviving east of the Rhine. These democratic Germans had always rendered unto the state what was the state's but they had not felt there was any need

---

[1] Enclosure to report by Koch to G.F.M. 13 September 1933, *G.F.M.* serial 9695, frames 682553-7.

[2] Koch to G.F.M. 17 December 1933, *DGFP*, C/II (London 1959), no. 132.

to express their allegiance openly. Now they began to feel the need to do this. Spina, the representative of the German Agrarians in the Cabinet, was the first to pronounce in May 1933[1] 'The storm which rages around our frontiers compels the nations of this State to draw together as equals among equals.' The Germans, he declared, did not consider themselves a minority but as an integral part of the State. Similar sentiments were expressed by Wolfgang Zierhut, a leading member of the German Agrarians in Parliament: 'We representatives of the Agrarian Union identify ourselves with the State,'[2] adding the assurance of their readiness 'in case of a conflict to defend, with our Czech fellow-citizens, every inch of our territory'. The party, he said, would stand firmly by the integrity of the State and its democratic institutions.

The Social Democrats, by far the largest and the most firmly rooted German party, now turned, together with the German Trade Union Federation, from more or less unintentional support of Czechoslovak democracy to become its deliberate and most determined advocates. Eugen de Witte, one of their members of Parliament, declared[3] the Party's readiness to protect and defend Czechoslovakia: 'Our policy of reconciliation, to which we firmly adhere, is the only one which the German population of this State can follow if it understands its interests correctly. Our policy of the closest possible association with the Czech proletariat is therefore the only road for us.'

The anniversary of the foundation of the State (28 October), offered a suitable opportunity for the party press to define the attitude of the German labour movement towards the State.[4]

Among the democratic States of Europe Czechoslovakia has a special relevance. In Central Europe she is now the last democratic stronghold of the rule of law, of a European outlook, of humanity and love of peace...It is for this reason that today we stand firmly by this State, not as a historic necessity, but as a factor in Central European politics whose importance we want to see strengthened, whose existence safeguarded and whose fate assured.

In conclusion it was said that the most important fact at the moment

[1] *Prager Tagblatt*, 16 May 1933.
[2] *Parliamentary Minutes* of 4 July 1933, pp. 38–41.
[3] *Parliamentary Minutes* of 26 April 1933, pp. 76–9.
[4] *Sozialdemokrat*, 28 October 1933.

was 'the existence of the State as a bulwark against Fascist barbarism'.

When Masaryk's period of office came to an end in 1934, the German parties represented in the Czechoslovak Government had of course no hesitation in voting for him again and the Christian Socials, who were then in opposition, joined in his re-election. Beneš, too, had now gained in popularity among the democratic Germans. This was shown in an article commemorating his fiftieth birthday:[1]

After the way events have developed in Europe during the last years, the German working population had to acknowledge how valuable it was that the foreign policy of the State was in the hands of a man who, like the President of the State, adhered to the tenets of democracy, who is anxious to pursue a policy of peace and understanding and had always shown a conciliatory attitude in national questions.

And in a Czech publication, Wenzel Jaksch said on behalf of the German Social Democrats:[2]

The fourth re-election of T. G. Masaryk as President of our State, to which the greater part of the votes of the minorities also contributed, proved by the large number of manifestations of sympathy the strength of the moral position of Czechoslovakia – in contrast to all dictatorships – in the wider area of human civilisation such as exists today... The German Social Democratic movement of this country has fought its way through historical obstacles to an absolutely positive relationship with the Republic and in view of the tragedy that has overtaken the German people this movement now has an interest, not merely from the view-point of cold reason but of warm sentiment, to see that this last island of democracy in the ocean of Central European Fascism is not overwhelmed.

However, even before the Nazi Party was dissolved the friend who was to help it to rise again had already appeared on the scene: on 1 October 1933 Konrad Henlein, an official of the German Nationalist (*deutsch-völkisch*) Gymnastics League, practically unknown and politically, at any rate, quite inactive until then, called for the formation of the 'Sudeten German Home Front', at the same time indicating his 'democratic' outlook by announcing that he himself would take over the leadership.

[1] *Sozialdemokrat*, 27 May 1934.
[2] Wenzel Jaksch, 'Náš bezpečnostní problém' (Our security problem), in *Dělnická Osvěta* (Workers' Education) (Prague 1934), 6, 906–7.

With all the experience the world has meanwhile gained of camouflaged Nazi and Fascist organizations there really ought to be no need to prove that Henlein was from the very first and without any wavering just as faithful a henchman of Hitler as the representatives of the 'true' Nazi Party in Czechoslovakia. Since this state of affairs, however plain it must appear, is still eagerly disputed – one can often read even in English publications that only 'Czech intransigence' gradually drove or forced Henlein into Hitler's arms in 1937 – it seems necessary to conduct a more searching examination of this chapter of Nazi politics.[1]

[1] Even a book published in London in 1972 (Keith Middlemas, *Diplomacy of Illusion: The British Government and Germany, 1937–39*) which is highly critical of appeasement policy, repeats despite all available evidence reflecting the true state of affairs all the fairy-tales about the 'moderate Henlein'. Middlemas calls him 'Leader of the Sudeten Germans' and, in his view, 'not necessarily a Nazi agent'. He says his real aim was an 'autonomous Sudetenland' inside the democratic state of Czechoslovakia. With such critics of appeasement policy those condemning it outright need not worry about the arguments of Chamberlain's defenders.

9 HENLEIN 'ANTE PORTAS'

Konrad Henlein may not have been a paid-up member of the Nationalist Socialist Party before 1933. If he was not, the reason is probably that as organizer of the 'German Gymnastics League' which included members of various parties as well as those who were of no party, he found a positive political commitment inconvenient, the more so since he had already evinced totalitarian predilections in that function. The League was not a general cover-organization for German gymnastic clubs of different political shades. The workers' sports clubs as well as Christian gymnastic clubs had their own organizations, and there were also separate liberal athletic clubs which rejected the 'Aryans only' rule of the nationalist organizations under Henlein's leadership. But even if Henlein was not formally a National Socialist before 1933, he had always been from top to toe the perfect Nazi official.

Henlein carefully hid the fact that he had a Czech mother. She was never mentioned by the newspapers subservient to him. This at any rate shows lack of truthfulness in the man who began his political career with the professed aim of working for 'the peaceful co-existence of the nations in this State' while at the same time refusing to reveal his most convincing qualification for this task. How much better equipped for it he would have appeared if he had openly declared that as son of a German father and a Czech mother he was by nature predestined to be the protagonist of national reconciliation!

Konrad Henlein was born in 1898 near Liberec, the son of a German book-keeper of the same name and his wife Hedwig, *née* Dvořáčková, the daughter of Edvard Dvořáček, a Czech book-keeper. The latter's parents, Henlein's great-grandparents, were František Dvořáček, a landowner and merchant living in Litoboř, a purely Czech village of 500 inhabitants, and his wife, also born a Dvořáčková. No particular importance is attached to all this in an ethnically mixed country where, despite mutual nationalist goadings under all governments, there were thousands of mixed marriages, but to Henlein the revelation of his ancestry by some of his opponents was embarrassing.

The Comradeship League

Henlein's emergence into public life coincided with the first general awareness of the existence of a semi-secret organization called the Comradeship League (*Kameradschaftsbund*, abbreviated KB). Until this time the League had blossomed in the dark. Henlein was a member of it, and it was to become a rallying point for those elements of nationalist youth, never amounting to more than a few hundred, who regarded themselves as its élite and in which masonic ritual was strangely combined with nationalist mysticism. Just as a legend has been built around Henlein, claiming he had nothing to do with Nazism, adherents of the KB have been and are still propagating the story that it had actually been a sort of anti-Nazi organization which was even proscribed by the Gestapo. The KB was not a Nazi organization within the strict party dogma, but it was just this circumstance which enabled it to come into the open in October 1933 as a sheet-anchor for the banned National Socialists. There could, however, be no question of a fundamental or in fact any sort of antithesis between the KB and the Nazi Party: simultaneous membership of both bodies was by no means incompatible. This was quite correctly described by Koch at the beginning of November 1933:[1]

In spite of the conflicts between the *Kameradschaftsbund* and the DNASP (Nazis) about claims to leadership of the Sudeten Germans there nevertheless exist, or existed, close cross-connections between the members of the *Kameradschaftsbund* and individual youthful leaders of the National Socialist movement.

To gain insight into the mentality of the KB members one need only look through the pages of their magazine *Die junge Front*, which was at that time quite obscure. Leadership, *Gefolgschaft* (something between team-spirit and subordination), discipline, heroic bearing, spirit of comradeship – there was an abundance of these and similar terms. True, there was indeed some sort of

[1] Koch to G.F.M. 8 November 1933, *DGFP*, C/ii, no. 51.

criticism of National Socialism but of a kind which its author, Walter Brand (Henlein's loyal assistant) would today not like to boast about.[1]

National Socialism has indeed gone farthest in fundamental appreciation of the things that matter, even if this has not come about through clear perception but rather through instinct. But the belief that the new can be attained with the means of the past, the dallying with democracy as a tactical step towards its conquest, again proves the truth of the adage that one cannot cast out the devil by coming to terms with Beelzebub.

The nub of the argument was that Brand considered Nazism to be insufficiently anti-democratic: it 'sullied' its idealogical purity, as it were, by coming into contact with parliamentarism.

Shortly after Brand, Henlein himself had appeared on the rostrum with a flood of typical nationalist phrases.[2] There can have been few occasions on which so much clashing of swords and revelling in words were combined in one essay, under the title 'The Education of our Young Men':

Place noble men, great ideas before the souls of youth, give them men, in the deepest and holiest meaning of the word, as leaders – and you will bring up a manly race, undaunted, heroic. . . The ceremony of the dedication of the young men should be the most solemn occasion of the year when they, grown to manhood and to dignity to bear arms, repose their vow of allegiance in the hands of the regional leader as the representative of the Supreme Fuehrer. Initiation into Germanic knighthood (*die germanische Schwertleite*) and knighting are the symbol. . . Unrelenting toughness with himself, obedience, loyalty to the Fuehrer and to his comrades are demanded of everyone. . . The Spartan who bore the responsibility for the valour of the young under his charge, the Germanic warrior who entrusted shield and spear for the defence of the tribe to his young vassal when he was admitted to the community of men, are ideals, noble enough to inspire our best men even now in the education of youth. . . We want lads with sharp eyes and smart bearing (*Kerle mit blitzenden Augen und schneidigen Zügen*). . . We look for the hero and despise the philistine. . . We want united heroic youth.

The political tendency of Henlein's Gymnastic League was made abundantly clear in a book published under its auspices in 1921: *German National Science, A Guide to Nationalist* (Völkisch) *Education*: 'The German Gymnastics League, just like other leagues and associations cultivating the German character, has chosen the

[1] In *Die junge Front* [St Georgenthal near Varnsdorf], no. 1 (1932).
[2] Konrad Henlein, 'Leibesübungen und ihre volkspolitische Bedeutung', in *Die junge Front*, no. 4 (1930).

Swastika, the sign and symbol of the victorious sun, as its badge.'
And Henlein's reaction to the emergence of the Third Reich is
equally clearly shown in his *Turnzeitung* (Gymnastic Newspaper) of
15 August 1933:

Beyond these frontier posts the bells are now joyfully heralding in a new era and
its minutes hurry full of hope towards the future... Germany has today entered
upon the path to freedom.

And men of this ilk wanted to persuade the world in October 1933
that they felt and fought for democracy! Unfortunately they
managed to persuade some people as late as 1938.

The Sudeten German Home Front

Not only did Henlein conceal his ancestry; he also claimed that the
establishment of the Sudeten German Home Front was entirely
his own idea.[1] This was not even true to the extent that his *final*
decision to enter politics was influenced by external circumstances.
In July 1933, on the occasion of a gymnastic jamboree at Žatec,
Henlein had been selected by the 'true' Nazi Hans Krebs as his
future assistant and this was the first occasion on which Henlein
attracted a certain amount of publicity. The circumstances are
described by Walter Brand in a post-war pamphlet in which an
attempt was made to depict Henlein as *integer vitae scelerisque
purus*.[2]

In July 1933 attempts were made by the National Socialists, notably by Hans
Krebs, to persuade Henlein to enter Sudeten German politics. Krebs envisaged
the formation of a Sudeten German People's Front, comprising all the non-
Marxist Sudeten German parties, under Henlein's leadership. This would have
given the two political parties threatened by dissolution, the German National
Socialists and the German Nationalist Party, the possibility of submerging in
this new League and thus protecting the body of their followers from the
persecutions they expected.

Whatever the background of all this secretiveness, the press was
able to report towards the end of September 1933[3] that negotiations

---

1 'Alone, free from any influence' he had composed his appeal, Henlein told an
astonished press-conference in Prague. *Konrad Henlein spricht* (Karlovy Vary
1937), p. 11.
2 Walter Brand, *Die sudetendeutsche Tragödie* (Nuremberg 1949), p. 22.
3 *Prager Tagblatt*, 21 September 1933, reprinted by Josef Fischer, Václav
Patzak and Vincenc Perth, *Ihr Kampf, Die wahren Ziele der SdP* (Karlovy
Vary 1937), p. 41.

had taken place in Prague between Henlein and Brand on the one hand and Krebs on the other. There was a clash of opinions between Krebs who wanted to ensure for himself and his followers the decisive share in the control of the new party, and Henlein who tried to make the compromised leaders of the Nazi Party understand that they would have to disappear if they wanted their political line to survive. Since he was unsuccessful in this endeavour, Henlein's first proclamation of 1 October 1933 appeared without the active co-operation of Krebs and Jung. This is not to say that he had acted alone and independently. At Krebs' post-war trial in Prague evidence that one of the authors of the appeal had been the Nazi journalist Karl Viererbl[1] (who shortly afterward fled to Germany and joined the editorial staff of the *Völkischer Beobachter*) was submitted.

A man as well-informed as Koch never had any doubt, of course, that Henlein's appeal had been prearranged with the Nazis. His first report of Henlein's appearance[2] mentions that

Konrad Henlein, the organiser of the Gymnastics Association, is trying with the support of the *Kameradschaftsbund* and the approval of the National Socialists Party Leaders here to unite the national Sudeten Germans under the name of a Sudeten German Home Front (*Sudetendeutsche Heimatfront*) if they are not compromised by undergoing prosecution.

A month later Koch judged[3] that after other attempts at unification had failed,

at the last moment Henlein...allegedly on his own initiative but actually urged on by the *Kameradschaftsbund* – issued a call to join the Sudeten German Home Front, which was to be a receptacle of the masses belonging to the dissolved parties. Youthful leaders of the National Socialists...who had at that time not yet been imprisoned, were inclined to join under the condition that they would be given leading positions.

Henlein's first public pronouncements were nothing but collections of the usual platitudes but they were precisely what Hitler needed at the time. At a press conference in Prague he went so far in his efforts to dispel Czech distrust that he underlined his positive

[1] See Robert Kvaček, 'K historii Henleinovy Sudetoněmecké strany' (About the history of Henlein's Sudeten German Party), *Dějepis v škole* (History in the school) (Prague), no. 5 (1957).
[2] Koch to G.F.M. 5 October 1933, *DGFP*, C/I, no. 484.
[3] Koch to G.F.M. 8 November 1933, *DGFP*, C/II, no. 51.

approach to democracy and even denied anti-semitic leanings by
protesting that the Sudeten German Home Front was of course
open to German Jews too.[1]

Quarrels in the Nationalist camp

From the moment Henlein entered the public arena he had to
defend himself against attacks from the old guard of the Nazi
Party, and this small-scale war only ended towards May 1938 when
Henlein finally triumphed over the opponents in his own camp
which was of course by then openly flying the Nazi flag. One of the
reports bruited about by the 'old' Nazis in Berlin had it that Henlein
was no anti-semite and even negotiated with Jews. The details of
these petty and trivial arguments are uninteresting but it is important that Hitler always and in all circumstances decided in favour
of Henlein and against his own praetorian guard. He realized very
clearly that his primary aim of removing the Czech obstacle to his
expansionist plans could never be achieved with the help of genuine
or 'old' Nazis who had lost most of their support even in their own
ranks, but only through the medium of a vaguely formulated
movement of national unity under the leadership of a man blindly
devoted to him.

Just as four years later (with greater success), so in 1933–4 Hitler
first directed his aggressive attentions towards Austria and tem-
porarily ignored Czechoslovakia. The Nazi old guard, now illegal
there, was of no political concern to him and at best only the subject
of charitable interest. How unjustified the 'old' Nazis' imputation of
slackness on Henlein's part really was is well illustrated by the
opinion expressed by the Austrian Hans Steinacher, who was in
charge of the *Volksbund für das Deutschtum im Ausland* (Association
for Germans Abroad) and acted as one of Henlein's most important
spokesmen in Berlin. What he had to say in 1934[2] successfully
demolished all versions of the 'honest Henlein' who had been outside the Nazi Party at least until 1937: 'Finally it must be remem-

---

[1] *Prager Tagblatt*, 10 October 1933.
[2] (Steinacher), Unsigned Note, *Zur sudetendeutschen Volkspolitik und deren
Moeglichkeiten. Zum Memorandum des Herrn Hans Krebs*, 26 June 1934,
G.F.M., serial 8772, frames 611321-7 and 611333-41.

bered that *Henlein offered to subordinate himself to the Führer some considerable time ago.*'

In Czechoslovakia Henlein of course took care not to make his Nazi contacts known. But when on 20 June 1934 he met the 'Sudeten German adviser' to the *Volksbund* in Bad Elster, on German territory, and while playing in Prague the rôle of the staunch democrat who would not dream of hob-nobbing with the Nazis, disclosed his real attitude:[1]

The accusation raised by certain people that the National Socialists were given no scope in the Sudeten German Home Front is wholly without foundation:

1. *Henlein* and his collaborators adhere to the *same National Socialist tenets* as certain agitators of the dissolved Parties.

2. Despite the (Prague Government's) ban on the political appointment of members of the dissolved Parties, the majority of the Sudeten German Home Front officials are former National Socialists.

3. He (Henlein) had asked the leader of the former National Socialist Students' League for a list of members whom they would like to have incorporated in his organization. This list has still not arrived.

4. Of the more than 100,000 members of the Sudeten German Home Front a great many were members of the dissolved National Socialist Party but *all were prepared, if necessary, to acknowledge themselves as Hitler's followers.*

At this time too, the first identifiable German subsidy was paid to Henlein's funds. The German Consul at Brno was not a little surprised when he received payments of 55,000 crowns (at that time about £400) which he was instructed to hand over to Franz Künzel, an assistant of Henlein.[2]

So far Henlein had steered clear of any concrete commitment about the programme for his movement which had sprung up with bombastic promises. (His true intentions could not of course be revealed.) In the autumn of 1934, however, he was awaiting the opportunity to hold a programmatic speech *à la* 'Nuremberg Party Rally'. But before this happened, a minor sensation took place: an interview of the most loyal citizen of Czechoslovakia Konrad Henlein, in a Czech right-wing newspaper.[3] It was literally an application of Hitler's formula 'The bigger the lie, the more likely it is to be believed'. German conscripts in the

---

[1] Steinacher to G.F.M. 27 July 1934, *G.F.M.* serial 9127 frames 641969–79.
[2] German Consulate at Brno to G.F.M. 29 September 1934, *G.F.M.* serial 9127, frames 642063–75.
[3] *Večer* (Evening newspaper) (Prague), 6 October 1934.

Czechoslovak Army were said to return from military service full of enthusiasm; Henlein suddenly discovered 'what good comrades the Czech fellow soldiers were and how decently the Czech officers treated them [the Germans]'. His party was of course utterly loyal:

I say clearly that I never had, and have now, anything in common with National Socialism...We are not a continuation of the Krebs Party, and let it be stated openly once and for all that Krebs and other leaders who deserted their followers are despised by us from the depth of our hearts...Whoever infringes the duty of loyalty to the State or shows that he has any connection with foreign organizations of whatever kind will be ruthlessly weeded out from the Sudeten German Home Front.

All this from the man who at Bad Elster a few months earlier had boasted of being at least as good a Nazi as Hans Krebs.

Henlein's 'Programmatic Declarations' were eventually given at a rally at Česká Lípa (Böhmisch-Leipa) on 21 October 1934, in exactly those words which, however obliquely formulated, were at that time needed to lull the Czech public into a feeling of security. The astonishing thing is that even now, after all the world has learnt of the techniques practised by the various masters of political camouflage, this speech is in many quarters still regarded as an expression of Henlein's true sentiments.

Pan-Germanism was just as bad as Pan-Slavism, proclaimed Henlein.[1] He and his followers ought not to be regarded, because of their German background, as second-class citizens, let alone as enemies of the State. No one had any such intention, but Henlein even demanded Czech recognition for having come to their aid, 'by having, in the interest of the consolidation of the State [*sic*] and of internal pacification, set a new political aim before the leaderless masses'. A polemic against Italian Fascism in Henlein's speech led to a denial of his lord and master: 'As regards German National Socialism, too, we have no hesitations in expressing fundamental reservations.' 'Certain reservations' which he was wise enough not to elaborate, were also made by Henlein about Liberalism but he wanted to state 'emphatically'

that we shall never, under any circumstances, abandon the liberal outlook, that is the unconditional respect for the rights of the individual as a basic factor in the determination of human relations in general and the relationship between

[1] Text of the speech in *Konrad Henlein spricht*, pp. 22–41.

117

citizens and authorities in particular...These declarations will explain the *fundamental differences separating us from National Socialism.*

It is odd, though, that these alleged 'fundamental differences' never emerged in any other form but these few words. Henlein who had been in Germany barely four months earlier now advanced a grotesque argument for not discussing conditions in Germany. Despite the fact that, never having been to Russia, he criticized Bolshevik reality, but was still able to say that since foreign travel apparently 'could be dangerous even for the most loyal citizen' he could not comment on conditions in the Third Reich: 'Through no fault of our own therefore, we do not know what conditions are like, for example, in Germany today and so we can hardly be expected to give detailed opinions without knowing the actual circumstances.' Then followed an attempt to cajole Beneš: 'I can content myself...with stating openly and plainly that *we have absolutely no interest at all in any sort of frontier revision.*' Henlein vowed to stand four-square behind the 'democratic–republican State system of Czechoslovakia'. The political demands which he then elaborated – a fair share in the administration, consideration for linguistic requirements – would have been trite if they had come from a real democrat. But no effort was too much for Henlein when it was a question of putting Czech minds at rest:

It goes without saying that the unity of the State and its leadership must be preserved. It is therefore quite senseless to suppose that self-administration could involve a separate Sudeten-German parliament or anything of that sort.

On the other hand, in order to cover up his real intentions, Henlein did not omit the veiled threat that whoever rejected the Sudeten-German hand so readily proffered, would have 'to bear the responsibility for the way in which things might then develop'.

Henlein's denial of Nazism, necessary for tactical reasons, caused no real or feigned indignation in Berlin. Extracts from his speech were indeed published, naturally leaving out any reference to 'reservations' about National Socialism:[1] these, coming from the man who had taken so decisive a stand on Hitler's side, were accepted in Berlin for what they were worth. But seven years were to elapse before Henlein, in a speech in Vienna,[1] revealed the motives which in 1934 made him deny his true aims:

[1] See e.g. the report in *Völkischer Beobachter* of 22 October 1934.

When during the great wave of persecution in the autumn of 1933 the leaders of the German National Socialist Party asked me to assume the leadership of the Sudeten Germans, the problem confronting me was: ought the National Socialist Party to continue illegally or should the movement take up the Sudeten Germans' fight for self-assertion and prepare for eventual return into the Greater German Reich under camouflage and outwardly in full legality? For us Sudeten Germans the only choice was the second way...No doubt...it would have been much simpler, instead of joining in this hard and protracted war of nerves, to dare the heroic gesture by acknowledging from the very beginning our allegiance as National Socialists and enter the Czech jails. Whether by such means the *political task of smashing Czechoslovakia as the key fortress in the ring of alliances against Germany* could have been solved as easily, too, seems to me doubtful. At any rate *it is a fact that within a few years the Sudeten Germans succeeded in undermining the internal stability of Czechoslovakia and in disrupting inner relations there to such an extent* that the country became ripe for *liquidation* as a first step towards the achievement of the New Order on the Continent... We knew that we could only win if we succeeded in turning 3½ Million Sudeten Germans into 3½ Million National Socialists, yet we also knew that in order to prevent interference by the Czech authorities and dissolution, *we had to dissociate ourselves outwardly from National Socialism.* That was the severest psychological stress to which I had to subject my followers. In an admirable spirit of discipline and with unshakeable confidence in me, my comrades realized what was at stake and saw, *behind the tactical moves of political manœuvring* forced on me the great goal of our path which was to lead us home into the Reich of Adolf Hitler.

Since the insinuations of the 'old guard' against Henlein showed no signs of abating after the speech at Lípa, Rudolf Hess, Hitler's deputy, decided on a drastic measure. At the beginning of March 1935 the '*Dienststelle* (Office) *Ribbentrop*' issued a circular with the following terse and unequivocal wording:[2]

You are informed by Party Comrade von Ribbentrop on behalf of Minister Rudolf Hess that, on principle and in all circumstances, all attacks by the German press on Konrad Henlein, the leader of the Sudeten German Home Front, must cease.

Hitler's confidence in Henlein did not waver until the very end[3] and very rightly so for he was and remained one of Hitler's staunchest paladins. But there was of course much more to it than the virtually

---

[1] Text in *Das größere Reich*, A series of lectures organized by the Academy of Administration in Vienna (Berlin 1943), pp. 36–52.
[2] *DGFP*, C/III, no. 525.
[3] Henlein committed suicide a few days after Hitler, on 9 May 1945, while under guard by the Americans at Pilzeň, by cutting his wrists.

119

unlimited trust which Henlein, despite all his alleged 'fundamental reservations' about National Socialism, enjoyed in Berlin. At the end of January 1935 Steinacher had called at the German Foreign Ministry[1] to suggest that a subsidy to Henlein of 300,000 marks, by Czechoslovak standards an astronomical amount (about £17,000) would not come amiss for the coming parliamentary election campaigns in Czechoslovakia. Under democratic conditions the Foreign Ministry would have indignantly rejected any such demand. Now their only concern was that the transfer of this large sum would not remain unnoticed. However, Henlein's requirements were eventually met – without any investigation or reduction. The suggestion that even a fraction of this huge amount of money which was smuggled into Czechoslovakia could be granted to a political party not in thrall to Hitler is too absurd even to be discussed. Encouraged by the generosity shown by the Reich, Henlein thought little of exceeding his preliminary estimate by 10 per cent and confirmed on 28 August 1935 in Berlin – foreign travel was apparently not quite so risky after all – the receipt of over 330,000 Reichmarks.[2] The Reich Finance Minister Schwerin-Krosigk wanted to negotiate with Hess about the apportionment of this subsidy between the State and the Nazi Party,[3] a further proof, if one be needed, that Henlein was put on the same level by Berlin as the Nazi Party, since the latter would hardly have been called upon to support an organization hostile to it.

In the meantime Henlein had also gained the support of one of the most influential men in the Czechoslovak Agrarian Party, a man who cared little enough for Henlein or the Germans as a whole, but greatly wished to see a right-wing régime established in the country. This was Viktor Stoupal, the leader of the Moravian wing of the Agrarians who was scarcely known to the public at this time. A German Foreign Ministry note of March 1935[4] discloses that

---

[1] Roediger (G.F.M.) to Koch 2 February 1935; Koch to Roediger 5 February 1935, *DGFP*, C/III, no. 482.
[2] For the text of the receipt see *G.F.M.* serial 6144, frame 459652.
[3] Note by Roediger, 4 September 1935, *DGFP*, C/IV, no. 285.
[4] Note of 8 March 1935, *G.F.M.* serial 6144, frames 459653-5, extracts printed in *DGFP*, C/IV, no. 285.

Friedrich Bürger, Henlein's agent in Berlin, had put the following question to the German diplomats:

The Czech Agrarians intend to direct the forthcoming election campaign against Beneš and aim to overthrow him. They themselves are too weak for that. They therefore wish to establish a link with the Sudeten German Home Front (Konrad Henlein) which would strengthen their position by bringing in 15 to 20 parliamentary seats. This would still not be sufficient, hence the German Agrarians (Spina) are also to be taken into this combination. Considerable opposition to this tactical alliance is felt by the Sudeten German Home Front, because Spina is...tainted by his former relations with Beneš. The Sudeten German Home Front now risks losing popularity by collaborating with the German Agrarians. On the other hand it will be in danger of dissolution if the proposals of the Czech Agrarians are not met since this Party alone has so far resisted Beneš' demand for banning the Sudeten German Home Front.

Henlein's emissaries, it was explained, would like to be able to convey the official attitude of the Reich and party authorities to Henlein to enable him to reach a decision. He would be prepared

if supported by the competent German authorities, to enter into an electoral alliance with the German Agrarians to conform with the wishes of the Czech Party so that...the Beneš party can be put out of action and, by collaborating with the Czech Agrarians in the Cabinet, an improvement in the external relations between the Reich and Czechoslovakia could perhaps be achieved.

The Sudeten German agents were referred to Hess: whether he actually did see them and if so, what he told them, can no longer be determined but the mere fact that Henlein contacted Berlin for guidance in a purely internal problem shows the degree of 'independence' of National Socialism which he had from the very beginning.

The Czechoslovak elections were planned for the middle of May 1935 but as late as the end of March it was by no means clear whether Henlein's party would be able to take part in them: not only Beneš but the German as well as the Czech Social Democrats were determined not to admit to democratic elections a substitute for the dissolved Nazi Party, which was equally manipulated from Berlin. The Agrarian Premier Jan Malypetr who belonged to the Bohemian wing of his party and did not have much influence in its counsels, took a neutral point of view under the pressure of the Moravian pro-Henlein Agrarians and invoked T. G. Masaryk's decision. The latter's word was accepted as final: the Sudeten German Home Front was not dissolved but admitted to the election. For a long time Henlein had tried in vain to make contacts with the President:

now the occasion was used by Henlein to send a telegram to Masaryk assuring him of undying loyalty in such terms as: 'From the first day of our political activity I have clearly and unambiguously explained our attitude towards the Czechoslovak State and its people. Only malevolence or deliberate incomprehension can see in our Party a political organisation endangering the State.'[1] It is unlikely that Masaryk was greatly impressed. The feeling that Henlein ought to be given his parliamentary reins probably influenced him more; if the need arose, his party could still be dissolved.

It was not until the beginning of April that the Government decided to admit Henlein's party to the forthcoming elections. Although that was certainly a mistake, a dissolution of his movement would not have done much good either, unless accompanied by really generous concessions to those Germans who were loyal to democratic ideals, and such liberality could hardly have been expected from any of the Czech parties in a pre-election period. In the event Henlein was only permitted to take part in the poll on condition that the Sudeten German Home Front changed its name, since the expression 'Front' could not be accepted in a democracy. Consequently he decided that his party should stand for election under the name of 'Sudeten German Party (SdP), Chairman Konrad Henlein'. This identification with Sudeten Germans as a whole ultimately did the latter untold harm but for the present it improved Henlein's chances considerably.

Undaunted by Hitler's repeated rebuffs the staunch 'old party comrades' in Czechoslovakia continued in their hopeless attempts to discredit Henlein or at least his close associates in Berlin. Of particular interest is a long memorandum[2] which arrived in Berlin a few days before the Czechoslovak elections, scheduled for 19 May 1935, which shows very clearly the 'genuine' Nazis' resentment at not having been offered the pick of the Sudeten German Party candidates. Details about the origin of the Henlein movement were here revealed:

Even before the dissolution of the German National Socialist Party leading personalities in it had started negotiations with Henlein...At that time Henlein

[1] Koch to G.F.M. 10 April 1935, *G.F.M.* serial 6144, frames 643700–8.
[2] Koch to G.F.M. 9 May 1935, *G.F.M.* serial 6144, frames 459660–8.

had promised to act in accordance with the traditions of the old Party and to accept leading National Socialists into the council of the new Party.

After complaints that Henlein had not kept to his promise fully, the lament continued:

It is assiduously stressed that this movement had been built up by Konrad Henlein out of nothing, that no movement had ever suffered such terrible persecution etc., while every school-boy knows that the core of the Sudeten German Home Front, were the 150,000 organised National Socialists of October 1933... The National Socialists are doing all the work of the lower echelons and are also fighting the election campaign.

The Elections of May 1935

Henlein was apeing Hitler even in the latter's disrespect for parliament. Like Hitler, who had stood aloof from parliamentary discussions, leaving them instead to the lesser breed, Henlein, the driving-force of his party, who made up to eleven election speeches a day, was not himself a candidate in the elections. That he considered beneath his dignity. On 19 May voting took place for both Houses of Parliament; a week later for the provincial diets and districts councils. Among the thousands of names appearing on the Sudeten German Party lists of candidates, there was not a single woman, just as in Nazi Germany. The election campaign too followed Nazi precepts, the only difference being that it took place in and was tolerated by a democratic State and was even protected by its police. The average voter could not fail to suppose that the movement was looked upon with favour by both Prague and Berlin, and that he might therefore mark his ballot paper with complete confidence.

The Henlein candidates were opposed by the Social Democrats, the German Agrarians, the Catholics (Christian Socials) and the Communists. The election result, as far as the Czechs and Slovaks were concerned, was a vindication of their political sense. Surrounded by authoritarian States, they chose democracy and ignored the extremist factions of right and left. Not so in the German sector. Against Hitler's agents in Czechoslovakia, skilfully camouflaged and aided on all sides, the German Activists fought a desperate rearguard action and succumbed. The remarkable feature of the result, however, was not so much that Henlein won but the size of his victory: a political group which until then had not been represented in Parliament at all, romped home with the largest number of votes, larger even than those cast for the leading Government party (Sudeten German Party 1,249,530 votes; Czechoslovak Agrarians 1,116,593). The Czechoslovak Social Democrats came third with 1,034,774 votes.

There is no doubt that for the party of a national minority to win more votes than the main Government party was an extraordinary achievement. In terms of parliamentary seats, however, under the system of proportional representation it obtained one mandate less (44, as against 45 for the Agrarians); this, in a parliamentary democracy, is of course the decisive factor. On the basis of votes cast for purely German lists of candidates the SdP would have obtained not less than two-thirds of the total German poll in Czechoslovakia, but the situation was not quite so clear-cut: the Communists, the international party *par excellence*, of course had adherents among the Germans, and there was also the small 'German Party of Zips' in Slovakia, which managed to hold out against Henlein as late as 1938 and gained one seat in the 1935 election.

All this may have accounted for 120,000 German votes, certainly not more; which leaves the share of the SdP still at 60 per cent. The German Social Democrats and Communists must therefore have lost votes to Henlein, as did to an even greater extent the German Agrarians whose vote was practically halved. A similar fate befell the Christian Socials and since this party had been in opposition since 1929, Henlein's success cannot simply be explained as the response of people disappointed with the results of German participation in the Government.

On the side of the Activists there were still 600,000 men and women, one-third of the German voters, who despite all promises and threats affirmed their faith in democracy. Counting the Zips German Party and the Communists (who gained 28 seats, 4 of which were held by Germans), the SdP stranglehold was further weakened. Although they lost 10 of their 21 seats, the German Social Democrats with 300,000 votes had shown how deep-rooted was their support among the German people. If German collaboration in the affairs of the state had not proved its worth by producing tangible results, such as the meticulously fair benefits awarded to the victims of the economic slump – not even Henlein complained of preferential treatment for the Czech unemployed – it is very probable that the German Activist parties would have been wiped out. Despite their setback, however, the principle of German–Czech democratic co-operation in the Government had shown its soundness and its broadly based support.

What, then, was the explanation for the undeniable triumph of the man who had been practically unknown until October 1933, who even in the May 1935 election had not himself stood as a candidate and whose party had nevertheless gained the highest number of votes? It was said at the time that the masses only applauded Henlein because they recognized Hitler behind him. But would it be true to deduce that the majority of the Germans had now irretrievably gone over to National Socialism? Such a conclusion would not be justified. The year 1935 was one in which Hitler achieved for the first time far-reaching internal and external successes and the Western Powers began to react to this provocative action by turning the other cheek. No one can say what the result of any sort of free elections in Germany or Austria might have been at that time, but Hitler's successes could not fail to have a psychological effect on those strata of the German population in Czechoslovakia which had never outgrown their resentment at the loss of German hegemony in the country and were by nature inclined towards nationalist hot-bloodedness. And nothing succeeds like success: many a German in Czechoslovakia who was no fanatical Nazi must have come away convinced that, as Hitler had proved, more could be obtained by a policy *à outrance* than one of loyalty to the State. To achieve 'more' of what was defined ambiguously as 'self-administration' was what the greater part of the Henlein voters wanted. That many of them had no positive attitude to the State in which they were living can hardly be denied but there were only few active irredentists among them. To many Sudeten German workers the Third Reich appeared less as the country of concentration camps than as a régime taking highly effective measures against unemployment. Compared with the achievements of a big State like Germany in this respect, those of Czechoslovakia must have appeared puny. A final factor was the suggestive power of a mass movement confident of victory and the disinclination of many people, especially in smaller places, not to 'conform'.

125

Czechoslovakia before Munich

Was Henlein's victory in any sense due to what the German Nationalists called 'the oppression of the Germans by the Czechs'? At the elections of 1925 and 1929 German Nationalist propaganda against what the Germans regarded as a policy of expansion had fallen flat and there is no reason to suppose that the election of 1935 would have seen a different outcome had the influence of the apparently irresistible Nazi advance been lacking. A few weeks before the Czechoslovak elections the Saar plebiscite resulted in an overwhelming majority for those favouring the immediate return of the territory to Hitler's Germany (90.39 per cent). The democratic parties of the Saarland, Christian Democrats and Social Democrats who, unlike the Activists in Czechoslovakia, were free of government responsibilities, implored the electorate to vote for the maintenance of the *status quo* which might have left the door open for a later return to a democratic Germany: only 8.83 per cent of the electors followed this appeal. Measured against Hitler's victory in the Saar territory, the 33 per cent of German votes cast, under extremely unfavourable conditions, for German–Czech democratic collaboration in 1935 do not show up badly even though the two results are not fully comparable.

The irruption into the Czechoslovak Parliament of a new political force of such sinister strength, a force which in its whole approach (many of Henlein's elected followers appeared in Parliament in jack-boots) was alien to Czechoslovak, or for that matter, any other democracy, in itself gravely disturbed internal relations. The size of his electoral victory and the conviction that under reasonably normal conditions a party of such standing could no longer be dissolved, gave Henlein a considerable fillip. Interspersing loyal gestures with provocative threats he assured Masaryk in a post-election telegram that he was going to operate 'only on the basis of the Constitution of our [sic] State'.[1] He immediately followed this up by summoning all newly elected SdP Members of Parliament to appear before him at Cheb to swear obedience to him personally before they had even taken the prescribed constitutional oath in Parliament.[2] Obviously it was intended to remind people of the moment when all 230 Nazi Reichstag deputies elected in the summer of 1932 had to appear before Adolf Hitler who, just like Henlein, had not himself stood as candidate.

The pipe-dream of the Moravian wing of the Czech Agrarians of creating a right-wing régime in Prague with the help of '15 to 20' Henlein parliamentarians, which, if realized, would have meant the capitulation of the country to the Third Reich, vanished into thin air when at the elections the Henlein party (SdP) emerged in a strength excluding any possibility of its being the tool of anybody else. The existing Government parties' determination to continue their coalition under all circumstances blocked the path of the SdP to power in the State and prevented it from undermining its constitutional foundations. But the policy of barring the SdP from all positions of power could only have the desired effect of strengthening democracy in the German camp if at the same time

---

[1] *Prager Tagblatt*, 21 May 1935. [2] *Prager Presse*, 9 June 1935.

far-reaching concessions were made to those Germans who remained loyal to the State. In fact only the Czech leftist parties were prepared to do this, while the Agrarians did not see their way to co-operating until Milan Hodža – politically talented, but of unreliable personal character – had become Premier in November 1935.

German participation in the new Government

Although the German parties which had been represented in the pre-election Government no longer stood for the majority of the German population in Czechoslovakia, their continued participation in the administration was never in question. Under normal conditions they would have resigned from the Government and returned in greater strength only after new elections. In the circumstances the existing democratic constellation had to be maintained at all costs, even if it meant Franz Spina remaining in the Government only as Minister without Portfolio and Ludwig Czech surrendering the Ministry he had taken over in 1934 (Public Works) for the less important Ministry of Health. The German Ministers played, as it were, the rôle of vicars of conciliation *in partibus infidelium* – they represented, and were regarded as representing, the interests of the whole German community.

A courageous warning

At the end of June 1935 Koch retired. While in office as German Minister in Prague he had tried, after Hitler's seizure of power in 1933, not to give unnecessary offence in Berlin. Now he evidently felt free to submit unpalatable truths to the Reich authorities. He had already told them before[1] that there were no serious issues between Germany and Czechoslovakia, but rather a continuous state of acute tension based on

> the instinctive mutual dislike of the Czech and German peoples which has existed for centuries and which no politician has yet been able to change and the fear of the Czechs of one day being smothered in the German encirclement. This fear among the Czechs also stems from the Middle Ages and has of late been greatly strengthened by Article 1 of the National Socialist Programme (Union of all Germans in one State).

His period of office almost over, Koch decided to deal a much

[1] Koch to G.F.M. 4 January 1934, *G.F.M.* serial 8911, frames 621830–4.

128

heavier blow in the form of a 10-page memorandum 'Causes and results of the fundamental anti-German attitude of the Czechs',[1] probably the most ominous warning ever sent to Berlin by one of the Reich's own representatives abroad. Koch began by calmly pointing out that Beneš was determined 'to continue to adhere to the anti-German tendency of his foreign policy, which he had shown since the beginning of his career', in order to kill any illusions Berlin might have cherished of a change in the Czech outlook:

It must be faced that with few exceptions...he can be sure of the Czech people's support. This political fact is rooted in the thousand-year-old Czech history which consists of nothing but the hitherto successful effort of the Czechs to maintain their independence in a geographically exposed position *vis-à-vis* the superior German nation...In the eyes of the Czechs their whole history is really only one continuous war against the Germans. This hereditary enmity is, as it were, every Czech's birth mark and is kept alive by the whole education system, by literature and political outlook. Hence that fundamental Czech fear of being 'germanized', virtually a psychotic state of fear, which is the only explanation for their political attitude.

Koch confirmed:

An objective evaluation of the facts of history must recognise that this basic Czech attitude, derived from experience, might not be correct in all details... but is in general at least understandable. All true German statesmen since the time of Charlemagne have recognized the truth of the statement formulated by Bismarck that the master of Bohemia is also the master of Europe...Over and over again attempts have been made either to incorporate this bulwark into Germany or at least to neutralise it in one form or another.

After a summary of the events leading to national independence in 1918 Koch continued:

No nation will forget a historical course of this sort, which, considering the smallness of the Czech people, may well be described as 'glorious'. A State which would not pursue the task envisaged at its inception, capitulates.

Hitler's peace overtures would only be regarded as camouflage by the Czechs:

As proof of their views the Czechs mention the support, shown...to the SdP by the VDA (the Association for the Germans Abroad). This, in their eyes, is the practical, the real policy of the Reich, anything else only serves to mask it... It is in vain that one tries to convince the Czechs that they are mistaken if they see everything simply as a preparation for war against them.

[1] Koch to G.F.M. 6 June 1935, *G.F.M.* serial 1976, frames 438523-32.

And these were Koch's conclusions:

It would be a mistake not to believe that the Beneš policy (of collective security) is in line with the deepest instincts of his people and that the Czechs see in it the only possibility of saving them from a German attack. One must not overlook the fact that well-planned and able Czech propaganda abroad has managed to present the Czechs to the world as a poor, small and harmless people, once more threatened by the pan-German ghost. Under these circumstances German steps against Czechoslovakia could easily mobilize world opinion against Germany. World opinion could without difficulty be made to believe that the 70 Million Germans encircling Czechoslovakia intend to impose their will on a mere 7 Million Czechs. Germany and Austria-Hungary sufficiently learned the lesson of the consequences of such misguided opinions from their experiences 21 years ago in the case of Belgium and Serbia... These facts and considerations might recommend special caution on the part of Germany in the treatment of any questions regarding Czechoslovakia.

These meditations were buried in the Foreign Ministry files and never shown to Hitler.

The Presidential election

In the late autumn of 1935, after Masaryk had resigned for reasons of age and before the election of his successor to the office of President of the Republic – constitutionally the task of both Houses of Parliament in joint session – the SdP made a new and extremely dangerous attempt to steer the country away from its democratic path and into one more acceptable to Hitler. The means employed were an alliance with the Czech right-wing. Masaryk's farewell message contained the significant warning: 'We need to show justice at home to all citizens of whatever nationality.'[1] At the same time he recommended Beneš as his successor.

The Czech right wing could not in fact muster any plausible candidate as an alternative to Beneš, but this did not deter the SdP from helping them to look for one. They even offered their support to the candidature of the Czech arch-chauvinist Kramář, if only Beneš could be kept out. Kramář, however, though old and ill (he died in 1937) still had enough sense of honour to turn down the suggestion that he should stand for 'President by the grace of Hitler'. Eventually a Czech nationalist was found, willing, at least for a few days, to be hitched to the SdP wagon. This was Bohumil Němec, a botanist of repute but politically a babe in arms. He had

[1] Klepetař, *Seit 1918*, p. 406.

130

been chairman of a body calling itself the 'Czechoslovak National Council', a cover-organization of various 'borderland associations' which the Germans considered, not without justification, as an organization for the spreading of Czech influence (*'Tschechisierung'*). Such was the paradoxical choice of the German Nationalists, but they would have allied themselves with the devil if he had been able to prevent Beneš, a determined opponent of Nazism, from becoming head of state.

It so happened that for a few days the leadership of the Czech Agrarian Party did fall into the hands of the ultra-reactionary right wing which lost no time in achieving an understanding with the SdP about Němec's candidature. But nothing came of all this, for the Agrarian Party soon regained its sense of political realism. The German Christian Social Party (in opposition), and the oppositional Slovak Hlinka Party, on whom the SdP had placed great hopes, declared themselves for Beneš. Faced by the general support for Beneš, Němec withdrew – in the event he would have been able to count on no one but the SdP! Beneš was elected President on 18 December 1935, in the first ballot, with 340 votes (out of 440, the SdP handing in empty ballot papers).

Henlein and Berlin

At the time the question whether Henlein was in fact in the pay of Berlin was a matter for conjecture. Only now, when the secret files of the German Foreign Ministry are open to inspection, is it possible to assess the extent to which Henlein, allegedly independent, was financially supported by the Reich. The granting of the enormous sum he demanded for his election campaign, with no questions asked, has already been mentioned. After his spectacular success Henlein's monthly stipend of 12,000 marks (actually 15,000, of which 3,000 went to his Berlin office) began to flow in regularly *via* the diplomatic courier. The first receipt[1] which survives is dated 30 September 1935; the later ones, in an unbroken series up to August 1938, were deposited at the German Legation in Prague.[2] But Henlein was evidently worth even more than that to the Reich. There were additional remittances under the heading 'For Welfare

[1] *G.F.M.* serial 6144, frame 459706.
[2] *Deutsche Gesandtschaft, Prag*, vol. 16/2, serial 3108.

Purposes'. Whole portfolios of securities were despatched to the SdP and in particular, the Reich financed Henlein's Prague newspaper *Die Zeit*, which first appeared on 1 October 1935. To give the journal a good start the Reich donated the equivalent of 250,000 marks,[1] followed by monthly subsidies of 10,000 marks. Henlein's 'independence' was so effective that even the paper's editorial staff salaries were fixed in Berlin.[2]

It is quite likely that Henlein and his henchmen would have done Hitler's work for less money or for none at all, but it is a fact that German diplomacy considered the SdP a paid outpost which should not deviate from the official German line. On the other hand the SdP leaders lived in perpetual fear of being ditched by their masters, and asked for 'guidance' whereas in Berlin it was apparently taken for granted that the party would know what to do without being told. Kreissl, one of the 'old' Nazis now sailing under Henlein's flag, complained to the Berlin Foreign Ministry[3]

that it was extremely difficult for the SdP speakers in Parliament and on other occasions to keep the interests of the Reich's foreign policy in mind when they are lacking any relevant information. It is therefore requested that Frank (Henlein's deputy) and Kreissl be received by a suitably high authority of the Foreign Ministry in the near future in order to obtain, in strict confidence, the necessary instructions.

Such touching trust doubtless received its reward for in its internal notes the Foreign Ministry left no doubt that in return for all the money spent it expected results:[4]

There can be no doubt that after his successful election Henlein cannot simply be left to his luck by the Reich but that as far as we are able we shall have to try to tide him over his present difficulties by giving him a good start and facilitating his political activity. In this context it should be noted that in view of the political alliance between Czechoslovakia, France and Russia the Reich also has a military interest in as compact and strong a Sudeten German group as possible – a point of view fully shared by the Reich War Ministry.

Henlein in London

In August 1935 the German Chargé d'Affaires in Prague learned

[1] Schwerin-Krosigk to Goebbels, 3 February 1936, *G.F.M.* serial 6144, frame 459806.

[2] Max Winkler to G.F.M. 23 March 1936, *G.F.M.* serial 6144, frames 459844-65.

[3] Note by Heinburg, 13 November 1936, *G.F.M.* serial 2381, frame 498963.

[4] Note by Roediger, 4 September 1935, *DGFP*, C/IV, no. 285.

that Henlein was going to England 'to get in touch with circles which were fundamentally opposed to the oppression of the German minority in Czechoslovakia'.[1] On that occasion Henlein appears to have been content to establish contact with a mysterious Colonel Graham Christie, a former British Air Attaché in Berlin, who seems to have been commissioned by somebody in London to sound out Henlein. In reality, though, it looks as if the interview went the other way round.[2] Unbiased as he might have been, Christie smoothed the path for Henlein, probably because he expected a diplomatic *quid pro quo*. At any rate this connection opened other doors to Henlein. Christie was certainly instrumental in obtaining an invitation from the Royal Institute of International Affairs for Henlein to deliver a lecture at Chatham House. That was by no means unusual because the Institute regularly invites V.I.P.s of one sort or another to express their views in order to give an exclusive circle of diplomats and diplomatic correspondents the opportunity to gain first-hand information about controversial problems. In Germany such invitations, which do not commit the Institute in any way, were and are still regarded as the hall-mark of approval for the visitor, and his appearance in such august surroundings naturally added greatly to Henlein's prestige.

In December 1935 Henlein went to London again to give the lecture and on 10 December the *Daily Telegraph* printed an interview with him in which he flatly denied ever having seen Hitler:

An emphatic declaration that the German political organisation in Czechoslovakia is entirely free from the influence of the Nazi party in Germany was made on his arrival in London yesterday by Herr Konrad Henlein...He described Pan-Germanism as 'disastrous'...'I have never at any time', he said, 'had any relations with the present German government. I have never seen Herr Hitler. I have never spoken with him, corresponded with him or negotiated with him in any way'...It is impossible to detach the German-speaking parts of Czechoslovakia from the Republic...Herr Henlein denied that he had recently been approached with a view to his entering the Government. No such invitation had been made. He was, however, perfectly willing at all times to co-operate loyally with the Government for the good of the Czechoslovakian Republic, provided the German minority received better treatment. 'But', he concluded 'this is almost the last chance of a peacable settlement'. If the German

[1] Stein to G.F.M. 21 August 1935, *G.F.M.* serial 9149, frame 643723.
[2] Due to age, illness and loss of memory Colonel Christie (who died in 1971) expressed himself unable to help clarify the matter. (Letter to the author of 7 May 1964.)

minority suffers further disappointment my party is likely to 'go radical' and adopt a policy of despair.

Into all this welter of feigned assurances of loyalty Henlein thus took care to incorporate an escape clause: if a murder had to be committed, it was bound to be the victim's fault. A similar story was concocted for the Chatham House audience. There the man who had pledged his obedience to the Nazi Party had the effrontery to declare[1]

Unfortunately fate has up to now failed to produce a fair solution in my country; and I must honestly admit that the blame rests with both nations, the Czechs and the Germans, as both sides had made many mistakes...I am firmly convinced that with honest goodwill these problems can be mastered...Their (*the Sudetendeutsche*) real mission lay in acting as mediator between their German mother country and the Czech people...We wish to work loyally with the State.

That he was not exactly speaking to an essembly of political innocents is shown by the vigorous questioning to which he was submitted after the speech and which touched on every weak spot in his position. He again firmly denied having any contact with the Nazi Party and swore by the territorial integrity of Czechoslovakia. He would like to point out, he assured his listeners, that he had already given his oath to the State as an officer (Henlein had in fact never served in the Czechoslovak Army and was not an officer) and there was of course no Aryan paragraph in the articles or constitution of his party.

Similar brazen lies were told in an interview Henlein later gave to the *Evening Standard*.[2]

We *Sudetendeutsche* are neither directly nor indirectly affiliated to the Fascists or National Socialists of any other country. We are neither in fact nor in sentiment the 'Bohemian Nazis' which some of our opponents are pleased to call us. We profess neither Hitlerism nor Fascism, but are loyal citizens of the State to which we belong and whose constitution we acknowledge and approve...The Magistrate of Prague has just excluded German and Jewish firms from municipal contracts. Following the example set in high places the country's industries are using the flimsy pretext of the economic crisis to dismiss their *Sudetendeutsche* employees.

The town administration of Prague had never issued any such

---

[1] For text, and summary of the disucussion, see *International Affairs* (London 1936), pp. 561–72.

[2] Konrad Henlein, 'Czechoslovakia's Germans', in *Evening Standard* (London), 17 March 1936.

decree. 'The country's industries' were largely in German hands, but there was never any report of any of the German manufacturers using the 'flimsy pretext of the economic crisis' for dismissing only their Sudeten German employees. (The sly addition of 'Jewish firms' in his complaint was obviously intended to fend off any possible accusation of anti-semitism.)

The questions put to Henlein at Chatham House may rightly have had critical overtones, but Christopher Bramwell, whom the Foreign Office had sent to the lecture to report on it,[1] found nothing suspicious about him. Without comment Bramwell repeated every lie he heard and added his own opinion: 'Herr Henlein impressed me in a general way by his moderation and freedom from the fanaticism one generally associates with the leaders of big popular movements.'

Henlein was also taken to lunch by Christie to meet Lord Stanhope, at that time Parliamentary Under-Secretary at the Foreign Office, and two leading officials of the Foreign Office, Mr (later Sir) Orme Sargent and Mr (later Sir) Clifford Norton. In Norton's notes[2] prominence is given to Henlein's deceitful assurance that 'he has no connection or affiliation with the German Nazi Party' – except that he had sworn fealty to it! This led to a Foreign Office official recommending to the Foreign Secretary (Hoare) that Beneš should be told in Geneva 'to give these fellows a straighter deal which, they say, is all that they want'. If this is at all typical of the Foreign Office outlook at that time (the advice was not taken up) it can no longer be a matter of surprise that Hitler's assurance about the Sudeten territory being his 'last territorial demand in Europe' was later also given credence.

Sargent had written earlier[3] that 'the Henlein Party is not Nazi'. Now, after the meeting with Henlein, he went a step further by informing the British Minister in Prague[4] that Henlein was 'on a

[1] Note by Bramwell, 10 December 1935, *Foreign Office Files (Czechoslovakia)*, F.O. 371, vol. 19463.

[2] Note by Clifford Norton, 10 December 1935, *Foreign Office Files (Czechoslovakia)*, loc. cit.

[3] Minute by Sargent, 24 May 1935, *Foreign Office Files (Czechoslovakia)*, F.O. 371, vol. 14492.

[4] Sargent to Addison, 12 December 1935, *Foreign Office Files (Czechoslovakia)*, F.O. 371, vol. 14493.

definitely anti-Nazi platform' – which was of course a travesty of truth. The Foreign Office, however, was convinced[1] that 'their (the Sudeten Germans') leader Henlein is a moderate and reasonable person'. It also thought that Czechoslovakia should sign the sort of agreement with Germany which Germany had concluded with Poland. Two Foreign Office officials suggested[2] that Czechoslovakia should find out whether an alleged German proposal for a non-aggression pact was still open and 'if it is, try to conclude if only for five years some sort of "standstill" agreement on the Polish model'. Czechoslovakia was thus to be driven like Poland into the enemy's camp and it is only a feeble excuse that at the time one did not know that it *was* the enemy. In fairness it should be mentioned that, however keen the British Legation in Prague showed itself about this idea, the Foreign Office did not pursue it any further.

On the whole, however, there was remarkable harmony between the line taken by the Foreign Office and the reports sent to London by the Prague Legation. These, especially as far as the Sudeten German problem was concerned, were – at least up to 1937 – often factually wrong on many essential points. The Sudeten Germans certainly did have many justified grievances but they were exaggerated out of all proportion by Henlein and his whole propaganda campaign – which was the decisive factor – was conducted with the sole aim of undermining a democratic State in the interest of the Third Reich. Anything that would have put the ethnic policy of Czechoslovakia into a favourable or even fair light was persistently omitted in the reports from Prague: thus the Foreign Office never learnt that the Germans in Czechoslovakia had in fact proportionately more schools than the Czechs and that – thanks to a German member of the Czechoslovak Government – unemployment relief and anti-crisis measures were allocated fairly between the nationalities. Nor was there any worthwhile mention of, let alone support for, the democratic German elements in Czechoslovakia and their unequal fight – not least in the interest of Britain herself – against

---

[1] Minute by O'Malley, 19 February 1936, *Foreign Office Files* (*Czechoslovakia*), loc. cit.

[2] Minute by Lambert and Gallup, 9 July 1935, *Foreign Office Files* (*Czechoslovakia*), loc. cit.

heavy odds. On the contrary, Henlein's sneering remark of 'splinter parties' was applied to them and R. H. Hadow, First Secretary of the British Legation in Prague, reported[1] that 'the German "splinter parties" did not even in 1929 command together 25% of the Sudeten German vote and at the last election were reduced to 10% thereof'. In reality the democratic parties had obtained 80 per cent of the German vote in 1929 and in 1935 their share was still 33 per cent – Henlein's propaganda tales were accepted at face-value. The accusations of the German democrats against Henlein were never reported by the British Legation and it seems that the German democratic press was not even read there. Any proof (which naturally could not be nearly as convincing as that available today) which the German democrats did produce of Henlein's association with Berlin was brushed aside. Eulogies of Henlein on the other hand abound. 'To judge by his personality,' wrote Hadow,[2] 'as well as by his speeches he seems to be a moderate and man of his word.' When Hadow reported[3] that Beneš had drawn his attention to the facts about the secret financing of Henlein from Germany, N. J. H. Cheetham of the Foreign Office could not see anything objectionable in it: the ' "sin" even if it has been proved, is not very deadly'. Generally, Cheetham averred, Beneš 'might even find some consolation in the fact that the main plank of Henlein's programme was loyalty to the Czechoslovak State'. Apparently he believed that himself for he added 'One wonders why Dr Beneš makes no attempt to take advantage of the moderation shown by Henlein himself before it is too late.' An official whose signature is illegible went so far as to add fatuously: 'If the facts [about the treatment of the Sudeten Germans] were more fully known in England there might almost be a general feeling of hope that Hitler would march in to put the matter straight – I exaggerate purposely to make my point clear.' Hadow at that time enquired[4] whether there was any objection

[1] Hadow to O'Malley 9 June 1936, *Foreign Office Files* (*Czechoslovakia*), F.O. 371, vol. 20374.
[2] Hadow to Hoare, 27 December 1935, *Foreign Office Files* (*Czechoslovakia*), F.O. 371, vol. 19493.
[3] Hadow to Eden, 31 January 1936, *Foreign Office Files* (*Czechoslovakia*), F.O. 371, vol. 20373.
[4] Hadow to O'Malley, 31 January 1936, Minute by Sargent, 5 February 1936, *Foreign Office Files* (*Czechoslovakia*), loc. cit.

to his establishing relations with Henlein. Far from objecting, Sargent was quite enthusiastic about the idea: 'This activity on the part of the Prague Legation is both unusual and refreshing.' Of course it would have been the right thing for British diplomacy to advise that Prague should make concessions to the Germans, but in fact ethnic justice was a far less vital subject than satisfying Henlein whose claims were invariably supported on the grounds that otherwise that 'moderate and man of his word' might be thrown over and replaced as Sudeten German leader by a 'real' Nazi firebrand. In reality that eventuality could not arise since Hitler knew quite well that his faithful paladin Henlein was the ideal man for the job.

Vansittart and Henlein

Even more important than his début at Chatham House was Henlein's introduction, through Christie, to Sir Robert (later Lord) Vansittart, the Permanent Under-Secretary of State at the Foreign Office. After the war broke out and Vansittart retired, he became widely known for his outspoken view that no Germans, not even anti-Nazis, could be trusted. It is easy to see now that this outlook contributed largely to the poisoning of public opinion against German émigrés during the Second World War. All the more interesting is a note penned by Vansittart about a meeting with Henlein in May 1938.[1] It clearly shows that he still had faith in him, at a time when Henlein had already openly espoused the Nazi cause. Vansittart, who prided himself on his expertise on German matters and his ability to see through any subterfuge connected with them, may well have been dismayed at being taken in by a man of the calibre of Henlein, and it is at least arguable that this experience may have helped to quicken in him the growth of what came to be known later as 'Vansittartism'.

His note about Henlein's first call on him does not convince one of Vansittart's exceptional perspicacity:[2]

He makes a most favourable impression. I should say that he was moderate, honest and clear-sighted. He speaks with a frankness and decision that inspire

[1] See p. 212.
[2] Eden to Addison, 27 July 1936, *Foreign Office Files* (*Czechoslovakia*), F.O. 371, vol. 20374.

confidence...Herr Henlein said that the Sudeten Germans...had never been German subjects, nor did they ever wish to be. They valued their liberties... They had no desire whatever to join Nazi Germany...Herr Henlein said that he had always been the advocate and the leader of the movement for reconciliation with the Czechoslovak Government...I think he is speaking the truth.

Henlein clearly again followed Hitler's precept on the relationship between the size of the lie and the likelihood of being believed and he was not even mistaken when his interlocutor was a man of outstanding intelligence.

Back home Henlein reported quite astonishing things about his meeting with Vansittart which are not corroborated by the latter.[1] Henlein seems to have deliberately bragged in order to impress Berlin. It is hardly credible that Vansittart could actually have assured him that the British Government was going to take up the Sudeten German problem in the League of Nations and that a directive was to be issued to the British press to discuss this question in the near future. No British official, no matter what his status, could ever have made any such statement to an outsider. At that time Anthony Eden was Foreign Secretary. To have expected that for the sake of the Sudeten Germans, let alone of Henlein, he would start proceedings against Czechoslovakia in the League of Nations is too grotesque to merit attention. To issue 'directives' to the British press was not possible even in war-time and no responsible official would have voiced any such desire. Vansittart spoke fluent German: hence there can have been no excuse of 'misunderstanding'. The conclusion that Henlein lied seems inescapable. The only point in his recital which does sound reasonably plausible is Vansittart's promise to 'advise and help' the Sudeten Germans – not, be it noted, the Sudeten German *Party* – although even to commit himself so far *vis-à-vis* Henlein was from a democratic viewpoint extremely unwise. Henlein maintained he had gained the impression that Vansittart's helpfulness was largely due to his fear that the Sudeten Germans would be drawn more and more into the Reich's orbit, but if this was indeed so, then Vansittart used the worst remedy possible.

Whatever the actual course of that interview, there is ample evidence in the Foreign Office files that Vansittart *did* help Henlein

[1] Stein (Prague) to G.F.M. 21 July 1936, *G.F.M.* serial 2381, frames 498892-5.

behind the scenes. Thus in a report to Anthony Eden[1] he says that 'France and this country can hardly be expected to fight in support of a policy so foolishly stiff and imprudent.'

The Berlin Olympic Games in the summer of 1936 provided a plausible reason for Henlein, as honorary president of his Gymnastics League, to go to Germany. He saw Hitler again (he had first seen him at a gymnastic festival in Stuttgart in July 1933, but perhaps had not spoken to him) and although no record of this meeting survives it can be safely assumed that it was more than a courtesy visit. To Neurath, the Foreign Minister, who received Henlein too, he expressed his satisfaction at being 'invited to see the Fuehrer, although in view of all the circumstances the Fuehrer could of course have only a few words with him.[2] It was however of great value to him (Henlein) to be able to report at home that he had spoken with the Fuehrer and that the latter had assured him of his sympathy.'

Henlein complained to Neurath that 'extremist elements who had connections with Germany largely hampered him in his work', but that he was determined to act mercilessly 'and had explained this to the party authorities here, too'. So much for his detachment from National Socialism into whose camp he was allegedly only pushed by Czech intransigence at the end of 1937. To Altenburg, a leading official at the Foreign Ministry, he boasted – and not without good cause – that 'thanks to the confidence he enjoyed everywhere in the Reich' he expected to have little difficulties in removing the hurdles which the 'old guard' of the Nazi Party put in his way in Czechoslovakia...

In conversation with Henlein, Neurath stated that the idea that 'the German Reich was going to solve the Sudeten German question in the immediate future by the sword' was erroneous. There could be no question that 'we should in the foreseeable future be embroiled in warlike enterprises for the sake of the Sudeten Germans'; the latter would just have to look after themselves. Henlein, who in all likelihood was better informed about Nazi strategy than Hitler's

[1] Vansittart to Eden, 18 July 1936, *Foreign Office Files* (*Czechoslovakia*), F.O. 371, vol. 20374.
[2] Minutes by Neurath (14 August 1936) and Altenburg (17 August), *G.F.M.* serial 2381, frames 499835–42.

own Foreign Minister, of course expressed full agreement and did not fail to repeat Vansittart's alleged assurance 'that the British Government was going to broach the Sudeten German question at the next League of Nations session'.

Towards the end of 1936 Vansittart seems to have been taken in by another intermediary, the German-Bohemian nobleman Max Hohenlohe-Langenburg, who was later to play an important rôle for the Reich during Runciman's stay in Czechoslovakia and even during the war, as a potential link with Britain. According to a report[1] by Eisenlohr, the new German Minister in Prague, Hohenlohe had approached Vansittart at the end of November 1936. Vansittart had allegedly asked him to contact Beneš and convey to him his (Vansittart's) recommendation that negotiations with the SdP begin without delay (which would of course have meant the betrayal of the German democrats and democracy as a whole). Hohenlohe is then said to have been received by Beneš who allegedly declared himself willing to see Henlein but asked for a precise formulation of his demands first. Eisenlohr expressed the justified fear that, confronted by the 'clever tactician Beneš', Henlein would get the worst of it. Actually no such encounter ever took place, nor is there any evidence that it was really planned.

To recapitulate: Henlein began by affirming his loyalty in Czechoslovakia. Then he did the same in Britain. Next his masters in Berlin still considered it advisable to hoodwink the British, but *vis-à-vis* the Czechs the visor could now be gradually lifted. An important step in this direction was Henlein's Prague speech on the 'Cultural Tasks of the Sudeten Germans'[2] which clearly showed signs of Nazi policy. Henlein gave his interpretation of German culture: it was of course the 'blood-and-soil' nonsense then prevalent in the Reich. 'Decadent asphalt literature' had become preponderant, Henlein complained, and was 'poisoning the purest springs of national life'; what was needed was 'art rooted in national soil'. The German broadcasts of the Czechoslovak Radio 'were not the mouthpiece of the Sudeten Germans', no doubt because the programme showed democratic tendencies. No mention was made by Henlein

[1] Eisenlohr to G.F.M. 4 December 1936, *G.F.M.* serial 3109, frames 630142-7.
[2] Speech of 23 February 1936, printed in *Konrad Henlein spricht*, pp. 129-51.

of the community of culture which was represented by names such as Goethe, Herder and Thomas Mann but rather of 'the great and indissoluble cultural community of the German people, irrespective of the structure of the State or the political régime in our mother country'. That was plain speaking, yet not plain enough for those who did not want to listen. When Henlein saw that he encountered no open protest, he went a step further. At a party conference at Cheb in June 1936 he assured his followers that the SdP would never enter into any anti-German front (thus equating Germany with the Third Reich) and that he would rather be hated with Germany than derive any benefit from the hatred of Germany.[1] (This was never reported to the Foreign Office by the Prague Legation.)

At that time Berlin no longer made any bones about letting the Prague authorities feel that the Reich fully backed Henlein. What was not made public, however, was the text of a greetings telegram the 'independent' Henlein sent to Hitler on New Year's Eve of 1937:[2]

> My Fuehrer! On the occasion of the New Year permit me to send you, my Fuehrer, my most sincere good wishes. In gratitude and loyalty,
> > Your faithful
> > Konrad Henlein

There may have been earlier such contacts between Henlein and Hitler, since in July 1936 Henlein sent Hitler a book with a hand-written dedication which is not likely to have been without some

---

[1] Report in *Die Zeit*, 23 June 1936.

[2] For Henlein's New Year greetings to Hitler, see *Deutsche Gesandtschaft Prag*, vol. 44/5. For Henlein's dedication cf. the letter by the head of the Reich Chancellory, Meissner, to Hitler's adjutant Schaub, of 17 July 1936: 'The enclosed illustrated book "Sudetendeutschland" has been sent by the leader of the Sudeten German Party as present for the Fuehrer. Attention is drawn to the printed dedication on the second page and the hand-written dedication by Henlein on the third. I would ask you to submit the book to the Fuehrer. A personal letter of thanks, drafted in his name, is enclosed. I should be grateful if you will arrange to have it signed by the Fuehrer and to return it directly to me so that I can have it sent back safely via the German Legation in Prague to his (i.e. Henlein's) address' (*Akten der Adjutantur des Führers*, 10/1*a*, Congratulatory letters etc., First Half of 1936, at the Federal Archive, Koblenz).

expression of loyalty to the Fuehrer. Hitler replied with a letter, but neither the book nor Hitler's acknowledgment survived the war.

Despite their external success the Henlein party underwent a severe internal crisis lasting throughout 1936. Basically it was the continuation of the conflict between the 'old Nazi fighters' and those who had jumped on the SdP band-wagon from the *Kamerad-schaftsbund*. Again the details of these internecine squabbles are far less interesting than the rôle of the German Nazi Party as a referee to whose judgment both sides submitted. The problem was resolved, in Henlein's absence, at a meeting in Berlin, in its outcome typical both of the extent of German interference in Sudeten German affairs and of Henlein's prestige – his praises were sung even by his opponent, the 'old Nazi' Hans Krebs. The outcome was that[1]

Herr Krebs declares his readiness to ensure that personal discords will be eliminated in the SdP and will inform Party Members arriving that Henlein personally as leader, as well as Henlein's decisions enjoy the complete confidence of Government authorities here and that this settlement in its present form corresponds to the views and wishes of the competent (Nazi) party authorities. At the beginning of the discussions in which...Krebs took part the competent Party authorities declared that Henlein now and in future enjoyed their full confidence unconditionally.

The Germans as the 'second nation' in the State

The efforts of the German members of the Czechoslovak Government, Czech and Spina, to ensure that in investments in the public sector special consideration was given to those particularly affected by the slump and thus to keep the Germans' faith in democracy alive, were rather unspectacular. In effect, however, they were of great help to the victims of the crisis living in the German ethnic area. The economic crisis had in general reached its nadir in the winter of 1933 and from 1934 a slow recovery took place. However, this upturn affected the heavy capital goods industries on Czech territory much sooner than the German industries which produced mainly consumer goods. In consequence unemployment among Germans in Czechoslovakia still remained relatively higher than among Czech industrial or Slovak agricultural labour. In these

---

[1] The whole conflict is documented in a volume of the German Legation in Prague (60/4), filmed in *G.F.M.* serial 3109.

circumstances it is certainly significant that during 1934/5 state expenditure on road repairs amounted to 14 million Czech crowns in the predominantly Czech areas, while the corresponding expenditure on German territory was 17 million crowns: for bridge-building work the figures were 9 as against 11 million crowns.[1] This reflects the influence exerted by German participation in the Prague Government.

Something more than economic palliatives was however required to assure Germans of all political creeds that they were not second-class citizens: the main need was to eradicate the idea that Czechoslovakia was merely the 'National State' of Czechs and Slovaks and nothing else. Kramář had fought for it in vain, when the Constitution was being drafted. Masaryk had flatly turned it down[2] and Beneš openly expressed his belief that he was the President of the Czechs as well as the Germans and all the other nationalities[3] in Czechoslovakia. To the powerful and generally chauvinistic bureaucracy, however, 'naše republika' (our Republic) meant something rather different from what Masaryk and Beneš wanted it to mean. Kamil Krofta, a historian of repute and free from party-political ties, who had succeeded Beneš as Foreign Minister, now took up what the Czech Social-Democrat leader Rudolf Bechyně had said in 1934[4] about the German as a 'State Nation'. In a lecture which he gave at a conference of German educationalists[5] Krofta referred to readiness to accept the Germans as 'second State Nation' (*zweites Staatsvolk*). He explained that the expression was not to imply that the Germans were to be second-class citizens, but that 'in accordance with their importance and numerical strength they did in fact occupy the second place in the State'.[6]

The Czechs now showed increasing awareness of the need for positive steps to further the aims of German Activism. In 1936 the absence of the German Christian Socials (Catholics) from the Government – a mistake which had been perpetuated since 1929 – was at last ended. The party entered the Government with Erwin

---

[1] Brügel, *Ludwig Czech*, p. 129. [2] See p. 80.
[3] *Prager Tagblatt*, 26 June 1936. See further p. 145 (Speech at Liberec).
[4] See p. 62. [5] *Prager Presse*, 22 May 1935.
[6] *Prager Tagblatt*, 18 July 1936. Edward Beneš, Aussig, 29 April 1935, 'Rede an die Deutschen in der Tschechoslowakei', printed in the collection *Gedanke und Tat* (Thought and Deed) (Prague 1937), vol. III.

Zajiček (Minister without Portfolio) as their representative. With him a generation of politicians who had not been involved in the ethnic conflicts of pre-1918 Austria came to the forefront on the German side. Only then did the possibility of a Government coalition on the Weimar model – i.e. between all German democratic parties represented in the Government: Social Democrats, Agrarians and Christian Socials – assume reality in Czechoslovakia. This coalition worked smoothly until the final defeat of the Activist camp in March 1938.

As soon as Beneš had assumed the office of President, in December 1935, he approached the task of speaking directly to the German population. Eisenlohr's report to Berlin[1] about Beneš' journey through Moravia may not have been greatly to the liking of the Reich authorities:

Beneš...took this opportunity to emphasise his objective attitude towards all nationalities of the State just as firmly as Masaryk used to do on similar journeys. At Eisgrub e.g. he said that the Germans were as close to him as the Czechs and Czechoslovakia offered both the same law and justice. At Nikolsburg he spoke in German, declaring the basic principles of his policy were the loyal and cordial co-operation of Germans and Czechs in their common homeland...he assured the people that 'he had confidence in Germans and in Czechs'. He was in favour of granting to the Germans everything they needed for their economic prosperity. Moreover, democracy in the State was the best guarantee for the Germans too.

More important still was a speech Beneš gave at Liberec in August 1936:[2] It was a significant statement of policy and raised great hopes. He repeated his view that the rule of law which the country enjoyed assured all nationalities of their own national and cultural way of life:

I emphasise that Czechoslovakia is a State in which no ethnic group's existence or culture is threatened, that the struggle of the minority nationalities is not one for their existence but solely one for political power and for a share in the government of the State. This is brought out clearly when Germans are referred to as equals among equals here. I know that our Germans have practical complaints, desires and demands. In matters of language and schools these factors are not of a fundamental nature and can be dealt with easily by means of sensible practice and this applies too to economic affairs. I have no hesitation in admitting that mistakes have been made which should not be repeated, for instance moving Czech workers and employers from Czech areas into German or mixed territory

[1] Eisenlohr to G.F.M. 18 June 1936, *G.F.M.* serial 3498, frames 020016-17.
[2] *Prager Presse*, 20 August 1936.

145

suffering from unemployment. As Head of the State I wish to be a mediator between both sides and their help...I look upon myself as Head of the whole State: I feel at home among you as if I were in Prague and it is my wish that you, too, should look upon me as one of you.

True enough, it was still a case of words, words, words – however weighty they were – the German members of the Government pressed for them to be followed by deeds. In November 1936 Hodža, the Prime Minister, announced in Parliament that the Government was going to adopt a more active nationalities policy.[1] Subsequent negotiations led to the Agreement of 18 February 1937 which will be discussed in the next chapter.

[1] *Prager Presse*, 12 November 1936.

11 DEMOCRACY IN RESISTANCE

Democracies are used to acting slowly and hesitantly, carrying out even overdue reforms only under a certain pressure. Pre-war Czechoslovakia was no exception to this rule. A Government decision to remove justified grievances of the German population could only be achieved by the German coalition parties when Czechoslovakia was threatened from within by Hitler's agent Henlein and from without by Hitler's decision to implement his programme as mapped out in *Mein Kampf*. This threat certainly led to some positive steps in the direction of more ethnic justice, but at the same time it made every concession to the Germans suspect to the Czechs – and not only to them – as it seemed that in the end only democracy's bitter enemy, German National Socialism, would benefit from them. Under normal conditions these concessions would most probably have needed even more time, but they would have had more solid and lasting foundations. The frightful dilemma of perhaps helping to strengthen the position of Hitler while carrying out reasonable measures in favour of the German population could never be entirely overcome until the fateful Munich Conference on 29 September 1938.

Apart from a fanatical minority, those who supported Henlein and hence Hitler at elections and on other occasions were really little more than passive camp-followers; on the other hand there did not exist any sizeable group of potential Henleinists who openly and unambiguously dissociated themselves from Nazism. The mere existence of the Henlein party made in some way even more difficult the attempts of the German Government parties to achieve full ethnic justice. The German democrats wished to obtain a larger share in the administration for the Germans, but not at the price of accepting anti-democratic elements. Among the German and the Czech coalition partners there was complete unanimity on one basic question: precisely because the justified aims of the Germans could only be attained in a democracy, the democratic basis of the State was not to be tampered with. The German democratic elements, aiming at restoring a German democratic majority, were willing to defer their old claim to territorial autonomy in the German ethnic area and even to cultural autonomy: if met it could in the circumstances only have led to the surrender of part of the country to Nazi rule. As Wenzel Jaksch put it later:[1] 'We don't want cultural autonomy for Nazi teachers to do what they like in the schools.'

The policy of '18 February'

After considerable preliminary work an Activist delegation under Dr Czech's leadership called on Hodža on 28 January 1937 to present a memorandum containing the demands of the German democratic parties.[2] They limited themselves to practical requirements. Above all the aim was to achieve all-round ethnic justice, priority in relief-work allocation to areas hit by the crisis, a more equitable representation for Germans in the public service and linguistic concessions. The result of the negotiations[3] has become associated with '18 February', the day when the bulk of these demands was accepted by the Government. The main concession was the acceptance of more Germans in the public service and the promise to allow German firms a proper share in the orders placed by the public sector. That the policy inaugurated on that '18 February' did not in the event produce any lasting success is not surprising, in view of the brief period (barely one year) in which it was valid and the unsettled conditions prevailing.

There were some undeniable improvements in the position of the Germans. Figures for public investments allocated at the beginning of 1938 show that there was no discrimination against them. Public investment in road and bridge building in the Czech area amounted to 109 million crowns (67%) and in the German area to 52 million crowns (32.4%). Expenditure on construction work was 42 million crowns (58.5%) for the Czech territory compared with 30 million crowns (41.5%) for the German territory. During the depression however, these orders were frequently

---

[1] *Sozialdemokrat* (Prague), 13 July 1938.
[2] For text see Brügel, *Ludwig Czech*, pp. 191–3.
[3] Text of Government decision in *Prager Tagblatt*, 21 February 1937.

awarded to metropolitan firms which brought their workers from Prague, so that the local unemployed derived little benefit. Prague firms were in general more efficient and could submit far lower tenders than local competitors. After 18 February 1937 all authorities issuing works contracts were freed from the previous requirement to choose the cheapest tender and were encouraged to insist on using local labour.

Statistical data on the increase of German participation in state administration after 18 February 1937 are not available, but even before that date the civil service was by no means an exclusively Czech preserve: in the judicature there had been since Austrian days a strong German element, which had continued to gain recruits. In view of the indifference, to put it mildly, with which many Germans regarded the Czechoslovak armed forces it is surprising to learn that there were 457 German officers, among them one General, in the Czechoslovak Army. This was 7 per cent of the active officer corps: the proportion of Germans in the Officer Reserve must certainly have been higher, although no figures are available. The German schools system was based on the exact proportion of the population, which of course meant that the number of people engaged in the country's educational service gave a true representation of the ethnic distribution in the State. Such favourable conditions, however, did not exist in any other sector.

Ludwig Czech, as Minister of Health, successfully insisted on an extension of his staff and proceeded to fill vacancies with suitable German candidates so that, when he resigned his office in April 1938, the proportion of Germans employed, at least in the medical and legal sectors, was not far short of the percentage of Germans in the total population (23.32%). These efforts by the German coalition parties were strongly supported by the Czech Social Democrats in the Ministries in their hands – Railways, Social Welfare and Justice – while the departments directed by the Czech Right were far less co-operative. The State Railways alone, for example, gave jobs to several thousand German labourers between 18 February 1937 and 28 February 1938.[1]

Towards the end of 1937 the German Activists successfully

[1] *Prager Presse*, 31 March 1938.

carried through Parliament a proposal to make the principle of proportional ethnic representation in the public service universally applicable.[1] Under normal conditions this would have been an important political and moral success. However, coming, as it did, shortly before the crisis situation of 1938, it had practically the same negligible effect as the Government's own decision (not carried out) to introduce by law the principle of ethnic proportionality in the civil service.[2] A peaceful development would quite certainly have led to increased conciliation in this respect, particularly since for the younger generation of Germans the Czech language was no longer an unknown quantity. It should not be overlooked, though, that – with the possible exception of Switzerland – even now there is not a single State of mixed nationalities in which these problems have been solved even moderately well. Those who today point to the old Habsburg monarchy as a refuge of ethnic justice would do well to ponder the fact that in old Austria with a German population percentage of only 35.6, the Germans accounted for no less than 81 per cent of the central bureaucracy.[3]

Henlein's press of course tried to ridicule the Government's concessions as quite inadequate. Ernst Eisenlohr, the German Minister in Prague, however, used the occasion to warn the SdP in terms which went about as far as a German diplomat could permit himself to go:[4]

It will be no easy matter for Konrad Henlein...to do the right thing. On the one hand party considerations compel him...to point out how little the concessions made to the Activists really mean...On the other hand he should *beware of not raising his demands so high that they could appear to jeopardize the central structure of the State (regional autonomy)*. For in this way...he would supply the Government...with the best pretext for charging the SdP with hostility towards the State and hence for rejecting any demand made by the SdP. At the same time the Government would certainly use this pretext to make it clear in London that it was not the Czechs' fault if, despite the will to appease the minorities, no further concessions could be made, but that the Henleinists were planning to disrupt the State.

[1] *Prager Tagblatt*, 19 November 1937.
[2] *Prager Presse*, 19 March 1938.
[3] Robert A. Kann, *The Multinational Empire* (New York 1950), II, 312.
[4] Eisenlohr to G.F.M. 21 February 1937, *Deutsche Gesandtschaft, Prag*, vol. 25/3.

It will be recalled that as early as 1922, when Czechoslovakia was not yet menaced by German nationalism, Koch, the German Envoy, said that in his opinion the Czechs could not afford to grant territorial autonomy to their German minority. This warning was now repeated by Koch's successor under circumstances which called for a good deal of moral courage on his part. Eisenlohr had come to Prague in early 1936 not very well-informed about the country and, hence, believing the slogans of Nazi propaganda about the alleged anti-German tendency of Czechoslovak policy and of Beneš personally. Confronted with the realities, he became a kind of advocate of the Czechs in Berlin. Reporting on a discussion he had with Beneš in April 1937, Eisenlohr wrote:[1]

Beneš explained that he was trying to solve the minorities question in such a manner that every nationality in this State should obtain that share in the institutions, offices and other benefits which corresponded to its proportional incidence in the total population. He had already instructed several Ministers to bear in mind when drawing up their budgets that the Sudeten Germans were entitled to more than 20 per cent of investment expenditure, in accordance with their numerical strength. It did admittedly happen that the intentions of the central authority were not always loyally obeyed in the province...But *by the end of his term as President (1942) he will have carried through the principle of full equality of nationalities in the State.* This he considered his official duty the fulfilment of which it was not necessary to negotiate...I (Eisenlohr) replied that...this would mean that by the end of his period as President, from being a fictitious National State such as she was today, Czechoslovakia would have become a State of Nationalities. Did he think that the Czech people could be brought to accept these concessions, however desirable they were? Beneš reported that he had never bothered, nor did he intend to do so in future, about the terminology of the National State as opposed to the State of Nationalities. No one had yet been able to explain to him clearly and unambiguously what a National State was, not even Kramář who at the peace negotiations had demanded the creation of a pure National State. He (Beneš) had rejected this even then, and that was the beginning of the conflict, never to be resolved, between him and Kramář. It is true that the Czechs would have to make sacrifices, but he was sure they would make them, for his people was reasonable and relatively easy to guide.

The implementation of these reasonable intentions would have hampered Hitler's plans to a certain extent; and the content of these plans was known to the inner circle of the SdP by the beginning of 1937 at the latest. On 2 March 1937 Henlein's deputy Karl

[1] Eisenlohr to G.F.M. *Deutsche Gesandtschaft, Prag*, vol. 60/3.

Hermann Frank called at the German Foreign Ministry and told one of the senior officials that[1]

yesterday he had been ordered to attend a meeting with the *Reichsführer* SS Himmler who had informed him that after discussion with Colonel-General Göring it had been decided that for the purposes of the Four-Year-Plan 25,000 Sudeten German farm-hands and 40,000 serving maids should be resettled immediately. He (Frank) had advanced objections on the grounds of foreign and national politics, since the Czechoslovak Government was bound to put obstacles in the way of executing the plan and it was also undesirable to deprive the Sudeten German ethnic group of something like 65,000 members who could render valuable service at elections etc. He was told that these measures were essential for carrying out the Four-Year-Plan and that *the Sudeten Germans would in any case be incorporated in the Reich in the not too distant future.*

Himmler's relevations probably did not come as a surprise to Henlein and Frank. At any rate Henlein took the hint and continued with his provocative, though still not quite unambiguous professions of loyalty not to Prague but to Berlin. His old pretence of being a good citizen of Czechoslovakia was increasingly replaced by carefully drafted statements which his followers could interpret as assertions of devotion to Nazism. In May 1937 he introduced the use of the Hitler salute (with the raised right arm), calling it the 'German salute' and assuring his audience that 'the German salute almost universally used was in no sense a provocation to the Czech people'.[2]

The more obvious the Henlein Party's attempts to wreck the policy of 18 February became (which after all brought concessions to the Germans), the more the democratic forces were determined to secure its success. Just as in the previous year, Beneš generally devoted the German and Czech speeches which he held up and down the country during 1937 to the need to satisfy justified ethnic demands. Speaking close to the Austrian border he said:[3] 'I have come here into overwhelmingly German territory to show that all our territories and all our communities, the welfare of all citizens, Germans as well as Czechs, are equally close to our hearts,' and at Cěský Krumlov in Southern Bohemia he assured his hearers that the Government was determined to implement all its promises:

When our Government puts these matters in hand and into operation, it does so of its own initiative and conviction. It does them for our citizens of German

[1] Note by Altenburg, 3 March 1937, *G.F.M.* serial 3653, frames 033170-2.
[2] *Die Zeit* (Prague), 23 May 1937.
[3] *Der Präsident in Südböhmen* (Prague 1937), pp. 59–61, 67.

tongue but above all, because they are clearly part and parcel of our democratic system...Look around in Europe! Which State has, like ours, managed after the war to avoid economic and social ruin, political risings and revolutions, the annihilation of the middle class, the abolition of personal and political freedom? ...Which States, after the war, have succeeded in maintaining so large a measure of liberties and rights for their minorities as we have, and which States prepare so calmly and efficiently for co-operation between majority and minority?

While the German Activist parties now stepped up their efforts to win the support of as many Germans as possible for the State, Henlein made for the first time the provocative move of sending an official SdP delegation to the Nazi Party Rally at Nuremberg in September 1937, no doubt in order to make it clear to the Prague Government that matters had now reached a critical stage. Shortly afterwards came the first encounter between Henlein and Premier Hodža, who had never before met the 'outsider' Henlein. Henlein came without special invitation – this he construed as a 'great sacrifice' – but there was no common ground between the two men and the talks ended fruitlessly.

Henlein again visits London

Towards the middle of October 1937 Henlein descended once again on London. In an interview in the *Daily Telegraph*[1] he still had the nerve to protest that he did not want any constitutional changes. His lecture to a study group at Chatham House was similarly deceitful:[2]

In reply to questions Herr Henlein specifically denied that his demands were totalitarian or precluded the recognition of other parties than the *Sudetendeutsche Partei* as representative of the German-speaking minority...The *Sudetendeutsche Partei*, Herr Henlein maintained, by no means sought to diminish Czech rights and privileges, but merely demanded equal rights and privileges for the German-speaking minority.

Asked whether Germany was not, with some justification, considered to be at the back of the *Sudetendeutsche Partei*, Herr Henlein maintained that at no time had Germany sought to influence or dictate his party's policy – or *vice versa*.

In reply to a further question he states his willingness to declare publicly... in the name of his party, that the *Sudeten Deutsche* were ready to work as loyal citizens of Czechoslovakia. Despite natural racial sympathy for Germany the

[1] *Daily Telegraph*, 15 October 1937.
[2] Report by R. H. Hadow, 14 October 1937, *Foreign Office Files* (*Czechoslovakia*), F.O. 371, vol. 21225.

bulk of the German-speaking population would, he felt, remain loyal to Czechoslovakia. This, however, depended to some extent upon the treatment they received from the rulers of the Republic.

This, as we shall see, was the same Henlein who a month later confided in Hitler that he wanted nothing more urgently than the incorporation even of the Czech areas of Bohemia, Moravia and Silesia into the Reich.

Later on at a dinner Henlein sat next to Sir Robert Vansittart and thus had the opportunity, during a three-hour discussion,[1] to dupe the clever British diplomat yet again:

The impression left upon me by Herr Henlein is always that of a decent, honest and moderate, or anyhow *relatively* moderate, man.

The qualification of his praise is gratifying. Henlein told Vansittart that things had taken a distinct turn for the worse and Vansittart was treated to a version quite different from that given to the Chatham House audience:

Well over 90% of them (the Sudeten Germans) were now in favour of complete absorption in Germany.

The valiant Henlein, however, was going to fight for autonomy within Czechoslovakia:

It was the only one (solution) for which he could work as a practical man, not because he thought it an ideal solution from the point of view of the majority of his supporters, but because it was the only policy that could be carried out without a European cataclysm in which all the frontier districts inhabited by his compatriots would be wiped out.

In case of violent German intervention France and the Soviet Union would come to the aid of Czechoslovakia and 'in the inferno everyone, including first and foremost the *Sudeten Deutsche*, would vanish'. His desire for autonomy, Henlein continued, could however only be realized when Austria was annexed to the Reich and Czechoslovakia surrounded. He seems to have been kept up to date about Hitler's immediate intentions. Only then according to Henlein were the Czechs likely to agree. He demanded that British influence be exerted on Beneš, for otherwise he (Henlein) could not guarantee to keep his followers under control. There is a report by

[1] Minute by Vansittart, 18 October 1937, *Foreign Office Files* (*Czechoslovakia*), F.O. 371, vol. 21131.

Henlein[1] stating that Vansittart had promised British intervention in Prague 'for the most far-reaching autonomy for the Sudeten Germans', while warning him that Britain would stand by France 'if the Germans invaded Czechoslovakia'. There is no mention of this in Vansittart's notes.

At any rate the outcome of this discussion was that British diplomacy decided to assist Henlein in his alleged aim of attaining autonomy within Czechoslovakia, and no effort was spared to persuade Prague to abandon part of its territory to a totalitarian and terroristic movement and thus to hasten the end of the last democratic bulwark in Central Europe.

British and French disagreements about Czechoslovakia
In its subservience to Henlein's wishes British diplomacy did not even hesitate to allow a conflict to develop between Britain and France. The French at that time did not incline so much towards appeasement as did the British. The British Foreign Office seriously believed that German aggression against Czechoslovakia could be forestalled if Henlein were given a seat in the Prague Government and it could not or would not see that the only result would have been to allow Hitler to take a decisive step forward in his plan for global domination – at no cost to himself. London suggested that the agreement of 18 February with the German Activists – an act meant to weaken Hitler's agent Henlein – ought to be followed by an act which would clearly lead to the weakening of democracy:[2]

it is obvious that the Czech Government, after reaching their agreement with the Activists, ought to have proceeded to enter similar negotiations with the Henlein Party.

Appropriate instructions were sent to Mr (later Sir) Basil Newton, the British Minister in Prague:[3]

We are...very disappointed that the February concessions to the Activists have not been followed up by agreements with the SdP.

Newton argued that to say this to the Prague Government would be

[1] Note by Altenburg, 6 November 1937, *DGFP*, D/ii, no. 13.
[2] Newton to Eden, 27 April 1937, Minute by Sargent, 5 May 1937, *Foreign Office Files (Czechoslovakia)*, F.O. 371, vol. 21128.
[3] Sargent to Newton, 16 June and 7 July 1937, Newton to Sargent, 21 May 1937, *Foreign Office Files (Czechoslovakia)*, F.O. 371, vol. 21129.

equivalent to interfering in Czechoslovakia's internal affairs and he was not prepared to do it. London brushed these scruples aside as 'over-cautious' and added the incredibly naive rider: 'Foreign opinion has yet to be convinced that the Henlein Party is fundamentally disloyal and that no co-operation with them is possible.' Soon afterwards Newton had to report a most disturbing occurrence:[1] he had been discussing the question of Henlein's entry into the Czechoslovak Government with his French colleague De Lacroix who had seriously warned him against recommending any such step. This, he said, would result in Czechoslovakia becoming Germany's vassal. Extreme displeasure was caused in the Foreign Office by this very sensible observation. Mr (later Sir Philip) Nichols, who later also became Ambassador to Czechoslovakia, minuted 'I am afraid it looks as though the French Minister...is giving utterance to some typically short-sighted French views.' An identical comment was sent to the Prague Legation ('We conceive this to be an exceedingly short-sighted view') and the British Ambassador in Paris, Phipps, was informed that Henlein's entry into the Government 'seems to us a decided step forward'. De Lacroix's reservations were therefore unhelpful and Phipps was instructed to intervene against them at the Quai d'Orsay – it was feared, not without reason, that De Lacroix may not have been acting entirely on his own initiative. British diplomacy continued its efforts to obtain an official repudiation of De Lacroix's views in Paris, but in vain. Vansittart, too, was extremely annoyed with the French Minister in Prague:[2] 'M. De Lacroix seems to play a disastrous role, and I wish we could get it altered.' The British Legation in Prague would have blamed Czechoslovakia and not Hitler, if Hitler had marched in:[3]

The bogey (*sic*) of a German attack upon Czechoslovakia, persistently and adroitly kept before Europe by President Beneš, takes on a less frightening aspect...The main danger of the peace of Europe being disturbed by a German attack upon Czechoslovakia, therefore, lies in a sudden incident resulting from

[1] Newton to Cadogan, 12 July 1937, Minute Nichols, 23 July 1937, O'Malley to Hadow, 5 August 1937, O'Malley to Phipps (Paris) 5 August 1937, *Foreign Office Files* (*Czechoslovakia*), F.O. 371, vol. 21130.

[2] Hadow to O'Malley, 10 August 1937, Minute by Vansittart, 24 August 1937, *Foreign Office Files* (*Czechoslovakia*), loc. cit.

[3] Hadow to Eden, 24 August 1937, *Foreign Office Files* (*Czechoslovakia*), loc. cit.

the irritation incessantly caused in Germany by the Czechoslovak Government's treatment of the *Sudeten Deutsche* minority.

Since no reassurances were forthcoming from Paris, Eden was furnished with a memorandum for a discussion he was to have with the French Foreign Minister Yvon Delbos. In this document it was emphasized[1] that 'We are...in favour of collaboration between the Czechoslovak Government and the SdP.' The French viewpoint was said to be 'contrary to the best interests of France and Europe as a whole'. Eden was to convince Delbos of all this in person, but the encounter did not take place so that the task devolved upon the hapless British Ambassador. The discussion between Phipps and Delbos ended in a complete fiasco for the British point of view.[2] Delbos, as Foreign Minister, strongly opposed any concessions to Hitler, and bluntly declared

It would be unreasonable to expect the (Czechoslovak) Government to take into their midst any of the SdP proper...nor could he (Delbos) recommend the Czechs to do this. It would be as though we brought pressure to bear upon Schuschnigg to give portfolios to Austrian Nazis who would finally explode his Government from within.

The Foreign Office had to concede that:

There is, in point of fact, a certain force in his argument that to apply pressure on the Czechoslovak Government to admit members of the Henlein Party is as if we were to bring pressure to bear upon the Austrian Chancellor to admit Austrian Nazis into the Cabinet, a thing which we have never dreamt of doing.

The idea of persuading France to agree to Henlein's entry into the Prague Government was therefore dropped; not however the general plan to sell the British appeasement policy to Paris: Sir Orme Sargent wrote, for example,[3]

The advice which we would like Delbos to join with us in giving to Beneš would be on general lines. Dr Beneš would be urged to enter into frank and full negotiations with Henlein, even to the extent of considering some scheme of administrative autonomy.

This line was pursued systematically even after the British Minister

[1] F.O. Memorandum, 9 September 1937, Sargent to Phipps, 1 October 1937, *Foreign Office Files* (*Czechoslovakia*), loc. cit.
[2] Phipps to Sargent, 19 October 1937, Minute by Bramwell, 22 October 1937, *Foreign Office Files* (*Czechoslovakia*), loc. cit.
[3] F.O. Memorandum Bramwell, 21 October 1937, Minute by Sargent, 26 October 1937, *Foreign Office Files* (*Czechoslovakia*), loc. cit.

in Prague drew attention for the first time to Henlein's subservience to Hitler:[1]

So far as the Henlein Party is concerned it is difficult to see how co-operation is possible so long as it continues its close association with Berlin.

A meeting between Eden and Delbos did eventually take place in Brussels[2] but no progress was made. Eden declared the situation in Prague to be dangerous 'if the Czechoslovak Government persisted in their present attitude towards the *Sudetendeutsche*'. He advanced a brilliant suggestion which he himself could hardly have taken seriously; if realized, it would have anticipated Munich by a year:

I had been thinking the situation over and wondered whether it might not be possible for *Great Britain and France to concert with Germany* in seeking to *find a satisfactory solution* to the problem. M. Delbos said that M. Beneš would no doubt be willing to listen to such concerted representation, although he could not be expected to heed threats.

At that time the ingenious plan to dissect the victim by arrangement with the murderer was premature – the Austrian *Anschluss* was still four months away. Newton, too, was now determined to prevent wiser counsel in the Foreign Office from gaining the upper hand:[3]

So far as the Czechs are concerned, would it not be in their real interest to get on better terms with Germany, *even at some cost to their independence*? Can they expect to maintain indefinitely the position of a bulwark against the spread of German influence southwards?

The darkening horizon

Henlein's 'Foreign Political Adviser' Heinrich Rutha had been arrested in October 1937, under suspicion of homosexual offences against juveniles, and had committed suicide while on remand. The unfavourable light which the whole affair threw on his movement had to be overshadowed somehow by Henlein and it seems that in order to whip up passions it was decided to provoke a clash with the police. According to Andor Hencke, the German Chargé

[1] Newton to Eden, 31 October 1937, *Foreign Office Files* (*Czechoslovakia*), loc. cit.

[2] Telegram by Clive (Brussels) to F.O. 4 November 1937, *Foreign Office Files* (*Czechoslovakia*), loc. cit.

[3] Newton to Sargent, 22 November 1937, *Foreign Office Files* (*Czechoslovakia*), F.O. 371, vol. 21132.

d'Affaires in Prague, the Czechoslovak Government had also been informed[1] that Henlein had been busy in London concocting a war plan with Ribbentrop, who had become German Ambassador to the Court of St James: 'Things in Czechoslovakia were to be brought to a head and the Sudeten German demands for autonomy pushed to the foreground of European politics.' Whether or not this report was accurate is less important than the fact that all indications point to previous collusion with Berlin about the planned 'action' or even to its origin there.

The desired *fracas* with the police came after a speech at Teplice-Šanov (Teplitz-Schönau) by Henlein, newly returned from London. An insignificant brawl was blown up into an intolerable act of 'despotism' by the police and trumpeted all over the Reich radio network before the Czechoslovak Government even knew anything about it. The German Minister in Prague himself seems to have had his doubts about the story of Czech police violence against Sudeten German innocence, though he could not very well say so directly:[2]

It appears from various conversations...that at present among the diplomats accredited here, including some well disposed towards us, greater credence is assigned to the versions of the Teplitz incident circulated by the Government... than to the arguments of the Sudeten German Party and to the Reich German press. More than once foreign colleagues have seriously asked whether this time it would not come to an armed conflict. Even leading personalities of the Sudeten German Party...were of the opinion that the Teplitz incidents might afford the occasion to bring the Sudeten German question to a head with the help of the Reich.

Henlein sent a provocative 'Open Letter' to Beneš which[3] was published in Germany before it was delivered at the President's office. He asserted categorically that the 'incidents of Teplice are intolerable for a self-respecting nation' and followed this up with the ultimatum

The practical demands which I, as responsible and through the elections of 1935 fully authorised spokesman of the Sudeten Germans, am raising as a result of yesterday's occurrences...are: immediate measures to realise the demand for autonomy made by me and my party.

The attempt to start a fire while blaming the fire brigade for the blaze is unmistakable.

[1] Hencke to G.F.M. 19 October 1937, *G.F.M.*, serial 3109, frames 629968–70.
[2] Eisenlohr to G.F.M. 22 October 1937, *DGFP*, D/II, no. 5.
[3] *Völkischer Beobachter*, Berlin, 20 October 1937.

Czechoslovakia before Munich

The Hossbach Protocol

While the German members of the Czechoslovak Government made every effort to have the promises of 18 February 1937 translated into administrative practice, Hitler was already issuing directives for the destruction of Czechoslovakia. These orders would not have been modified, let alone cancelled, as a consequence of *any* Czech concessions to the German minority or even to Henlein, for Hitler was not even remotely interested in the allegedly pitiable state of 'his' Germans in Czechoslovakia. The document of 5 November 1937,[1] which has become known as the Hossbach Protocol (after the Colonel who minuted it) clearly sets out Hitler's decision that 'for the improvement of our politico-military position' – and not for the liberation of German fellow-nationals smarting under a foreign yoke – 'our first objective, in the event of being embroiled in war' (which Hitler could of course arrange at the drop of a hat) 'must be to overthrow Czechoslovakia (*die Tschechei*) and Austria simultaneously...The assault upon the Czechs (*der Ueberfall auf die Tschechei*) would have to be carried out with "lightning speed".'

Hitler was also the first to envisage the expulsion of millions of people from their homes in Czechoslovakia:

Even though the population concerned, especially of Czechoslovakia, was not sparse, the *annexation of Czechoslovakia* and Austria would be an acquisition of foodstuffs for 5 to 6 million people, on the assumption that the *compulsory emigration of 2 million people from Czechoslovakia* and *1 million people from Austria* was practicable.

This, however, was not Hitler's first expression of his determination not to allow the Czechs to remain in their own country. The former President of the Danzig Senate, Hermann Rauschning, recalls[2] that in summer 1932 he had heard Hitler announce that

We shall never be able to make grand politics without a firm, steel-hard power centre, a centre of 80 or 100 millions of Germans living in an enclosed area! My first duty therefore will be to create this centre which will not only make us invincible but ensure for us once and for all the decisive ascendancy over all European nations...Part of this centre is Austria. That is a matter of course. Bohemia and Moravia however, also belong to it...In all these areas there is today a large majority of alien tribes, and if we want to put our Great Power on a permanent basis, it will be our duty to remove these tribes. There is no reason why we should not do so. The technical possibilities of our time will enable us

[1] Note by Hossbach, 10 November 1937, *DGFP*, D/I, no. 19.
[2] Hermann Rauschning, *Hitler speaks* (London 1939), p. 42.

160

to carry out these resettlement plans comparatively easily...The Bohemian-Moravian basin, the Eastern territories bordering on Germany, will be colonized by German farmers. The Czechs will be settled in Siberia or Wolhynia [a marshy area in Poland]...The Czechs must be expelled from Central Europe.

The Hossbach Protocol was of course 'top secret' and it is very unlikely that Eisenlohr in Prague knew anything definite of Hitler's plans. It seems, however, that he must have had an inkling of what was going on, because the warnings he uttered at just about this time sound remarkably like arguments against Hitler's views and intentions. To persuade the Nazis to behave differently may have been to emulate King Canute, but at least Eisenlohr's reports do prove that there were some German diplomats who did not pour oil on the flames but sincerely tried to avoid the catastrophes by spreading the truth. A discussion between Eisenlohr and Beneš in November 1937 has been minuted in detail by the former, beginning with a summary of his own views.[1] As regards Czechoslovak internal affairs, Eisenlohr limits himself to mentioning Beneš' conciliatory attitude. But in his introduction he points out that even if Beneš' statements were not made in good faith and only under the pressure of the foreign political situation, they would still be of practical importance. He considered these statements to be really true, however,

for the simple reason that a politician of his experience must long since have realised that the most important condition for the maintenance of the State which he helped to create must be a permanent good relationship with the German people outside and inside the borders...For this reason I am also inclined to assume that he really wishes to improve the position of the German minority. From his point of view, of course, he doubtless pictures the relationship to the German Reich and the legal position of the German racial group within Czechoslovakia differently from us...If the view is correct which I have expressed above, namely that Beneš wishes to improve the position of the German minority from the point of view of well-understood State interests and that therefore his efforts, even if they do not go all the way with ours, at least run parallel part of the way, the further question arises as to whether he is in a position to awaken in the Czech people the understanding necessary to carry out his intention. This question remains completely open. At the present time only this much can be said, that every manifest intensification of the German pressure on Czechoslovakia and every attitude on our part which can be construed, even remotely, by the perpetually watchful suspicious elements on the other side as a desire for aggression, will unite the Czech people in fear and hatred not only of us but of their own Sudeten German fellow citizens as well.

[1] Eisenlohr to G.F.M. 11 November 1937, *DGFP*, D/II, no. 23.

I could only imagine a change in the attitude of the Czechs towards the Sudeten Germans, if, in addition to the silent pressure which the growing power of the Reich exercises on the Czechs, there could be added the *confidence that we have no wish to touch the Czech nation and the Czechoslovak frontiers.*

The tenor of this solemn and carefully worded warning resembles that of his predecessor Koch's farewell-message,[1] and also agrees with the utterances of all other German diplomats accredited to Prague since 1918. But it fell on even less fertile ground: in fact, much of what Eisenlohr told Berlin never reached the Fuehrer.

Henlein's report to Hitler

Again it is no coincidence that a few days after the Hossbach conference of 5 November 1937, when Hitler outlined his intention to 'overthrow' Czechoslovakia, he received a memorandum from Henlein in which Hitler's plans were supported in much detail. Reading that document, one cannot help gaining the impression that Henlein had actually been asked to submit arguments to show that a solution of the Sudeten German problem within the existing framework of Czechoslovakia and without German intervention was not possible. Henlein also used this opportunity to forestall any possible attempts by the 'old' Nazis to dislodge him from his position as the Fuehrer's sole executive organ. Such was the background of his long memorandum 'for the Fuehrer and Reich Chancellor'.[2] Hitler was informed – no doubt because he wanted to be – that 'an understanding between Germans and Czechs in Czechoslovakia is practically impossible and a settlement of the Sudeten German question is only conceivable on a German basis'. In order to under-pin his argument, Henlein again used the precept of the direct proportion between the size of the lie and the probability of its being believed. The Prague Government at that time included three German Ministers who were anything but tools of the Czechs, but that did not deter Henlein from asserting that since 1933 'Czech internal policy has been unequivocally and systematically directed towards the de-nationalization and annihilation of the Sudeten Germans.' More than that: 'Incontestable information proves that

[1] See pp. 128–30.
[2] Enclosure in letter by Henlein to Neurath, 19 November 1937, *DGFP*, D/II, no. 23.

Beneš is determined to solve the Sudeten German question in the sense of the mission of the Czech nation and State by completely annihilating the Sudeten German racial group.' There is a striking similarity between this and the 'call for help', by means of which the 'Austrian Henlein' Seyss-Inquart[1] was supposed to have unleashed the German invasion of Austria on 11 March 1938.

Henlein then enlarged on the extent to which the Sudeten Germans (of course considered identical with his own party) were 'Nazi orientated' and in fact organized in a 'National Socialist Party'. The SdP was constrained to disguise their 'avowal of Nazism' and 'critics in the Reich' might still perhaps find 'blemishes in the National Socialist attitude of individual Party members'. Henlein had already committed himself at least as decisively to the Nazi creed in June 1934,[2] but what was new was his *cri de coeur* that

The dilemma in the external appearance of the SdP is deepened by the fact that internally it desires nothing so much as the incorporation of the Sudeten German area, and even the *whole Bohemian, Moravian and Silesian area into the Reich*, but that outwardly it has to support the maintenance of Czechoslovakia and the integrity of her frontiers and to attempt to set up an aim, having some semblance of political reality, for its own internal political struggle.

The movement which pretended to strive only for the concession of rights allegedly withheld from the Sudeten Germans thus openly admitted its real aim: to deprive the Czechs of *their* right to self-determination.

In this document on 19 November 1937 Henlein conveyed to Berlin the 'Sudeten Germans' desire to be a 'factor in the Nazi Reich policy'. But only one day earlier, in an interview with the American journalist Otto Tolischus, he wanted him and through him the readers of the *New York Times*[3] to believe what he had put across in London a month before: that he and his followers were thoroughly loyal and democratic citizens of Czechoslovakia:

The Sudeten German Party's stand towards the Czechoslovak State, Mr Henlein said, always had been positive and unequivocal...We are in opposition to the present Government...but we fight on the basis of the State for a just order within it and for organic democracy...The unity of the State and the State's leadership must naturally be preserved, he admitted, but said that

---

[1] *DGFP*, D/1, no. 358.   [2] See p. 116.
[3] Otto Tolischus, 'Not against the State, Henlein declares', *New York Times*, 19 November 1937.

State unity did not mean centralisation, and autonomy, he believed, far from alienating the Germans from the State, would greatly strengthen the State-consciousness...I have always declared that we stand unequivocally for a democratic republican form of a Czechoslovak State. We believe in democracy ...The SdP is not an appendix of either National Socialism or Fascism, but wholly a natural movement of long standing. With all the respect paid to me in Germany, for instance, nobody there would think of giving me orders and instructions.

The only true sentence was the last one. No one in Germany ever had any *need* to give him orders and instructions: he did Hitler's job without any instructions.

A fateful step in British appeasement policy was the visit of Lord Halifax, Lord President of the Council, to Germany in November 1937. It was his first contact with German reality and, unfamiliar as he was with Nazi tactics and subterfuges, he immediately misjudged it. His report on his visit to Hitler at Berchtesgaden on 19 November[1] differs little from the notes the German interpreter made for Hitler (Halifax had received an English translation of these notes). The only remarkable deviation is Hitler's hope, registered by Halifax, that 'reasonable elements' in Czechoslovakia would make it possible for the Sudeten Germans to 'enjoy a status which would safeguard their position'. There were two lies in this statement: that Hitler was looking forward to the further existence of the Czechoslovak State and that the Sudeten Germans needed something to safeguard their – in reality very firm – position.

This is how, later, Neville Chamberlain, when not inhibited by any considerations of parliamentary tactics, assessed the situation (in a letter to his sister of 26 November)[2]:

Both Hitler and Goering said separately and emphatically that they had no desire or intention of making war and I think we may take this as correct, at any rate for the present. Of course they want to dominate Eastern Europe; they want as close a union with Austria as they can get, without incorporating her in the Reich, and they want much the same thing for the *Sudeten Deutsch* as we did for the Uitlanders in the Transvaal.

Shortly afterwards (29 and 30 November) Camille Chautemps, the French Premier, and Yvon Delbos, the Foreign Minister, were

---

[1] Halifax's Report on his visit to Germany, *Cabinet Committee on Foreign Policy*, F.P. (36), *Cab.* 24/626, no. 39.
[2] Middlemas, *Diplomacy of Illusion*, p. 137.

in London to discuss the situation with their British colleagues.[1] Much time was devoted to the problem of Czechoslovakia and to Halifax' German impressions. Chautemps was a weak man and hardly contributed to the exchange of views, but Delbos told the British many things they did not like. According to the (unpublished) minutes another strong-willed man, the British Prime Minister Neville Chamberlain, did most of the talking. There was a definite difference of opinion between Chamberlain and Delbos, but their exchange of views was a 'dialogue of the deaf'. Delbos, as later events showed, correctly described Hitler's plans: Halifax on the other hand first repeated Hitler's remarks to the effect that the Sudeten Germans could be made perfectly happy inside Czechoslovakia and then expressed his conviction that Hitler 'was not bent on early adventures'. He had been 'surprised at the moderation of Herr Hitler's remarks on this point'.

This blind confidence in the words of a man who had broken his promises on numerous occasions was too much for Delbos. He said he had secret information from a neutral country about the real intentions of the Nazi leaders. According to them, Austria was soon to be absorbed by means of a 'plebiscite'. This prophecy was fulfilled three months later. In Czechoslovakia, the German aims 'would be achieved by stages, though the final objective was the annexation of the territory inhabited by the Sudeten Germans'. 'There would be,' Delbos said, 'the introduction of Ministers with Nazi tendencies, a kind of federation, a quasi-autonomy of fact, if not of right. This would be followed by autonomy pure and simple, and then by attachment to the Reich.'

In his reply Chamberlain had nothing whatever to say to these gloomy forecasts. He only pointed out that British public opinion was not in favour of war for the sake of Czechoslovakia. Moreover he had the feeling that the Sudeten Germans were not getting fair treatment from the Czechs. Chamberlain did not even know that there were three German Ministers in the Czechoslovak Government.

Delbos reacted to these irrelevancies with the remark 'What Germany really wanted was to absorb the (Sudeten) German

[1] Visit of French Minister to London, F.P. (36), *Cab.* 24/626, no. 40.

territory and not that Sudeten Germans should receive better treatment.' Here Eden interjected: 'there was a feeling here that the Sudeten Germans had certain grievances which ought to be dealt with'. Perhaps one should advise the Prague Government to act in this direction? Chamberlain added that he did not think 'that there would be an act of aggression' (because of the Sudeten Germans). He was in favour of 'some reasonable form of local government' not knowing that this had always existed. His next sentence reflected his absolute inability to see the facts of the situation:

He (the Prime Minister) agreed with M. Chautemps that we could not request Czechoslovakia to grant autonomy to the *Sudetendeutsche*. He did not, in fact believe that the Germans would go so far in their demands as that.

Credo quia absurdum est (I believe it *because* it is absurd) seems to have been Chamberlain's secret motto. Delbos' answer was to the point: 'If now Czechoslovakia gave satisfactory treatment to the Sudeten Germans, Germany would find some other pretext against her.' Delbos was supposed to go to Prague in December where he wanted to advise the Government not to give Hitler any pretext for a pretended 'outbreak of temperament', but to make reasonable concessions, compatible with the integrity of the State. Eden was against the first part of the advice (to avoid giving a pretext for a Nazi action). Delbos should simply say in Prague that one should do everything possible 'to meet the legitimate grievances of the Sudeten Germans'.

Delbos answered with a remark which must have been news to the British Ministers: the Germans were represented in the Prague Government. Eden was not impressed by any facts destroying his arguments. He had never bothered to inform himself about real conditions, but now he said he 'thought that the number of Sudeten Germans who favoured the present régime was not very large'. At the last election 33 per cent of the German electorate had 'favoured the present régime'.

It was a tragedy for mankind that the Chautemps Government, with Léon Blum as Vice-Premier and Delbos as Foreign Minister, lasted only until the middle of March 1938. It was replaced by the short-lived second Government of Léon Blum whose Foreign

Minister Joseph Paul-Boncour was, like Delbos, a firm opponent of tendencies to appeasement. With Delbos or Paul-Boncour at the Quai d'Orsay in summer 1938 there would never have been the pilgrimage to Canossa renamed Munich. Unfortunately at the beginning of April George Bonnet took over...

At the same time as Delbos tried in London to open the eyes of the leading British statesmen the German Minister in Prague had the decency – useless, indeed dangerous, in view of his employer's real intentions – to confirm the good intentions of the Prague Government in his reports to Berlin.[1] Eisenlohr emphasized that disturbances were 'actually only to be feared from possible Sudeten German incidents and from the persistent attempts of the Sudeten German press agency to make use of our [i.e. the Reich's] newspapers for the airing of their grievances'. He expressed the hope that 'in this matter we maintain an iron calm'. A month later he quoted, without comment, Beneš' observation[2] that

his (Beneš') aim was to attain for the Germans the status of full equality of rights and contentment within the State. Though he would not tolerate any interference...still, in view of Germany's natural interest in (the minority) and on account of common concern that no disturbing factor in our relations should arise from this source, he was always prepared to discuss minority questions with us in a friendly fashion.

Three days later Eisenlohr warned that as regards foreign politics, concessions to Germany might not be easy to obtain from Beneš, but internally the President wanted to carry out 'pacification':[3]

I am quite certain that he (Beneš) will make concessions under pressure of the foreign political situation and that he alone is capable of realizing them...He has made the internal appeasement of the country the aim of his Presidency, and that not just from today...For the time being all he says regarding the matter is that he wishes to secure for the Sudeten Germans the full enjoyment of their constitutional rights and their full participation in the State.

Hodža, the Prime Minister, was more communicative, but, as Eisenlohr reported, he had taken a decisive stand against territorial autonomy. Interwoven with Hodža's train of thoughts, Eisenlohr skilfully conveyed his own warnings against the 'autonomy' slogan:

The country [Eisenlohr reported Hodža as saying] was too small to allow itself

---

[1] Eisenlohr to Weissäcker, 12 November 1937, *DGFP*, D/II, no. 19.
[2] Eisenlohr to G.F.M. 18 December 1937, *DGFP*, D/II, no. 34.
[3] Eisenlohr to G.F.M. 21 December 1937, *DGFP*, D/II, no. 38.

to be 'atomised'...In times of crisis the State would fall into pieces; the fortifications were without exception in the autonomous border areas. This is the Czech view of the question: that autonomy for this State would virtually mean suicide. One had to know this view-point in order to understand that autonomy could never be achieved here by peaceful means...In my opinion the Sudeten Germans would therefore be better advised to delete the ambiguous expression 'autonomy' which means different things to different people and which excites distrust and discord, from their vocabulary and instead talk of the matter which really lies at their heart.

In February 1938 Eisenlohr sent a new and even more outspoken warning to Berlin:[1] he was worried lest the 'conforming' German press might be unable to keep certain promises of moderation in their tone:

Something at least can be prophesied with certainty: If the German press starts to use aggressive language once more...it would necessarily nourish the Czech people's fears of an impending German attack...It is traditional that the Czechs, if they scent danger, unite against anything German and cling closer to their allies.

The bleak year 1938

The year 1938, one of the blackest years in the history of democracy, began with two most disturbing events in Czechoslovakia – both on New Year's Day. *Venkov* ('Countryside'), the paper of the Czech Agrarians, had prepared one of the newspaper enquiries then popular for its New Year's issue: 'What would you wish for Czechoslovakia in the twentieth year of her existence?' Among those asked to contribute was Konrad Henlein who had never before been approached by a Czech newspaper. His answers[2] were rather cautious and non-committal, but the fact that the organ of the strongest government party had given him, as it were, the accolade of respectability, had a traumatic effect. What was even worse was that Rudolf Beran, the party's chairman, wrote an article[3] in which the possibility or intention was mooted, albeit in a veiled form, that the Czech Agrarians at least might count on the SdP as a possible Government partner. What did put the cat among the pigeons was the sentence 'When under our democratic electoral system more than 1.25

---

[1] Eisenlohr to G.F.M. 11 February 1938, *Deutsche Gesandtschaft, Prag*, vol. 85/3.

[2] *Venkov*, 1 January 1938.

[3] *Venkov*, 1 January 1938, reprinted in *Mnichov v dokumentech*, II (Prague 1958), no. 7.

million Germans have given their confidence to the SdP, one has to accept the fact and draw the appropriate conclusions from it.' Had the same number of votes been given to the Communists Beran would hardly have suggested drawing 'the appropriate conclusions from it'. To isolate the SdP, as a fascist body alien to a democracy, had been the guiding principle of the Government and all democratic parties. The change was unmistakable. Almost the entire Czech press angrily rebutted Beran's suggestion, which had all the characteristics of a *ballon d'essai*. Despite its tentative character, the article had far-reaching effects: the German Activists, especially of course the German Agrarians, felt the ground was being pulled away from under their feet. Beran at that time also conferred with Eisenlohr behind the backs of the President, the Premier and the Foreign Minister and in these discussions with the German envoy he was rather more frank. Two of these talks between Beran and Eisenlohr have since become known in some detail through Eisenlohr's reports.[1] According to them, Beran had at first revealed a rather generally formulated desire for closer ties with Germany but had hastened to qualify this by pointing out that despite their opposition to Communism 'the Agrarian Party...could not undertake the hazard of breaking off treaty relations with Soviet Russia before knowing whether its efforts were appreciated by us'. Regarding the Sudeten Germans, Beran merely said that he did not think the minorities question insoluble. At the second meeting he 'desired to know on his part whether Berlin was really inclined towards an understanding with Czechoslovakia'. Only in this case 'could a dissolution of the pact with Soviet Russia be considered'. His next step, however, was ominous for democracy: he assured Eisenlohr that 'his Party had now taken up the fight for the liquidation of the German Social Democrats as a Government Party' and it wanted to expel this party, the last German partner in the Czechoslovak Government coalition, 'in order to facilitate understanding with the Sudeten German Party. Germany must help to liquidate Marxism.'

On 12 February 1938 Schuschnigg, the Austrian Federal Chancellor, had been 'invited' to see Hitler at Berchtesgaden. Exactly one month later Austria had ceased to exist. Under the shattering

[1] Eisenlohr to G.F.M. 27 February and 27 March 1938, *DGFP*, D/II, nos. 62 and 105.

impact of the Austrian *Anschluss*, bringing in its wake a radical deterioration of Czechoslovakia's strategic position and a deadly threat to the last Germans living in freedom, the German Social Democrats called an emergency conference in Prague, which affirmed its resolution[1] 'to defend, jointly with the democratic forces of the Czech people and sustained by our alliances, the independence of our country to the last'. After Hitler's threatening reference, before the Reichstag on 20 February 1938, to the 10 million 'unredeemed Germans' it was clear that Czechoslovakia was going to be the next victim of Nazi aggression.

In a telegram Beneš was assured by the German Social Democrats of their 'unconditional loyalty':

In this critical hour for the maintenance of peace in Europe we consider it our duty to pledge ourselves again to the support of your policy of democracy and peace and the understanding of nations. We feel at one with you and the whole Czechoslovak people in the determination to maintain the independence of the State and the inviolability of its frontiers under all circumstances...We are convinced that the Republic, of its own strength and its own will, in collaboration with all democratic forces irrespective of their national origin, will continue to the end on its successful course for the achievement of full national equality.

In his reply Beneš said:

I agree with you that the attainment of national equality is a matter of our internal relations and that we have sufficient positive forces of our own to establish and maintain a régime of equality of rights. That, also, is the actual meaning of democracy. Loyalty to the democratic principle appears to me the best guarantee that our State will always be able to count on having adequate forces to protect itself and solve its problems in its own way.

Statements of this kind were never reported to the Foreign Office by the British Legation in Prague.

The end of Activism

The German Agrarians and the Christian Socials were not unanimous in their reaction to events in Austria. In view of the Catholic character of the régime overthrown there, the Christian Socials were naturally deeply worried and they might well have withstood the pressure of their own defeatist, anti-democratic wing if the German Agrarians had given them moral support. In the event, however, after severe internal struggles, that party succumbed to the machina-

[1] *Sozialdemokrat*, 19 March 1938.

tions of its own chairman Gustav Hacker, who proclaimed on 22 March 1938, that his party was leaving the Czechoslovak Government and 'joining as a whole the SdP under the leadership of Konrad Henlein'.[1] This internal *putsch* left Spina no alternative but to resign from the Government, although he did not follow the SdP call. Spina died a few months later embittered and disillusioned, in the middle of the crisis manufactured by Hitler.

The self-immolation of the Christian Social Party was not quite so straightforward, but after the Agrarians' *volte face* much of its resistance crumbled away. On 23 March the defeatists finally gained the upper hand. Their parliamentary representatives duly joined the SdP ranks,[2] with the exception of Zajiček, who resigned from the Government the day after Spina.

With the disappearance of the two non–Socialist Activist parties Henlein's claim to be the Sudeten Germans' sole spokesman had gone a long way towards being substantiated. But his success was not yet complete. The small but irrepressible German Liberal Party, with one representative in Parliament, was written off by Henlein as negligible, but the German Social Democrats could not be ignored. They were to be fought to the bitter end and Henlein, the self-appointed 'guardian of German interests' laid his anathema upon them:[3]

The last two German splinter Parties...who were the only ones to preserve a miserable semblance of existence apart from our powerful united movement, *are no longer regarded by us as part of the Sudeten German national group.* In particular the German Social Democrats can no longer be counted among the Germans of this State...

It is difficult now to imagine what was meant for the simple worker to remain loyal to democratic ideals. During this period when the majority of employers were supporters of Henlein and used all kinds of blackmail to persuade their workers into his party, people dare not associate themselves with anything other than the SdP. Nevertheless some 200,000 German workers did remain in the German free trade unions which resisted all attempts to enforce *Gleichschaltung* (conformity).

In the oppressive aftermath of Hitler's successful Austrian coup

[1] *Prager Tagblatt*, 23 March 1938.   [2] *Prager Tagblatt*, 24 March 1938.
[3] *Die Zeit*, 26 March 1938.

171

the bi-annual regular conference of the German Social Democratic Party opened in Prague on 26 March 1938. Ludwig Czech, now 68 years old and ill, who had led the party since 1920 and represented it in the Government since 1929, was replaced as party chairman by the younger Wenzel Jaksch. No change in the party's outlook was involved as was shown by a message of loyalty to Beneš,[1] carried unanimously:

The Party Conference of the united German Social Democratic Workers' Party offers its greetings and its expression of love and admiration to the President of the Republic. The Party again pledges its loyalty to the Republic and declares its unshakeable determination to defend our democracy and freedom with all the force at its command.

Jaksch's political report proved that the party – just like Beneš himself – had now placed all its hopes in the expectation that the Western powers, purely from considerations of their own safety, would not abandon Czechoslovakia, but uncertainty about the short-term and long-term future nevertheless weighed heavily. Dr Czech had left the Government; he could, however, have been replaced by another nominee of the Party. Although the SdP had not succeeded, in its striving after total power, in forcing the Social Democrats to capitulate, they did their utmost to deprive them of all influence and eliminate them wherever possible. Eventually representatives of the SdP told Hodža that the German Social Democrats would have to disappear from the Government: the SdP was 'the only authorised representative of the Sudeten Germans' and the Social Democrats continued membership in the Government was 'absolutely intolerable and disturbing'.[2] It was not internal dissension but external threats and blackmail which ended the democratic co-operation between Germans and Czechs in the Government.

Henlein's meeting with Hitler

On the occasion of the 'happy turn of events' in Austria Henlein sent a letter of congratulation to Ribbentrop[3] promising to show his

[1] *Sozialdemokrat*, 27 and 29 March 1938.
[2] Discussion with Hodža, minuted from memory, 6 April 1938, *G.F.M.* serial 2369, frames 494413-21.
[3] Henlein to Ribbentrop (from Hof, in Bavaria), 17 March 1938, *DGFP*, D/II, no. 89.

gratitude to Hitler by 'redoubled efforts in the service of Greater German policy'. On 28 March Henlein was received by Hitler in Ribbentrop's presence. What happened on that occasion can only be gathered from the one report in existence, written by Henlein himself[1] and thus not altogether reliable; but he certainly interpreted Hitler correctly by quoting:

that he intended to settle the Czechoslovak problem in the not too distant future. He could no longer tolerate Germans being oppressed or fired upon.

Germans were not being oppressed or fired upon, but one extra lie in the whole edifice of terror and blackmail mattered little. What was more significant was that Hitler no longer limited himself to the Sudeten Germans: it was the *whole* of Czechoslovakia which he intended to 'deal with' in his own manner.

To Henlein's objection that he (Henlein) could only be a substitute, Hitler replied: 'I will stand by you; *from tomorrow you will be my Viceroy* (Statthalter) ...The purport of the instructions which the Fuehrer has given to Henlein is that *demands should be made by the SdP which are unacceptable to the Czech government*...Henlein summarised his view to the Fuehrer as follows: '*We must always demand so much that we can never be satisfied*'. The Fuehrer approved this view.

Hitler was then said to have assured Henlein that 'he was the rightful leader of the Sudeten German element', and enjoyed his complete trust.

On the following day, 29 March, Henlein saw Ribbentrop and on this occasion Eisenlohr among others was present. 'With reference to the principles imparted to Konrad Henlein yesterday afternoon by the Fuehrer' – the minutes do not say to what extent, if at all, these were revealed – Ribbentrop stated that the Reich 'would tolerate no further suppression of the Sudeten Germans by the Czechoslovak Government'. The formation of concrete demands to be put before the Prague Government was left to the SdP – the show was evidently carefully planned. Henlein 'was the expressly recognised leader of the Sudeten German element, recently confirmed by the Fuehrer' to whom the Reich Government would not give any detailed instructions (no longer necessary, Hitler had just seen to it).

[1] Report note (unsigned and undated), *DGFP*, D/II, no. 107. Note of the G.F.M. of 28 March 1938, loc. cit., no. 106. Note by Ribbentrop of 29 March 1938, loc. cit., no. 109.

It was a matter of drawing up a maximum programme which would guarantee as its final aim total freedom for the Sudeten Germans. The final object of the negotiations to be carried out between the SdP and the...Government would be, by the scope and step-by-step specification of their demands, to avoid entry into the Government.

The Reich Government for its part must decline to appear *vis-à-vis* the Prague Government, or London and Paris, as 'the representative or pacemaker of the Sudeten German demands', said Ribbentrop, after the Reich Government had done precisely that and was going to do it again much more emphatically. That 'no confidence could be placed in the assurances of Beneš and Hodža' was a statement clearly intended for Eisenlohr. He, nevertheless, despite these 'instructions' and the broad hints of Hitler's real intentions, did not cease to advocate an utterly fair solution of the Sudeten German problem within the framework of the existing constitution and on the basis of the assurances received from Beneš and Hodža.[1]

[1] See p. 207.

12 CZECHOSLOVAKIA'S RÔLE IN NAZI FOREIGN POLICY

It seems appropriate to consider now the political relations between Nazi Germany and Czechoslovakia. Since Hitler's rise to power the internal and external aspects of the German–Czech problem had become so intertwined that it was becoming more and more difficult to distinguish between them.

A Non-Aggression Pact?

It had always been the aim of National Socialism to eliminate the obstacle presented by Czechoslovakia to its plans for world domination by undermining her security through the exacerbation of the country's internal difficulties. In order to give their victim a false sense of security, during the early 1930s the Nazis 'played it cool': they deliberately created the impression that Czech affairs in general and the Sudeten Germans in particular were of little interest to them. The deception did not quite succeed – those responsible for Czechoslovak foreign policy were after all conversant with *Mein Kampf* – and when Anthony Eden arrived in Prague in March 1935, Beneš assured him that his country was going to continue in its pro-Western policy. If, however, the Germans were given *carte blanche*, they would progressively take over the whole of Europe. Hitler would not remain content with the German frontier areas of Czechoslovakia, Beneš told Eden, the whole State was a thorn in his side:[1]

I bear the burden of German proximity, but I bear it in the interest of all. That is why I always advise Paris to come to terms with Germany.

[1] Note by Beneš about his talks with Eden, 4 April 1935, *G.F.M.* serial 2028/III, frames 44440-518. (This is a German translation of the Czech original, which, together with other Prague files, fell into the hands of the Nazis in March 1939.) See also Earl of Avon, *The Eden Memoirs, Facing the Dictators* (London 1962), p. 173.

175

Czechoslovakia before Munich

During those years there were only three discussions between Hitler and the Czechoslovak Minister in Berlin, Vojtěch Mastný. The first of these started unpropitiously with Hitler protesting against Czech allegations of collusion between the Nazis of the Reich and those of the Sudeten areas. Since, however, at that moment Hitler had been Reich Chancellor for only a week, he seems to have felt the need to put his visitor somewhat at ease by assuring him that the Nazi Party in Czechoslovakia was 'completely independent, and that he had nothing to do with it', and he went on to tell Mastný that he 'wanted friendly relations with his neighbours'.[1]

In the following autumn Mastný was able to inform Prague that 'unofficially' he had been offered a Non-Aggression Pact between Germany and Czechoslovakia; this had been suggested he said, by 'a very noteworthy German source' in Hitler's entourage.[2] Prague's equally unofficial reply was the Czechoslovakia could not conclude such a pact without the concurrence of France. Bilateral (never multilateral) pact offers were part of Hitler's strategy: in this particular case and at that time it might have been useful for him to protect his left flank while he was dealing with Austria. Whenever Hitler went one step further on his road of 'dynamic expansion', he always made sure that soothing offers were made to all and sundry at the same time: thus, when he left the League of Nations he also assured the world that 'the German Government and the German people...further declare that they are willing at any time, through the conclusion of pacts of non-aggression, entered into for the longest periods, to secure the peace of Europe'.[3]

In order to calm the European States which had been agitated by the 'weekend surprise' of the German occupation of the Rhineland (7 March 1936), Hitler declared in his subsequent speech in the Reichstag that 'the German Government repeats its offer

[1] *Europäische Politik 1933–1938 im Spiegel der Prager Akten*, ed. Friedrich Berber (Essen 1942), p. 20. (Since many records are printed here incompletely, without any indication of omissions, so that their sense is often distorted, this collection of Prague files – published by the Nazis to prove their own innocence – cannot be considered as a sound historical source.)

[2] Note by Köpke, 14 November 1933, *DGFP*, C/II (London 1959), no. 68, Koch to G.F.M. 17 November 1933, *G.F.M.* serial 9151, frames 643900-1.

[3] Norman H. Baynes (ed.), *The Speeches of Adolf Hitler, April 1922 – August 1939* (London 1942), II, 1091.

to conclude with the States bordering Germany in the East non-aggression pacts similar to that with Poland'.[1] This of course included Czechoslovakia, but when Mastný took up the idea seriously, the Reich Foreign Minister Neurath could only offer evasive replies.[2]

The Berlin Foreign Ministry studiously ignored reports it got from Prague where the newly appointed German Envoy Ernst Eisenlohr had a three-hour discussion at his first encounter with Beneš on 21 February 1936.[3]

According to Eisenlohr's summary of this, Beneš had spoken to him with the obvious intention of refuting the stories spread by Nazi Germany about Czechoslovakia, and of making it more difficult to put them about in the future:

His policy after the foundation of the...State, he said, had had perforce to be a policy within the framework of the League of Nations and one leaning towards the Western Powers, and not France alone, as was believed in Germany. To incline towards British as well as French policy had always appeared to him particularly important since he saw in British policy the necessary corrective to French policy, the exaggerations and errors of which he clearly recognized. Were he ever to publish his memoirs, the documents included therein would show on how many occasions he had urged moderation and a more yielding attitude on the French statesmen...Admittedly, he said, Czechoslovakia had received a small piece of German territory...but he had advocated that in exchange Germany should receive a far larger portion of Bohemia with a population many times greater than that of the small Hultschin territory [which Germany had to cede to Czechoslovakia in 1919]. Lloyd George had told him that he was unable to understand this and had frustrated his plan...He had always been in favour of a German–French *détente* and had always supported it; in this respect, too, we in Germany did him an injustice...He was quite open-minded about Germany, he said. He well knew what German culture had meant and still meant for his people. He was compelled, he said, to pursue a policy which gave his country security and the time required to consolidate the still somewhat fluid structure of the State. But the fact that he inclined towards the Western Powers did not mean that he adopted a hostile attitude towards Germany. On the contrary, he had repeatedly tried, both in his public reports to Parliament and in his conversations with German Ministers – he named Stresemann and Curtius – not only to establish normal relations with us, but to go further than that and make them more friendly. For seventeen years he had repeatedly stretched out his hand; he had admittedly received friendly answers in private conversations but never once in public. This reproach he levelled at those who conducted German policy.

[1] Ibid. p. 1298.
[2] Note by Neurath, 20 March 1937, *G.F.M.* serial 1941 frames 433837-8.
[3] Eisenlohr to G.F.M. 23 February 1936, *DGFP*, C/IV (London 1961), no. 580.

After that Beneš turned to the Goebbels legend of Czechoslovakia as a Soviet air-base:

> The Pact with Russia [concluded in 1935] was referred to by Beneš as the result of the deep-rooted fear of us [i.e. the Germans] among his people. As for himself, he had no doubt but that Czechoslovkia's culture was Western and could never be Russian-orientated; he was determined to fight Communism ruthlessly in his own country...He could have had a military agreement (with Soviet Russia)...(but) he had refused.

Beneš emphatically stated that there were no airfields at the Russians' disposal and no Soviet military aeroplanes in Czechoslovakia:

> He was going to tell me quite bluntly his reason for it...assuming a conflict broke out one day, how would Czechoslovakia's moral position look if she allowed herself to become a Russian arms dump?

A few weeks later Eisenlohr sent a 14-page memorandum on 'Czechoslovakia in the present European Crisis'[1] to Berlin which again contained many remarkable judgments quite contrary to what official German propaganda wanted the world to believe. Eisenlohr described the difficulties of a young State requiring a long period of consolidation. Every aspect of National Socialism was to the Czechs 'distasteful, frightening and hateful' – the Fuehrer principle, as also the attitude to traditional democratic forms, the racial principle and the emphasis on the unity of the whole German community (*Volkstum*) with the dissemination of this idea across the frontier. The immediate dangers which, in the Czechoslovak view, threatened Czechoslovakia from Germany were threefold:

> the danger of an attack from without, the *Anschluss* of Austria to Germany which would encircle this country politically, economically and culturally, and the fear that the Sudeten German Party, which comprises 70 per cent of the German minority and is also a consequence of National Socialism, could be used as a lever to weaken or even to burst asunder the fabric of the State from within ...The crucial factor in any Czech policy is its relationship with the German people, that is to say, nowadays, with the Reich. The Czechs have always regarded themselves as an 'island in the German sea'. Experience has taught them that they can only hold their own if they are either living on good terms with the Germans or, with powerful and reliable foreign aid, defending themselves against the German community...The Czech people...continued on this path for more than a thousand years, constantly at odds with the Germans, and yet always protected by them through all the vicissitudes of Western history. But to be at peace with the German community concealed a deadly peril, that of absorption by an alien, higher culture...It is necessary to maintain tense, even

[1] Eisenlohr to G.F.M. 16 April 1936, *G.F.M.* serial 9144, frames 643061–74.

178

hostile relations with the German community in order not to be overpowered by it and in order to preserve the ethnic (*völkisch*) identity of the Czechs which in the course of history has so often appeared to be almost lost and has yet been recovered again and again with remarkable tenacity.

No Czech would have pleaded his country's cause more eloquently than did Hitler's envoy in Prague. However hostile the Czech people might, in general, be to Germany, Eisenlohr estimated that they were too experienced politically and that fear had made them too clear-sighted 'to see things other than as they are'. Beneš was 'certainly not the man to run his head against a brick wall'. Eisenlohr thought that Beneš could be counted on to make concessions to the Germans in the country if he could thereby save its independence.

The Haushofer–Trauttmansdorff Mission

At the end of 1936 two of Hitler's emissaries – Albrecht Haushofer and Count Trauttmansdorff – had appeared twice in Prague to negotiate with Beneš about the possibilities of a political *rapprochement* between Germany and Czechoslovakia. This mission took place with Hitler's approval, in fact on his orders.[1] Haushofer, son of the founder of 'Geopolitics', had little knowledge of the internal problems besetting Czechoslovakia; Trauttmansdorff, on the other hand, a member of the old Austrian aristocracy who had found a job in the German Ministry of Labour, was better acquainted with them. Haushofer was at that time working for the *Dienststelle Ribbentrop* – a rival organization to the German Foreign Office until Ribbentrop became Foreign Minister himself. This defrayed both Haushofer's and Trauttmansdorff's expenses. In April 1936 Haushofer presented a rather fanciful memorandum, *Politische Möglichkeiten im Südosten* ('Political Possibilities in the South-East') in which only the references to Czechoslovakia are of interest here. In May 1938 Haushofer warned Ribbentrop in vain against adventures and was shortly afterwards denounced as 'politically

[1] See Haushofer's *Bericht uber Verbandlungen in der Tschechoslowakei* (Report about negotiations in Czechoslovakia), Berlin, 9 January 1937. This report and other relevant data used here can be found in the Albrecht Haushofer File of the Library of Congress, Washington, Dept. of Manuscripts, no. 11 249. The material available here has been most instructively used by Gerald L. Weinberg, 'Secret Hitler – Beneš Negotiations in 1936–37', *Journal of Central European Affairs*, Boulder (U.S.A.), January 1960, pp. 366–74.

unreliable'.[1] In 1944, he was arrested as a member of a German resistance group and executed on 21 April 1945.[2] In the light of the author's tragic end one might therefore imagine that the memorandum of April 1936 was an act of disguised resistance. It is, however, difficult to discover anything in it beyond suggestions for German expansion into the south and south-east of Europe. Haushofer did not regard as quite impossible an attempt in Prague 'to break the encirclement of Germany'. He therefore recommended the conclusion of a non-aggression pact with Czechoslovakia, which as 'confirmation and extension of the existing Arbitration Treaty [of 1925]' would have looked harmless, and a 'German–Czech compromise' (*Ausgleich*), according to which 'Germany would agree not to raise the boundary question for an appropriate period of time in return for the complete cultural autonomy and economic equality of the Sudeten Germans' – in other words, permitting Germany to interfere openly in the internal affairs of Czechoslovakia. After returning from his first visit to Prague, Haushofer's report included a sentence providing the classic definition of Hitler's misuse of the Sudeten German problem for his wider imperialist aims:

Should it be desirable, for whatever reasons, not to reach agreement [about a non-aggression pact], it would be best to protract negotiations and if necessary render them nugatory by tightening the screw of Sudeten German demands.

It is impossible not to realize that the continual escalation of political demands by Henlein was precisely what Hitler had ordered Henlein in March 1938.[3]

Haushofer and Trauttmansdorff first went to Prague on 13 and 14 November 1936 and talked to Beneš and Krofta, the Foreign Minister.[4] Judging by Haushofer's notes, Beneš spoke to his visitors of his attitude to Germany, the German question and the pact with

---

[1] Note by Likus, August 1938, Files of the *Dienststelle Ribbentrop*, *G.F.M.* serial 314/1, frames 190639–40.

[2] Rainer Hildebrandt, *Wir sind die Letzten* (subtitled: From the life of the resistance fighter Albrecht Haushofer and his friends') (Neuwied 1949), p. 206.

[3] See p. 173.

[4] Edvard Beneš, *The Memoirs of Dr Beneš* (London 1954), pp. 15–20, 46–7. This also contains the text of the draft treaty between the two countries which was sent to Berlin.

Moscow, as he had previously told Eisenlohr. In general he tried to disarm Hitler's emissaries by showing a co-operative spirit: he was ready 'to negotiate today with Germany about a non-aggression pact', even without a new 'Western Locarno', i.e. a German pact with Britain and France. Haushofer noted that Beneš was willing to talk with his visitors about the 'delicate subject' of the Sudeten Germans. 'The Germans belong to our State... We want the Germans to be satisfied.' Further details were to be discussed at the next meeting.

On his return to Berlin, Haushofer reported to Himmler and Hitler. To the latter he submitted a summary of aims which he thought could be achieved: a bilateral non-aggression pact, independent of a new 'Western Locarno' and subject to a Czechoslovak reservation regarding the League of Nations Covenant, Czechoslovak neutrality in the – most improbable – event of a Russian attack on Germany or 'in case of a conflict with Russia over Spain', although should Germany attack Russia, Haushofer thought that Czechoslovak neutrality could not be obtained: this was perhaps meant as a warning to Hitler. Further issues on which results could be expected were, according to Haushofer, a curb on the activities of the political émigrés, a trade agreement and, finally, 'improvements – through German influence – in the situation of the Sudeten Germans'. Hitler crossed out the non-aggression pact, changed the order of some of the other points and omitted any comment on the Sudeten German question – he was clearly much more interested in preserving this issue as an excuse for future manœuvres. Although he had rejected the non-aggression pact, Hitler agreed to a resumption of contacts with Prague.

Discussions were resumed on 18 December but ended inconclusively. Beneš himself mentions the second meeting in his memoirs and there are fragments of his own minutes recorded at the time – some in facsimile – in Communist publications,[1] as well as a note by Haushofer, 'Outcome of Prague'. It appears that Beneš gave a long academic lecture to his visitors about the Sudeten German problem and then dealt with their objections to the 'tendencies to

[1] Jaromír Hořec, *Cesty zrady* (Paths of Treason) (Prague 1957), pp. 136–9. (A more detailed English version in *Germany and Czechoslovakia, 1918–1945, Documents on German Politics* (Prague 1965), pp. 97–111.)

spread Czech influence' (*Tschechisierungstendenzen*). He is said to have stressed German equality in the educational system – two colleges of higher technology for eight million Czechs and the same number for three million Germans – and Trauttmansdorff agreed that in this respect the Germans had everything they needed.

Except for the final conclusions, Haushofer's minutes about this lengthy meeting to a large extent tally with Beneš' notes. Hitler was unlikely to derive much pleasure from reading that

while one may notice at most a certain anxiety but no serious desire for an understanding among the Czechs as a whole, the decisive individual – a personality of stature (*eine Persönlichkeit von Format*) – looks further and makes efforts to secure better relations, naturally as cheaply as possible. It is clear to him that without better treatment of the Sudeten Germans, an improvement in the relations between Berlin and Prague cannot be obtained.

Haushofer and Trauttmansdorff had brought to Prague the draft of a treaty to be concluded between the two States which was, however, so carelessly drafted that it did not even designate the Czechoslovak State correctly. Would it mean, Beneš asked, the termination of the Czechoslovak treaties with France and the Soviet Union as well as the withdrawal of Czechoslovakia from the League of Nations? When he declared that this was out of the question, his visitors were said to have reassured him that it was not necessary; it would be quite sufficient if Czechoslovakia, should a crisis occur, did not implement the commitments laid down in the treaties she had concluded with the other countries. They also said that Germany would be 'content' with cultural autonomy for the Sudeten Germans; this throws a significant light on the 'non-interference in internal affairs' offered by Hitler at the same time.

The two visitors finally urged Beneš to send his counter-proposals for a new bilateral treaty to Berlin. Beneš did so, sending his draft via Mastný: it merely reaffirmed the mutual obligations arising out of the Arbitration Treaty of 1925 and the Kellogg Pact of 1928, outlawing war. All this was of course useless to Hitler because it left the existing treaty structure intact. When Haushofer reported to Hitler the latter showed little interest and resignedly Haushofer had to note in the margin of his minute: 'Reported to Fuehrer,

January 1937. Order received to delay matters. – To be carefully preserved.'

On 5 February 1938, the day after his dismissal as Foreign Minister, Neurath signed his last instructions to Eisenlohr.[1] These confirmed the continued validity of the German–Czechoslovak Arbitration Treaty of 1925: the question had been examined by the German Foreign Office and it had been decided that, unlike the analogous treaties with Belgium and France (which Hitler had torn up together with the Locarno Pact), the Arbitration Treaties with Poland and Czechoslovakia 'should be regarded...as still in force'. This might 'prove an inconvenient restriction on our freedom of action', added Neurath; on the other hand, abrogation of the treaty would in the present circumstances cause an international sensation, which was most undesirable since (this was, of course, not mentioned in the instructions) it would have made the German plans for aggression all too obvious. Eisenlohr was however to avoid any further acknowledgement of the continuing effectiveness of this treaty.

This admission, from a competent authority, that Germany was still bound to submit any conflict with Czechoslovakia to arbitration, definitely proves that Hitler's later actions – at first tolerated and then actively supported by Chamberlain and Daladier – ran counter to international law. Moreover, when Germany invaded Austria in March 1938, Goering as well as Neurath (the latter in the name of his absent successor Ribbentrop) solemnly assured the Czechoslovak Minister in Berlin that German action was concerned solely with Austria and was not going to affect Czechoslovakia in any way.[2] Mastný, of course, hastened to convey these statements to Prague where Czechoslovak diplomacy, with London's help, tried to tie Berlin down to this 'guarantee'.[3] At their trial at Nuremberg after the war both Goering and Neurath claimed that their

---

[1] Neurath to Eisenlohr, 5 February 1938, *Documents and Materials relating to the Eve of the Second World War* (Moscow 1948), I, 46–9.

[2] Eisenlohr to G.F.M. 12 and 13 March 1938, Note by Neurath, 14 March 1938, Note to Mackensen, 16 March 1938, *DGFP*, D/II, nos. 72, 74, 78 and 85.

[3] Note by Neurath, 14 March 1938, Woermann (German Embassy, London) to G.F.M. 15 March 1938, *DGFP*, D/II, nos. 81 and 84, cf. Neville Chamberlain's statement in the House of Commons of 14 March 1938, *Parliamentary Debates (Hansard)*, vol. 333, cols. 50–1.

declarations could only be regarded as valid within the context of the circumstances at the time, i.e. the occupation of Austria.[1]

'Clearing up the Czech question'
Even before Hitler informed his Generals on 5 November 1937 that his immediate aim was 'to overthrow Czechoslovakia and Austria simultaneously', using the expression 'assault upon the Czechs'[2] (*Überfall auf die Tschechei*), detailed plans had been drawn up for such an attack; they cannot be explained away on the grounds that a General Staff must be prepared for every eventuality. In June 1937 the German War Minister Blomberg, hardly on his own initiative, had signed a 'Directive on the Combined Preparation for War of the Wehrmacht',[3] which began with the remarkable admission that 'Germany need not take into account an attack from any side'. This was tantamount to saying that German rearmament was not intended for purposes of defence. Nevertheless, according to Blomberg, 'constant preparedness for war on the part of the German Armed Forces' was necessary in order to 'meet attacks at any time and to be able to exploit militarily any favourable opportunity that may offer itself'. Plans were made for 'Operation Red' based on the West, and 'Operation Green' based on the South-East. Having expressly denied that Germany was in any danger of attack, Blomberg defined the aims of 'Operation Green' as follows:

With the object of warding off an imminent attack by a superior combination of enemy forces, the war in the East may begin with a *surprise German military operation against Czechoslovakia*. The necessary conditions to justify such an action politically and in the eyes of international law [*sic*] must be created in advance... The task of the German armed forces is to make preparations in such a way that the whole weight of all forces *can invade Czechoslovakia quickly and unexpectedly, and with the utmost force*... The aim and object of the surprise attack... must be – defeating the enemy armed forces and occupying Bohemia and Moravia – to eliminate from the outset and for the duration of the war the

---

[1] *Judgment of the International Military Tribunal for the Trial of German Major War Criminals* (hereafter *IMT*), Cmd. 6964 (London 1946), p. 19; *The Trial of German Major War Criminals*, part II (London 1946), pp. 3, 228; V (London 1946), 118; IX (London 1947), 106–7; X (London 1946), 50–1; XVII (London 1948), 130–1, 186; XIX (London 1948), 305–6, 468; XXII (London 1950), 427.

[2] See p. 160.

[3] Nuremberg Document C175, *Documents on International Affairs, 1939–46*, I (London 1951), 7–13.

Czech threat to the rear of operations in the West and to deprive the Russian air force of the most important of its bases in Czechoslovakia.

The 'final aim' was to conquer Czechoslovakia in a short time by exploiting her ethnic divisions. It was therefore merely a question of 'exploiting' the internal difficulties of the country for the purpose of subjugating her, not in order to 'liberate' those fellow-Germans who were alleged to be cruelly oppressed.

Hitler's 5 November Directive resulted in a 'Supplement' (dated 7 December) to Blomberg's Instructions of June which emphasized that 'Operation Green' now had priority. The intention to attack was openly admitted, although the troops were to be left in the dark about the actual date. Some days later followed an appendix to the 'Supplement', a new Directive which declared with quite unusual brutality that an aggressive war was planned:[1]

When Germany has achieved complete preparedness for war in all fields, then the military conditions will have been created for carrying out an *offensive war against Czechoslovakia* so that the *solution of the German problem of living space* can be carried to a victorious end, even if one or the other of the Great Powers intervene against us...Should the political situation not develop, or only develop slowly, in our favour, then the execution of 'Operation Green' from our side will have to be postponed for years. If however a situation arises which, owing to Britain's aversion to a general European war...creates the probability that Germany will face no other opponent than Russia on Caechoslovakia's side, then 'Operation Green' will start before the completion of Germany's full preparedness for war.

The military objective was always 'the speedy occupation of Bohemia and Moravia with the simultaneous solution of the Austrian question in the sense of incorporating Austria into the German Reich'. In detail the operation was to run as follows:

The bulk of the field army is to be employed in the attack on Czechoslovakia... The aim is a *strategic and sudden attack* on Czechoslovakia properly *prepared in peacetime*...The bulk of the *Luftwaffe* will be committed against Czechoslovakia.

In General Jodl's diary an undated note, presumably made just after the occupation of Austria,[2] quotes Hitler as saying that after the incorporation of Austria 'he is not in a hurry to clear up the

---

[1] Directive by Supreme Commander of the *Wehrmacht*, 21 December 1937 (Germany's Preparations for War), *DGFP*, D/VII (London 1957), no. 634.
[2] Document PS-1780, *IMT*, XXVIII, 495.

Czech question'. Austria had to be digested first, but preparations for 'Operation Green' were to be pushed forward 'energetically' and to be adapted to the changed circumstances. Provision was still to be made for 'exploiting militarily any favourable political opportunity' and 'Britain's aversion to a general European war' had put 'Operation Green' into the foreground even before Austria was fully digested.

On 21 April the matter was again discussed by Hitler and Blomberg's successor, Keitel.[1] From the political point of view three possibilities for 'clearing up the Czech question' were envisaged, none of them – needless to say – peaceful. The first, a 'strategic attack out of the blue without any cause or possibility of justification', was rejected; it would have created world-wide hostility which 'could lead to a serious situation'. Equally undesirable was the second choice of 'action after a period of diplomatic discussions which gradually led to a crisis and to war': this would give the opponent time to prepare. There remained only the third possibility: 'Lightning action based on an incident (for example the murder of the German Minister in the course of anti-German demonstrations)'. *Faits accomplis* must convince foreign powers of the hopelessness of any military intervention. Since Berlin was quite aware that the Czechs were unlikely to oblige the Germans by murdering their envoy, it must have seriously considered having him murdered by German 'volunteers' and blaming the Czechs for the crime. A German military order of August 1938[2] speaking of the 'timing of the incident' seems to confirm this theory.

On 20 May 1938 Keitel submitted to Hitler a new draft of the Directive for 'Operation Green'.[3]

It is not my [i.e. Hitler's] intention to smash Czechoslovakia by military action in the immediate future without provocation, unless an unavoidable development of political conditions within Czechoslovakia forces the issue, or political events in Europe create a *favourable opportunity which may perhaps never occur again.*

It was thus a rather different formulation of the old idea of acting with lightning speed on the basis of a (prearranged) incident and the exploitation of the prevailing situation.

[1] Note by Schmundt, 22 April 1938, *DGFP*, D/II, no. 133.
[2] See p. 242.
[3] Keitel to Hitler, 20 May 1938, *DGFP*, D/II, no. 175.

Czechoslovakia in Nazi foreign policy

The May 1938 Crisis

Although Hitler's decision on 5 November 1937 to destroy Austria and Czechoslovakia could not be known, the reference in his Reichstag speech on 20 February 1938 to the 'ten million unredeemed Germans in the adjacent States', followed within less than a month by the occupation of one of these States, could leave no doubt in any one's mind that it would be Czechoslovakia's turn next. Can one deny in these circumstances that Czechoslovak defence preparations were anything but desperately urgent measures necessitated by the Nazi menace and by no means a 'provocation which Hitler could not tolerate'? What really happened in the May crisis of 1938, still so often discussed?[1] To the historian W. V. Wallace it was

clear...that before the May crisis nothing had been further from the Czechoslovak Government's mind than a military demonstration. In so far as it considered military matters at all, it had been in terms of Hitler's possible intentions ...The May crisis was of Hitler's making.

The first news of German troop movements against or near Czechoslovakia did not come from Czechoslovak, but from British observers, and Sir Nevile Henderson, the British Ambassador in Berlin, sent them on to London. Henderson is notorious for having fallen prey to the most ludicrous illusions about Hitler and he was thus the last person to take mere anti-German rumours seriously. The fact that the first news about German troop concentrations reached the British and not the Czechoslovak Government was confirmed by the Foreign Secretary, Lord Halifax, when he informed the Cabinet on 22 May:[2]

In the evening of May 19th reports were received from H.M. Consulate Offices at Munich and Dresden to the effect that German troops were concentrating in

[1] The account given here is based primarily on the following publications and their respective sources (generally the published German and British diplomatic papers), R. G. D. Laffan, *The Crisis over Czechoslovakia, January to September 1938* (*Survey of International Affairs, 1938*, vol. II) (London 1951); Gerald L. Weinberg, 'The May Crisis, 1938', *Journal of Modern History*, (September 1957), pp. 213–25; Boris Celovsky, *Das Münchner Abkommen von 1938* (Stuttgart 1958); W. V. Wallace, 'The Making of the May Crisis of 1938', *Slavonic and East European Review* (June 1963), pp. 368–90; Henderson B. Braddick, *Germany, Czechoslovakia and the 'Grand Alliance' in the May Crisis, 1938* (Denver 1969).
[2] *Cab. 23/93*, no. 25 (1938), meeting of 22 May 1938.

Southern Silesia and Austria and that leave has been suspended for Sunday, May 22...According to the latest information available at the War Office in London, units of 11 German divisions have been traced moving towards the frontier in Bavaria and Saxony and one class of reservists had been called up in Leipzig.

This by itself would demolish any theory that the Czechs deliberately carried out a provocative though partial mobilization which jeopardized peace. It is not known whether Czechoslovakia based her actions solely on information from Britain or whether she had her own sources too.[1] What created most alarm was the fact that – in contrast to the secrecy normally surrounding such manœuvres – Leipzig newspapers published reports during the critical periods of troop movements, even though they were said to be small.[2]

Not surprisingly Prague suspected that there was more behind it and Krofta telephoned to Eisenlohr on 20 May to express his Goverment's concern about German troop concentrations in Saxony. Eisenlohr considered his alarm unjustified but promised to make enquiries. The British Ambassador in Berlin who called on the State Secretary Weizsäcker on the same day was told that the whole story was 'pure nonsense' and a similar reply was given by Weizsäcker to Mastný, who also mentioned troop movements in Silesia and Lower Austria. A courteous tone prevailed in these talks, but it changed when Mastný called on Ribbentrop shortly afterwards. The German Foreign Minister indulged in threatening tirades, accusing the Czechs of inventing the stories because they themselves were pursuing military plans:

If the existence of such tactics were to be confirmed, they could have only one result with the German Government, that these troop concentrations...would take place with *lightning speed*...I left the Minister in no doubt that the present development of the Sudeten German problem might lead inevitably to the most serious consequences.

[1] The Czechoslovak collection of documents relating to Munich, *Mnichov v dokumentech*, II (Prague 1958), 44, contains two reports about alleged German troop movements, but mentions Bavaria only. There is no indication as to whether other reports were available nor whether the Czechoslovak Government based its decision on these two reports.

[2] Cf. *Leipziger Tageszeitung* of 18 May 1938, 'Call-up for Active Service in 1938', and two days later a report about a reinforcement of the Zeitz garrison as well as an appeal for 'Volunteers for the *Luftwaffe* and Signal Troops'. The *Leipziger Neueste Nachrichten* reported on 19 and 20 May that the Zeitz garrison had been reinforced by the 1st Battalion of no. 11 Infantry Brigade, and this is also mentioned in the *Neue Leipziger Zeitung* of 20 May 1938.

Mastný's report home about this menacing attitude must have influenced the decision of the Government in Prague which was then in session with Beneš presiding. On the same day the SdP, on a flimsy pretext, broke off the sham negotiations it had been conducting with the Czechoslovak Government about a fresh approach to the country's problems: no doubt this again was due to collusion with Germany. The Czechoslovak General Staff which was after all responsible for ensuring the country's safety, demanded that five age-groups of reservists should be called up. On the strength of German explanations that all reports of German troop movements were 'pure nonsense' the Prague authorities decided to call up only one class and some specialist troops.

It seems likely that in May 1938 Hitler was not yet ready to make his planned 'assault' on Czechoslovakia, yet grounds for suspicion remain: 'categorical German assurances' did not remain categorical, and what was brushed off as 'pure nonsense' became 'routine exercises' or 'peace-time manœuvres'.[1] There is one feature which is even more striking: on the evening of 20 May Basil Newton, the British Minister in Prague, telegraphed to London that the latest reports of the Czechoslovak General Staff stated that the 7th and 17th German Infantry Divisions were marching in the direction of the frontier between Bavaria and Bohemia. On 16 May Hitler's adjutant Schmundt had asked Zeitzler (later Chief of the German General Staff) which divisions could be mobilized against Czecho-slovakia within twelve hours and Zeitzler had submitted a list the next day in which the 7th and 17th Divisions were shown first and second.[2] It would seem that the Czechoslovak General Staff received reliable though incomplete information emanating directly from German General Staff sources.

Nor is it without significance that Newton now strongly supported the Czechoslovaks *vis-à-vis* London. Since coming to Prague in 1937, he had not only loyally carried out the appeasement in-structions sent to him from London, but he had sincerely believed

---

[1] 'It is true that during the present spring period troops in the whole of Germany are being sent to training camps and that there, or on the way there, they are holding exercises.' Weizsäcker to Eisenlohr, 24 May 1938, *DGFP*, D/II, no. 206.

[2] '7th, 17th, 10th, 24th, 4th, 14th, 3rd, 18th, 8th PZ (Panzer) and Geb. (Moun-tain troops)'. Zeitzler to Schmundt, 16 May 1938, *IMT*, xxv, 419.

them to embody the right policy. He now judged correctly what was happening: the Prague Government, he wired home on 24 May,

were surely not only within their rights in taking such counter-measures, but they owed it to their own population to do so. To have waited might not only have been an unjustifiable risk, but it might in the long run have made inevitable the taking of still more 'provocative measures'.[1]

The German Government could not seriously maintain that the call-up of one age-group of reservists constituted an act of aggression towards Germany. Earlier Newton had already pointed out that the attitude of Prague was guided neither by chauvinism nor despair: the Government was perfectly stable. No responsible Czech could wish now or in the future to bring matters to a head.

It is interesting in this connection to consider Neville Chamberlain's reaction to the crisis of May 1938. According to his biographer, Chamberlain, notorious for his illusions about Hitler, made the following entry in his diary on 28 May:[2]

I cannot doubt in my own mind (1) that the German Government made all preparations for a coup, (2) that in the end they decided, after getting our warnings, that the risk was too great...But the incident shows how utterly untrustworthy and dishonest the German Government is.

Prague was determined to deal with provocations quietly. On the day after mobilization in Czechoslovakia, two SdP couriers had been recklessly tearing along the road from Cheb to Františkové Lázně (Franzensbad). When the gendarmerie tried to stop them the men drove on. Shots were fired which killed them although the gendarmes had been aiming only at their tyres. It is understandable that the SdP would want to organize an impressive funeral for the two men. But that was not all: the German Military and Air Attachés were present in their official capacities and laid wreaths on the coffins in the name of the Fuehrer, complete with swastika-decorated crêpe. This challenge to the sovereignty of an independent State was ignored by the Czechs, thanks to Anglo-French pressure.[3]

Even Eisenlohr seems to have lost his head during those hectic days. He reported on 23 May that 'Beneš and the General Staff,

[1] Newton to Halifax, 24 May 1938, *DBFP*, 3/1, no. 304.
[2] Keith Feiling, *The Life of Neville Chamberlain* (London 1946), p. 354.
[3] 'The red ribbons on the wreaths bear the plain name Adolf Hitler in gold letters. Above it is the swastika and the symbol of the Fuehrer's banner.' (*Die Zeit* (Prague), 26 May 1938.)

in agreement with the French, against opposition from their own Government, had ordered military measures...to demonstrate the solidity of the French alliance even at the risk of letting loose a war in Europe.' He had, however, sent a sensible warning to Berlin on the 21st, advising the Nazi authorities 'for the present against application of German measures, since no threat of any kind to Reich security exists'. He also tried very soon to make amends for his mistaken assessment of the situation on the 23rd: he had learnt 'from a completely reliable source' that as late as 19 May Beneš had attached no importance to the reports about German troop movements and had given no thought to military counter-measures: it was only after British warnings had reached him that, on the 20th, he changed his mind. 'The decisive factor confirming the view that Czechoslovakia was militarily threatened by Germany came from London and not from Prague. According to the above account the part played by Beneš appears to me in a somewhat more favourable light than it had hitherto done. He is not the instigator but partly the victim of a deception.'

Ribbentrop was, of course, less conscientious than his envoy in Prague. According to his own notes, in two discussions with Sir Nevile Henderson on 21 May he reviled the Czechs as 'people of an inferior race' (*minderwertiges Volkstum*) who 'day after day were spilling the blood of defenceless Germans'. Henderson reporting to London added something quite different: the German Foreign Minister had said that the Czechs would be 'exterminated, women, children and everybody'.

At Berchtesgaden Hitler studied the draft for the execution of 'Operation Green' and informed Keitel on 23 May that while the basic plan would remain unchanged, the element of surprise was to be brought out more sharply and the defensive fortifications in the west 'hurried on'. Sometimes after the 21st Jodl noted in his diary that Hitler's intentions had undergone a change as a result of the 'Czech operation of 21 May'. This is the only available and not very convincing evidence for the hypothesis that Hitler was influenced by the partial Czechoslovak mobilization: he had, after all, already decided on aggression. In reality things remained as arranged, as one can see in the directive to Keitel. According to Jodl, Hitler received Henlein on the 22nd, no doubt to brief him

191

for his interview with Hodža on the following day. After his return to Berlin Hitler held a conference on 28 May at which he repeated his contentions of 5 November 1937. Erich Kordt, Ribbentrop's *chef de cabinet*, obtained a full report from one of those present at that meeting, where Hitler is said to have announced that Germany would have to be militarily ready within two months: 'I shall then proceed to smash Czechoslovakia'.[1] Two unexpected results of Prague's decision may have caused his special wrath: the precision with which the Czechoslovak mobilization (in which Sudeten Germans as well as Czechs had taken part) had proceeded and then the fact that Britain had shown surprising interest in the Czechoslovak situation.

On 30 May Hitler signed the revised version of the Directive for 'Operation Green' which now began with the much more characteristic words

It is my *unalterable decision* to smash Czechoslovakia by military means in the near future. It is the business of the political leadership to await or bring about the suitable moment from a political and military point of view.

This was followed by declarations similar to the previous ones on the exploitation of favourable opportunities, should they arise sooner, and of 'lightning' action. Since Hitler's decision to remove the Czechoslovak obstacle to his plans had been just as 'unalterable' before 21 May as it was afterwards, one gains the impression that he chose these words deliberately because of their mesmerizing effect on him. The draft for the new directive of 18 June stated that Germany was not threatened from outside. Hitler's immediate aim remained the 'solution' of the Czech question from 1 October onwards, although this was qualified by the words:

I shall however only decide to act against Czechoslovakia (*die Tschechei*) if I am firmly convinced...that France will not march and hence England will not intervene either.

While even that decision need not necessarily have been 'unalterable', it does provide grounds for the belief that by remaining firm instead of giving in again, Britain and France could at that late date still have prevented the catastrophe which the capitulation of

[1] Erich Kordt, *Wahn und Wirklichkeit* (Stuttgart 1948), p. 12; *Nicht aus den Akten...*(Stuttgart 1950), p. 228.

Munich meant not only for Czechoslovakia but for the Western Powers and the cause of democracy.

In all the discussions between Hitler and his Generals about the most opportune way to attack Czechoslovakia in time of peace, the existence of an Arbitration Treaty, which made a peaceful settlement of all disputes between the two States obligatory, does not seem to have been mentioned.[1] This appears to have caused misgivings even to the German Foreign Office and after Hitler had expressed his 'unalterable decision', expert opinion was expressed by Friedrich Gaus, the chief legal adviser, to the effect that Germany had made it clear to Czechoslovakia that she felt bound by the provisions of the treaty even though the Locarno Pact had been abrogated. 'After the matter had been submitted to the Fuehrer however, it was decided not to close the question in this way' (i.e. by denouncing the Treaty – for this would have made Germany's aggressive intentions patent to the world). The Memorandum's final conclusions left no doubt:

From the foregoing procedure it is obvious that, should the question become acute, Czechoslovakia could substantiate with strong arguments our express and repeated recognition of the continuing validity of the Treaty.

The Treaty of Arbitration places both States under the strict obligation to submit points of controversy of all kinds either to a Court of Arbitration or to a Conciliatory Commission. The political significance of this obligation lies above all in the fact that France and Czechoslovakia have...expressly confirmed a violation of Germany's obligation under the Treaty...as a *casus foederis*. It cannot be overlooked that the Treaty of Arbitration might have unfavourable repercussions in a conflict between Germany and Czechoslovakia, especially in so far as Germany's disregard of it would provide a convenient formal legal basis for a French intervention.

It was eventually recommended that, should a suitable opportunity occur, a statement that the 'applicability' of the Treaty was 'extremely doubtful', should be made, but this does not alter the fact that the German Foreign Office must have been aware that any action of the sort contemplated by Hitler, whether before or after 21 May, ran counter to the treaty obligations assumed by the Reich. A circular was subsequently sent to several German missions abroad in which they were confidently informed of the contents of

[1] Memorandum by Gaus of 13 June 1938, Circular by Weizsacker of 25 June 1938, *DGFP*, D/II, nos. 268 and 269.

the Memorandum and advised that 'even now' (25 June) an abrogation of the Treaty was not planned. But an abrogation of a treaty, even if unilateral, implies its previous validity.

In a sense, 21 May 1938 can be regarded as a turning point. Hitler's despotism and the Western Powers' complaisance caused Czechoslovakia's internal and external problems to merge. During the following months everything that happened on Czechoslovak soil was to become a world problem.

13 BRITAIN CAPITULATES TO HITLER

The occupation of Austria had made Czechoslovakia's military and political situation much more difficult. It would have helped if the Western Powers had uttered a firm 'Thus far and no farther' but nothing of the kind occurred. Conciliatory Czechs would have been willing to accept exhortations from the British and French Ministers[1] to make concessions to the Germans had it not been so obvious that what was in reality urged was surrender to Henlein and through him to Hitler. For example Basil Newton, the British Minister in Prague, had pressed Beneš in March 1938 to accept members of the SdP into the Government of democratic Czechoslovakia,[2] at a moment when the desertion, thanks to Henlein's intimidation, of the non-Socialist Activists into the SdP camp made the prospects for democracy in Czechoslovakia even gloomier. The continued existence of German Social Democracy thwarted Henlein's ambition to be recognized as the sole German spokesman in Czechoslovakia, though he did succeed in ousting the German Social Democrats from the Government.[3]

If in 1938 Prague had been familiar with the minutes of the British Cabinet and Cabinet Committee meetings of the time (in fact available for research only since 1969) Beneš would probably have given up all hope and capitulated in March or April 1938. In January 1938 the Cabinet Committee on Foreign Policy discussed suggestions for a 'general settlement' with the Third Reich. As a result instructions were sent to Sir Nevile Henderson, the British Ambassador in Berlin, signed by Anthony Eden, authorizing him to hint to the German rulers that even colonies could come their way if they

[1] During the short period of Blum's second Government (13 March – 9 April 1938) France affirmed her solidarity with Prague.
[2] Newton to Halifax, 20 March 1938, *DBFP*, 3/1 (London 1949), no. 100.
[3] See p. 172.

behaved.[1] These instructions were signed and despatched on 12 February, the day Hitler was blackmailing Schuschnigg at Berchtesgaden. They were not countermanded even when part of the truth about this encounter became known in London. Consequently on 3 March Henderson tried his best to interest Hitler in the British proposals – with no success whatsoever. A few days before he resigned as Foreign Secretary, Anthony Eden had submitted a memorandum to the Cabinet Committee on Foreign Policy called 'German contribution to General Appeasement'[2] in which in all seriousness the following suggestion regarding Czechoslovakia was made:

Germany should be asked [as a contribution to 'General Appeasement! *Author's note*] to conclude with Czechoslovakia an arrangement analogous to the German–Austrian Agreement of July 1936 and to the German declaration to Belgium of October 1937.

These far-reaching proposals had not been discussed with the Czechoslovak Government at all, just as at Munich the Great Powers unilaterally partitioned her. The German–Austrian 'Agreement' of 11 July 1936[3] had first opened the door to the acceptance of Nazis (Seyss-Inquart and Glaise-Horstenau) in official positions and later made possible the German invasion under the pretext of an alleged call for help from Seyss-Inquart. Hitler's promises to respect the neutrality of Belgium[4] in exchange for that country's abrogation of her alliances with Britain and France were not worth the paper on which they were written. For the British Government, however, they were a shining example applicable to Czechoslovakia even though the latter's Foreign Minister had always angrily rejected suggestions that the country should go 'the Belgian way'. Moreover, Eden's memorandum contained a statement of principles taken over from a policy statement of October 1937 then prepared for the British Ambassador in Berlin but shelved:

[1] Eden to Nevile Henderson, 12 February 1938, *Cabinet Committee on Foreign Policy*, F.P. (36), *Cab*. 24/627, no. 52.

[2] Memorandum by Secretary of State for Foreign Affairs, F.P. (36), *Cab*. 24/627, no. 51.

[3] Text in *DGFP*, D/I, no. 152.

[4] German Note to Belgium, 13 October 1937, *Documents on International Affairs 1937* (London 1939), pp. 190–1. For Krofta's statement (22 October 1936) that Czechoslovakia 'cannot and shall not follow Belgium's example' see *Survey of International Affairs 1936* (London 1937), p. 284.

It would not be our intention, in discussing this problem with Germany, to imply that we regard the present territorial disposition in Central and Eastern Europe as rigid and unchangeable for all time. But we should make it clear that we would not condone any change in the international status of a country achieved by force against the will of the inhabitants, or any forcible interference in its internal affairs. Any change in the existing situation, if such is necessary must in our view be a change negotiated between the Governments concerned.

The last part of the last sentence is the only safeguard against a sell-out in the Munich fashion, but the rest of this statement is a foretaste of Munich. This signified a remarkable change in Eden's outlook, for his Private Secretary noted in his diary[1] a discussion in Eden's office a year earlier dealing with Czechoslovakia when the consensus of opinion among those present had been not to urge Czechoslovakia to conclude an agreement with Germany 'as Beneš might interpret this as encouragement to desert from France and Russia or as committing Great Britain to stand by him if negotiations failed'. The same source quotes Eden's defence of the Foreign Office (8 November 1937) against Chamberlain's complaints that it 'never made a genuine effort to get together with dictators. Eden said it was useless and impossible to do so unless and until we were strongly armed.' Nothing had changed between November and February, Britain was still not armed, but it was now thought possible to tell Hitler that the *status quo* could be changed in his favour. In Eden's formula he could even have seen connivance at a planned forcible occupation of Austria, because in Hitler's eyes such a step would not have been contrary to the will of the inhabitants.

All Neville Chamberlain's naive expectations that Hitler or Henlein would 'not go so far' as to insist on autonomy for the Sudeten Germans were obvious fallacies, for the British Government had been told *expressis verbis* what Hitler's real intentions were. A German anti-Nazi whose semi-official function enabled him to travel freely and to speak to well-informed people in Germany reported regularly to the Foreign Office what he had seen and heard. Ernst Jäckh, who brought these reports, was regarded as trustworthy

[1] *The Diplomatic Diaries of Oliver Harvey 1937–1940* (London 1970), pp. 18–19, 58.

by British diplomats.[1] Ernst Woermann, a German career diplomat who in spite of formal membership of the Nazi Party was not one of Hitler's blind followers, was Chargé d'Affaires in London in January 1937 and told Jäckh in confidence and perhaps with the hope that he would warn the British that 'in a few years time Germany would have to attack Czechoslovakia in order to penetrate into the Danube basin. She would not, however, do this until she had assured herself of Great Britain's friendship. She would be prepared to risk French and Russian intervention as long as we [Britain] stood aloof.' In March 1937 Jäckh hurried to tell the Foreign Office that in conversation with him, Neurath, the German Foreign Minister, had said Czechoslovakia '*esse delendam*'. In September 1937 Woermann told Jäckh that the Czechoslovak situation could 'not be considered as permanent' – the alleged 'oppression' of the Sudeten Germans was never mentioned. In March 1938 Woermann was even more outspoken. Slices of Czechoslovakia would go to Germany, Poland and Hungary. The rest would hardly be able to continue an independent existence, and so it would be best to partition it between these three states. 'Such a policy might lead to a world war, but that depended on Great Britain. Hitler's task was to prepare the situation and choose his time so that Great Britain could be kept out.' So the British statesmen could be in no doubt of the situation. They preferred to ignore the warnings.

After the invasion of Austria it was not difficult to see that Czechoslovakia was the next target. The Foreign Office tried in vain to induce the Government to issue some sort of warning to Hitler.[2]

On 20 February, immediately after Hitler's occupation of Austria, Lord Halifax, who had become Foreign Secretary on Eden's resignation submitted a memorandum entitled 'Possible measures to avert German action in Czechoslovakia' to the Cabinet Committee on Foreign Policy.[3] After discussing the various possibilities he

[1] Survey of information submitted by Ernst Jäckh, September 1938, *Foreign Office Files* (*The Sudeten Crisis*), F.O. 371, vol. 21714.
[2] Harvey, *Diplomatic Diaries*, p. 116.
[3] Text as App. 1 in *Cabinet Committee on Foreign Policy*, F.P. (36), *Cab.* 24/623, pp. 181–94.

came to the conclusion that as far as Britain was concerned nothing could be done. France was committed by treaty to come to Czechoslovakia's aid if Germany attacked. Great Britain was committed by the Locarno Pact to come to the assistance of France if attacked by Germany, but there was no corresponding obligation to France in the case of that country declaring war on Germany following an invasion of Czechoslovakia. A solemn, strong and unambiguous British declaration to join France in such a case even without a treaty commitment would in all probability have had the effect of deterring Hitler, at least for the moment. Many people were asking for such a declaration, because they saw in it the minimum of deterrent necessary after Hitler had been allowed to swallow Austria. Halifax admitted in his memorandum that a new British commitment 'might considerably reduce the danger of war', but it was too great a risk for him. Halifax's unwillingness to do anything is even more unbelievable because in his memorandum he showed he had no illusions about Hitler's intentions, namely to incorporate Czechoslovakia into Germany – 'passing perhaps by way of some kind of intermediate autonomous régime'. He suggested Prague should be pressed to introduce just such a régime!

In the Foreign Secretary's opinion the Czechs would have to treat the Sudeten Germans in a way which 'will leave the German Government with no reasonable cause for complaint'. This was written on the day of Hitler's march into Austria. Schuschnigg too had tried his hardest to 'leave the German Government with no reasonable cause for complaint'. Instead of a new British commitment Halifax wanted Czechoslovakia to come to an 'agreement' with Germany 'rather earlier than later'. The reasoning in Halifax's memorandum was only another way of saying that his Government had already written Czechoslovakia off. If she could be induced to make concessions, it was said, it would be difficult for Germany

to enforce a solution of the question since in that event Germany would have less reason to risk the hazards of war in order to obtain what she could have some hope of obtaining by peaceful means.

When the Cabinet Committee on Foreign Policy discussed Halifax's memorandum on 18 and 21 March 1938[1] Sir Thomas

[1] F.P. (36), *Cab.* 24/623.

Inskip, Minister for the Co-ordination of Defence, confessed that he 'could see no reason why we should take any steps to maintain such a unit (Czechoslovakia) in being'. Inskip also asked the Prime Minister whether he had some information about German intentions: would they be satisfied with taking over the Sudeten German territories only or did they want to absorb the whole of Czechoslovakia. Neville Chamberlain answered:

The seizure of the whole of Czechoslovakia would not be in accordance with Herr Hitler's policy, which was to include all Germans in the Reich but not to include other nationalities.

To Chamberlain it seemed likely that Hitler wanted to absorb the Sudeten German territory and to reduce the rest of the country to a 'condition of dependent neutrality'. This was said at a secret meeting of a Cabinet Committee and certainly represented the Prime Minister's real view. It was, therefore, absurd when thirty years later Lord Butler, who was not present at that meeting, tried to vindicate the honour of his then leader in these words:[1]

He (Chamberlain) was fully aware... that the Sudeten problem might not be the real issue and that Hitler might have ambitions far beyond the restoration [sic] of Sudeten rights.

Or did perhaps Lord Halifax suspect Hitler of bigger ambitions when he said at the meeting on March 18, 1938:

If... a satisfactory solution of the Sudeten problem was reached we might offer in that event to join with Germany in guaranteeing Czechoslovakia's independence.

Whereupon Neville Chamberlain exclaimed:

If Germany would obtain her *desiderate* by peaceful methods there was no reason that she would reject such procedure in favour of one based on violence.

At the next meeting of the Committee Chamberlain decided to tell the French that Britain would not accept additional commitments:

The German view appeared to be that if the Germans in Czechoslovakia were guaranteed autonomy in cultural and other matters... a satisfactory solution might be reached, and that Germany would respect Czechoslovakia's independence, provided the Sudeten Germans were accorded real equality of treatment.

[1] Lord Butler, *The Art of the Possible* (London 1971), p. 65.

At the same time (20 March) Chamberlain developed his ideas in a letter to his sister.[1] After saying that he had abandoned any thought of guaranteeing Czechoslovakia because that country just could not be saved, he described what he would like to say to Hitler:

The best thing you can do is to tell us what you want for your [*sic*] Sudeten Germans. If it is reasonable we will urge the Czechs to accept and if they do, you must give assurances that you will let them alone in the future.

To this he added an expression of his willingness in such circumstances 'to join in some joint guarantee with Germany of Czech independence'. A month later he told the French Ministers that Hitler would either not give a guarantee or would not feel bound by it...

The whole matter was then discussed by the full Cabinet[2] and on 22 March it approved the ambiguous declaration Neville Chamberlain was to make in the House of Commons two days later. The limits of Britain's legal commitments were stated, but it was indicated that there might be situations forcing the country to go beyond them. This could be misunderstood and has been misunderstood. Exactly one week after the occupation of Austria Halifax warned the Cabinet against any 'policy involving a risk of war'. Lord Halifax believed or pretended to believe he had a better recipe, namely to 'induce the Government of Czechoslovakia to concentrate on producing a direct settlement with the *Sudetendeutsch*' who for him were identical with the Henleinists. The French should be persuaded to support British pressure in Prague.

In addition, it might be possible for the British and French Governments to approach the German Government with a view to acceptance of the settlement in Czechoslovakia.

This ingenious idea was accepted by the Government after Chamberlain had referred to a report of the Chiefs of Staff Sub-committee according to which British help would not prevent a Czechoslovak defeat in war: 'All this showed that if a decision was taken to guarantee Czechoslovakia, we should be in a most dis-

---

[1] Middlemas, *Diplomacy of Illusion*, p. 188.
[2] *Cab.* 23/93, Minutes 15 (38), 18 (38) and 21 (38), Meetings of 22 March, 6 April and 27 April 1938. Partly quoted by Ian Colvin, *The Chamberlain Government* (London 1971), pp. 112–13.

advantageous position when we came to implement it.' Yet at the Munich Conference Chamberlain, who refused to guarantee the well-protected frontiers of Czechoslovakia did not hesitate to extend a British guarantee to a defenceless Czechoslovakia.

At one of the next Cabinet meetings of 6 April Lord Halifax suggested a 'joint approach to Dr Beneš' to satisfy Henlein, though he added 'it was clear that Dr Beneš and his Government were doing their utmost' to meet German demands. He did not suggest a *démarche* in Berlin in the form of a warning, but regarded it desirable 'also to say something in Berlin as to the genuineness of Czechoslovak efforts'. He was, however, quick to produce arguments against any such activities, namely that 'we should exercise some caution in allowing Dr Beneš to draw us into expressing an opinion as to the details of his proposals'. Consequently, the Cabinet followed his advice and decided that 'however reasonable those proposals might be, Herr Hitler might want more'.

The draft of Halifax's letter to the British Ambassador in Paris, asking him to secure French collaboration in bringing pressure to bear on Prague, underwent some interesting changes. The version of 8 April[1] still envisaged a settlement leaving Czechoslovakia at least formally intact. It would certainly have been difficult to get French approval for anything else. Accordingly the draft spoke of 'steps to settle the problem of the German minority, and indeed of the other minorities in Czechoslovakia on lines which offer some hope, at least of a peaceful solution within the present frontiers of the Czechoslovak State'. Even Henlein's dependence on Berlin was explained as a favourable factor:

the fact that he (Henlein) has closer relations than hitherto with the National Socialist leaders in Germany would make it more likely than before that any agreement reached with him would not be regarded with disfavour by the German Government.

When the Foreign Office learned that Léon Blum's Government, in which Paul-Boncour was Foreign Minister, had fallen the letter was redrafted and the reference to a solution within the existing boundaries eliminated. Georges Bonnet, the new Foreign Minister,

[1] First and second draft of Foreign Office communication to Phipps (Paris), 24 March and 8 April, in *Foreign Office Files* (*The Sudeten Crisis*), F.O. 371, vol. 21714. Final text (Halifax to Phipps, 11 April 1938), *DBFP*, 3/1, no. 135.

obviously seemed more amenable to ideas of appeasing dictators. Now nothing more than the hope was expressed of reaching 'a settlement of the German minority problem by direct negotiations with Herr Henlein or with those who spoke for him'.

A few days after Henlein had proudly proclaimed that National Socialism inspired all his feelings and thoughts (see below) Lord Halifax reported to the Cabinet Foreign Office information on that point: 'Henlein was more and more coming under the influence of Herr Hitler.' That he never had been under any other influence had been obvious to British correspondents in Prague but not to British diplomats.

As a result of British pressure, the Prague Government accepted Henlein's party as a political partner. It began with a speech by Hodža, the Premier, in which he announced[1] that the Government was to elaborate a 'Minority Statute' with the aim of assembling and improving all the various regulations concerning the national minorities. Hodža then announced that the new code would be called 'Nationalities Statute',[2] a term which implied that the true character of the state was multiracial. This was not enough to placate the SdP whose principle had always been to ask for more than could be conceded. So it is not surprising that nothing came out of the first meetings of the Premier with SdP representatives at the beginning of April 1938.[3]

In the artificially overheated atmosphere which followed the occupation of Austria it would have been a Herculean task to create the conditions necessary for serious negotiations, even if the SdP had been willing to accept a settlement. The Czechs, for their part, were ready to be conciliatory, thanks rather to the exigencies of the situation than to their own insight. Beneš had told the British Minister that 'he had long held that Czechoslovakia could not be a national State, but he had to educate the Czech Parties, especially those over which he had most influence'. In the Cabinet it was

[1] *Prager Presse*, 29 March 1938, Newton to Halifax, *DBFP*, 3/1, no. 103.
[2] Chief of the *Wehrmacht* High Command to German Foreign Ministry, 8 April 1938, *DGFP*, D/11, no. 121. Newton to Halifax, 8 April 1938, *DBFP*, 3/1, no. 131.
[3] Notes by Kundt on discussion with Hodža, 1 and 6 April 1938, *G.F.M.* serial 2369, frames 494409–12.

already realized that his programme (i.e. the Nationalities Statute) meant the end of the conception of a National State.[1] It has already been explained that while the country was never officially designated a 'National State', the bureaucratic practice had generally been to regard it as such, i.e. to favour the Slavs. It has been shown too that Beneš[2] was convinced from the beginning that Czechoslovakia would have to rely on the co-operation of all her ethnic groups. How far could Prague go without seriously jeopardizing her own freedom as well as the whole cause of democracy? To what limits were the Western Powers, unwilling or unable to understand that Hitler and the SdP were not interested in any concessions but in destroying Czechoslovak democracy, prepared to go to exert pressure on Czechoslovakia? The British Minister in Prague seemed to be in two minds about it. While certain of his reports recommended the neutralization of Czechoslovakia as 'the least evil', others[3] showed that the truth had dawned on him. He had discovered that the real issue was not the improvement of the position of an allegedly discriminated minority what mattered:

Even so apparently innocent a demand as that for cultural autonomy for the Sudeten Germans could, for example, be used, if granted, for the wholesale introduction of *Mein Kampf* as well as of a swarm of National Socialist propagandists to influence and organize the Sudeten German population. It is partly on account of this fear that any genuine concession is merely the thin end of the wedge, which, apart from a temperamental obstinacy, renders the Czechs so determinedly uncompromising...

Probably to reassure London, the Prague Government sent a memorandum in April explaining the principles of Czechoslovak policy regarding the minorities in the past and future.[4] The Czech majority of the country had always been aware, it was said, that the State was not, and could not be, racially homogeneous:

The Czechoslovak majority never had a pure National State in mind; its ideal had always been the democratic State, guaranteeing justice to all citizens and hence also to all nationalities.

The memorandum then pointed out how meticulously the political

[1] Newton to Halifax, 22 April 1938, *DBFP*, 3/I, no. 154.
[2] See p. 61.
[3] Newton to Halifax, 12 April 1938, *DBFP*, 3/I, no. 140.
[4] Memorandum on the Nationality Policy of the Czechoslovak Republic, handed over by Jan Masaryk on 26 April 1938, *DBFP*, 3/I, no. 160.

institutions corresponded to ethnic distribution and that the Germans in Czechoslovakia had proportionally more German schools than the Germans in Germany. Fairer arrangements in proportional and general representation of the minorities in the administration were promised but a territorial division along racial lines was rejected.

Henlein openly professes National Socialism

Henlein's long speech at the main session of the SdP rally at Karlovy Vary on 23 and 24 April 1938 was a retrospective survey full of half-truths, downright lies and tendentious distortions, culminating in what was really an ultimatum to the Czechs.[1] He started by implicitly asserting that everything the Germans had owned in 1918 was theirs by right – which would have given them completely unjustified privileges in the new State. The Czechs, Henlein claimed, would have to revise their 'erroneous historical myths', and, for good measure, abandon their idea of being a bulwark against the 'so-called' German expansion to the East (*Drang nach Osten*); he also called for a change in foreign policy 'which has hitherto lined the Czechs up with the enemies of the German people'. Putting it more bluntly, he demanded that the Czechs capitulate before aggressive German nationalism and surrender their defences. Besides this 'treble revision' the Government must unconditionally fulfil the following eight demands before Henlein would be prepared to discuss peace:

1. The establishment of full equality of right and status between the German *Volksgruppe* (ethnic group) and the Czech people in the State.
2. The recognition of the Sudeten German *Volksgruppe* as a legal person (*Rechtspersönlichkeit*) to safeguard this equal status in the State.
3. The demarcation and delineation of the area of compact German settlement.
4. The establishment of German local government in the German area, to cover all aspects of public life as far as the interests and affairs of the German *Volksgruppe* are concerned.
5. The provision of legal protection for those citizens who live outside the confines of their ethnic group.
6. The removal of injustices done to the Sudeten Germans since 1918 and compensation for damage suffered as a result of these wrongs.

[1] The passages quoted are taken from the brochure *Der Lebenswille der Sudetendeutschen* (Karlsbad 1938), containing the text of the speeches delivered at the Karlovy Vary rally on 23 and 24 April 1938.

7. The recognition and realization of the principle: German public officials in the German area.

8. Full freedom to profess membership of the German race (*Volkstum*) and the German outlook on life (*Weltanschauung*).

Apart from the last point, which, divested of its nationalist jargon, simply meant freedom to adhere to the tenets of National Socialism, there were, doubtless among these demands many issues about which negotiations between a democratic party and a democratic government would have been possible. But in each formulation, however harmless-sounding, there was a carefully concealed totalitarian trap. There was no need to demand 'full freedom to profess membership of the German *Volkstum*' – no one in Czechoslovakia had denied the Germans the right to regard themselves as Germans – but in its coupling with the ambiguous '*Weltanschauung*', by which of course the Nazi 'outlook' was meant – the right to deny freedom to those who thought otherwise – lay the real *hubris*. Here Henlein threw off his last mask. In 1934 he had, in order to deceive both Czechs and British, pretended to have 'fundamental reservations' against the principles of National Socialism.[1] Now he asserted that the Sudeten Germans no longer wished to stand aloof from a creed 'which all Germans in the world embrace with joy'; even more explicitly, he said:

Like the Germans all over the world we too acknowledge the National Socialist interpretation of life which inspires all our feelings and thoughts and in pursuance of which we wish to build the life of our national group.

In various speeches on 1 May 1938 Henlein drove home his Karlovy Vary declarations by emphasizing that they were his *minimum* demands.[2]

We are Germans [he said], and because we are Germans, we profess the German, that is the National Socialist way of life.

The German Minister in Prague, however, even used this occasion to urge Berlin not to push matters too far. Having warned Berlin before against the formulation of a programme of territorial autonomy,[3] Eisenlohr no longer dared condemn Henlein's Karlovy Vary demands. He did however try to base his argument for a peaceful solution on the acceptance of Henlein's vague reference to

[1] See p. 118.   [2] *Die Zeit*, 3 May 1938.   [3] See p. 150.

a settlement 'within the framework of the law'. He had to tread warily:[1]

> The most important factor for a peaceful development...seems to me Henlein's explicit declaration that in putting forward his demands he had not been guided by the intention to burn all bridges, for both in the Sudeten camp and in the Czech camp, and also abroad, the opinion has gained ground that the Henlein Party was conducting only mock negotiations (with the Government) but intended to step up its demands in order to make an agreement impossible.

It had been decided on 28 March that Henlein should act in exactly this way. Hitler's orders were that 'demands should be made which were unacceptable to the Czech Government.' Eisenlohr had not been present at that meeting, but might have heard of this formula and only played the rôle of the uninformed when warning:

> If the correctness of this assumption were confirmed, it would be impossible for the Czechoslovak Government to persuade its own people of the need to be conciliatory. The SdP would lose the moral support of world opinion, particularly in England, and the tension between Sudeten Germans and Czechs would reach such a degree that an acute danger of an explosion would arise...Anglo-French pressure will make it easier for the Czechoslovak Government to persuade the parties of the Czech Left to make concessions. Thus it could be expected without exaggerated optimism that, when the excitement of the local elections is over, a continuation of the negotiations – provided both sides are really sincere – could achieve a transformation of this State into a community where the various nationalities enjoy equal rights. Sensible representatives of the Czech Left are ready for it. Time would then have been gained, the dangerous tension decisively relieved and the State in its new form could prove whether, in the face of the action of the diverging centrifugal forces, it can remain viable.

One cannot but respect Eisenlohr's efforts. He was after all Hitler's representative in Prague but he had the courage to present unpalatable warnings to his master.

Daladier and Bonnet in London

A week after the Karlovy Vary meeting a conference of British and French Ministers took place in London at which the Czechoslovak problem was high on the agenda. The published minutes make embarrassing reading.[2] After this outspokenness at Karlovy Vary

---

[1] Eisenlohr to G.F.M. 3 May 1938, *G.F.M.* serial 3653, frames 033003-5.

[2] Record of Anglo-French Conversations held at 10 Downing Street, on 28 and 29 April 1938. *DBFP*, 3/1, no. 164 (passages referring to Czechoslovakia on pp. 212–34).

there could no longer be any doubt that Henlein had lied to his British hosts in London. The real question in Czechoslovakia was not sectional aspirations but the outright demand, clearly directed against Anglo-French interests, that Czechoslovakia should desert the defence front against Nazi Germany. The French on this occasion – Daladier and even his Foreign Minister Bonnet, later a determined appeaser – saw things in their true light, but their British partners Chamberlain and Halifax remained blissfully optimistic. Daladier openly stated that Henlein was not going to be restrained by any sort of concession: his real aim was the destruction of Czechoslovakia. The British, however, rejected all French proposals to embark on a more determined course of action. Chamberlain did not even hesitate to put forward contradictory excuses for his inactivity. He pinned all his expectations on exerting pressure on Prague (which involved no risk to London) but when the French suggested that Hitler be approached to give an undertaking not to break off negotiations, Chamberlain rejected this as useless. Hitler would not give any guarantees or, if he did, he would ignore them. This was in sharp contrast to the appeasers' trust in Hitler's word, but it did not betoken a change of heart; it was only a sign of their disinclination to do anything. Lord Halifax was appalled when he realized how great the differences were between the proposals of the Prague Government and Henlein's 'postulates' but instead of coming to the only correct conclusion, i.e. that Hitler and Henlein would never be satisfied with piecemeal concessions, he did exactly the opposite by suggesting increased pressure on Prague. Henlein's demand for freedom to pursue Nazi activities shocked neither the French nor the English. No matter how far the British and French Governments diverged in other respects, they were united in their decision to 'press' Prague, although even here there was an essential difference. France wanted this intervention in order to be able to say that everything possible had been done, while Britain clung to the illusion that Central Europe would be pacified if Prague made enough concessions to Henlein. The outcome of the meeting was meagre. It was agreed to intervene jointly in Prague and to ask Berlin to exert a moderating influence on the SdP. Should the Germans refuse, attention was to be drawn to the dangers which violence might produce.

The results of the London Conference were brought to Berlin's notice by the British Ambassador with the utmost circumspection. Their impact was of course nil. Ribbentrop replied, in a blustering speech, with a flat refusal to influence the SdP.[1] There was no need to show any such consideration in Prague. Krofta, the Foreign Minister, was urged by Newton to be more conciliatory toward the SdP and told that the military possibilities of aiding Czechoslovakia were slight.[2] The French Minister, who called separately, at least spoke of concessions which would not affect the integrity of the state.[3] Since Krofta did not appear compliant enough, Newton repeated his arguments to Hodža and to Beneš.[4]

The British Cabinet was informed on 5 May of the discussions with the French.[5] Lord Halifax mentioned the decision to put pressure on Prague but could not say that pressure would also be brought to bear on Hitler. Moreover, even the fact that the German Government was to be asked to restrain the SdP was not mentioned by Halifax. Most probably he feared that some Cabinet Ministers would be frightened. But he added: 'It would be very useful if the Germans would tell us at some time *what would satisfy them.*' This glorious idea was immediately taken up by the Prime Minister who supported the Foreign Secretary with the words, he 'wanted, if possible, to get the Germans to say *what kind of settlement would be acceptable*'.

Henlein's last visit to London

Eisenlohr had to explain to Newton, his British counterpart in Prague, that the latter's idea of 'neutralizing' Czechoslovakia was absurd.[6] Such a plan might work for Switzerland, said Eisenlohr, but not in a country surrounded on three sides by Germany. It thus fell to a German diplomat to demonstrate the fallacy of their

---

[1] Note by Ribbentrop, 11 May 1938, *DBFP*, D/11, no. 154. Henderson to Halifax 12 May 1938, *DBFP*, 3/1, no. 206.
[2] Newton to Halifax, 9 May 1938, *DBFP*, 3/1, no. 195.
[3] Georges Bonnet, *Défense de la Paix, De Washington au Quai d'Orsay* (Geneva 1946), p. 120.
[4] Newton to Halifax, 10, 17, and 18 May 1938, *DBFP*, 3/1, no. 200,223, 226,227 and 229.
[5] *Cab.* 23/93, Minute 22(38), Meeting of 5 May 1938.
[6] Newton to Halifax, 10 May 1938, *DBFP*, 3/1, no. 201.

views to the British, but the British remained obdurate. Towards the end of May Halifax wanted to make the idea of 'neutralization' more palatable to Jan Masaryk, the Czechoslovak Minister in London, by trying to persuade him that 'this might be represented as the contribution of the Czechoslovak Government to the peace of Europe'.[1] Shortly before, obviously inspired reports appeared in the American press affirming that British foreign policy was in favour of ceding the Czechoslovak border areas inhabited by Germans.[2] That the source of these reports was 10, Downing Street was never denied.

If the slogan of a 'stab in the back' was ever justified, this was the occasion. Czechoslovak democracy was slowly and pitilessly abandoned. Henlein was invited to speak in London again although his Karlovy Vary demands had been a frank enough admission that he had been hoaxing the British for years. Before his departure for London he assured the German Foreign Office that 'he would deny in London that he is acting on instructions from Berlin'.[3] In this case he was as good as his word, particularly in a four-hour talk with that renowned 'expert' on German questions, Sir Robert Vansittart. Did Vansittart recognize now that his previous favourable reports on Henlein were based on a misjudgment of the man? Vansittart, who had issued many warnings of Nazi intentions, was still incurably blind in Henlein's case, though the speech in Karlovy Vary had made him suspicious for a short time. 'Henlein's speech of last night', he wrote, 'may be regarded...as showing that he is completely in the hands of the German Nazi Party.'[4]

But this seems to have been quickly forgotten. Vansittart not only encouraged Henlein, who in his opinion was 'completely in the hands of the German Nazi Party', to come to London, he even wrote behind the back of the Foreign Secretary to the Prime Minister

[1] Halifax to Newton, 25 May 1938, *DBFP*, 3/i, no. 315.
[2] In an unpublished essay 'Czechoslovakia and Germany, 1933–45', G. L. Weinberg quotes from the papers of the former Secretary of State, Cordell Hull, deposited at the Library of Congress, a report by the head of the London United Press Bureau, who heard Chamberlain himself express this view. (Reprinted here by kind permission of Prof. Weinberg, University of Michigan.)
[3] Note by Weizsäcker, 12 May 1938, *DGFP*, D/ii, no. 155.
[4] Memorandum Vansittart, 25 April 1938, *Foreign Office Files* (*The Sudeten Crisis*), F.O. 371, vol. 21716.

recommending that he receive Henlein's aristocratic helper Max Hohenlohe. On 12 May 1938, Sir Alexander Cadogan, Vansittart's successor as Permanent Under-Secretary at the Foreign Office, noted[1] (*for* Van *read* Vansittart, *for* H Halifax):

Went to see Horace Wilson [Chamberlain's adviser] about message I had from PM [Prime Minister] as to suggestion he had received that he should talk to Hohenlohe, who might influence Henlein. (I had found out that the 'suggestion' came from Van) Horace showed me letters from Van to PM, in which former said he had been approached by Henlein, who wanted to come over here, that he had spoken to H, who approved. (H. said nothing to me about it) and that he had therefore answered encouragingly. I said I didn't see any positive harm, and if Henlein had been encouraged it might be bad now to put him off.

The next day Cadogan again had something to say about Henlein in his diary:

Press now have it that Henlein is here. Talked to Rab Butler [at that time, Parliamentary Under-Secretary of State, Foreign Office] about it, and he saw Van and told him not to press Henlein too hard...(Rab) says Henlein's points should be a basis for discussion. (This better than I expected) So I don't want Van to tell Henlein to come off his eight points altogether: that will go straight back to Berlin, who will think we are double-crossing them...Corbin [French Ambassador] at 4.15...impressed that French *must* press Czechs, and that delay is dangerous.

Henlein's 'eight points' included the recognition of National Socialism (currently demonstrating its brutal methods in Austria) in a democratic State, but Foreign Office Ministers and officials considered that *all* these eight points could and should form a 'basis for discussion'. There seem to have been no reproaches when Vansittart met Henlein again. Had he reproached Henlein for his earlier denials of Nazi leanings, Vansittart would surely have taken care to record it, but there is no mention of it in Vansittart's notes on his talk with Henlein. (These notes were published eight years before Vansittart's death, but he never commented on their publication.) It seems that he regarded his long conversation with Henlein as his private affair, because only four days later, after promptings from Halifax he submitted a report upon it with the words:[2] 'These are my impressions from the Henlein visit, for which

[1] David Dilks (ed.), *The Diaries of Sir Alexander Cadogan 1938–45* (London 1971), p. 76.
[2] Note by Vansittart, 17 May 1938. Original in *Foreign Office Files* (*The Sudeten Crisis*), F.O. 371, vol. 21719 (containing unpublished note for Halifax).

you asked yesterday.' From the reproduction of this remarkable document the editors of the publication omitted the first sentence. It ran as follows:

I have been on very friendly terms with Herr Henlein for some years past and have seen him frequently during his visits to London.

Vansittart claimed to have told Henlein that

I had of course noticed that he had of late been no longer ostensibly the moderate Henlein whom I had known and appreciated in previous years. He (Henlein) said that he had always been the apostle of conciliation

and Vansittart, swallowing this blatant lie,

hastened to assure him that I knew this to be true...He is indeed under considerable pressure...but...I retained the general impression...that I was, as in previous years, speaking to a wise and reasonable man. I found Herr Henlein far more reasonable and amenable than I had dared to hope...we parted on terms as friendly as ever.

It is obvious that Vansittart still had not grasped that ever since 1933 Henlein had been nothing but Hitler's tool. Vansittart surpassed himself by concluding that 'we have now a real chance...if only the Czechoslovak Government will take the opportunity'. The same idea reappears in another note rather more prudently expressed, which was published in a book based on Vansittart's posthumous papers:[1]

'If only the Czechoslovak Government will take the opportunity,' reflected Sir Robert, 'We shall be helping both Herr Henlein and ourselves by putting really strong pressure on Berlin not to interfere with any acceptable solution.'

At long last pressure in the right place was envisaged, though in a context which was a travesty of the real situation. What Vansittart reported to the Foreign Secretary was even worse and reflects an amazing lack of judgment. Vansittart must have known that Henlein had lied to him over all those years when protesting that he had nothing to do with National Socialism. In spite of this Vansittart again gave credence to his lies in May 1938. Lord Halifax told the Cabinet about it:[2]

Published text in *DBFP*, 3/1, App. II. (The discussion with Henlein took place on the 12th, in the course of a dinner party.)

[1] Ian Colvin, *Vansittart in Office* (London 1965), p. 209. Colvin also notes that Sir Alexander Cadogan had assured him that ' "Van" was soon cured of his illusions' about Henlein. This is not borne out by events.

[2] *Cab.* 23/93, Minute 24(38), Meeting of 18 May.

Vanstittart had formed two conclusions from his conversation: first, that Dr [sic] Henlein had *no instructions from Berlin* and second, that Dr Beneš could get an agreement of a useful character if he would only act quickly.

As a civil servant Vansittart cannot be made responsible for the foreign policy of the Government he served, but he must take the blame for the absurd advice which he gave them. He seems to have taken particular pride in his astuteness in warning Henlein against getting involved in foreign policy and demands to compensate the Sudeten Germans for losses allegedly sustained since 1918; he advised him to leave both issues alone. Nor should Henlein expect, Vansittart said, that he would be permitted to build a Nazi State within a democracy. Henlein pretended to be convinced: he had in fact received valuable hints on what to avoid saying in order to continue enjoying British patronage.[1]

---

[1] Vansittart's public references to Henlein after the war were few and prevaricating. On 15 June 1953 a letter from Vansittart appeared in *The Times*. In it he put forward the unconvincing excuse that he only tried to disillusion Henlein of any idea 'that England was not interested in the Czechoslovak crisis' and maintained that he had always warned him. This is contradicted by Vansittart's own notes of October 1937, published for the first time in the present book. A few days after his letter to *The Times*, Vansittart's former colleague Sir Walford Selby drew attention to the evasive character of Vansittart's account and asked about his negotiations with Henlein in October 1937 (*The Times*, 20 June 1953). Lord Vansittart preferred to ignore this challenge. In his posthumously published autobiography (which describes events only up to 1936), *The Mist Procession* (London 1958), Vansittart recalls 'when Henlein came into view as their [the Sudeten Germans'] Leader, a dreary gymnast. The Czechs suspected what I found out later – that he was in Nazi pay... When I did find out, Henlein's monthly subsidy was 15,000 Mark, not much on which to run a Movement' (p. 470). There is no evidence in Foreign Office files that Vansittart ever found out anything about Henlein's backers, and Henlein was not restricted to a monthly subsidy of 15,000 mark – quite a big sum for Czechoslovak conditions. He had in fact received over 330,000 mark to cover his election expenses in 1935, more than any other Czechoslovak party had at its disposal for this purpose (see p. 120.) In his earlier book, *Bones of Contention* (London 1945), Vansittart said: 'I spent some time during his [Henlein's] visits here trying to frighten him and to keep him from contact with British appeasers. He was however too poor a figure to be anything but a German stalking-horse, groomed for the crisis of 1938' (p. 111). In a broadcast of 1948 Vansittart recalls that 'a stalwart friend of mine got hold of Henlein, the *Sudetendeutsche* leader, and kept him on a string while I told him that Britain and France would fight, and war would flatten his Sudetenland. We hoped that he and his master, Hitler, might be put off. Then we turned him over to Mr Churchill. Unfortunately Henlein got off the string sufficiently to see the appeasers who undid our handiwork.

Vansittart was also instrumental in arranging meetings between Henlein and three politicians who were opposed to appeasement: Churchill, the Liberal leader Sir Archibald Sinclair and Sir Harold Nicolson, then a Member of Parliament. To Churchill[1] Henlein 'offered to give his word of honour that he had never received orders or even recommendations (*Weisungen*) from Berlin'. He also developed proposals relating to autonomy which could not have been more innocuously worded. Nicolson had met Henlein before and had shown, in a letter to the Foreign Office, that he failed to see through him. He called Henlein[2]

a serious and reliable person, and one whose control over the Bohemian Germans is a thing which, I imagine, we and France desire to maintain.

That, indeed, was in 1936 and in the meantime Henlein had openly acknowledged his allegiance to National Socialism. This *volte face* did not deter Nicolson from entering in his diary on 13 May 1938:[3]

I give a tea party...for Henlein, I have invited Spears, Mark Patrick [Cons. M.P.], Duncan Sandys, Macnamara [Cons. M.P.] and Godfrey Nicholson. Henlein arrives at 4.40 followed by Press men. We all sit around, have tea, have sherry and talk till 6.40. Henlein tells us (1) that his ideal solution would be a direct arrangement between himself and the Czech Government, giving local autonomy to the Sudeten Germans within a defined area. Such autonomy would cover all local interests but would not affect federal interests such as finance, foreign affairs and defence. Similar autonomy would be given to the Hungarian, Polish and Ruthenian minorities. This cantonal system would be absolutely democratic and upon an electoral basis. (2) That should these direct negotiations fail, then he would be prepared to accept an international commission and a plebiscite upon the Saar precedent. He would not wish to join Germany, although many of his followers desire it. If both (1) and (2) fail, he sees no alternative but German occupation which he well knows means war.

We tell him that British opinion will probably support his (1) and (2) but will turn against him if he makes demands which are impossible of fulfilment. For instance, we do not understand certain points in his Karlsbad speech such as

---

By then, too, Hitler had taken the measure of Britain and France' (Lord Vansittart, 'A Morally Indefensible Agreement', *The Listener*, 4 November 1948). The allegedly 'stalwart' friend was no doubt Colonel Christie. Henlein spent the evening of 13 May in the company of ten unnamed persons, to whom Vansittart's observation might well apply (*The Times*, 14 May 1938).

[1] Churchill's note about his meeting: *DBFP*, 3/1, App. II, pp. 633–5. See also his reference in *The Gathering Storm* (*The Second World War*, vol. 1), p. 223. Churchill's interpreter on this occasion was Prof. Lindemann (Lord Cherwell).

[2] Nicolson to Strong, 14 February 1936, *Foreign Office Files* (*Czechoslovakia*), F.O. 371, vol. 20373.

[3] Harold Nicolson, *Diaries and Letters 1930–1939* (London 1966), pp. 340–1.

that in which he claims a directing voice in Czech foreign policy and that in which he expressses sympathy for a Nazi *Weltanschauung*. He explains the first by saying that what he meant was that the Sudetens could not approve of a pro-Russian and anti-German policy and would claim the right to protest against attack upon Germany. But they did not claim more than to voice their opinion in this respect. They did not claim to overrule the majority. On the second point he said that they approved of the social and class legislation of the Nazis, but not their anti-God and antisemitic measures.

What is so amazing is not the impudence of Henlein's lies, which were in glaring contrast to demonstrable facts, but that these lies were swallowed without protest by British intellectuals and Members of Parliament. Even the way in which Nicolson formulated his query revealed his fundamental inability to grasp the seriousness of the situation: Henlein had never merely expressed 'sympathy' for the Nazi *Weltanschauung*; he had *identified* himself fully with it as inspiring 'all our feelings and thoughts'.

While he was in London Henlein also called on Jan Masaryk at the Czechoslovak Legation. The latter reported to Prague[1] that Henlein had assured him of his willingness to come to an understanding. The Karlovy Vary speech had been forced on him by events in Austria and the excitement of his own followers. He wished Masaryk to believe that he remained loyal to the State and would proceed democratically...One lie more or less was no longer of much consequence.

On the day Henlein played his rôle as 'moderate' *vis-à-vis* Vansittart, Hodža again received a delegation from the SdP. He informed them that the draft of the Nationalities Statute was almost ready and that it would be discussed with the SdP and other interested parties and then laid before Parliament. It appears that the SdP delegation sent back a report containing the following characteristic sentences:[2]

The decisions are to be taken at the end of June 1938. The following suggestion is therefore the only practicable one; when the SdP receives the Nationalities Statute, it will reject it as inadequate for negotiations and instead submit its own

[1] See Robert Kvaček, *Osudná mise* (Fateful Mission) (Prague 1958), p. 27. A similar report was sent by the U.S. Ambassador in Britain (Kennedy to Hull, 14 May 1938, *Foreign Relations of the United States, 1938*, I (Washington 1955), 498–500).

[2] Kvaček, *Osudná mise*, p. 49, quoting from the files of the post-war trials of the SdP members.

autonomy proposal. If this is turned down, Konrad Henlein will demand a plebiscite. The moment Henlein raises this demand, unrest will break out. This can then be prevented only if the Great Powers, to whom Henlein will turn for support, act at once and give their approval, or if the Reich acts at once. *For us there can be no question of a peaceful settlement within the framework of the Czechoslovak State.*

Eisenlohr was no doubt unaware of this plan, but he summarized it quite accurately, *sub rosa*, in the disguise of a report on a meeting he had with Hodža:[1]

Do the leaders of the Sudeten German Party desire the settlement (*Ausgleich*) on the basis of equality of rights, or *will they only make a pretence of negotiating and keep raising new demands so as to make an agreement impossible*, and then call for help from the Reich? This is the question that is being put forward everywhere by the press, by politicians and by diplomats. And it is suspected by the overwhelming majority that the question is to be answered in the negative, as conversely it seems generally to be assumed that the Sudeten German Party only acts on instructions from the Reich Government and that every point in Henlein's Karlsbad speech has been dictated by Berlin.

In a discussion with the SS leader Werner Lorenz, the head of the *Volksdeutsche Mittelstelle* (a secret agency, giving directives to 'Germans abroad'),[2] Henlein was no less frank than his 'negotiating delegation': no disguise was required here. Henlein asked for advice on what to do 'if the Czechs...suddenly concede all my demands and present, as counter-demand, entry into the Government?' – but before this would be answered he came forward with his own suggestion which apparently found favour in Berlin: 'If the Czechs yield on all points, I shall answer "Yes" with the demand that the foreign policy of Czechoslovakia be modified. The Czechs would never accede to that.' In fact, Henlein had already urged a change in Czechoslovak foreign policy although he had decided for the time being to keep this demand in the background.

It has already been shown that Henlein never really thought of negotiating,[3] but this was confirmed again by a Berlin journalist

[1] Eisenlohr to G.F.M. 13 May 1938, *DGFP*, D/11, no. 158.
[2] Note by Lorenz, 3 June 1938, *DGFP*, D/11, no. 237.
[3] Middlemas (*Diplomacy of Illusion*, pp. 242 and 253) alleges Czech unwillingness to negotiate with Henlein, while the SdP 'appeared willing to resume the interrupted negotiations'. Later on the 'Sudeten leaders' had allegedly 'resumed negotiations', while 'Prague continued to be unreasonable'. This is a complete travesty of the truth. No attempt is (or could be) made to substantiate these amazing allegations.

called Lojewski who had been in Prague at the beginning of June 1938. He reported to the German Foreign Office about a meeting with Wilhelm Sebekovsky, who was in charge of the SdP press:[1]

Dr Sebekovsky...is looked upon as the intellectual leader of the extremist wing of the Sudeten German Party, which is pressing for direct action by the Reich as soon as possible. Dr Sebekovsky therefore counts at present as the most essential man in the Party, the *éminence grise* who prepares the interviews which Konrad Henlein gives...In answer to my explicit enquiry he explained that the present negotiations with the Prague Government could only be regarded as a tactical game. The strategic line was fixed, it is to join the Reich. Anything else was a mere manœuvre and subordinate to this aim.

Whenever in his internal memoranda Vansittart insisted on firmness in dealings with the Third Reich – and he did that frequently – Lord Halifax paid no attention. But when he recommended acting in favour of Henlein, he found willing ears and his advice was immediately taken up. Sir Nevile Henderson, the British Ambassador in Berlin, had sent an optimistic report and Vansittart contradicted him with common-sense:[2]

It is a delusion to believe that 'once the Sudeten problem was settled, Germany would be a saturated State'. Events just won't work out that way.

This was ignored and when although maintaining his own illusions about Henlein, Vansittart issued warnings about dealing with Germany a few days later, the warnings were brushed aside and the private illusions transformed into official political actions.[3] When Britain had shown for once some firmness in the May crisis he wrote:

The best way to deal with Germany is firmness. The last days have shown that it pays and that no other method does...It is, however, now of first-class importance to put renewed pressure on the Czechs to come forward and meet Henlein quickly. Herr Henlein is now in urgent need of having his hand strengthened and it would be profitable to anybody if we did the strengthening. The message received from his friend this morning was that only we can do so owing to our own friendliness to him and the interest that we have always taken in the *Sudeten Deutsche* question. In a word, the Germans have got their tail

[1] Lojewski to Aschmann, 7 June 1938, *G.F.M.* serial 1977, frame 439165–76.
[2] Henderson to Halifax, 12 May 1938, *DBFP*, 3/1, no. 208. Note by Vansittart, 20 May 1938, *Foreign Office Files* (*The Sudeten Crisis*), F.O. 371, vol. 21719.
[3] Memorandum by Vansittart for Halifax and note by Halifax, 23 May 1938, *Foreign Office Files* (*The Sudeten Crisis*), F.O. 371, vol. 21721. Halifax to Newton, 23 May 1938, *DBFP*, 3/1, no. 293.

down, though only for the time being. If Mr. Beneš will be constructive, he ought with any fortune to find the *Sudeten Deutsche* more accommodating, for of course they are well aware that Germany is beginning to back down. If, however, Mr Beneš does not come forward quickly, the crisis may boil up again if Germany feels that her face is not being saved.

Vansittart was probably the only person who believed Hitler might back down in the days when he was in fact formulating his 'unalterable decision' to destroy Czechoslovakia, but Lord Halifax immediately wanted from Vansittart and Cadogan suggestions for 'any further action we can usefully take at Prague'. The same day a telegram went to the British Minister in Prague saying that it looked as though Berlin' intends to go slow for the time being', but advising Prague 'to come forward with the most generous offer and attempt to clinch a settlement'.

When the British Ambassador in Berlin reported some stories about Communist influence in Prague[1] which he had heard from Neurath, the former Foreign Minister, Vansittart again partly warned against and partly spread illusions:

The Germans should not be allowed to get away with this poisonous and silly stuff. The more they think they can make us swallow it, the more likely they are to try to press Henlein away from moderate demands.

Henlein might not have known or understood that in 1938 Vansittart was no more the leading official of the Foreign Office: Chamberlain had arranged that he be 'kicked upstairs' into insignificance by making him 'Chief Diplomatic Adviser to His Majesty's Government' on 1 January 1938.[2] He still, however, had the ear of the Foreign Secretary, and through Vansittart's private intelligence service Henlein communicated with the Foreign Secretary until the beginning of August 1938, presenting in the service of Hitler the most fantastic inventions which were promptly taken as undeniable facts. Henlein's emissaries came with personal messages for Vansittart and went back with his answers. The Foreign Secretary only received translated extracts from Vansittart who later carefully destroyed all traces of his contacts with Henlein

[1] Henderson to Halifax, 27 May 1938, *DGFP*, 3/1, nos. 323 and 324. Note by Vansittart, 29 May 1938, *Foreign Office Files* (*The Sudeten Crisis*), F.O. 371, vol. 21722.
[2] Harvey, *Diplomatic Diaries*, pp. 63–4.

and his friends – not a single line of it has survived in the 'Vansittart papers'.[1] Only the names of two of the intermediaries can, thus, be established. One of them was Henlein's permanent London representative Walter Brand. Perhaps more important was the Bohemian aristocrat Max Hohenlohe, an owner of large estates whose English education and impeccable manners obviously made a big impression on the British diplomats he met. Vansittart never seems to have found out that he was one of the most skilful Nazi agents. There might have been other intermediaries. Vansittart took everything they submitted at its face value and on Vansittart's advice so did Halifax. They never even considered the possibility that these constant complaints about alleged Czech intransigence might have been tactical steps in Hitler's strategy. They always believed that in helping Henlein they prevented Hitler from carrying out his plans.

On May 26 Vansittart presented[2] a long personal message from Henlein full of lies and culminating in the peremptory demand 'Please ask the British Government urgently through your friends to make the strongest representations in Prague before it is too late.' Vansittart conceded that Henlein perhaps exaggerated 'the guilt of the Czechoslovak Government' but recommended that his advice be accepted because otherwise he might be 'driven away from his London attitude and proposals on to his second line of demand, i.e. for a plebiscite, which it was well realised was more unobtainable and much more dangerous'. This was all pure fantasy: Henlein had no first or second line of demands, he always did what Hitler needed at the moment. Nevertheless, the British Minister in Prague was alarmed by a telegram from the Foreign Secretary, fixing even the day when the Prague Government had to satisfy Henlein:

You should therefore make immediate representations to the Czechoslovak Government in the light of this knowledge, without revealing its source, and make it clear that a definite and concrete proposal on Saturday [28 May] is absolutely indispensable for the prospects of an acceptable and therefore peaceful solution.

[1] The author was able to study the Vansittart papers, deposited in Churchill College, Cambridge, by kind permission of Lady Vansittart.

[2] Memorandum by Vansittart for Halifax, 26 May 1938, *Foreign Office Files* (*The Sudeten Crisis*), F.O. 371, vol. 21723. Halifax to Newton, 27 May 1938 (unpublished telegram in same volume).

Czechoslovakia before Munich

On 31 May Vansittart could report again that one of Henlein's associates had come to London for two interviews with him.[1] Predictably, the emissary said that everything would be all right in Prague if Beneš were to stop making difficulties. In Vansittart's words the visitor had brought 'the repeated and most explicit assurances from Herr Henlein that he abode by all he had said to me in London'. He would make no demands in the field of foreign policy or compensation. 'The point about (Nazi) *Weltanschauung* would not be unduly pressed or stressed.' So not even Vansittart said it would be abandoned; nevertheless his conclusions were that as far as Henlein was concerned 'these points can be considered to be eliminated from the Karlsbad speech'. Hence Vansittart's suggestion for 'pressing Dr Beneš very strongly, in conjunction with the French, to go ahead at once with the negotiations on the London line'. That even concessions on the imaginary London line would have meant the Nazification of a democratic state was not taken into account. On the contrary, Vansittart thought that an unfavourable reply from Prague would create 'an exceedingly bad impression here and nobody would believe that the question was sincerely tackled by the Czech Government'. On the same day Halifax informed Newton in Prague that the questions of foreign policy, reparation and *Weltanschauung* did not figure in the proposals and that Henlein had thus reduced his programme so that a reasonable compromise was possible, provided it was reached without delay. As if this were not enough, Halifax lost no time in inciting Paris against its Czechoslovak ally by urging 'energetic steps' – in Prague, not Berlin. The ground in France was now becoming more fertile for such seeds, as Bonnet had seen the Czechoslovak Envoy Osuský a few days earlier[1] in order to demand that Czechoslovakia come to an agreement with the Sudeten Germans *coûte que coûte*. Halifax's intervention assured Bonnet of British support in his appeasement of Hitler: he now talked to Osuský in an even more threatening way and gave him a memorandum to transmit to

[1] Memorandum by Vansittart for Halifax, 21 May 1938, *Foreign Office Files* (*The Sudeten Crisis*), F.O. 371, vol. 21723. Halifax to Newton, 21 May 1938, *DBFP*, 3/1, no. 353.

[2] Bonnet, *Défense de la Paix*, p. 156. Phipps to Halifax, 27 June 1938, Memorandum by Halifax, 9 July 1938, *DBFP*, 3/1, nos. 447 and 472.

Prague: the time was propitious (it said), Henlein had 'only' mentioned internal autonomy.

Newton, however, contradicted this cheap optimism by pointing out that the Karlovy Vary speech was being distributed in the original text in the form of a pamphlet. 'I fear,' he said,[1] 'that even if question of *Weltanschauung* does not figure in them [the demands] it would be rash to regard it as eliminated...For tactical reasons they may refrain from bringing up every point in first stage of negotiations.' One of the most impertinent inventions of Henlein in his communications with Vansittart was the fairy tale about the 'danger' of his replacement by the 'old' Sudeten Nazi Hans Krebs. In reality, Krebs, living in Berlin, had been banned by Hitler from all political actions and only tolerated as a minor official of the Ministry of Interior. As a blind follower of Hitler he never dared to interfere in matters reserved by Hitler for Henlein. Nevertheless Vansittart blindly accepted what Henlein wrote to him, and so Newton was informed in this sense:[2]

Have received information to the effect that Herr Krebs is trying by every possible means to oust Herr Henlein from the leadership and to drive him off his moderate policy. The pressure on Herr Henlein is so hard that it is necessary that he should score a personal success in his negotiations with Herr Beneš in order that he may be enabled to retain his moderating influence and personal position against the extremist.

In the middle of June Vansittart reported to Halifax that Henlein thought the situation would be 'immensely eased by a declaration of the (Prague) Government that they are negotiating on the double basis of the Nationalities Statute [the Government proposals] and the Karlsbad points'. Varsittart added: 'I see no reason why such a declaration should not be made, and we might suggest it to Dr Beneš.' Accordingly, a sentence was added to a prepared telegram to Newton:[3]

Any influence you may feel able to bring to bear on the Czech Government to

[1] Newton to Halifax, 7 June 1938, *Foreign Office Files* (*The Sudeten Crisis*), F.O. 371, vol. 21724.

[2] Memorandum by Vansittart for Halifax, 7 June 1938, Halifax to Newton, 10 June 1938, *Foreign Office Files* (*The Sudeten Crisis*), F.O. 371, vol. 21724.

[3] Memorandum by Vansittart for Halifax, 14 June 1938, and note by Ivo Mallet 'I have added a sentence to this effect to the draft telegram C5692'. *Foreign Office Files* (*The Sudeten Crisis*), F.O. 371, vol. 21724.

meet Henlein's...demands would no doubt improve the atmosphere for the negotiations.

And so it went on until the end of July 1938:[1]

They (the Nazi leadership) are pressing Henlein to work up sympathy for a plebiscite in Great Britain. Henlein, on the other hand, wants the present negotiations to succeed; he is against a plebiscite and *Anschluss*. He feels that success depends upon the broad acceptance of his eight points...Indeed, he can hardly accept less if he is to retain control of his own people...Henlein, Frank and others...hope inwardly the Great Britain and France will oppose the idea of a plebiscite...but...fear lest this should encourage further stubbornness on the part of Mr Beneš and lead to the rejection of their minimum demands...Henlein will certainly give us warning before he takes any such step [ask for a plebiscite because of Czech intransigence and lacking British support. *Author's note*]. (16 June)

There is clearly a case for further and pressing action on our part...Henlein has evidently lost faith in Beneš again...I urge strongly in any case pressing Beneš as urgently as we can. (21 June)

Henlein no longer trusts Hodža – this is disastrous...Judging from the lack of results up to date and from the amazing way in which the Czech Government is playing with fire, it would seem that Henlein's convictions are not far wrong... He says that he will have no alternative but to demand a plebiscite for an *Anschluss*...He says that he will have staked his faith on his friends in London for nothing (I in no way quarrel with him for saying this). Both he and his chief colleagues still want to avoid a plebiscite; they want a successful end of the present negotiations in spite of *Reich* opposition...We can now only hope to hold him by regaining his confidence, and this can only be done by showing that we really have the power to stop the Czechoslovak Government's clumsy trickery...Henlein no doubt overstates his case. The significant thing is that the moderate Henlein *should* be talking like that. (12 July)

What Hitler and Henlein did was not classified as 'playing with fire' or 'clumsy trickery' by Vansittart. These expressions were reserved for the desperate attempts of the Prague Government to evade in the interest of peace and world democracy what was demanded of them, namely to commit suicide. Whenever Hitler's lieutenant Henlein managed to approach the British Foreign Secretary with the help of Vansittart, his tactics of blackmail were successful: Newton in Prague always got instructions to intensify the pressure on the Czechoslovak Government to surrender to Nazi demands.

Let us now return for a short moment to the Czechoslovak scene.

[1] Notes by Vansittart, 16 June, 21 June and 12 July 1938, *Foreign Office Files* (*The Sudeten Crisis*), F.O. 371, vols. 21724, 21725 and 21727.

Although the local elections could not be postponed indefinitely, the decision to hold them during the crisis on the last two Sundays in May and on 12 June was an unwise one. As a result the campaign, particularly on the German side, was conducted entirely on a political plane, as if problems of local administration did not exist. In many of the smaller places intimidation by the SdP effectively prevented any but their own lists of candidates from being put forward – the necessary ten signatures for submitting a list of candidates could not be found among democrats, as people dare not identify themselves publicly with a political party opposing Henlein. As an illustration of the methods used by the SdP it may be mentioned that on the occasion of Henlein's fortieth birthday in 1938 the employers at Aš (where he lived) closed their factories and led their workers to pay homage to him.[1] In this atmosphere of fear and terror it was gratifying that about 12 per cent of the Germans voted against Henlein, mostly in favour of the Social Democrat candidates.

When the British Cabinet met on 25 May, the Foreign Secretary acquainted the other members with his new theory on the validity of military commitments.[2]

The British view was that a war would be unprofitable, and that was the French view also...The French engagement [the treaty with Czechoslovakia of 1925. *Author's note*] had been entered into many years ago in totally different circumstances, when Germany was still disarmed...It was desirable, therefore, if possible to obtain a release of the French from their obligations and its contingent consequences.

This meant that one should accept commitments only if no risk was involved in them, but that it was desirable to run away from them if the danger of having to do something arose. Just six weeks before this, Hitler had arranged a 'plebiscite' in Austria which had the result he wanted. Undeterred by this experience, Lord Halifax

---

[1] *Volkswille* (Karvoly Vary), 5 May 1938. The Henlein terror is described in a letter by W. Jaksch in *Manchester Guardian*, 15 June 1938, partly reprinted by Laffan, *The Crisis over Czechoslovakia*, pp. 154–5. Further details about intimidation are given by Alexander Henderson, *Eyewitness in Czechoslovakia* (London 1939), pp. 84–97.

[2] *Cab.* 23/93, Minute 26(38), Meeting of 25 May. See Colvin, *The Chamberlain Government*, p. 130. Halifax used the same argument about French treaty obligations on 25 May, when speaking to Jan Masaryk. See p. 210.

now started to play with the idea of a plebiscite on the future of the Sudeten Germans. He realized that this might be dangerous to Beneš. What he did not apparently realize was that, in the current situation, anything weakening or destroying Beneš' position was also dangerous to Britain and to world democracy.

If at some point a strong demand should be made for a plebiscite, he doubted if it could well be resisted with sufficient support from public opinion here. On the other hand, he also felt that for Dr Beneš to concede a plebiscite under German duress would be very damaging.

A few days after the German Minister in Prague had tried to explain to his British colleague that from a British point of view any idea of 'neutralizing' Czechoslovakia was wrong – this had been duly submitted to the Foreign Secretary – Lord Halifax found this 'solution' quite attractive:

He (Halifax) had been pondering, therefore, as to whether at some point Dr Beneš might not be well advised to make the best offer he could to the *Sudeten Deutsch*, but to add that he realised that the offer was of no use if large blocks of the citizens of the country were to remain discontented, and, consequently, that he would be willing to put to them the question as to whether they would prefer the settlement he offered or the *Anschluss* with [*sic*] Germany.

A second point which he thought was worthy of consideration was whether Dr Beneš might not work for a provisional settlement for five years, with a plebiscite at the end...He would, however, like to see the Czechoslovak State move into a position of neutrality which, like the neutrality of Switzerland, would be witnessed by the big nations concerned. Under such a system the alliances would automatically disappear.

Making the British position in Europe still more precarious! The Prime Minister hastened to add that he 'was thinking on these lines'. If the Germans, he said, could be 'satisfied' with the Czechoslovak State from the 'point of their foreign policy, it might be possible to get a settlement in Europe'.

Lord Halifax lost no time in making practical suggestions as to how Czechoslovakia could be neutralized. Phipps, the Ambassador in Paris, was asked to win over the French Foreign Minister[1] to a scheme which would leave intact the French and the Soviet commitment to come to the aid of Czechoslovakia against unprovoked aggression but would relieve Czechoslovakia of her contractual obligations to enter a war against Germany should France or the

[1] Halifax to Phipps, 17 June 1938, Phipps to Halifax, 18 June 1938, Campbell (Paris) to Halifax, 6 August 1938, *DBFP*, 3/1, no. 421, 429; 11, no. 601.

Soviet Union be involved in a military conflagration with her. It was the most naive attempt imaginable to snatch away from Hitler the argument of Czechoslovakia being 'the aircraft-carrier' of an allegedly aggressive Soviet Union, and this attempt was made behind the back of both Prague and Moscow (though it was hoped that with the help of France the Soviet Union could be induced to accept this proposal). Phipps did his best to explain the matter to Bonnet who first gave an evasive reply and, when pressed by his British allies, said 'no' to the whole proposal.

Here we must deal with an argument which the appeasers liked to use in their attempts to browbeat Prague. Even after a victorious war, they said, Czechoslovakia would hardly be reconstructed in the present fashion.

What therefore would be the use of a war? There was no logic at all in this reasoning; British firmness, instead of the weak policy of Chamberlain and Halifax, would in all probability have prevented war, not brought it about. Yet even if Hitler had attacked Czechoslovakia despite Britain's support for the principle of collective defence against unprovoked aggression, the main aim of the democracies in such a war would have been to liberate the world from the threat represented by an aggressive régime in Germany not the maintenance or re-establishment (however much the Czech patriots might have longed for it) of Czechoslovakia on the old lines.

This simple truth which the responsible politicians refused to see was clear to the unpolitical soldiers. A War Office memorandum of September 1938 stated.[1] 'Our real object is not to save Czechoslovakia – that is impossible in any event – but to end the days of the Nazi régime.'

The Nationalities' Statute

During June and July 1938 there were fruitless discussions between the Government and the SdP delegates on the Nationalities' Statute. The Government hesitated to put all its proposals on the table at once, but handed them to the SdP piecemeal. There is little point now in analysing them in detail since they were never seriously considered: suffice it to say that the SdP demand for the 'recognition

[1] Middlemas, *Diplomacy of Illusion*, p. 384.

of the Sudeten German *Volksgruppe* as a legal person' by setting up a *Volkstag* (People's Assembly) as a sort of special Parliament was met half-way by the Government's suggestion for national *curiae* with special rights in the provincial diets which were to be formed in Bohemia and Moravia–Silesia. This solution could not have satisfied the totalitarian aspirations of the SdP. Hodža and his Government, however, wanted to convince Britain that they were willing to concede as much as was possible without endangering the safety of the State. What the SdP demanded and what the Government was constrained to accept as 'the basis for negotiations'– real negotiations in fact never took place – would have meant the disintegration of the State and the installation of Nazi rule in the German-inhabited districts, later to be annexed by Hitler.

In the heart of Central Europe, next door to an armed neighbour continuously on the watch for an aggressive outlet, the travesty of a State, as demanded by Henlein, could not have survived for a week, or as the British Minister in Prague, not usually prone to hyperbole, put it:[1] 'Such a system existed no where in the world and might obviously effect horizontal cleavage in the State if indeed it were administratively practicable at all.'

Newton directed London's attention to the fact that while the SdP documents submitted to Hodža did not mention 'foreign policy' or the Nazi *Weltanschauung* (this was now hardly necessary), it did, contrary to the 'agreement' made in London, claim 'restitution'.[2] Halifax had simply 'overlooked' that. When Newton called on Beneš to convey to him British admonitions to come to an agreement with Henlein without further delay, Beneš produced the SdP Memorandum and read out to the British Minister what the document had to say about the *Volkstag*: this separate Sudeten German Parliament in the midst of a democratic state would have introduced the so-called 'Aryan paragraph', created a thoroughly totalitarian régime and wound up its activities by 'legally' proclaiming an *Anschluss* to Germany.[3] One would have thought this, at any rate, should have startled the British Foreign Secretary, but Halifax

---

[1] Newton to Halifax, 14 July 1938, *DBFP*, 3/1, no. 486.
[2] Newton to Halifax, 15 June 1938, *DBFP*, 3/1, no. 415.
[3] Newton to Halifax, 3 June 1938, Halifax to Newton 8 and 16 June 1938, *DBFP*, 3/1, nos. 373, 384 and 416.

informed Newton: 'If the functions of a *Volkstag* could be satisfactorily limited and defined, they (the Czechs) need surely not be afraid of the mere name.' To image that Hitler's henchmen would have agreed to 'satisfactory limitations and definitions' and have respected them is absurd enough, especially when it is remembered that in April the Prime Minister had told the French that it would be useless to ask Hitler for guarantees since he would either not give any or ignore them. Later Halifax seems to have had second thoughts about the matter; he wrote: 'I had in mind a form of provincial Parliament, exercising a limited jurisdiction over a definite territory. The *Volkstag* as outlined... would seem to be something quite different.'

Yet Newton was not instructed to tell Beneš that London would support him against the attempt to set up another Nazi Reichstag in his country. Halifax merely enjoined the Minister 'not to commit yourself with regard to it'.

In effect the British Government was undeterred by all previous experiences with Hitler and Henlein, and saw only one way of settling the dispute: the Czechs had to blindly accept all the Nazi demands whatever their consequences. The Cabinet minutes for 13 July record:[1]

He (Halifax) felt that the only thing to be done was to continue to maintain pressure on Dr Beneš, both directly and through the French Government.

Any kind of pressure on Hitler was not mentioned even as a vague possibility.

It was at this time that Robert Boothby, M.P. (now Lord Boothby) had a long conversation in Prague with Beneš who rightly complained of the dangers of this one-sided approach. Boothby lost no time in informing the Prime Minister.[2]

It is right that you should put pressure on us now [Beneš said]. This is an international question. But it would be dangerous to give Hitler the idea that pressure is always going to be put on us and never on him.

No attention was paid to this warning by Neville Chamberlain or by Halifax, who received a copy of Boothby's letter.

[1] *Cab.* 23/94, Minute 32(38), Meeting of 13 July 1938.
[2] Robert Boothby, *I Fight to Live* (London 1947), p. 153. Boothby to Chamberlain, 27 July 1938, in *Foreign Office Files* (*The Sudeten Crisis*), F.O. 371, vol. 21730.

By the end of July 1938 Vansittart finally seems to have begun to doubt the sincerity of Henlein's assurances. He transmitted to Halifax[1] what he had learnt from Hohenlohe about Henlein's 'more liberal-minded and moderating influence', but he did not add his own comments even when repeating Hohenlohe's fairy tale that Henlein was 'frightened for his own life', allegedly endangered by the Nazis from the Reich. Vansittart implored Hohenlohe to go back to Czechoslovakia as soon as possible to get 'Henlein out of his present depressed and angry mood'. In the end it was agreed that Colonel Christie, who had been the go-between in all matters concerning Henlein, should meet Henlein, Hohenlohe and Brand, Henlein's London representative, in Zurich on 5 August.

Christie had for years been of decisive help to Henlein, but at the Zurich meeting he must have lost faith in him. According to Henlein's notes (which were found in his house and published in Prague some years ago),[2] Christie accused Henlein of having deceived him. Henlein retorted by talking of Czechoslovakia as a 'state of crooks and criminals' (*Gaunerstaat, Verbrecherstaat*) and an 'abortion of a state' – to which, three months earlier, he had vowed loyalty in London. The time had come, he threatened, 'to rob the British of any illusion that stability could be achieved in a combined State under Czech sovereignty'. It was not merely a question of the Sudeten Germans – said the man who until then had always maintained that he had only the Sudeten Germans in mind – it was above all the problem of 'Germany versus Czechoslovakia'

which would exist even *if there were no Germans in Czechoslovakia at all*. In the long run Germany cannot tolerate such an abscess on its body...no other State

[1] Memorandum by Vansittart for Halifax, 26 July 1938, *Foreign Office Files* (*The Sudeten Crisis*), F.O. 371, vol. 21729.
[2] Václav Král (ed.), *Die Deutschen der Tschechoslowakei 1933–1947* (Prague 1964), no. 172.

would put up with this provocation for ever...If England thinks that she must protect this State come what may, then England will bear the blame for an extension of the conflict.

Henlein graciously agreed to delay the call for a plebiscite for another month, but true to his promises to Berlin, he stoutly denied Christie's accusation that he received instructions from Germany. This would agree with a report from the German Ambassador in Paris[1] that Christie was deeply disillusioned with Henlein and considered him a puppet of Berlin. It had taken a remarkably long time for Christie to realize the truth.

Christie's own notes about the Zurich conversations,[2] submitted by Vansittart to Halifax, do not register Henlein's words about a 'state of crooks' etc. but basically confirm Henlein's description of the conversations. Christie, however, wrote something which for obvious reasons is not contained in the report Henlein submitted to his masters in Berlin:

Henlein is in favour of a settlement by negotiation and is against a plebiscite. He must, however, under German pressure, demand a plebiscite. He is under no illusions as to his own fate in the event of an *Anschluss*. He would never be tolerated by the radical Nazis in the Reich and would disappear from the political leadership.

Henlein surprised Christie by offering to act as mediator between Berlin and London:

On three different occasions he (Henlein) has been asked by Hitler, Goering and Ribbentrop how exactly he had come to secure such personal success in London ...It was obvious that there were certain considerations...of prestige which prevented Berlin and London coming together. He asked me whether I had any proposals to make, i.e. whether I could advise him what steps could be taken by Germany towards a *détente*. If I could tell him now or after proceeding to London bring back to him any concrete proposals, he felt sure he could put it through to the Reich Government with the best prospects of a good understanding, but the matter should be taken in hand at once.

Surprised at this unexpected suggestion, Christie says he advised Henlein against it, at least for the moment. First he should help to

[1] Welczeck to G.F.M. 9 August 1938, *G.F.M.* serial 1613, frames 369658-60. (This report was also part of the prosecution's evidence at the Nuremberg 'Wilhelmstrasse' Trial as Doc. NG-3359.)

[2] Report by Christie on conversation with Henlein, 8 August 1938, submitted by Vansittart to Halifax, *Foreign Office Files* (*The Sudeten Crisis*), F.O. 371, vol. 21731.

bring about an internal settlement: 'It was in the capacity of an independent leader of a loyal German minority in Czechoslovakia that he could work with much likelihood of success for Anglo-German relations in the future.' Christie first regarded Henlein's curious offer as a 'naive desire of increasing his position with the Reich Government', but heard afterwards from a German friend that this move had been agreed beforehand in Berlin. This might have disillusioned both him and Vansittart who had information from 'a very well informed *Sudetendeutsche* source' to the effect that 'Henlein and his negotiators are at present completely at the hands of Berlin'. Vansittart told Halifax that 'a clear stand by this country can still...ensure European peace. This view is based not only on my own judgement but on several good German sources.'

Runciman in Prague

From June 1938 onwards, Lord Halifax considered sending an 'independent' British expert to Prague to settle the dispute between the two sides. He obviously thought that the legal government of a democratic state had the same standing as a totalitarian irredentist movement, operating within that state while paid and directed by an aggressive neighbour. As a former Viceroy of India Halifax regarded an ex-Governor of an Indian province as the best man for the job. Newton, however, was reluctant to submit this suggestion to the government to which he was accredited, and it was accordingly dropped.[1]

The Czechoslovak Government knew only too well that in the unequal struggle with Hitler it had to rely on the support of the Western Powers. It thus considered it wiser not to refuse outright when, in the second half of July, London suggested the Czechoslovak Government should jointly with the SdP ask the British Government to send a mediator in the person of Lord Runciman[2] – an act of interference unprecedented in the history of diplomatic relations. Beneš and Hodža did at least succeed in convincing London that they could not act together with the SdP in this manner; it was also arranged that Runciman was not to appear as a

[1] Halifax to Newton, 18 June 1938, Newton to Halifax, 21 June 1938, *DBFP*, 3/1, nos. 425 and 431.
[2] Halifax to Newton, 18 July 1938, *DBFP*, 3/1, no. 508.

230

mediator, let alone referee, between the Government and an opposition party, but merely as an 'independent adviser'. On the other hand Prague had to accept the untrue and humiliating statement made by Chamberlain in the House of Commons that the Czechoslovak Government had asked for Runciman.[1]

Viscount Runciman of Doxford had not the slightest qualification for a task which would have been beyond a far abler man. He had been in the Government several times, but he had no knowledge of Central Europe nor the complex question of minorities. This alone need not have disqualified him, if he had had the ability to conduct or at any rate initiate negotiations, but not only did he show no sign of this he even lacked the elementary tact one would expect from a British politician in so delicate a situation. When the SdP, at one of his sojourns in the castles of Sudeten German landowners, arranged for a demonstration to welcome him and had instructed the crowd to greet him with the Hitler salute, Runciman responded from the balcony in the same fashion.[2] He probably regarded it a simple act of courtesy.

Runciman's mission would have had some sense if it had aimed systematically at spinning out negotiations until the end of September, thus robbing Hitler of the possibility of attacking while weather conditions were favourable. Runciman, however, was always pressed by London for quick results. Although this had not been laid down beforehand, from the time of his arrival in Czechoslovakia (3 August) Runciman accepted the SdP on the same footing as the Czechoslovak Government. His discussions with the latter seem to have been limited to exhortations to be accommodating to the former and to recommence 'negotiations' for a nationalities' statute. These duly took place – with the same success as before. An SdP delegation under Ernst Kundt naturally tried to win Runciman's favour, disguising their demands as harmless attempts to obtain justice for the Germans. In order to drive home their views Henlein's collaborators extended their official contacts and arranged weekend trips for Runciman to visit the estates of German aristocrats who sympathized with or were members of the SdP. Other landowners,

[1] *Parliamentary Debates* (*Hansard*), House of Commons, 26 July 1938, vol. 338, cols. 2250–63.
[2] Kvaček, *Osudná mise*, p. 178.

equally disgruntled at the loss of their titles and the reduction of their landed property because of the land reform, were invited to these gatherings. All this naturally created ample opportunities for unobtrusive propaganda.

In a formal sense Runciman and his mission were independent of the British Government, but nobody took this seriously. Runciman obviously represented official British policy; he did not, however, seem to have received any directives as to what kind of procedure and what sort of proposals London expected from him. Chamberlain and Halifax believed that he wholeheartedly supported their policy of appeasement. Only Runciman's principal adviser Frank Ashton-Gwatkin received some kind of advice before leaving for Prague: Vansittart recommended that he cultivate relations with Henlein.[1]

Henlein himself showed no desire to meet Runciman, and so after a fruitless week in Czechoslovakia the latter told Kundt that he would finally like to have a talk with Henlein.[2] K. H. Frank had given instructions that such an encounter should be avoided as long as possible, and Kundt accordingly claimed that Henlein was abroad. Since Runciman would not be put off with excuses, a meeting with Henlein was eventually arranged for 18 August at Hohenlohe's Rothenhaus Castle. For a long time the only account available of what went on there was a note by Ashton-Gwatkin[3] which said nothing essential and threw no light on Runciman's attitude. According to Ashton-Gwatkin, Henlein played both the peaceable man of honour and the uncompromising champion of the eight Karlovy Vary demands. A more recent Prague publication contains for the first time the text of Henlein's notes about that meeting. They show that Runciman by no means swallowed blindly everything Henlein tried to tell him and that he stood up to him well. In discussions with Runciman, Henlein avoided expressions

---

[1] Information kindly supplied to the author by Mr Ashton-Gwatkin, 6 May 1971.

[2] Hencke to G.F.M. 13 August 1938, *G.F.M.* serial 1613, frames 386971-2. Hencke to G.F.M. 12 August 1938, *DGFP*, D/II, no. 349.

[3] Note by Ashton-Gwatkin, 18 August 1938, *DBFP*, 3/II, App. II, pp. 656-7. Notes about conversation between Konrad Henlein and Lord Runciman, written on 19 August 1938, printed by Král, *Die Deutschen in der Tschechoslowakei*, no. 184.

like 'a state of crooks', but he did bring up the tale of the 'deliberately induced pauperization of the Sudeten Germans'. The Czechs, he said, had advocated 'the extermination of the Sudeten Germans and the destruction of their homes' – although submitting no proof of this. Henlein insisted that he knew 'for certain that the highest political and military circles (of the State) wanted war'. Runciman was said to have asked Henlein 'in astonishment' what made him imagine that, and Henlein assured him that this was not based on imagination but on information derived from 'the most reliable sources' – so reliable indeed that they still cannot be traced.

When Henlein denounced the Government's offer as worthless, Runciman replied that 'any Englishman would have seized at them and then have asked for more'– not exactly what Henlein, who had never wanted an agreement at all, had in mind. When he told Runciman that the slogan *Heim ins Reich* had to be understood in its context, Runciman replied that 'in Germany, too, things were not exactly as our people would wish them to be'. Tendentious descriptions of Sudeten German misery were countered with the dry statement that 'there was temporary economic trouble everywhere, even in England'. That Runciman had a mind of his own is corroborated by the account of an official in the Czechoslovak Foreign Ministry, quoted by a Prague author.[1] An unnamed member of the Mission was said to have mentioned to him that Runciman was thinking of an international conference at which Britain and France would guarantee the independence of Czechoslovakia within her existing frontiers in return for her neutralization and autonomy for the Sudeten Germans.

Much to the chagrin of the SdP, Runciman could not well refuse to receive representatives of the German Social Democrats.[2] A few days later, Jaksch, as party leader, and Taub, the General Secretary

---

[1] Kvaček, *Osudná mise*, pp. 137–8.
[2] *Sozialdemokrat*, 8 August 1938. The British journalist Alexander Henderson who worked in Prague in 1938 recounts in his book *Eyewitness in Czechoslovakia* (p. 145) that on 3 August, on being asked whether he was going to talk to the German Social Democrats, Runciman looked perplexed as if he had never heard of their existence. Finally he explained that they had not contacted him so far. The text of their memorandum, which has never been published in full (for extracts see Laffan, *Crisis over Czechoslovakia*, p. 173), was kindly put at the author's disposal by Mr Robert Stopford who was a member of the Runciman Mission.

and Vice-President of Parliament sent him a lengthy memorandum. It expressed the point of view of all Germans opposed to Hitler and Henlein, and differed appreciably from Henlein's list of demands. What the Social Democrats desired did not go beyond what a substantial minority like the Germans could reasonably claim: equal status for their language, guarantees for a proportional share in the civil service, democratic self-administration entailing the maximum of civic rights and a policy of industrial reconstruction. The memorandum restated these demands, adding,

On the other hand, as German democrats we are aware that in return the vital interests of the Czech people must be acknowledged from the German point of view. It would be a tragedy for the whole of the German people if a currently prominent political trend...were to force through a solution which was not guided by the spirit of equality of rights but by the desire for German hegemony in Central Europe. This would bury all hopes for a conciliation between Sudeten Germans and Czechs for an indefinite period.

Attention was drawn to the results of the 1929 elections, which had taken place under normal economic and political conditions, when over two-thirds of the German voters had of their own free will united in support of those political parties which accepted the Czechslovak State and its democratic form of government:

Such an electoral result ten years after the founding of the state can be regarded as proof that given the conditions of European stability, the minorities problem in Czechoslovakia was by no means of dramatic urgency.

Runciman most probably paid no attention to the memorandum, but the personal appearance of the German Socialists showed him that he could no longer regard Henlein as the undisputed spokesman of all the German inhabitants of the country. He was confirmed in this view by Erwin Zajiček, former Christian-Social German member of the Czechoslovak Government, who managed to obtain an interview with him. Representatives of the German Trade Union Federation[1] also successfully convinced the Runciman Mission that a German democratic trade union movement existed in Czechoslovakia and identified itself with the State.

Since no compromise was possible between the totalitarian aspirations of the SdP and the desperate efforts of the Czechoslovak Government to resist the enemy, Runciman was powerless to speed

[1] *Prager Tagblatt*, 1 September 1938.

up the 'negotiations'. The SdP took good care not to give prominence to its principal demand – the right to profess National Socialism. There was, of course, no question of any renunciation of this claim: silence about it was simply a tactical move, because Runciman would have accepted it much less readily than Henlein's more harmless demands for 'legal status' and 'self-administration'.

Runciman's most prominent collaborator, Frank Ashton-Gwatkin, was recalled to London for consultation, but before he went he had a long discussion with Henlein on 22 August. Ashton-Gwatkin was the Foreign Office's expert on trade negotiations (in this field he had collaborated with Runciman before and that had been the reason for Runciman's wish to have him in Prague), but totalitarian movements and their tactics were completely alien to him and Henlein was easily able to mislead him. He showed no surprise when the SdP leader first mentioned the possibility of the incorporation of the German-speaking areas of Czechoslovakia or even the whole of Bohemia, Moravia and Silesia into Germany, although Henlein pretended that he would 'vastly' prefer local autonomy within the existing frontiers. Ashton-Gwatkin equally accepted at its face value Henlein's 'emphatic denial'[1]

(1) that he was a dictator, (2) that he had any sympathy with the terror of the German Nazis, (3) that he would ever permit any Jew-baiting (*Judenhetze*), (4) that he aimed at political totalitarianism or anything other than honourable treatment of opponents and opposition as long as they dealt fairly with him. He [Henlein] believed that an honest opposition had useful functions of criticism.

Henlein was not asked how all these pious sentiments could be reconciled with his profession of National Socialism and so it is hardly surprising that Ashton-Gwatkin wrote to London on 23 August:[2] 'I motored to Marienbad to see Henlein. My talk with him was extremely interesting...I like him. He is, I am sure, an absolutely honest fellow.'

Henlein did not mention any of these ruses in the notes he made after that interview – his record can now be studied in facsimile in a Moscow publication.[3] According to these notes Ashton-Gwatkin

---

[1] Note by Ashton-Gwatkin, 22 August 1938, *DBFP*, 3/II, App. II, pp. 657–9.
[2] Ashton-Gwatkin to Strang, *DBFP*, 3/II, App. II, p. 664.
[3] *Documents and Materials relating to the Eve of the Second World War*, I (Moscow 1948), 156–60.

quite seriously proposed sending the 'moderate' Henlein to Hitler in order to persuade the Fuehrer not to make an inflammatory speech at Nuremberg. The man who had promised not to dabble in foreign affairs was now asked to do so:

Ashton-Gwatkin asked whether, if the Czechs in the coming week betrayed no intention of coming to terms, K.H. [i.e. Henlein] was prepared *to sound out the Fuehrer* as to the desirability of a meeting between British representatives and the Fuehrer *at which not only the Czechoslovak question need be discussed.*

K.H. asked what other possible point of discussion he had in mind.

A.-G.: He could not say definitely, but he supposed *an air pact, the colonial question and an armament agreement.*

Henlein now raised his price: he could not do anything before the week was out and then only at the express invitation of the British Government. (That the Czechoslovak Government might object, was not considered.)

Ashton-Gwatkin duly flew to London where it was thought that Runciman was the appropriate man to see Hitler; he however declined. In the meantime K. H. Frank, who from the beginning had pursued the policy that it was 'the duty of the Sudeten German Party to convince his Lordship that the Nationality Problem in Czechoslovakia cannot be solved within the State',[1] had himself been talking to Hitler in Berlin. After seeing Hitler, he gave two absolutely different versions of Hitler's attitude. Helmut Groscurth, of the *Abwehr* (Military Counter-Espionage), noted in his diary under 27 August.[2]

Visit by K. H. Frank. He reports about his visit to the Fuehrer on August 26. The Fuehrer is determined to wage war (*Fuehrer ist zum Krieg entschlossen*). He *gives orders to arrange incidents in Czechoslovakia.* Insulted Beneš. He wants to catch him alive and to hang him personally on the rope.

As Frank did not know that Groscurth was one of the military conspirators against Hitler he might in this case have spoken the truth. The lies were reserved for the British:

[1] Halifax to Newton, 25 August 1938, Newton to Halifax, 26 August 1938, *DBFP*, 3/II, nos. 686 and 695 (Runciman's refusal to intervene with Hitler). Enclosure to letter by Bürger to Altenburg, 17 August 1938, *DGFP*, D/II, no. 366.

[2] Frank's evidence about his visit to Hitler, 10 October 1945, Huremberg Trial Doc. PS-3061, *IMT*, XXXII, 11. Helmut Groscurth, *Tagebücher eines Abwehr-Offiziers 1938–1940* (Diaries of an officer in the *Abwehr*) (Stuttgart 1970), p. 104.

Frank said [to Ashton-Gwatkin] that Herr Hitler would welcome peaceful solution of Sudeten question if it came quickly. Further Herr Hitler would welcome visit from Henlein provided Henlein can bring a definite statement of what His Majesty's Government propose, i.e. (a) if Lord Runciman really intends to help Henlein to find solution on basis of Karlsbad eight points, and (b) as regards a general Anglo-German settlement if Henlein would bring list of subjects which His Majesty's Government would be prepared to discuss with Germany.

To be so much in the centre of events added to Henlein's feeling of self-importance. He was also present at Rothenhaus Castle, when Frank spoke to Ashton-Gwatkin. The – let us say, unusual – idea that the British Government could use a Nazi adventurer like Henlein as their *postilion d'amour* to Hitler had come after all from Ashton-Gwatkin four days before Frank visited Hitler. Neither Runciman nor Ashton-Gwatkin were shocked when Frank came with this grotesque suggestion. Henlein made full use of the unique situation by boldly insisting that the British Government should recommend Prague to accept the 'eight demands' – including the freedom to profess National Socialism – as the basis for negotiations. Ashton-Gwatkin was of course not empowered to give so far-reaching an undertaking and even Runciman who had a second talk with Henlein lasting only sixteen minutes,[1] merely declared his readiness to consult London. Neither of the two British negotiators, however, protested at Henlein's demands regarding the Karlovy Vary programme, probably because neither realized what they really signified: that one democratic government should exert pressure upon another to legalize anti-democratic National Socialism. In his own notes Ashton-Gwatkin found the eight points 'unobjectionable' although of those concerning the *Volksgruppe* and the *Rechtspersönlichkeit* (ethnic group and legal personality) he admitted that 'both these conceptions are very obscure to me'.[2] It would have been easy to find someone to explain these things to him. What he certainly could not have known was that ten days earlier Weizsäcker, the State Secretary in the German Foreign Office, had minuted:[3]

During a conversation with Ribbentrop on August 19 he explained to me that

[1] Troutbeck to Halifax, 29 August 1938, *DBFP*, 3/11, no. 706.
[2] Ashton-Gwatkin to Strang, 29 August 1938, *DBFP*, 3/11, App. 11, pp. 665–7.
[3] Note by Weizsäcker, 19 August 1938, *DGFP*, D/11, no. 374.

the Fuehrer was firmly resolved to settle the Czech affair by force of arms. He designated the middle of October as the latest possible date because of technical reasons governing air operations.

At that time Sir Nevile Henderson was very concerned in Berlin as to whether London was doing enough – to destroy democracy in Central Europe. On 22 August 1938 he wrote:[1] 'I wonder sometimes whether we are backing Henlein enough in London.'

Beneš' 'Third Plan'

Meanwhile Beneš had decided towards the middle of August to intervene in the 'negotiations' with the SdP. He let them know[2] he would agree to the immediate acceptance of the German language as of equal status with Czech, an increased intake of Germans into the administration of the State and so on. His only demand was an 'armistice' of two months to create a calmer atmosphere. This was highly embarrassing to the SdP. Again they asked Berlin what to do and Ribbentrop, on whom the German Chargé d'Affaires in Prague, Hencke, called at the unusual hour of 1 a.m., was understandably annoyed:

He did not like to be approached so often by the Sudeten German Party for advice. Henlein had already received clear instructions and therefore it is not fitting that one gentleman after another kept appearing from Prague to obtain decisions on individual questions. Henlein and his people must learn to stand on their own feet.

As regards Beneš' initiative, Henlein was to be guided by the general directive given to him 'to keep on negotiating and not to let the ties break, but always to demand more than the other side could concede', and he was to emphasize again that the 'eight points' were merely a minimum programme. It will be seen that Henlein took this advice to heart.

Beneš obviously resolved on active intervention in order to impress Runciman, who under pressure from London continually urged 'concessions' without giving much thought to their character

---

[1] Nevile Henderson to Halifax, 22 August 1938, *Foreign Office Files* (*The Sudeten Crisis*), F.O. 371, vol. 21743. Quoted by Mark Arnold-Forster, 'How we helped Hitler', *The Guardian*, 1 January 1969.

[2] Note by Altenburg, 18 August 1938, *DGFP*, D/II, no. 369. Note by Mitis, Appendix to *DGFP*, D/II, no. 378. Note by Hencke, 19 August 1938, in Král, *Die Deutschen in der Tschechoslowakei*, no. 183.

and possible consequences. Until then Beneš had avoided all contacts with the SdP. Now he had lengthy discussions with Kundt
and Sebekovsky on 24, 25 and 30 August[1] intended as preliminaries
for an agreement which would then be concluded by the Government. Although his success proved to be of short duration, Beneš
did in fact perplex the SdP delegation because they found themselves at a loss to produce any serious counter-arguments to his
statements. Even Hencke had to tell Berlin that 'Beneš gave the
delegates of the Sudeten German Party the impression of sincerity'.
Above all, Beneš made a point of refuting thoroughly the allegation
that he was anti-German. At the final meeting he handed the SdP
delegation his draft for an agreement. Of course, he had no completely fresh panacea to offer: his 'Third Plan' merely went a few
steps further in the direction of the Karlovy Vary demands and he
assured his visitors that 'he would not object if the Sudeten German
Party for its part publicly announced that the eight demands would
be fulfilled'. To the point 'profession of National Socialism' he
referred only indirectly by promising to reinstate officials allegedly
dismissed because of their membership of the banned Nazi Party.
The new proposals envisaged the division of Bohemia and Moravia–
Silesia into *Gaue* (cantons), three of which would have had a German majority. There would have been a double administration for
these *Gaue*: an elected 'President' to represent local autonomy side
by side with a state official as head of the administration. There is
little doubt that National Socialism would thus have gained control
over at least part of Bohemia. The SdP delegates promised to reply
by 2 September: even Frank had to admit that 'in his opinion...
they (Beneš' proposals) could not be rejected out of hand', while
Kundt commended the proposals by saying that 'their realization
would in actual fact mean the fulfilment of the eight Karlsbad
demands'.[2] Henlein, however, 'described Beneš' latest proposals as

---

[1] Hencke to G.F.M. 26 and 27 August 1938, *DGFP*, D/II, nos. 391, 398.
Deutsche Gesandtschaft, Prag, fascicle 62/1 (this includes the unpublished
SdP note about the discussion of the 30 August). Edvard Beneš, *Mnichovské
Dny* (Days of Munich) (Prague 1968), p. 178; French edition: *Munich*
(Paris 1970), p. 122.
[2] Hencke to G.F.M. 30 August 1938, *DGFP*, D/II, no. 407. Eisenlohr to
G.F.M. *DGFP*, D/II, no. 417. Newton to Halifax, 2 September 1938, *DBFP*,
3/II, no. 746. Laffan, *Crisis over Czechoslovakia*, p. 236.

inadequate in their present form' and the official SdP reply, disguised as a counter-proposal, insisted on the unconditional acceptance of the eight postulates.

Beneš' 'Third Plan'[1] contained many sensible features which would not have meant a surrender of democracy: language concessions, an increased quota of German officials, a loan for the relief of distressed areas. But what caused Beneš to make the ominous *Gau* offer, which would have abandoned part of the country to totalitarian forces? The explanation may well be that Runciman, who so far had merely been pressing for concessions, might have produced his own plan which could have shown even less consideration for the desire of a democratic state not to capitulate. Kundt and Frank adhered to the directive not to sever ties and were therefore opposed to outright rejection; Henlein, on the other hand, had clearly decided for it, since Ashton-Gwatkin had told him 'very confidentially' that Lord Runciman himself was 'ready to produce a scheme by some given date (say 15 September), should the two parties have failed to reach an agreement on the present basis'.[2]

Chamberlain and Halifax would undoubtedly have asked Czechoslovakia to make every concession, but when Halifax learned that Henlein was to see Hitler almost as the spokesman of the British Government, to broach issues like the question of the colonies, he informed Runciman that there could be no question of Henlein being sent on any such mission, after he had already given instructions to remind Kundt of Henlein's promise not to meddle in foreign affairs.[3] He also rejected Henlein's attempts to blackmail Prague *via* London about the Karlovy Vary programme. Nevertheless, he did not only not object to Henlein's journey to Berlin, but even expressed wishes as to what Henlein should tell Hitler, namely

that he (Henlein) believed Great Britain desired an Anglo-German agreement and that he further believed that a settlement of the Czech question might well open the way for such an agreement.

[1] The first plan had been the memorandum sent to the British Government in April 1938 (see p. 204), the second plan the proposals of Hodža, given to the Henlein delegation in June (see p. 226).
[2] Newton to Halifax, 1 September 1938, *DBFP*, 3/II, no. 732.
[3] Halifax to Newton, 25 and 29 August 1938, *DBFP*, 3/II, nos. 688, 710.

German military preparations

In Prague meanwhile feverish but fruitless attempts were made to square the circle: how to make the sacrifices demanded by the Western Powers and at the same time not jeopardize the country's survival. There were civilians and officers in Germany who had preserved a sense of humanity and reality, and who did their best to avert the catastrophe they saw approaching. Ewald von Kleist-Schmenzin, later to become one of the participants in the unsuccessful rising of 20 July 1944, went to London to warn the British about Hitler's schemes. Had Hitler resorted to force, a Generals' revolt was planned which would have had a better chance of putting an end to the Nazi reign of terror than the heroic but hopeless attempt six years later, if only Chamberlain had not helped Hitler to gain another bloodless victory.[1] But other members of the German *Wehrmacht* were at that time concerned about entirely different matters. A conflict had arisen between the *Luftwaffe* and the Army about the timing of the 'X-order' which was to start the onslaught on Czechoslovakia. On 24 August Colonel Alfred Jodl – later hanged at Nuremberg as one of the Major War Criminals – wrote a 'report note' ('*Vortragsnotiz*').[2]

The *Luftwaffe*'s endeavour to take the enemy air force by surprise on their peace-time air fields in the first wave of attack on Czechoslovakia, justifies the *Luftwaffe*'s objection to all measures in advance of the 'X-order' and the demand that the 'X-order' itself be given sufficiently late on X-day minus 1, so that the fact of Germany's mobilisation will not be known in Czechoslovakia on X-day minus 1.

The Army's efforts tend in the opposite direction. It intends to let the *OKW* (Army High Command) carry out between X-day minus 3 and X-day minus 1 such advance measures as will ensure the rapid and smooth working of mobilisation. Therefore the *OKW* also demands that the X-order be given to the Army not later than 2 p.m. on X-day minus 1.

While one side wanted the order for the attack not later than 2 p.m. on the day before, the other wanted it no earlier than sometime in the afternoon. Jodl commented

Operation Green will be set in motion by an incident in Czechoslovakia which will provide Germany with a pretext for military intervention.

[1] For details see Hans Rothfels, *The German Opposition to Hitler* (London 1961), pp. 56–63; Gerhard Ritter, *The German Resistance* (London 1958), pp. 80–112.

[2] Report note by Jodl, 24 August 1938, *DGFP*, D/II, no. 388.

This could still be taken to mean that the opponent was expected to cause an incident of some sort or at least make it possible for the Germans to allege that one had taken place. But what follows leaves no doubt that, in accordance with the Directive of December 1937[1] to carry out 'a strategic and sudden attack on Czechoslovakia', the incident was to be organized by the Germans themselves:

The determination of the day and hour of this incident is of extreme importance. It must fall within a period of general weather conditions favourable for...our superior *Luftwaffe*, and the hour must be selected so that it is known to us authentically by noon on X-day minus 1. It can then be countered by the spontaneous issue of X-order on X-day minus 1 at 1400 hours.

On X-day minus 2 the *Wehrmacht* contingents will receive a preliminary warning only. Should the Fuehrer decide to proceed in this manner, no further discussions are called for, because in this case no preliminary measures must be taken by us before X-day minus 1 which could not be explained away on harmless grounds, for otherwise the incident would appear to be instigated by us. Absolutely necessary preliminary measures would in these circumstances have to be ordered a considerable time ahead and also disguised with numerous exercises and manœuvres...

If for technical reasons the incident is to take place in the evening, X-day could not be the next day but will have to be the day after...

The purpose of these notes is to *emphasize the interest of the Wehrmacht in this incident* and that it will have to be informed of the Fuehrer's intentions in time, unless the Abwehr-Abteilung (counter-intelligence) *is being entrusted with the organisation of incident anyway.*

'For the improvement of our political and military position' and without any mention of the alleged need to liberate the oppressed fellow-Germans, Hitler, in November 1937, had proclaimed his aim 'to overthrow...*die Tschechei*'. Even though documentary evidence about that decision became available only after the war, the intentions preceding it had long been plain. Jodl asked for Hitler's views in his memorandum and was informed on 31 August 1938 that Hitler 'would act in conformity with these statements'. If one bears in mind that the plans to put millions of people to a hideous death in gas chambers were referred to even in the most confidential internal documents only as *Sonderbehandlung* (special treatment), the open brutality with which the timing of a convenient incident as a pretext for an aggressive war as discussed here is particularly revolting.

[1] See p. 185.

15   SEPTEMBER 1938

During those September days of 1938 one blow after another fell on the last remnants of Central European democracy. As if it were the most natural thing in the world, it was announced[1] that Konrad Henlein, formally still the citizen of a democratic state, was about to have political talks with Hitler at Berchtesgaden. He went there on 1 September at the wish of Halifax and Runciman, who really believed that Henlein was the man to 'assuage' the Fuehrer. Ashton-Gwatkin reported that he had found Henlein ready to convey written messages from Runciman to Hitler. Lord Runciman would inform Beneš that Henlein was going at his (Runciman's) request:

Lord Runciman believes in Herr Henlein's genuine desire for peace and he hopes that Herr Henlein's attitude may influence Herr Hitler and that to convey a message to the effect that Lord Runciman trusts negotiations and that settlement of Sudeten question may lead on to settlement of questions now outstanding between Great Britain and Germany.

Beneš records in his memoirs that he received a letter in exactly these terms from Runciman. What Runciman did not write to Beneš was that he had given Henlein two written messages in German, a language not normally used by British negotiators. In these messages Hitler was *expressis verbis* conceded a voice in the settlement of an independent country's internal problem:

(First message)   The object of Lord Runciman's mission is to assist both parties to reach a settlement on the basis both of the Karlsbad eight points and of new proposals of Czechoslovakian Government. As regards Herr Henlein's suggestion that His Majesty's Government might intervene, their position is that they are reluctant to pronounce on the merits of any proposals that may be put forward by both sides.

[1] Troutbeck (Prague) to Halifax, 29 August 1938, Newton to Halifax, 1 September 1938, *DBFP*, 3/II, nos. 706, 731, 732. Beneš, *Mnichovské Dny*, pp. 194, 461; French edition, pp. 136, 341. Runciman's belief of being able to 'intimidate' Hitler with the help of Henlein is, however, rendered there only as '*afin d'avertir Hitler*'.

The legal government of an independent country and an irredentist terroristic party in the pay of an aggressive neighbour were for Runciman simply 'both parties' and 'both sides'. The message continued:

Both Lord Runciman and His Majesty's Government are however very anxious that a settlement should be found at the earliest possible moment; and Lord Runciman is making every effort to this end. Lord Runciman would be glad if Herr Henlein could convey this message to Herr Hitler and he hopes Herr Hitler will give approval and support to the continuance of negotiations.

(Very confidential) In order to convince Herr Henlein and Herr Hitler that Lord Runciman and also His Majesty's Government are sincere in their determination to promote a quick and comprehensive settlement Lord Runciman desires to inform Herr Henlein very confidentially of his readiness to produce a scheme by some given date (say September 15) should the parties have failed to reach an agreement on present basis.

(Second message) As regards the general question of Anglo-Czech [sic] relations Lord Runciman would be glad if Herr Henlein would tell Herr Hitler that he (Herr Henlein) believes that Great Britain desires an Anglo-German agreement and that he further believes that a settlement of the Sudeten question will open the way to such an agreement. Lord Runciman is not in a position to given any list of subjects which His Majesty's Government would be prepared to discuss. The actual initiative and programme of such discussions would presumably have to be arranged between the two Governments through their own channels.

These documents, probably unique in the history of diplomacy, represented the implementation of wishes expressed by Lord Halifax.[1] In his memoirs Beneš describes a visit Runciman paid him on 1 September. Beneš protested against Runciman's initiative (not knowing that Halifax was behind it) which practically invited Hitler to intervene in the internal affairs of Czechoslovakia. Runciman explained that he took this step on his own responsibility, in order to 'intimidate Hitler' with the threat that if the conflict between Prague and Henlein were not cleared up the Great Powers might take it into their hands.

During this period[2] both Runciman and the British Minister in Prague did their utmost to persuade Beneš that further concessions were inevitable. If at the Nuremberg Nazi Party rally Hitler were to ask for a plebiscite or the right of the Sudeten Germans for self-

[1] See p. 240.
[2] Newton to Halifax, 3 and 4 September 1938, *DBFP*, 3/II, nos. 753, 758, also Beneš, *Mnichouské Dny*, pp. 201–3; French edition, pp. 141–2.

determination, British opinion, Newton declared, would consider that plausible. Beneš recalls Newton's statement that Prague would have to agree to the Karlovy Vary programme 'if that's necessary'. Although London had always refused to officially sanction these demands, they were now repeatedly brought home to Beneš together with the assurance, for which in fact there was no evidence at all, that there was no choice between 'acceptance of the Karlsbad programme or war'.

Meanwhile Ashton-Gwatkin was busy providing London with fresh illusions about Henlein's sincerity and usefulness from the British point of view.[1]

(Henlein) is simple and honest and may succeed with Hitler where the more crafty would fail...Henlein is anxious to disassociate his movement from identification with the Reich Nazis and he repudiates absolutely the spirit of persecution. He will probably go to 'Parteitag' this year...because he thinks himself a moderating influence.

Instead of expressing satisfaction with Beneš' Third Plan which incorporated certain democratic safeguards, Runciman expressed irritation because, as he complained, 'it was covered with boltholes and qualifications'.[2] Jan Masaryk reported from London that Sir Robert Vansittart had reproached him bitterly because Prague could not make up its mind.[3] To a British diplomat, far removed from the danger zone, the problem of suicide appeared so much simpler than to Beneš, who was expected, nay pressed, to commit it. One thin ray of hope for democracy seemed to come from Bonnet's declaration[4] of 3 September at Pointe-de-Grave, stressing French determination to fulfil all treaty commitments.

His affirmation would hardly have made the impression it did

---

[1] Newton to Halifax, 1 September 1938, *DBFP*, 3/ii, no. 734.
[2] Runciman to Halifax, 30 August 1938, *DBFP*, 3/ii, no. 723.
[3] Masaryk's report which, together with the remaining archives of the Czecho-slovak Foreign Ministry, fell into the hands of the Germans when they occupied Prague, was published in a Nazi propaganda collection (*Europäische Politik 1933–1938 im Spiegel der Prager Akten*, no. 153): for this publication see above p. 176. A comparison with the full text, as now available in the files of the German Foreign Ministry shows that the meaning of Masaryk's report of 31 August 1938 has been distorted in the Nazi publication. German translation of full text in *G.F.M.* serial 1809/1, frames 412022–3. Vansittart does not seem to have made a note about the conversation.
[4] *Documents on International Affairs 1938*, ii (London 1943), 178.

in Prague, had it been known that the day before he had said exactly the opposite to the German Ambassador Welczek,[1] whose observation that 'the only satisfactory solution of the Czech question' was the 'annexation of the Sudeten German regions to the Reich' was received by Bonnet not with a protest but with the comment that once autonomy was achieved, annexation would follow automatically. Although he restated France's obligations towards Czechoslovakia, Bonnet is said to have implored the German Ambassador not to force France into a position where she would have to fulfil them. Once the Sudeten German question was cleared up, it would surely be possible to accommodate Germany in other ways, e.g. in the question of colonies!

According to a British account of this meeting, Bonnet is thought to have declared that if Beneš did not accept Runciman's verdict, whatever that was, France would consider herself freed from all treaty commitments to Czechoslovakia. Since the German Ambassador, who was obviously the man most interested in such concessions, did not report this, it is doubtful whether Bonnet actually used such language. Although Bonnet denied the authenticity of the German report on that meeting before the Investigating Commission of the French Senate in 1947,[2] he never commented on the British version published in 1949 and never revealed his own version of this interview.

Henlein had returned from Berchtesgaden to Aš late on 2 September, but he did not condescend to receive Ashton-Gwatkin, who had been anxiously waiting for news, until the 4th. What he told the British diplomat about his encounter with Hitler[3] bore little enough resemblance to the truth. They had 'agreed' on a peaceful solution provided 'full autonomy' was granted to the Sudeten Germans (Henlein's supposed preference) or that they were given the opportunity of a plebiscite. Hitler did not at this stage want to

---

[1] Welczek to G.F.M. 2 September 1938, *DGFP*, D/II, no. 422; Phipps to Halifax, 2 September 1938, *DBFP*, 3/II, no. 747.

[2] *Les événements survenus en France de 1933 à 1945, Témoignages et documents recueillis par la Commission d'Enquête parlementaire* (Paris 1947–52), Annexes, tome IX, pp. 2600–740.

[3] Newton to Halifax, 4 September 1938, *DBFP*, 3/II, no. 765. Note by Ashton-Gwatkin, 4 September, and enclosure to letter by Ashton-Gwatkin to Strang, 6 September 1938, in Appendix III of same volume.

discuss Anglo-German relations, said Henlein – a week earlier Frank had told the British at Rothenhaus the exact opposite, but in the meanwhile a warning had come from London that Henlein should not be used as spokesman for the British. Hence Hitler pretended not to be interested or allowed Henlein to convey that impression.

The 'Fourth Plan'

Even before Hitler's speech at Nuremberg, Ashton-Gwatkin and Runciman had both begun to put into operation those measures which might maintain peace as Hitler understood it. Runciman found a way to exert more pressure on Beneš: to dispel the suspicion of bias which his frequent sojourns at the castles of German feudal landowners had created, Runciman accepted an invitation from the Archbishop of Prague, Karel Kašpar, to spend a weekend at his country seat near the capital. Though a Czech patriot, the Archbishop had never been politically active. On 4 September he sent Beneš a memorandum which, he said, Runciman had handed to him as his 'final proposal'.[1] It provided for the division of the State into autonomous Czech, Slovak and German areas. The Ministries of Foreign Affairs, Defence and Finance were to be responsible for all three regions. The integrity of the State was to be guaranteed – how that was to be done was not explained. Under normal conditions the proposal would have merited serious study, but in the prevailing circumstances its realization could only have led to the progressive dismemberment of a democratic State. Whether Runciman really believed or did not believe that Hitler would be satisfied with these proposals, Beneš at least knew then what to expect of Runciman.

On 5 September he again received Henlein's emissaries Kundt and Sebekovsky. On the same day the Government uneasily accepted Beneš' own formulation of the 'Fourth Plan', a last, almost despairing attempt to yield to Anglo-French pressure while saving as much as possible of the things that mattered.[2]

[1] Kvaček, *Osudná mise*, p. 158. Beneš, *Mnichovské Dny*, pp. 203–4 (French edition, p. 142).
[2] See the comparison between the Karlovy Vary Programme and the Fourth Plan in Laffan, *Crisis over Czechoslovakia*, pp. 240, 245. For the text of the Fourth Plan see *Documents on International Affairs 1938*, II, 178–84; for Beneš' reminiscences, see *Mnichovské Dny*, pp. 205–12 (French edition pp. 143–8).

This draft, too, contained proposals which would have been praiseworthy under any circumstances; for example, equality for all languages spoken in the country was to be guaranteed. But there were again dangerous concessions to the Nazis and their misguided supporters in the West. The 'state within the state' which had always been feared was promised through the indirect means of a right of appeal granted to the 'national *curiae*' in the various autonomous bodies. They were to enjoy the right to air their grievances.

The obnoxious 'freedom to profess National Socialism' was to be rendered innocuous by the formula that the autonomous bodies were to be charged with 'facilitating and promoting the fullest possible development of the social characteristics and capacities of the various nationalities on an equal footing within the framework of the common State'.

I was aware [wrote Beneš later] that I succumbed in this struggle against Nazi totalitarianism and for the rescue of Czechoslovak democracy, to the exaggerated and improper pressure of the democractic British and French Governments which – striving for the maintenance of peace – forced us to concessions clothed in the mantle of ethnic justice and having as their real aim the destruction of our State and national existence.

The implementation of the plan would have meant, in Beneš' words, the introduction of a totalitarian system in parts of the country, followed by the total loss of the territory.

I presented this plan [Beneš continued] to the SdP not only to convince the British and French Governments that we did not play an insincere game, but also because I was almost sure – observing the attitude of Hitler, Henlein and Frank – that our Pan-Germans would not accept even this Plan. I wanted to convince the French and the British Governments that not even the biggest concessions...could satisfy either Berlin or the Sudeten Pan-Germans. I saw in it the only and last way – if any existed at all – to bring the Western Powers and the rest of the world onto our side should an armed conflict break out between us and Germany.

The announcement of the Fourth Plan caused grave concern among the German democrats in Czechoslovakia. They realized that if carried out, it would mean the end of the democratic way of life in the German areas of the State. The German Social Democrats got in touch with their Czech colleagues and two delegates, Jaromír Nečas and Robert Wiener, were sent to Paris to point out the disastrous consequences of the ill-advised French pressure.[1] They met Léon Blum, the leader of the French Socialists, and gave him a detailed report on the Czechoslovak situation, imploring him to work for a change in French policy. Blum was spokesman for the strongest political party in France at that time, but this party was not represented in the Government. Thus there was not much chance of help from the Socialists in France.

Blum was opposed to concessions to the dictators and had told the British Ambassador in Paris that 'if they [i.e. His Majesty's Government] made it abundantly clear to Hitler that German aggression would inevitably bring in Great Britain, he would never dare attack Czechoslovakia'.[2] When his party colleagues from Czechoslovakia appealed to him, he telephoned Daladier in their presence and tried to convince the Prime Minister of the gravity of the crisis. Daladier sought shelter behind the argument that renewed pressure had become necessary because the Third Plan offered fewer concessions than the earlier ones. This suggestion, no doubt invented by the Nazis, had first been channelled to London, whence it had duly reached Paris.[3]

Beneš had calculated rightly when he had hoped to win Runciman for the Fourth Plan, although he was to be disappointed in his hope for definite support from London. Immediately after studying the plan Runciman had telegraphed to London that 'while it is true that proposals of Czechoslovak Government differ in some respects from those which I have been preparing, the general line is the same'.[4]

To the SdP the Fourth Plan caused grave embarrassment: even they had hardly expected that their demands were going to be met in so far-reaching a manner (according to Beneš, one of the SdP members is said to have burst out with 'My God, he's given us everything!'). An outright refusal to negotiate would have been unwise because at that time Runciman's continued goodwill was

[1] The following account is based on information supplied to the author by the two emissaries, Jaromír Nečas and Robert Wiener, independently of each other, after their return from Paris to Prague.
[2] Phipps to Halifax, 9 September 1938, *DBFP*, 3/II, no. 816.
[3] Newton to Halifax, 30 August 1938, *DBFP*, 3/II, no. 717.
[4] Newton to Halifax, 9 September 1938, *DBFP*, 3/II, no. 813. See also Runciman's report (21 September).

still considered important. Even the hyper-radical Frank hesitated.[1] Both Beneš and Runciman urged the SdP to commit themselves before Hitler gave his speech – awaited with much trepidation – at Nuremberg, but the SdP was not prepared to grant them this favour. The dilemma was eventually resolved by the 'incident' of Moravská Ostrava (Mährisch-Ostrau) which, they said, had to be 'cleared up' before negotiations could be resumed at all.

It is part of the tactical make-up of totalitarian movements that suitable incidents can be arranged at the drop of a hat or they can at least be alleged to have taken place. The similarity between the non-events of Teplice in October 1937 and those of Moravská Ostrava on 7 September 1938 is striking. If the latter had any basis of fact, it merely involved the manhandling by the police of a Sudeten German deputy in the course of organized street brawls.[2] Even the Runciman Mission was speedily able to convince itself of the triviality of the affair. But, instead of drawing the logical conclusion and explaining to his Government that the SdP was not to be taken seriously as a negotiating partner, Ashton-Gwatkin redoubled his efforts to bring the Czechoslovak Government and the SdP back to the conference table. The Government was dissuaded from holding an official enquiry into the Ostrava 'events': it could only have ended with the SdP being held up to ridicule. Instead, disciplinary punishment was meted out to the completely innocent local police chief and a number of his subordinates. On the same day Goebbels and Goering spoke at Nuremberg. Goebbels proclaimed that 'the trend of developments in Czechoslovakia is particularly menacing ...Prague represents the organizing centre of Bolshevik plots against Europe',[3] while Goering's inflammatory speech against that country contained passages of invective unusual even by Nazi standards:

[1] Hencke to G.F.M. 6 September 1938, *DGFP*, D/II, no. 440. Frank's comments are contained in Hencke's report to G.F.M. of 7 September 1938, *DGFP*, D/II, no. 438. Beneš, *Mnichovské Dny*, p. 218; French edition, p. 152.
[2] Footnote in Newton's report to Halifax, 8 September 1938, *DBFP*, 3/II, no. 801. Runciman's belief that the incident was organized by the SdP is expressed in his report (21 September).
[3] *Documents on International Affairs 1938*, II, 189–91.

We know how intolerable it is that *that little fragment of a nation* down there – goodness knows where it hails from – should persistently oppress and interfere with a highly civilized people. But we know that it is not *these absurd pygmies* who are responsible: Moscow and the *eternal Jewish–Bolshevik* rabble are behind it.

If they had not been sure of it before, the Franks and Kundts could now be certain that their lord and master was no longer interested even in sham negotiations.

The fateful 'Times' *leader*
In the meantime the democratic position had been weakened even further by a leading article in *The Times*[1] which, in order to restrain Hitler from resorting to force, recommended giving him what he wanted voluntarily. To provide so unscrupulous an opponent with justification at the height of the crisis was an act of the crassest political irresponsibility. The story of that disastrous blunder has since then been fully and remarkably frankly revealed[2] but the question whether and to what extent Chamberlain and the whole British Government were implicated remains unresolved. The first version of the article, written by A. L. Kennedy, one of the foreign sub-editors, and appearing in the early editions, adhered to the traditional tone of the newspaper, advancing the main argument hidden in a subordinate clause of a text which consisted of a series of otherwise unobjectionable statements. After discussing the Czechoslovak situation it was suggested that in view of the obvious 'German' desire – if required, Nazis and Germans were equated – for more than the mere removal of grievances, the Prague Government should reflect whether an entirely new solution ought not to be considered: 'that of making Czechoslovakia a more homogeneous State by the secession of the fringe of alien populations who are contiguous to the nation with which they are united by race'. Late at night the Editor, Geoffrey Dawson, a determined protagonist

[1] 'Nuremberg and Aussig', *The Times*, 7 September 1938. (Aussig was mentioned because Henlein had planned an SdP rally there after the conclusion of the Nazi Party rally at Nuremberg.) Similar views, though not so precisely formulated, had already been expressed by *The Times* in a leader on 3 June 1938.
[2] *The History of the Times*, IV, pt II (London 1952), 929ff. See also John Evelyn Wrench, *Geoffrey Dawson and our Times* (London 1952), pp. 371–2 (with extracts from Dawson's diary).

of appeasement, evidently thought that the conventional policy of understatement ought to be abandoned for once. In the later London editions he gave the article a sharper edge, adding that the proposal to make Czechoslovakia into a more 'homogeneous' State 'has met with favour in certain circles'. And to make quite sure that no doubt could arise, Dawson wrote that this advantage 'would far outweigh the disadvantages resulting from the loss of the Sudeten German districts'.

What all this really amounted to was that the most influential British newspaper had saved Hitler and Henlein the trouble of formulating their main argument for the cession of Sudeten German territory (and also, incidentally, by using the plural they anticipated the surrender of other 'alien populations' to Hungary and Poland). The article gave the impression that the mysterious 'certain circles' were either directly within or at least close to the British Government. It seems, however, that it was not inspired by the Government, for Lord Halifax, when speaking to the Cabinet, called it 'an unhappy leading article'.[1] But Jan Masaryk did not succeed in obtaining an official disavowal of the newspaper's proposals until he had had two interviews with Halifax.[2] Yet no *démenti* could shake Hitler's conviction that he no longer had anything to fear from London and consequently nothing from Paris. More than thirty years later, in order to make amends, *The Times* correctly formulated what ought to have been done in 1938:[3]

Britain should not have taken up the General's [Mason MacFarlane] idea [of killing Hitler] but should have done something much more substantial in 1938. It should, against the advice of this newspaper at the time, have stood firm at Munich. That would really have affected history.

Hitler's Nuremberg speech

Compared with Goering's, Hitler's speech at Nuremberg was almost restrained. His immediate aim now was to isolate Czechoslovakia, and hence he no doubt found it advisable not to alienate Chamber-

[1] *Cab.* 23/95, Minutes 37(38), Meeting of 12 September 1938. Colvin, *The Chamberlain Government*, p. 149.

[2] Note 1 to Halifax' despatch to Chilston (Moscow), 8 September 1938, *DBFP*, 3/11, no. 808. According to this even Runciman had reported to London that the *Times* article had aggravated an already difficult situation.

[3] *The Times*, 6 August 1969 (in the leading article 'Should we have shot Hitler?').

lain by intemperate language. All the same, he peremptorily
demanded[1] 'that the oppression of three and a half million Germans
shall cease and that its place shall be taken by the free right of
self-determination'. The man who oppressed the whole German
nation was hardly qualified to become incensed about events
elsewhere, but not even the Great Powers safe from his aggressive
intentions dared tell him this. In any case the claim that the Germans
were oppressed in Czechoslovakia was as untrue as his assertion
that the handing over of defenceless people to a tyranny was in line
with 'the free right of self-determination'. Hitler was astute enough
not to commit himself to any concrete demand; he could thus keep
the world guessing as to what he really wanted. Designed for this
purpose – on the one hand to pacify the West, on the other to keep
them in suspense – was his declaration that 'it is the business of the
Czechoslovak Government to discuss matters with representatives
of the Sudeten Germans and in one way or another to bring about
an understanding'. In appreciation of such moderation London and
Paris were prepared to overlook the incitement to open rebellion:

The poor Arabs are defenceless and perhaps deserted. The Germans in Czechoslovakia are neither defenceless nor are they deserted; and folk should take
notice of that fact.[2]

Lord Halifax's first impression of Hitler's speech was in his own
words 'that it may signify early demand for plebiscite'.[3] He sat down
and wrote in longhand a telegram to Newton asking whether the
objections of the Prague Government to the whole idea of a plebiscite arranged by Hitler could be overridden, if means could be
devised of assuring reasonable and fair conditions for holding a
plebiscite or – in other words – if anybody could succeed in de-
Nazifying Hitler. Newton gave the obvious answer: 'It would be

[1] Laffan, *Crisis over Czechoslovakia*, pp. 305–7; *Documents on International Affairs 1938*, II, 191–8; Baynes (ed.), *Speeches of Adolf Hitler*, pp. 1487–99.
[2] Without trying to give a source, Middlemas (*Diplomacy of Illusion*, p. 331) states that in Western Bohemia 'the Czech police fired on crowds listening to the broadcast in the open air. Six were killed and twenty seriously wounded.' There is no truth in this story, obviously based on Newton's telegram to Halifax of 13 September (*DGFP*, 3/II, no. 844) which says however something entirely different.
[3] Halifax to Newton, 13 September, 1938. Newton to Halifax, 14 September 1938. *Foreign Office Files*, vol. 21782.

difficult to persuade the Czechs that any reasonable and fair conditions could be devised for wording a plebiscite.' It was as simple as that, but, as we shall see, it proved not only difficult but impossible to persuade both Halifax and Chamberlain of it.

How did the British Government react to these developments? The Cabinet had not met between 26 July and 30 August. At the latter meeting[1] Ministers discussed whether Hitler should be told that if he invaded Czechoslovakia Great Britain would join France in her defence. Lord Halifax had to admit that 'many moderate Germans' (a curious description of Hitler's German adversaries) were convinced that if Britain did this there would be no further attempt to coerce Czechoslovakia. Chamberlain likewise said that 'many people in this country and in Germany' were convinced that war could be prevented by British action. He read a letter by Robert Boothby who referred to a German industrialist, desperately demanding such a step on Britain's part. But Chamberlain always had at hand a well-sounding argument in favour of inaction.

No state, certainly no democratic state, ought to make a threat of war unless it was both ready to carry it out and prepared to do so.

This would have been an excellent doctrine if accompanied by the declaration that no democratic state ought to capitulate to threats from a dictator. The position of the Cabinet Ministers, unable to see that lack of action brought more risks than anything else, was strengthened by Sir Nevile Henderson, the Ambassador in Berlin, who had been called to the meeting to give his opinion. He was almost always in favour of doing nothing at all:

His own view was that Herr Hitler had made up his mind to settle the Sudeten German question before the winter, but that he had not decided what steps he should take to this end...He agreed very strongly with the view that we must assume...that Herr Hitler had not yet decided to use force...*Herr Henlein was not entirely in Herr Hitler's pocket* although some of his followers were. Threats could only strengthen the extremists...

Duff Cooper (First Lord of the Admiralty) was in favour of energetic action. Disregarding that, Chamberlain said in summing up that the Cabinet unanimously considered that the threat which

[1] *Cab.* 23/94, Minutes 36(38), Meeting of 30 August 1938, partly quoted by Colvin, *The Chamberlain Government*, p. 140.

would most probably have saved the situation should not be made. 'It was very important,' Chamberlain pontificated, 'not to exacerbate feeling in Berlin against us.'

The Cabinet met again on 12 September a few hours before Hitler spoke at Nuremberg.[1] The meeting was strongly influenced by no less than three passionate appeals from Henderson, who had been present at the Nuremberg rally, not to do anything at all:

For Heaven's sake send no more instructions as on May 21st...*The solution lies at Prague, not in Berlin today*. Henlein himself has the plebiscite solution up his sleeve if Beneš will not agree to something amounting to the Karlsbad programme. This is better than driving Hitler over the edge with another May 21st.

Goering assured me that no aggression is contemplated and certainly no sudden one. But if Beneš goes on 'havering' that is what will provoke Hitler...The solution lies in Prague...Both Ribbentrop and Goering told me that Henlein has reassured Hitler about Runciman, so that I feel that Hitler will give Runciman credit [for a solution of his own. *Author*] and wait...None of us can even think of peace again until Beneš has satisfied Henlein and *Henlein wants peace* and will agree with Beneš if the latter is made to go far enough...It is revision by war or revision by peaceful means, which in fact means compulsion of Prague and not Berlin, because compulsion here settles nothing.

A further message, despatched two days later, again warned against any action, because that would only drive Hitler to greater violence or greater menace. That 'settlements' with such a maniac might be dangerous did not enter Henderson's head. He only dreaded an order to speak frankly to Hitler: 'If he has decided, that will not alter his decision. If he has not decided, that will help him to do so.' Instead Henderson announced his intention of telling Neurath, the former Foreign Minister, that 'His Majesty's Government...still have confidence in Hitler's sincerity in his desire for peace.' After having seen Goering that day, Henderson hastened to send a second message on 10 September. Goering had assured him the Germans would not attack Czechoslovakia – he gave these 'assurances' either before or after his speech calling the Czechs 'these absurd pygmies'. According to Goering, Henlein had 'informed' Hitler that the Czechoslovak army would revolt against the Government and install a military dictatorship, ask Runciman to

---

[1] *Cab.* 23/95, Minutes 37(38), Meeting of 12 September 1938. *Cab.* 24/278, C.P. 196(38), Memorandum by the Secretary of State for Foreign Affairs, 11 September 1938, partly quoted by Colvin, *The Chamberlain Government*, pp. 148–9. A garbled version of the first Henderson letter is printed by Laurence Thompson, *The Greatest Betrayal* (New York 1968), p. 133.

leave the country and 'might murder Henlein'. Nevile Henderson believed any nonsense, but he did not believe Hitler had any bad intentions.

Accepting Henderson's 'expert' advice, the Cabinet once more decided to do nothing. Again Chamberlain had no difficulty in finding a convincing explanation for that:

Any serious prospect of getting Herr Hitler back to a sane outlook would probably be irretrievably destroyed by any action on our part which would involve him in what he would regard a public humiliation.

The dangerous enterprise of publicly humiliating Hitler would have saved several million lives...Two days later Chamberlain embarked on an action which was far more risky than a public humiliation and had disastrous results.

Even without Hitler's reference to the poor, downtrodden Arabs, the tenor of his Nuremberg speech was clearly a signal for rebellion in the German areas of Czechoslovakia.[1] On the evening of the 12th, immediately after he had finished, unrest broke out near the German border in Western Bohemia, spreading on the following day into the interior of the country as far as Karlovy Vary; however trouble remained almost entirely limited to that region. On 13 September martial law was proclaimed in some districts of Western Bohemia, followed on the 14th by a pitched battle around the SdP headquarters at Cheb where a huge store of arms had been concentrated. On 15 September order had been restored everywhere: the whole uprising had been the work of a few desperados who could have been rendered harmless very much sooner had not the authorities kept the use of force to the absolute minimum. There was nothing spontaneous about the disorders and the broad masses of the people remained passive. It could in no sense be called a 'popular revolt'.

Meanwhile the SdP should have resumed negotiations with Hodža, the Czechoslovak Prime Minister, on 13 September; instead he received over the telephone an ultimatum from Frank

[1] A note by Weizsäcker (10 September 1938) mentions that the SdP had instructions 'to provoke and create incidents'. The provocations were to reach a climax 'by Tuesday' (i.e. the day after the Hitler speech). (*Nuremberg Doc. NG-2749.*) The report referred to local events and came from a provincial official, but its validity was no doubt general.

in Cheb: the SdP would be prepared to continue 'negotiations', provided martial law was lifted and the State Police withdrawn; in other words, if National Socialism was allowed free rein.[1] Six hours 'grace' was granted to the Government for acceptance or refusal. Hodža, however, did not fall into Frank's trap: he did not angrily reject his suggestion (thus supplying him with the excuse that the Czechoslovak Government had turned down his overtures): he merely asked that a SdP delegate be sent to Prague. This was, of course, the last thing Frank was prepared to do.

Undaunted, the Runciman Mission continued its efforts to get the SdP and the Government to meet again. On the evening of 13 September, Ashton-Gwatkin with two other members of the Mission – Geoffrey Peto and Ian Henderson – went in search of the elusive Henlein. At Aš they did not find him, but they did find a *pronunciamento* signed by him which declared that 'in view of the events of the last forty-eight hours' the SdP delegation considers its task at an end. The British Mission rushed back to Cheb where at 2 a.m. on the 14th they found Frank, who tried to explain to them that all was over now, since the Government had let his six hours' ultimatum expire without replying. Later that morning Henlein himself emerged and was naively asked by the British Mission whether he still counted on their mediation. He did, Henlein assured them, but a new situation had arisen: the Karlovy Vary programme was now out of date (everything was out of date as soon as conceded) – it was no longer a question of self-administration but of self-determination and a plebiscite.[2] The British delegation's promise that they could still persuade the Prague Government to withdraw the police made little impression on Henlein. On the same day (14 September) he issued a *communiqué* saying that negotiations could only be resumed on the basis of self-determination: the fulfilment of the Karlovy Vary demands was no longer enough.[3]

While Ashton-Gwatkin and his colleagues went post-haste to Prague to report to Runciman, Henlein, Frank and some of the other SdP leaders crossed the unguarded frontier into Bavaria,

[1] Notes by Altenburg, 13 September 1938, *DGFP*, D/ii, nos. 466, 467.
[2] Newton to Halifax, 14 September 1938, Ashton-Gwatkin to Strang, 17 September 1938, *DBFP*, 3/ii, nos. 860, App. ii.
[3] Eisenlohr to G.F.M. 15 September 1938, *DGFP*, D/ii, no. 491.

formally breaking off their last ties with the Czechoslovak Government.

The Berchtesgaden meeting

The idea of a direct and personal appeal to Hitler must have been in Chamberlain's mind for some time.[1] Sir Alexander Cadogan, then Permanent Under-Secretary of State in the Foreign Office, noted in his diary on 8 September[2] Chamberlain's saying that instead of sending a written warning to Hitler, 'he should go himself'. Cadogan was in favour of this idea, but Vansittart was opposed, using the word 'Canossa'. On 10 September Chamberlain acquainted Sir Samuel Hoare (Lord Templewood), the Home Secretary, with his plan to pay a personal visit to Hitler.[3] Hoare, himself an appeaser, was sceptical and spoke of a 'great political risk in intervening in a way that was quite likely to fail'. Chamberlain was undeterred by this warning but does not seem to have told Hoare what he intended to say to Hitler. Two days later the Cabinet met. On the 13th a Cabinet committee met twice. On none of these occasions did Chamberlain mention his plan to visit Hitler. The Cabinet was only informed on the 14th, one day before the fateful Berchtesgaden encounter.

Had Chamberlain gone to Berchtesgaden in order to warn Hitler of the possible consequences of his aggressive intentions, he would have done a service to mankind. Nothing of the sort was in his mind. Hitler is certainly not a very reliable witness, but for once he might have spoken the truth when he told the Polish Ambassador (at that time an ally) that he had expected Chamberlain to come with a warning:[4]

[1] Middlemas (*Diplomacy of Illusion*, pp. 300 and 315), quoting from the unpublished papers of Sir Horace Wilson and Sir Thomas Inskip (Lord Caldecote), says that Chamberlain mentioned his intention to visit Hitler first on 28 August in conversation with Wilson. Halifax was informed on 1 September, Hoare and Simon the following week.

[2] *Diaries of Sir Alexander Cadogan*, p. 95. A slightly different version is printed in Colvin, *The Chamberlain Government*, p. 147.

[3] Viscount Templewood, *Nine Troubled Years* (London 1954), p. 300. Colvin, *The Chamberlain Government*, p. 148.

[4] Lipski to Beck, 20 September 1938, *Papers and Memoirs of Józef Lipski, Ambassador of Poland, Diplomat in Berlin 1933–1939*, edited by Waclaw Jedrzejewicz (New York, 1968), p. 408.

(Hitler) remarked that he was taken aback to a certain extent by Chamberlain's proposition to come to Berchtesgaden. It was, of course, impossible for him not to receive the British Prime Minister. He thought Chamberlain was coming to make a solemn declaration that Great Britain was ready to march.

The minutes of the Cabinet meeting,[1] held on 14 September show, however, that Chamberlain went to Germany in an absolutely defeatist spirit. At Nuremberg Hitler had spoken but vaguely about self-determination, but the British Prime Minister was prepared for sacrifices not even hinted at yet by Hitler. He told the Cabinet beforehand that he wanted to say at Berchtesgaden that: 'We were neither pro-Czech nor pro-Sudeten German. Our business was to keep the peace and find a just and equitable settlement.'

He did not seem to understand that peace was not an abstract thing but somehow directly connected with Hitler's aggressiveness. Chamberlain foresaw that Hitler might fulminate against Beneš and express mistrust of Czech promises. In this case the Prime Minister would suggest the establishment of an international body to supervise the implementation of any agreement reached. If Hitler insisted on a plebiscite, Chamberlain left no doubt of his readiness to oblige. After all the experiences with plebiscites arranged by Hitler he still thought that this was in any circumstances a democratic measure:

He thought it was impossible for a democracy like ourselves to say that we would go to war to prevent the holding of a plebiscite. Further, the presence within their boundaries of a homogeneous, disciplined and easily moved people ...was not a source of strength to Czechoslovakia...He doubted whether Czechoslovakia would ever have peace so long as the Sudeten Germans were part of the country.

Here the Foreign Secretary should have intervened and drawn the attention of the Prime Minister to the fact that his ideas amounted to a violation of Great Britain's international commitments: the Covenant of the League of Nations bound all members 'to respect and preserve territorial integrity' of the other members. Lord Halifax kept silent. If he did not know the Covenant, some of the eminent legal experts of the Foreign Office could have told him about it. It seems that they did not do so either. Nor did any member of the Cabinet. Opposition came only from Hore-Belisha,

[1] *Cab.* 23/95, Minutes 38(38), Meeting of 14 September 1938. Partly quoted by Colvin, *The Chamberlain Government*, pp. 152–4.

Secretary of State for War, who said that all this was 'part of a relentless plan on the lines of *Mein Kampf*' and Duff Cooper who declared that 'the choice was not between war and plebiscite, but between war now or war later'.

Sir John Simon, Chancellor of the Exchequer, wanted to know what would happen to the rest of Czechoslovakia after such an amputation. 'The Czechs might...prefer to die fighting rather than accept a solution which would rob them of their natural frontiers.' The guarantee which Chamberlain had in March refused to give to a Czechoslovakia able to defend herself would then be given to a country unable to defend herself for a single day:

The Prime Minister said that the only answer which he could find was one which he was most unwilling to contemplate, namely, that this country should join in guaranteeing the integrity of the rest of Czechoslovakia...The value of the guarantee would lie in its deterrent effect. Czechoslovakia should be guaranteed by France, *Russia*, Germany and Great Britain and would become a neutral state.

The value of a British guarantee which could not be implemented would lie in its 'deterrent effect' – Chamberlain obviously thought that Hitler would not find out that the British guarantee was an empty gesture. But as Hitler was supposed – together with the Soviet Union – to join in this guarantee, Czechoslovakia would definitely have been out of any danger. This is the only conclusion one can draw from Chamberlain's reasoning. To include the Soviet Union (without asking her) in any guarantee was a fundamental change in British policy, but nobody said a word about it. It at least demolishes the Communist argument that the policy leading to Munich amounted to a sort of conspiracy against the Soviet Union.

When the question was asked whether other national minorities in Czechoslovakia were not also likely to demand plebiscites, the omniscient Prime Minister answered that 'he did not contemplate that any such demand would be made'. More competent observers did not overlook the fact that the Polish and Hungarian governments were acting with Hitler and fomenting unrest among the Poles and Hungarians living in Czechoslovakia, but Lord Halifax was sure 'that the other minorities in Czechoslovakia were content at the moment'. He added, however, that the idea of a plebiscite was infectious.

The Cabinet approved the line Chamberlain intended to take when speaking to the German dictator, but in fact at Berchtesgaden he acted quite differently.

Chamberlain had gone to see Hitler in order to find out how the latter thought the Sudeten Germans' right to self-determination should be implemented. But when he arrived at Berchtesgaden, the situation had changed again. Henlein had called for the annexation of the Sudeten German areas by Germany[1] and since the Sudeten Germans wanted this, Hitler could not of course deny them their dearest wish. He informed his visitor that he was going to settle the question 'one way or another' in the near future, accepting even the risk of war. The predominantly German areas must to go Germany; afterwards the Germans who had remained on the 'wrong' side of the border would be exchanged for Czechs. So Hitler first formulated the idea that an inhabitant of Czechoslovakia would have to give up his home if he belonged to the 'wrong' nationality. Needless to say, Hitler tried to arouse Chamberlain to indignation with talk of so-called Czech 'atrocities' to which some 300 Germans had already fallen victim. It seems that the Prime Minister was taken in by this fairy tale. Hitler agreed, once the British Government had accepted the principle of cession, to discuss the details of its execution with Chamberlain. The latter explained that he had first to consult his own and the French Government and also to see Runciman. The question of consulting the Prague Government was not mentioned.

On 17 September Chamberlain reported to the Cabinet on the Berchtesgaden meeting. According to this report, he did not feel deceived by the sudden 'change of situation' engineered by Hitler. His impressions were excellent. Here are extracts from the official minutes:[2]

---

[1] Henlein to Hitler, as well as Henlein's proclamation in *Documents on International Affairs 1938*, II, 205–6, 15 September 1938, *DGFP*, D/II, nos. 489, 490. The encounter between Hitler and Chamberlain at the Berghof, on 15 September 1938, has been the subject of a vast number of studies so that a detailed description is not called for. The narrative is based on the notes taken by Hitler's interpreter Schmidt (*DGFP*, D/II, no. 487), the books by Laffan and Celovsky already mentioned and the following publications: J. W. Wheeler-Bennett, *Munich, Prologue to Tragedy* (London 1948), Keith Eubank, *Munich* (Norman (U.S.A.), 1963), and Henri Noguères, *Munich or the Phoney Peace* (London 1965, trans. from the French edn of 1963).

[2] *Cab.* 23/95, Minutes 39(38), Meeting of 17 September 1938. Extracts in: Philip Howard, 'How Britain drifted to the tragedy of Munich', *The Times*,

Czechoslovakia before Munich

It was impossible [Chamberlain said] not to be impressed with the power of the man (Hitler)...The Prime Minister had formed the opinion that Herr *Hitler's objectives were strictly limited*...When he had included the Sudeten Germans in the Reich he would be *satisfied*...The Prime Minister said that the impression left on him was that Herr *Hitler meant what he said*...The Prime Minister's view was that Herr *Hitler was telling the truth*...It was immaterial to him [Chamberlain told Hitler] whether the Sudeten Germans stayed in Czechoslovakia or were included in the Reich. What the British people wanted was a peaceful and a just settlement...The Prime Minister said that Herr *Hitler would prove to be better than his word*...

In May 1938 Chamberlain had complained in his diary how utterly untrustworthy and dishonest the German Government was.[1] Five days before he had spoken at the Cabinet meeting about the difficulties of bringing Hitler back to a sane outlook,[2] but now, in order to get his policy approved he told the Cabinet things about Hitler's truthfulness which he could not possibly have believed himself. Only one member of the Cabinet – Duff Cooper – was unimpressed by the Prime Minister's report. 'Hitler's promises,' he said, 'were quite unreliable.' Hitler had also promised not to attack Austria and had done so afterwards: 'There was no chance of peace in Europe as long as there was a Nazi régime in Germany.' No one paid any attention to these warnings, only Lord Winterton, Chancellor of the Duchy of Lancaster, noting that the arguments in favour of accepting Hitler's demands could 'equally be used to justify acquiescence in the invasion of Kent or the surrender of the Isle of Wight'. The Marquess of Zetland, Secretary of State for India, feared the consequences of British support for demands for self-determination: 'The Indian Congress Party would not be slow to take advantage of such a declaration on our part.' Lord Halifax, a former Viceroy of India, understood this remark much better than he understood Hitler's intentions. He assured the noble Marquess that it was 'undesirable to burn too much incense on the altar of self-determination', but declared it 'impossible to lead the country into war against this principle'. Chamberlain finally wound up the discussion by stating that 'acceptance of the principle of self-determination was not an abject surrender'.

Meanwhile Henlein had issued two proclamations from Bavaria.[3]

1 January 1969; Mark Arnold-Forster, 'How we helped Hitler', *The Guardian*, 1 January 1969; Colvin, *The Chamberlain Government*, pp. 155–9.

[1] See p. 190. [2] See p. 256. [3] See p. 261 n. 1.

The first was full of inventions about Czech 'atrocities' against 'defenceless Germans'. The second was remarkable for two reasons. First, because Henlein alleged that the whole Czech people was to blame for the misfortune which had allegedly befallen the Sudeten Germans – the first attempt in fact to formulate the doctrine of a nation's collective responsibility for the real or alleged deeds of its rulers. Secondly, because he introduced the slogan '*Wir wollen heim ins Reich!*' (We want to return to Germany). This had no historical foundation whatever: the Germans in Bohemia, Moravia and Silesia had never belonged to Germany. Nevertheless the formula was 'to rebound on its inventor's head' in the winter of 1945/6 when even Germans in no way associated with National Socialism were driven out of newly restored Czechoslovakia – 'back' to what was left of Germany.

Henlein had sent his manifesto to Hitler with a covering letter suggesting that the Fuehrer should demand from Chamberlain the immediate surrender of those Czechoslovak districts with a German majority – according to the old Austrian census of 1910. German occupation was to be effected within 24 or 48 hours. It is noteworthy that Henlein wanted these steps to be applied only if 'approved as a *short-term solution* by you, my Fuehrer', i.e. a preparation for the occupation of what Hitler later called '*die Rest-Tschechei*'.

From Berchtesgaden Chamberlain summoned Runciman to London 'for consultations'.[1] He left Prague, accompanied by Ashton-Gwatkin, on 16 September.

Chamberlain did not hasten to inform the Czechoslovak Government of his talks with Hitler. Beneš and his Government had ample reasons to fear the worst. The truly monumental lack of understanding shown so far by the responsible men in London and Paris encouraged the Czechoslovak Government to fear that the Western Powers might accede to, or at least not oppose, Hitler's demand for a plebiscite in the German-speaking areas of Czechoslovakia. However democratic the notion of a plebiscite may be, in the prevailing circumstances there was no question of obtaining a free vote. Nazi intimidation was rife in the German area and every prominent democrat had already been driven from them.

[1] Halifax to Newton, 14 September 1938, *DBFP*, 3/II, no. 882.

On 14 September, the day on which Chamberlain's plan to visit Hitler became known, Beneš had a discussion with Newton. The latter reported to London that[1]

in the course of our conversation Dr Beneš mentioned that some Sudeten Germans lived in areas such as Egerland which in his opinion could have been excluded from Czechoslovakia without endangering the existence of the State. During the Peace Conference (1919) he personally had suggested...[2] their exclusion but the suggestion had never been seriously discussed nor had it been agreed to by other members of the delegation...Their exclusion now would of course be no adequate solution and would in any case be impossible in the present circumstances as such a precedent could not be admitted.

Naturally Beneš had to keep up appearances by rejecting the 'Egerland' solution in advance but the possibility that he really wanted to show London the way to a comparatively painless compromise cannot be altogether excluded.

In his memoirs, Bonnet states in his own defence that another alleged 'mediation attempt' took place. The French diplomat who was supposed to have conveyed the message of mediation, however, promptly repudiated his former chief. According to Bonnet sometime before the Anglo-French conference began on 18 September (the exact date of the interview is uncertain), Beneš is said to have mentioned to De Lacroix, the French Minister in Prague, that an area with 900,000 German-speaking inhabitants might be ceded.[3] De Lacroix refuted this version after the war. According to him, Beneš gave him roughly the same account of the Egerland (Cheb) situation of 1919 as he gave Newton. That means that in 1938 he did not suggest the cession of this territory. When, however, De Lacroix looked up his Prague despatches in the French Foreign Ministry after the war he discovered that his report on the conversation with Beneš 'had been faked in a way which might lead to the belief that what in retrospect Beneš had said about 1919 had in reality the character of a solution proposed by him' for the situation of 1938.

Less circumspect than Beneš but still emphasizing to Newton[4]

---

[1] Newton to Halifax, 15 September 1938, *DBFP*, 3/II, no. 888.
[2] See pp. 40 and 45.
[3] Bonnet, *Défense de la Paix*, pp. 237ff. Statement by De Lacroix in *Évenements*, II, 266ff.
[4] Newton to Halifax, 16 September 1938, *DBFP*, 3/II, no. 902.

that he did not wish to be quoted and that he was 'only thinking
aloud', Hodža expressed much the same views in their talks on
16 September. According to Newton, the Czechoslovak Prime
Minister stated that

if some territorial secession was absolutely insisted upon as a *sine qua non* of a
peaceful solution with Herr Hitler it might in the last resort be feasible to
surrender Egerland and other areas...the areas could be drawn to include
from 800,000 to perhaps even 1,000,000 inhabitants.

The Germans still remaining in the Czechoslovak State could then
benefit from the provisions of the Fourth Plan: 'self-determination
could be granted within the present State by means of the Government's last offer'. All this strengthens the impression that when
Prague realized that the Western Powers would not object on
principle to territorial concessions, it wanted to give them an idea
of what it considered acceptable. At the time the Western Powers
paid no attention to these diplomatic moves.

Deeply disturbed by the unhelpful attitude of the Western Powers,
Nečas, the Socialist Minister, had in the meantime decided to go to
Paris again and also to visit London. Since, however, his contacts
were almost entirely restricted to socialist circles, his chances were
not very bright. In France the Socialists were not represented in
the Government and in Berlin Labour was in opposition.[1] On 15

---

[1] Early in September, the National Executive Committee of the Labour Party,
in joint session with the General Council of the T.U.C. and the Parliamentary
Labour Party Executive at Blackpool, drafted a joint declaration, insisting
that 'the British Government must leave no doubt in the mind of the German
Government that it will unite with the French and Soviet Governments to
resist an attack on Czechoslovakia' (cited in John F. Naylor, *Labour's International Policy* (London 1969), p. 241). On 19 September the National
Council of Labour, at that time jointly constituted by the Labour Party and
the T.U.C., issued a manifesto, espressing 'dismay at the reported proposals
of the British and French Governments for the dismemberment of Czechoslovakia under the brutal threat of armed force by Nazi Germany and without
prior consultation with the Czechoslovakian Government, which is a shameful
betrayal of a peaceful and democratic people and constitutes a dangerous precedent for the future' (Laffan, *Crisis over Czechoslovakia*, p. 351). This was
followed two days later by a new declaration expressing 'profound humiliation'
in view of the British Government's treatment of Czechoslovakia. 'This is a
shameful surrender to the threats of Herr Hitler. Although the Czechoslovak
Republic has gone to the extreme limit of concessions...the British Government has set aside all consideration of freedom, equality and justice, and has

265

September Nečas flew to Paris, going on to London on the 17th, where he supplied the Labour leaders with arguments to support their position. In Paris he had the more formidable task of communicating to Léon Blum or any other accessible politician a desperate compromise proposal which Beneš had entrusted to him. The President had obviously jotted down his ideas in a great hurry on a piece of paper,[1] warning Nečas never to reveal that the plan had come from him or indeed from any Czechoslovak source at all. Nečas was to destroy the piece of paper: 'The whole idea is extremely dangerous and if carelessly divulged, it would be a catastrophe.' Since Beneš realized that 'at the moment when we accept the principle (of territorial cessions) Daladier and Chamberlain might yield to Hitler and give him everything', they would have to be persuaded to suggest to Hitler that he be satisfied with small portions of Czechoslovak territory. Beneš had an area of 1,500 to 2,300 square miles in mind: the Munich Agreement was to deprive Czechoslovakia of 16,000 square miles, nearly 30 per cent of her territory (including the areas which had to be ceded to Hungary and Poland). He said, however, that Germany would have to accept more Germans from the remaining Czechoslovak territory – 'at least one and a half to two millions' – democrats, Socialists and Jews remaining in Czechoslovakia.

If Beneš had been able to give the matter more thought, so confused a project would never have been put on paper. He could not seriously have thought that any French politician would submit such a proposal to his Government as his own. After the war Blum put the affair into an altogether different perspective[2] and it is quite possible that because of its complexity Nečas never even told Blum of the plan sketched out to him by Beneš. According to Blum, Nečas gave him a map 'from Beneš' (which need not be taken

consented to the virtual destruction of the Czechoslovak State. This is not merely the sacrifice of a gallant democratic people, it is the sacrifice of vital British interests...' *Keesing's Contemporary Archives* (1938), pp. 32–4.

[1] In an attempt to discredit both Beneš and Nečas the Communists reproduced this paper in fascimile, thus leaving no doubt about its authenticity. J. Pachta and P. Reimann, 'O nových dokumentech k otázce Mnichova' (About new documents concerning the question of Munich), in *Příspěvky k dějinám KSČ* (Contributions to the history of the Czechoslovak Communist Party), I (1957), 104–33.   [2] *Évenements*, I, 256.

literally) showing the limits of tolerable territorial concessions. This map no longer exists but it is very likely that the areas which it indicated as 'cedable' lay outside the belt of fortifications; in other words, a relatively small territory. Blum's secretary, André Blumel, handed this map to Daladier before the French Prime Minister left for London, but as far as can be ascertained it was not used during the Anglo-French discussions and after the war Blum declared that Daladier had ignored it.

Daladier himself gave three quite different explanations. After the war[1] he stated that on 17 September a French journalist had given him a proposal originating from Beneš. Its contents were not specified. The circumstances surrounding this episode suggest that the intermediary can only have been a French journalist who lived in Prague until the time of Munich and died shortly afterwards. It is of course possible that Beneš tried several ways of contacting Daladier. But on 27 September 1938 the latter had told the American Ambassador in Paris[2] that 'some time ago' he had received a communication from the Czechoslovak President informing him that he (Beneš) would not object to the surrender of the border areas outside the fortress belt. This might be an allusion to one of the two maps allegedly given to Daladier or to both of them. In his recollection of 1938, however, which appeared 23 years after the event,[3] Daladier's version had clearly been influenced by the publications which had appeared in the meantime. He described how on the morning of 18 September, before his flight to London, Blumel handed him a message from Blum which had originally come from Nečas. This message, accompanied by a map, indicated that a compromise solution might be reached by the cession of three border strips: one in the north-west, another in the north-east of Bohemia, and a third in Silesia. The total population involved was about one million. Daladier said that he was greatly taken aback by all this, since such a proposal might well have led to even greater demands; for just that reason (*pour les raisons que j'ai dites*) it had been rejected at the London conference. It can however be proved

[1] Ibid. p. 33.
[2] Bullitt to Hull, 27 September 1938, *Foreign Relations of the United States, 1938*, I, 686–8.
[3] Edouard Daladier, 'Munich', *Candide* (Paris), 7 September 1961.

from the very detailed minutes of that conference that neither this nor any similar project was ever discussed there. At any rate, since Hitler was eventually given much more, the rejection of an alleged Czechoslovak suggestion could hardly have been motivated by Daladier's *'raisons'*. What he alleged to have received from Blumel does not tally with the note Beneš had given to Nečas and which did not specify any details of the territory to be ceded.

Prague's desperate attempts to stave off or at least to mitigate the disaster threatening may be understandable enough, but they in no way influenced the Western Powers' actions.

The Anglo-French transfer proposals

The minutes of the Anglo-French Conference of 18 September[1] made no reference to any initiative by Prague or anybody else to surrender any territory. It is very unlikely that so important an argument, if tabled by the French or the British, would have been overlooked. Reporting on his talks with Hitler, Chamberlain said he had gained the impression that there was no alternative to granting self-determination to the Germans in Czechoslovakia. After the French delegation had discussed the matter among themselves for several hours, Daladier declared that he could not accept the demand for a plebiscite but he agreed 'that it might be possible to consider some sort of cession of a part of the territories occupied by the Sudeten Germans. This agreement would, however, be conditional upon the necessity of prior consultation with the Czechoslovak Government.' The idea of consultation was dropped, but not that of cession. The French Premier explained that he could exert no pressure on Prague without a British guarantee of the new frontiers. After another prolonged pause in the joint negotiations, Chamberlain announced that his Government was prepared to grant such a guarantee, provided Czechoslovakia accepted the proposals submitted to her. Such lack of logic could hardly be surpassed: the Western Powers declared their inability to assist Czechoslovakia when she was well-armed with good strategic frontiers, yet they were ready to 'guarantee' her borders when disarmed and helpless.

Only at this stage did Chamberlain make concrete suggestions: all

[1] Record of Anglo-French Conversations held at 10 Downing Street, 18 September 1938, *DBFP*, 3/II, no. 928.

districts with a German-speaking population of more than 50 per cent were to go to Germany. The possibility that Hitler might wish to use criteria other than those of the Czechoslovak census for the determination of the percentages was not even discussed. Understandably enough, Daladier was taken aback. Supposing Prague refused, a critical situation could arise – war might break out and France would find herself compelled, in case of German aggression, to come to the aid of Czechoslovakia. This prospect upset Chamberlain too, not so much on account of German aggression, but because of its possible repercussions, and he asked Daladier 'whether he contemplated that it might be left to Dr Beneš to take a decision which would certainly involve France and might perhaps also involve this country in war after he had refused to take the advice which had been given to him?' Daladier assured him 'that the strongest pressure would have to be brought on Dr Beneš to see that the Czechoslovak Government accepted the solutions proposed'. The existence of a German–Czechoslovak Treaty of Arbitration which had to be invoked to settle any conflict between the two countries was ignored. That same night instructions went out to Newton in Prague[1] informing him that 'after recent events the point has now been reached when the further maintenance within the boundaries of the Czechoslovak State of the districts mainly inhabited by *Sudeten-Deutsch* cannot in fact continue any longer without imperilling the interests of Czechoslovakia herself and of European peace'. He was to tell the President that 'you (Beneš) may prefer to deal with the *Sudeten-Deutsch* problem by the method of direct transfer'.

Prague had rejected the idea of a plebiscite, but, curiously, it was still inferred that an even more far-reaching proposition would be accepted. Nothing was said about areas where there were large numbers although not a majority of Germans. The decision of the London conference was to be conveyed to Czechoslovakia only after France had given her approval. This was obtained the following day by Daladier and Bonnet in the French Cabinet against strong opposition, notably from Georges Mandel. In the British Government a similar opponent to appeasement was Duff Cooper, who

---

[1] Halifax to Newton, 19 September 1938, *DBFP*, 3/11, no. 947, *Documents on International Affairs 1938*, 11, 213–14.

nevertheless remained in the Government until after the Munich agreement, i.e. when in his view there was nothing left to save. The French Ministers who voted against capitulation, especially Mandel and Reynaud, presumably stayed in office because they thought they could help, lest worse befall and perhaps hoping Czechoslovakia might turn down the suicidal 'advice' offered to her. The Czechs pinned their hopes on the possible fall of Daladier and a change of Government in Paris which might remove the threat of this 'advice'.

The question of a guarantee

The question of a British guarantee for Czechoslovakia's new frontiers was child's play for Chamberlain: he imagined a guarantee which did not guarantee anything and did not commit anyone. Reporting the conversations with Daladier and Bonnet to the Cabinet on 19 September,[1] he said that the guarantee should be formulated as vaguely as possible. 'It would, of course, be for us to determine what constituted unprovoked aggression.' Lord Halifax added that 'a guarantee did not exclude peaceful solutions of any minority question'. This was another way of saying that it would not prevent the Beck régime in Poland or the Horthy régime in Hungary from blackmailing Czechoslovakia after Hitler's fashion. To underline the point, Chamberlain answered some critical remarks from Hore-Belisha with the statement:

It was not right to assume that the guarantee committed us to maintaining the existing [He meant the 'newly proposed'. *Author's note*] boundary of Czechoslovakia. The guarantee was merely related to unprovoked aggression... Its main value would lie in its deterrent effect.

How 'deterrent' the effect of the British guarantee was became obvious on 15 March 1939, when Hitler occupied Prague. But six months before that day Halifax quoted what Jan Masaryk told him after hearing the British–French proposals: the Czechs would rather fight than agree to a large surrender of territory. Halifax's comment was that Masaryk had obviously not thought of the guarantee.

The 'thoroughness' with which the Cabinet investigated the situation is illustrated by the statement in the minutes that there was a discussion about the Soviet–Czechoslovak treaty. 'The

[1] *Cab.* 23/95, Minutes 40(38), Meeting of 19 September 1938, Colvin, *The Chamberlain Government*, pp. 159–61.

French Ministers referred to a definite treaty and not, as Lord Runciman had understood from Dr Beneš, merely an understanding.' Nobody bothered to ring up the Foreign Office to find out the facts.

Two days later the Cabinet met again.[1] Neither the Prime Minister nor the Foreign Secretary informed their colleagues that the Czechoslovak Government had meanwhile rejected the advice to capitulate and drawn attention to the fact that according to international law all conflicts between Germany and Czechoslovakia had to be settled by arbitration. This had been foreseen in the arbitration treaty between the two countries, signed at Locarno in 1925 and still recognized as binding even by the Third Reich.[2] Knowledge of this fact relevant to the situation was withheld from the Cabinet together with all news about the ultimatum, presented to Beneš by the British and French Ministers at 2 a.m. that very morning (see below).

Chamberlain quoted Hitler as saying at Berchtesgaden that he was not interested in the non-German minorities in Czechoslovakia: 'If Herr Hitler maintained this attitude, these minorities should not present any immediate difficulties.' (Chamberlain had apparently forgotten and his listeners, too, that he had spoken quite otherwise when returning from Berchtesgaden. He had told the Cabinet on 17 September[3] that if the Sudeten Germans were to be given what Hitler misnamed 'self-determination', the same concessions would have to be made to the Hungarians, the Poles and the Slovaks – who were not a 'minority' like the other ones.) Now he said Hitler could reverse his alleged lack of interest in non-German minorities when meeting the Prime Minister again, but 'he did not think that Herr Hitler was likely to take up this attitude'. In Chamberlain's view nothing which could make his position more difficult was ever 'likely'. Should Hitler bring in the other minorities of Czechoslovakia, he (Chamberlain) would point out that this was in contradiction to his previous 'limited' interests in 'his' Germans

[1] *Cab.* 23/95, Minutes 41(38), Meeting of 21 September 1938, Colvin, *The Chamberlain Government*, p. 161.
[2] Reply of the Czechoslovak Government, 20 September 1938, in *DBFP*, 3/II, no. 987, *Documents on International Affairs 1938*, II, 214–16. Ultimatum in Telegram Halifax to Newton, 21 September 1938, ibid. pp. 216–17.
[3] See p. 262.

only. Should Hitler insist on an immediate solution of the alleged problem of the non-German minorities, the Prime Minister would return to London to consult his colleagues. When at Godesberg Hitler took this – in Chamberlain's view – unlikely attitude, the Prime Minister had forgotten his promise to return to London to consult his colleagues.

Returning to the question of a guarantee for a truncated Czecho-slovakia, Chamberlain said the guaranteeing powers would in effect 'have the right to determine whether the guarantee operated in a particular case'. A joint meeting of the guarantors should decide whether 'unprovoked aggression' had taken place. How any aggression could have been prevented or even curbed by such a tortuous procedure, remained the Prime Minister's secret. At least he understood that his ideas would give Hitler a veto against any action, and so he changed his original proposal: the joint guarantee should be given by Great Britain, France, and the Soviet Union and Germany should be 'invited' to sign a non-aggression pact with Czechoslovakia. (It goes without saying that Czechoslovakia was never informed of Chamberlain's grandiose plans nor of his rather original interpretation of international commitments.) He wanted France

to invite Russia to follow the French example and to modify her treaty with Czechoslovakia to conform with the arrangements now proposed. It was possible that Russia refuses to agree to this arrangement, but she should be invited to do so. So far as he (Chamberlain) could see, such a guarantee was unobjectionable from Herr Hitler's point of view, unless he intended to commit an act of un-provoked aggression against Czechoslovakia and wished to destroy it.

Should Hitler make difficulties about a Soviet guarantee, the Prime Minister promised to refer back to the Cabinet. The whole Cabinet was in favour of inviting Moscow to share in the joint guarantee, and it was decided that the Prime Minister should speak to Hitler thus. When Chamberlain met Hitler at Godesberg, he did not even dare to mention the name of the Soviet Union.

The Runciman Report

How far had Runciman's impressions of Czechoslovakia influenced Chamberlain in his decisions? Did they influence him at all? When speaking to the French visitors, the Prime Minister did, of course, refer to Runciman, if only in fairly general terms, but it is at the very least odd that Runciman himself, just back from Prague, was not called to attend the conference. Some writers[1] have erroneously stated that as early as 16 September (the day of his homecoming) Runciman gave the British Government the advice contained in his report dated 21 September. In fact, on the 16th there was only an informal meeting between Chamberlain, Halifax, Simon, Hoare and some officials.[2] Chamberlain reported on the Berchtesgaden encounter in much the same terms as a day later at the meeting of the full Cabinet. While the meeting was in progress, Lord Runciman entered, fresh from Prague, and took part in the deliberations. In his absence Chamberlain had formulated what he would 'recommend' him to do:

> The Prime Minister said that the most convenient course would be if Lord Runciman made a pronouncement to the effect that after all that had happened and the incidents which had taken place, it was impossible that the Sudeten Germans and the Czechs would settle down together, and that a plebiscite was the only way out. He thought that this might make matters easier for the Czech Government.

After having been informed about the preceding discussion, Runciman reported on the interview he had had with Beneš that very morning. Then he told the meeting of a proposal he had received from a Czech banker who thought Henlein's Karlovy Vary demands could somehow be fitted into the State as it existed. He made no proposals of his own and did not react in any way to what would have been 'the most convenient course' for Chamberlain. When the latter repeated that 'a plebiscite offered the only solution', Runciman gave an evasive reply. To Halifax's question whether 'apart from Hitler' it would in Runciman's view 'be possible to look forward to the Czechs and the Sudeten Germans settling down to live together happily', Lord Runciman gave the cryptic answer that 'he thought not, unless someone who was not a local politician assumed responsibility for law and order'. On this day (but on this day only) Chamberlain was obsessed with the idea of a plebiscite

---

[1] Laffan, *Crisis over Czechoslovakia*, p. 334, Celovsky, *Münchner Abkommen*, p. 349.
[2] *Cab.* 27/646 (*The Czechoslovakia Crisis*), Notes of informal meetings of Ministers, 38(5), 16 September 1938.

which according to all reports Hitler had not even mentioned at Berchtesgaden:

> The Prime Minister said that Herr Hitler told him if a plebiscite was granted he would not worry his head on what was left of Czechoslovakia. He, the Prime Minister, believed that this really represented Herr Hitler's view.

After having heard what Hitler was supposed to have said, Runciman conceded that 'if once you accepted the principle of self-determination, there was no alternative to a plebiscite'. Then he left the meeting.

It is interesting to compare the minutes of this meeting with Chamberlain's statement about it in the House of Commons on 28 September.[1]

> I came back to London next day (September 16), and that evening the Cabinet met and it was attended by Lord Runciman who, at my request, had also travelled from Prague on the same day. Lord Runciman informed us that although, in his view, the responsibility for the final breach in the negotiations at Prague rested with the Sudeten extremists, nevertheless in view of recent developments, the frontier districts between Czechoslovakia and Germany, where the Sudeten population was in an important majority, should be given the full right of self-determination at once. He considered the cession of territory to be inevitable and thought it should be done promptly.

It is true that Chamberlain returned to London on the 16th, and it is also true that Runciman travelled the same day from Prague to London. Everything else in Chamberlain's description of events is, to say the least, not in accordance with the facts. It is not even true that the full Cabinet met that evening. The words Chamberlain put into Runciman's mouth were not spoken on the 16th, i.e. before the Cabinet had accepted such a line, but were quotations from Runciman's published proposals dated 21 September. For obvious reasons Chamberlain had ante-dated them. The Cabinet met on the 17th and heard Runciman. Duff Cooper, one of those present, wrote in his diary:[2]

> At the Cabinet Meeting on September 17th Runciman was present and described his experiences...He was interesting, of course, but *quite unhelpful as he was unable to suggest any plan or policy.*

[1] *Parliamentary Debates (Hansard)*, House of Commons, 28 September 1938, vol. 339, col. 25.
[2] Viscount Norwich, *Old Men Forget, The Autobiography of Duff Cooper* (London 1953), p. 229, quoted by Colvin, *Vansittart in Office*, p. 255.

This is confirmed by the minutes of this Cabinet meeting. If Runciman had come back from Prague with the impression that Czechs and Germans could not go on living in the same country and that, therefore, the German-inhabited areas should be ceded to Germany, this was the occasion to say so. Instead, Runciman told the meeting that 'there was no point in putting forward any further plan at the present time'. The only concrete idea he expressed was the possible cession of the frontier districts of Cheb and Aš to Germany – he mistakenly believed that they were inhabited by 800,000 Germans (in reality they had only 110,000 inhabitants according to the census of 1930). On plebiscites Runciman was sceptical.[1]

At the present time he doubted whether free expression of opinion was possible ...The transfer of these areas (Cheb and Aš) to Germany would almost certainly be a good thing. On the other hand the Czech army would certainly oppose any transfer of territory very strongly. Dr Beneš had said that they would fight rather than accept it...Czechoslovakia could not continue to exist as she was today. *Something* would have to be done, even if it amounted to no more than *cutting off certain fringes*...He thought that there was a *considerable percentage of people in the German area who did not wish to be incorporated in the Reich.*

A letter from Runciman to Chamberlain and an analogous letter to Beneš signed on 21 September and published the next day has become known as the 'Runciman Report'. Between the 17th and 21st there must have been some 'briefing' in private from Chamberlain for Runciman to be prepared to suggest what according to Chamberlain he had already suggested on the 16th. This becomes apparent from the minutes of the Cabinet meeting of 21 September:[2]

The Prime Minister reported that Lord Runciman proposed to write him a letter reporting on the work of his Mission and setting out the views which he had formed. *He had seen a draft of this letter, in an incomplete form.* He suggested that the letter would *probably* be found to be suitable for incorporation in a White Paper...which would have to be published before Parliament met.

It seems that Chamberlain had not only seen a draft of the 'Runciman letter' in an incomplete form but the letter itself. He was not satisfied with it and asked Lord Runciman to make basic changes in his proposals. Eventually Runciman substantially complied with this request. The Foreign Office archives[3] contain a ten-page letter

[1] See p. 273.   [2] See p. 271 n. 1.
[3] *Foreign Office Files* (*The Sudeten Crisis*), F.O. 371, vol. 21741.

from Lord Runciman to the Prime Minister dated 20 September and duly signed 'Runciman of Doxford'. Pages 1–4 and 6–10 are identical with the beginning and end of the letter which was finally published on 21 September.[1] Page 5 of the letter of 20 September has not been preserved. It had obviously contained Runciman's original proposals. As the other pages (with the exception of the still shorter pages 1 and 10) had only 21 lines, it is most unlikely that Lord Runciman went into great detail here. The missing page has been replaced by a much longer text (the definitive letter has fifteen pages), written on Foreign Office paper, partly typed and partly in Ashton-Gwatkin's handwriting. The text later inserted in the letter introduced a criticism of the Czechoslovak nationality policy which for lack of space could hardly have been included in the original text. Then came a rejection of the idea of a plebiscite (most probably also new) and finally Runciman's proposals for the cession to Germany of frontier districts 'with an important (German) minority' Runciman still did not accept Chamberlain's reasons for handing over to Germany *all* the Czechoslovak territory with a German majority, but the expression of his real or alleged opinion certainly helped the Prime Minister. On 29 September Chamberlain tried to create the impression in the House of Commons that he had only been following Runciman's advice, while in reality, Runciman's final recommendations were an attempt to fall into line with Chamberlain's intentions. Mr Ashton-Gwatkin does not remember the details of what happened in 1938,[2] but he distinctly remembers Runciman telling him, as guidance, that he wanted to back up Chamberlain's policy. Afterwards Runciman seems to have regretted the degree to which he had become identified with Chamberlain. Some telephone conversations between Jan Masaryk in London and Beneš in Prague had been intercepted in Berlin, transcribed and quickly given by Goering to the British Ambassador who passed the transcripts on to London. For obvious reasons both Beneš and Masaryk had been careful in their conversations and so Goering's 'scoop' caused no sensation. But the following passage from a tele-

[1] *DBFP* 3/II, App. II, no. IV; *Documents on International Affairs 1938*, II, 218–24.
[2] Information kindly supplied by Mr Ashton-Gwatkin to the author in a personal interview, 6 May 1971.

phone conversation which took place on 23 September 1938 is not without interest:[1]

JAN MASARYK: The old Lord has rung me up.
  He has been deceived as much as you.
BENEŠ: The Lord who was with us?
MASARYK: He has been slighted in the most shameful manner.
BENEŠ: I felt it.
MASARYK: Yesterday he still thought that we should only have to cede up to 75 per cent. I told him about the 50 per cent. He collapsed and wept.

('To cede up to 75 per cent' meant a cession to Germany of districts where the German population was at least in a majority of three fourths, while '50 per cent' meant the more radical solution of ceding all districts with a German majority of at least 51 per cent.)

A few days later as a result of textual analysis only, and with no inside knowledge whatsoever, the American writer Dorothy Thompson stated that she thought something was wrong with the Runciman Report.[2] She called it an 'illogical document', 'apparently made to order to fit the agreement which had already been reached between Hitler and Chamberlain. It is not the basis of the Anglo-French proposals, but is an apology for them.' Pointing to the fact that the tone of the middle passages varied drastically from that of the first section, she called it a 'rigged report'. Commenting on her criticism, a British official in New York likewise said that there was 'surely a break or hiatus in that report'.

These hasty last-minute changes – most probably a result of pressure from the Prime Minister – may explain some of the contradictions in Runciman's published letter and the degree to which it differed from the views he expressed in an unguarded moment in the Cabinet meeting of the 17th. An example is the sentence 'History has proved that in times of peace the two peoples can live together on friendly terms'. The advisability of eliminating this may have been overlooked; hence it remained in a document which otherwise tried to prove the opposite view. In the letter Runciman declared that the Fourth Plan could have meant the successful conclusion of his mission to Prague; however,

---

1 *Foreign Office Files* (*The Sudeten Crisis*), F.O. 371, vol. 21741.
2 *New York Herald Tribune*, 1 and 3 October 1938. Fletcher (British Library of Information, New York) to Leeper (Foreign Office), *Foreign Office Files* (*The Sudeten Crisis*), F.O. 371, vol. 21745.

responsibility for the final breach must in my opinion rest upon Herr Henlein and Herr Frank and upon those of their supporters inside and outside the country who were urging them to extreme and unconstitutional action.

In the circumstances it would have been logical for him to recommend the implantation of the Fourth Plan within the existing State, but without Henlein and Frank who had run away. Whether Runciman's criticism of Czechoslovak conditions, later interpolated into the letter in order to vindicate Chamberlain's course, was justified or not, it did not warrant his conclusion that disaffection had reached 'a point where the resentment of the German population was inevitably moving in the direction of revolt'. Was it really bad enough to justify an appeal to Berlin? Runciman himself confirms in his report that there was no oppression of Germans in Czechoslovakia and that they were not intimidated. On the other hand, the very existence of German democrats who rejected Hitler and Henlein and whose representatives had been received by Lord Runciman was not mentioned.

It has been suggested that pre-war Anglo-French policy towards Czechoslovakia was influenced by a kind of guilt-complex arising out of the 1919 Peace Treaties. Was Chamberlain perhaps out to restore to the Sudeten Germans the right to self-determination allegedly denied to them in the settlement after the First World War? All evidence points to the conclusion that nothing of the sort was ever contemplated. Sir Nevile Henderson, the British Ambassador in Berlin, told Ribbentrop quite bluntly that 'England was utterly indifferent to the Sudeten Germans or the Czechs'.[1] This goes for Chamberlain too: who had assured Hitler at Berchtesgaden that Great Britain was not interested in whether the Sudeten Germans remained in Czechoslovakia or were transferred to Germany. What Chamberlain wrote in a private letter to his sister certainly reflected his true feelings much better than official pronouncements, because it was not intended for publication:[2] '*I didn't care two hoots* whether the Sudetens were in the Reich or out of it.'

---

[1] Note by Ribbentrop, 3 September 1938, *DGFP*, D/II, no. 425.
[2] Feiling, *Life of Chamberlain*, p. 367; Iain Macleod, *Neville Chamberlain* (London 1961), p. 238.

Prague forced to capitulate

The Anglo-French proposals caused deep dejection in Prague, where even the pessimists had not expected such a development. People doubted whether the whole plan was intended seriously: perhaps it was merely a *ballon d'essai* to test the willingness of Czechoslovakia to resist such demands? The general consensus was tersely expressed in the headline of the main Czech newspaper's leading article: 'Unacceptable!'[1] The real victims, however, would not have been the Czechs who at least could have kept their homes and hopes, but the German opponents of National Socialism, who, in a terribly literal sense, would have lost the ground from under their feet. The German Social Democrats' reaction was a cry of despair in the form of an 'urgent appeal' to the British and French envoys:[2]

We turn to the Governments of Great Britain and France with the question of what is to become of the 400,000 Sudeten Germans who, trusting in the solidarity of the French nation and in the declaration of the British Prime Minister...on 24 March 1938, adhered until the last moment, with heroic sacrifices, to the ideal of democracy.

On 24 March 1938 Mr Chamberlain declared himself for a solution of the Sudeten German question within the structure of the Czechoslovak constitution. Building upon the word of the spokesman for Great Britain, we Sudeten German democrats have striven for a peaceful solution of the Sudeten problem within the structure of the Czechoslovak State. Now the British and French Governments have put forward the claim that the German districts of Czechoslovakia shall be surrendered to Germany. We raise the question whether, when these demands are met, the 400,000 German democrats are to be included: for this would mean their destruction.

What is to become of these people? Are the Governments of Great Britain and France willing to hand over the last free Germans in Central Europe to the vengeance of the conqueror? Do they wish to accept the moral responsibility for the massacres which must inevitably break out there...

In Prague it was apparently thought that the Chamberlain–Daladier proposals were not necessarily their last word. This illusion did not last long. At 2 a.m. on 21 September, the two Western envoys, in accordance with their instructions, called on Beneš to inform him bluntly that an appeal to the German–Czechoslovak Arbitration Treaty, suggested as a way out by the Prague Govern-

[1] *Lidové Noviny* (Prague), 20 September 1938.
[2] *Sudeten-German Newsletters* (Prague), no. 12, 22 September 1938 (published by the German Social Democrats in English).

ment, was useless and that there was no choice for him but to give way. The French Minister spoke a shade more sharply than his British colleague, for he declared that if Czechoslovakia's rejection of the Anglo-French proposals led to the outbreak of war, Prague would be responsible and the French Government – contrary to its treaty obligations – would not intervene. A heated discussion between Beneš and his two nocturnal visitors ensued and Beneš later wrote of this interview:[1]

The French Minister handed me the message of his Government with tears in his eyes; he had every reason to weep over the end of a twenty-year-old policy to which we had remained faithful unto death. What the British Minister felt at that moment I did not know. He was cool; while his French colleague spoke, he kept looking at the floor. I had the impression that both of them were ashamed to the bottom of their hearts of the mission they had to discharge in the name of their Governments.

This meeting went on until nearly 4 a.m.; at 6.30 a.m. the Government met to discuss the situation. At noon[2] the two Ministers insisted on seeing Beneš again and by 5 p.m. Czechoslovakia announced her submission to the demands of the Western Powers. Even so, Krofta's acceptance was not unconditional: it contained certain essential reservations. Prague accepted the plan 'as a whole' (*comme un tout*), emphasizing that the guarantee promised in the note was part of it (*en soulignant le principe de la garantie*). Although this was to become of rather academic interest in the disaster that was to overwhelm the country, the fact that Czechoslovakia's acceptance was not unconditional remains of historical importance.

Bonnet later asserted that Prague had practically asked for this extraordinary pressure from Paris and London so that it could point to *force majeure* as the reason for its unpopular decision to capitulate. This was hotly contested by De Lacroix who explained that on this occasion, too, one of his despatches had been 'edited' by the Quai d' Orsay so as to deprive it of its real meaning. The rather involved course of events has been succinctly described before[3] and it is

[1] Beneš, *Mnichovské Dny*, p. 262, French edition, p. 179.
[2] Laffan, *Crisis over Czechoslovakia*, pp. 355–9.
[3] Ibid. pp. 359–62; Celovsky, *Münchner Abkommen*, pp. 358–69; Eubank, *Munich*, pp. 301–3. Bonnet's version has been denied by Hodža on at least two occasions: in a letter to *Europe Nouvelle* (Paris), 19 October 1938 and in discussion with J. W. Wheeler-Bennett in 1941. Míla Lvová, in 'K otázce t.

sufficient to say here that Prague's demand for a clear statement of British and French requirements was natural – their precise formulation might have shown the Western Powers their inevitable consequences. As far as France was concerned it was also hoped that if things were made plain to the Daladier Government, it would shy away from an outright repudiation of its treaty obligations. Beneš himself expressed the conviction[1] that no efforts should be spared to make it clear to the West that Hitler wanted far more than just the Sudeten German districts.

Godesberg

It is difficult to believe that on his return from Berchtesgaden, Chamberlain really did write 'I got the impression that here was a man who would be relied upon when he had given his word.'[2] On 22 September 1938 Chamberlain went to Godesberg to confront the German dictator again.

Before Chamberlain went to Godesberg his brief for the meeting was prepared by Sir Horace Wilson and accepted by the Cabinet Committee (Chamberlain, Halifax, Hoare, Simon).[3] According to the brief, Chamberlain planned to tell Hitler that he had no intention of making a final settlement without consulting Beneš through diplomatic channels. Furthermore, he intended to plead 'for a more favourable principle of transfer than the 51 per cent majority already accepted' (i.e. more favourable to Czechoslovakia and her German democrats), for 'some withdrawal of German troops from the frontier' and the immediate dissolution of the Sudeten German Freikorps. Frightened at his own courage, Chamberlain did not say a single word to this effect at Godesberg. When he told

zv. objednaného ultimátu' (About the question of the so-called ordered ultimatum), *Československý časopis historický* (Czechoslovak Historical Journal), 3 (1965), 333–49, quotes a letter by Beneš to Hodža from 1943 according to which Alexis Léger, previously the leading official in the French Foreign Ministry, told Beneš in Washington that he was able to testify to Bonnet's telephonic intervention with the French Minister in Prague, charging him to call on Hodža and to provoke enquiries so that it could be said 'that the request for the declaration that France would not fulfil her obligations had come from the Czechoslovak Prime Minister'.

[1] *Mnichovské Dny*, p. 265; French edition, p. 183.
[2] Feiling, *Life of Chamberlain*, p. 367; Macleod, *Chamberlain*, p. 329.
[3] Middlemas, *Diplomacy of Illusion*, p. 361.

Hitler how he had persuaded the Czechs to accept the cession of territory he received a rude shock. Hitler insolently informed him 'that he was sorry to say that this plan could not be maintained'.[1] It was of course the same manœuvre Hitler had used before in his dealings with Chamberlain. The reaction of the Prime Minister – who had obviously failed to understand Hitler's technique – was bitter. The details of the Godesberg negotiations have been told too often to require repetition here. We need merely note that Hitler now also put forward the claims of Hungary and Poland for the rectification of their frontiers with Czechoslovakia and further-more demanded unconditional German occupation of the Sudeten German areas by 1 October. Afterwards plebiscites could be held, e.g. in Brno and Jihlava (Iglau). Here Hitler had again got the better of Chamberlain, for while he had previously kept silent about the criteria to be followed in determining German population per-centages he now insisted that the 1918 *status quo* be regarded as their basis. In practice this meant going back to 1910, the date of the last Austrian census when Brno was still a German town, in order to obtain data for a decision to be taken twenty-eight years later.

The discussions at Godesberg, during which Hitler did not hesitate to utter war threats, went less smoothly than those at Berchtesgaden. Chamberlain's annoyance at Hitler's attitude was not the only reason for this: it is clear that he was conscious of circumstances which ought to have forbidden *any* surrender to Hitler's blackmail. An extremely significant altercation during the Godesberg talks is mentioned briefly in Sir Ivone Kirkpatrick's memoirs:[2]

At one point Mr Chamberlain said drily: You assume that every Sudeten wants to join the Reich. What do you propose to do if the Sudeten Social Democrats prefer to remain in Czechoslovakia? Schmidt (the interpreter), foreseeing a fresh outburst, translated this question: The Prime Minister asks a theoretical question. I repeat, my Fuehrer, a purely theoretical hypothesis. Supposing there were some Social Democrats who did not want to join the Reich, how would you propose to deal with them? Hitler made a noise, a sort of angry

[1] German notes about the Godesberg negotiations in *DGFP*, D/II, nos. 562, 583. British notes in *DBFP*, 3/II, nos. 1033, 1073.

[2] Ivone Kirkpatrick, *The Inner Circle* (London 1959), p. 117. German notes about the Chamberlain–Hitler discussion do not go to the length of Sir Ivone's account, but dispose of it with Hitler's assurance that he would gladly do without those Germans who wanted to stay in Czechoslovakia.

snort, and replied: It's an impossible hypothesis. But if there were such men, I should not want them in the Reich.

Chamberlain therefore *knew* that not all Germans in Czechoslovakia wanted 'to go back' to Germany. He described these people quite correctly as Social Democrats, although anti-Nazi feelings were not limited to them. The argument that Chamberlain actually believed his mission as one aimed at realizing just demands therefore loses its validity. He in fact knew the arguments to refute the dictator's threats, but he capitulated to them instead.

A written formulation of Hitler's demands was handed to the Prime Minister who had asked for such a document at the second Godesberg conference.[1] It was in the form a memorandum but of such peremptory character that even Chamberlain had to complain that

it was couched in the language of a conqueror who dictated his will to the conquered, laid down everything in precise terms, and left no time for discussions on measures for the peaceful and orderly execution of the existing basic plans.

Although there were lively exchanges between Hitler and Chamberlain the latter eventually accepted Hitler's sham concessions and his assurance, which became notorious, that 'it was the last territorial demand which he would make in Europe'. Chamberlain promised to convey the memorandum to Prague 'in his capacity as mediator', without adding any recommendation of his own.

The memorandum again contained deliberate ambiguities but Hitler's true intentions were revealed in the paragraph calling for a 'plebiscite' in a vaguely defined area (districts with preponderant German majorities were to be surrendered unconditionally by 1 October): 'All persons who were residing in the area in question on 28 October 1918, or were born there prior to this date will be eligible to vote' – so that for example Czechs who had moved to the overwhelmingly Czech city of Brno after 28 October 1918 would have had no vote. The future of the whole area was to be decided by a simple majority. This would have meant that even if districts actually expressed a preference for Czechoslovakia they would still have had to go to Germany if the area as a whole had voted for incorporation into the Reich – but any 'difficulty' here would have

[1] Memorandum handed by the Fuehrer to the British Prime Minister, *DGFP*, D/II, no. 584.

been smoothed out by Nazi methods anyway. The whole memorandum was an attempt to achieve by gradual means what Hitler was to seize with one blow on 15 March 1939.

Two days after his return from Godesberg Chamberlain received the Canadian High Commissioner in London.[1] The latter gathered that Chamberlain had reluctantly come to the conclusion that Hitler's profession of limited objectives was not sincere and that he had far wider ambitions. Nevertheless, the Cabinet papers show that after Godesberg the Prime Minister trusted or at least pretended to trust Hitler even more than after Berchtesgaden. Reporting to the Cabinet on 24 September,[2] he spoke of Hitler's intense dislike for the Czechs: 'He had lived among them for many years and had no faith in them.' God knows who had told the Prime Minister the story that Hitler had ever lived among the Czechs. When he mentioned his idea of a German–Czechoslovak non-aggression pact, Hitler said he could not sign such a pact unless the demands of the 'other minorities' had been carried out. To everybody else this would have been a clear indication of Hitler's real aims, but the Prime Minister only repeated, contradicting once again his own report on Berchtesgaden, that 'Herr Hitler had not even mentioned these other minorities' then. In all seriousness Chamberlain presented these conclusions:

Herr Hitler had a narrow mind and was violently prejudiced on certain subjects, but he *would not deliberately deceive a man whom he respected* and with whom he had been in negotiation, and he was sure that Herr Hitler now felt some respect for him...The crucial question was whether Herr Hitler was speaking the truth when he said that he regarded the Sudeten question as a racial question which must be settled and that the object of his policy was racial unity and not the domination of Europe...*The Prime Minister believed that Herr Hitler was speaking the truth*...He thought that he had now *established an influence over Herr Hitler* and that the latter trusted him and was willing to work with him.

Those who still try to find excuses for the appeasers should not overlook these misjudgments which were responsible for so much misery. Asked by Duff Cooper whether the inclusion of France, Russia and Britain in a joint guarantee had been mentioned at Godesberg, the Prime Minister had to admit that 'Russia was not mentioned'. That was his way of carrying out Cabinet decisions.

[1] Vincent Massey, *What's Past is Prologue* (London 1963), p. 261.
[2] *Cab.* 93/95, Minutes 92(38), Meeting of 24 September 1938; for extracts see Philip Howard in *The Times*, 1 January 1969, Mark Arnold-Forster in *The Guardian*, 1 January 1969, Colvin, *The Chamberlain Government*, pp. 162–3.

Only Duff Cooper contradicted Chamberlain's optimism:

No confidence could be placed in Hitler's promises. He was certain that Herr Hitler would not stop at any frontier which might result from the proposed settlement.

This was nothing but common sense. Duff Cooper urged a general mobilization. Chamberlain answered that this suggestion should be discussed at the next meeting on 25 September (Sunday). It was never mentioned again.

The atmosphere of uncertainty prevailing in Czechoslovakia cleared late on the evening of 23 September when general mobilization was proclaimed. This took place while the Godesberg talks were still going on, and the Czechs were sure that it could not have happened without at least the connivance of the French and British Governments. It was assumed that they had finally realized what Hitler's real intentions were. In fact the Czechoslovak mobilization was only ordered after London and Paris had expressly withdrawn their previous 'counsel' not to mobilize and in diplomatic parlance this was, of course, equivalent to advice to meet the German threat by a call to arms. In the course of the heated second discussion with Hitler at Godesberg, Chamberlain plainly stated, in the face of all the evasions of the German dictator, that the responsibility for these preventive measures was Hitler's.

Henlein's exhortations to the Sudeten Germans to sabotage the Czechoslovak mobilization orders failed just as completely as his incitement to mutiny ten days earlier. The Czech politician Hubert Ripka wrote afterwards[1] that the Germans had followed their orders to mobilize just as readily as their Czech fellow-countrymen.

New Anglo-French discussions

Since another Anglo-French conference was due to take place in London on the evening of 25 September, Prague lost no time in making its attitude towards Hitler's Godesberg ultimatum clear. Their memorandum rejecting the demands was presented at the

[1] Michael Killanin (ed.), *Four days* (London 1939), pp. 96–8. Leopold Amery, in his memoirs (*My Political Life*, 3 (London 1955), 273), mentions that 'Jan Masaryk...told me that their German Social Democrats were coming forward enthusiastically for mobilization.'

Foreign Office by Jan Masaryk on the afternoon of the 25th.[1] Naturally, Masaryk's note could not repudiate what Prague had been forced to accept on 21 September but it could, and did, find ways to weaken the impression of surrender by stressing that it had been 'accepted under extreme duress' and that there had not been 'time to make representations about its many unworkable features'. It had been agreed to with a heavy heart and in the belief that no further demands would be made of Czechoslovakia.

The Anglo-French discussions began on the evening of the 25th[2] with Daladier's statement that Hitler wanted not merely to destroy Czechoslovakia but to subjugate the whole of Europe. However, the French Premier lacked the courage of his own convictions: no final decision was reached. Instead Daladier accepted Chamberlain's suggestion to make one more attempt to appease Hitler. Before the latter's next big speech, arranged to take place on the 26 September in the Berlin Sports Palace, it was planned to send him a message through Sir Horace Wilson, a close personal confidant of the Prime Minister with the official rank of 'Chief Industrial Adviser' and without any sort of diplomatic experience. Not surprisingly, this mission too was a failure.[3]

It is worthwhile recounting Daladier's arguments in opposition to Chamberlain's. With regard to the territory which was to be ceded to Hitler without even the pretence of a plebiscite, Daladier recalled that

there were many democrats in this area. Were they to be left to the axe and the executioners of Herr Hitler? It is essential to safeguard our honour by ensuring the departure of these democrats and also...that those Czechs who wished to do so should also withdraw.

On 25 September the British Cabinet met twice, in the morning and afternoon, before Daladier and Bonnet arrived in London and late in the evening after the first conversation with them.[4] Not a word was said about a British mobilization. Halifax surprised the

---

[1] Jan Masaryk to Halifax, 25 September 1938, *DBFP*, 3/II, no. 1092, *Documents on International Affairs, 1938*, II, 235–6.

[2] Record of an Anglo-French Conversation held at 10 Downing Street on 25 and 26 September 1938, *DBFP*, 3/II, nos. 1093, 1096.

[3] Notes by Schmidt about the discussion between Sir Horace Wilson and Hitler, 26 and 27 September 1938, *DBFP*, 3/II, nos. 1118, 1129.

[4] *Cab.* 93/95, Minutes 43(38) and 44(38), Meeting of 25 September 1938, Colvin, *The Chamberlain Government*, pp. 163–5.

meeting by indicating that he was not sure he still agreed with the Prime Minister. He was against further pressure on the Czechs to accept Hitler's terms. Lord Hailsham (Lord President of the Council) disturbed the general complacency by reading out a long list of Hitler's broken promises for the years 1935 until 1938: 'He did not feel we could trust Herr Hitler's declarations in future.' If Czechoslovakia rejected Hitler's ultimatum and France intervened in her favour, Britain ought in his view to come to France's assistance. Earl Stanhope (President of the Board of Education), who had kept silent so far, contradicted him, assuring the meeting there was a big difference between Hitler's previous promises and the present ones, for 'the Prime Minister had clearly exercised a considerable influence on him'. Stanhope was not the only one present who lived in a cloud-cuckoo land of his own imagination. He was quickly outdone by Sir Kingsley Wood (Secretary of State for Air) who proclaimed that the Prime Minister's visits had 'made a considerable impression in Germany and had probably done more to weaken Nazism than any other event in recent years'. In reality Chamberlain's pilgrimages to Hitler had destroyed the last possibility – a well-prepared *putsch* of the German generals – to get rid of Nazism.

As in previous meetings, Duff Cooper was critical of Chamberlain's policy. The Czechs should be told that Hitler's terms were intolerable and that if attacked they would be helped: 'He thought that the future of Europe, of this country and of democracy was at stake.' He was supported by Hore-Belisha who stated the truth Chamberlain did not want to hear: 'Czechoslovakia was a democracy, which was inspired by the same ideals as this country and shared our opposition to Nazi tyranny.'

The Prime Minister, however, stuck to his guns. 'He thought that Herr Hitler wanted peace and if the point at issue was not very large he might be induced to accept some compromise.' In the second meeting, which did not start before 11.30 p.m., the Prime Minister reported on the negotiations with the French. He now admitted the possibility that 'there was some element of bluff in Herr Hitler's attitude', but he assured the Cabinet that 'anything in the form of a threat would destroy any chance of acceptance of the appeal' which Horace Wilson had to take to Berlin.

287

Czechoslovakia before Munich

On the evening of the 26th Hitler spoke in the Berlin Sports Palace. The Western Powers were presented with a skilful mixture of threats and lies diluted with palliatives. Whereas at the Nuremberg Rally two weeks earlier, Hitler's aim had been to drive a wedge between Czechoslovakia and the West, there was now no longer any need for restraint. He attacked Beneš personally in the wildest terms: the Czechoslovak crisis was really his doing.[1] While foreign correspondents and diplomatists could only report that the Czechs showed admirable restraint, Hitler ranted against them: 'Whole stretches of country were depopulated, villages are burnt down, attempts are made to smoke out the Germans with hand-grenades and gas.' He alleged that 214,000 Germans had fled during the last few days, while 'nearly 600,000 Germans had to leave Czechoslovakia' during the previous years – 'otherwise they would have had to starve'. No one dared ask how it was possible that such a mass emigration had remained completely unknown to the outside world until 26 September 1938.

London and Paris bothered little about these revelations or the unusual way in which Hitler spoke of the head of another state. They were, however, alarmed by his open threat to take what he wanted by force. But instead of reminding Hitler of his obligations under the German–Czechoslovak Arbitration Treaty of 1925 and reassuring Czechoslovakia that aid would be forthcoming if Hitler attacked her, they tried to calm Hitler with the assurance that he could have everything he wanted without resort to arms. Hitler had calculated quite astutely the seductive effect his public promise, first given to Chamberlain at Godesberg, that he had no further territorial demands in Europe, would have. What he had previously said with brutal frankness in *Mein Kampf* about territorial demands and the stronger credibility of big lies (compared with small ones) was, of course, not known either to Chamberlain or to Daladier. Hence the inclusion of the notorious 'We certainly don't want any Czechs' in his speech was even more effective in reassuring the Western world.

Under the influence of Hitler's threats Chamberlain's resistance again collapsed. In a statement[2] which he rushed out immediately

---

[1] *Documents on International Affairs, 1938,* II 249–60; Baynes, *Speeches of Hitler,* II, 1508–27. [2] *DGFP,* D/II, no. 618.

after the Sports Palace speech he thought it 'incredible that the peoples of Europe...should again be plunged into a bloody struggle over a question on which agreement had already been largely obtained'. His proposals, he declared, would 'satisfy the German desire for the union of the Sudeten Germans with the Reich without the shedding of blood in any part of Europe'.

This was followed by a message to Prague to warn Beneš[1] that

German troops will have orders to cross the Czechoslovak frontier almost immediately, unless by 2 p.m. tomorrow (28 September) the Czechoslovak Government have accepted German terms. That must result in Bohemia being overrun and nothing that any other Power can do, will prevent this fate for your own country and people.

On the same evening (27 September) Chamberlain broadcast that famous speech[2] in which he said

how horrible, fantastic, incredible it is that we should be digging trenches and trying on gas-masks here because of a quarrel in a far-away country between people of whom we know nothing...

Before this, Newton in Prague had handed a mediation proposal to Krofta.[3] According to this German troops were to occupy that part of Czechoslovakia which lay outside the fortifications belt by 1 October. A mixed Anglo-German–Czechoslovak Commission was to meet within the country on the 3rd to decide on further cessions and these were to be concluded by the 10th. Negotiations about guaranteeing the new frontiers were to begin as soon as possible. In London's view this was to be a joint Anglo-French–German undertaking. (In April Chamberlain had told the French that Hitler would not abide by any guarantee given.)

Obviously the Czechs had hoped, though they had not said so, that Hitler's unbridled aggressiveness would induce London and Paris to withdraw the transfer proposals they had made on 19 September. Now this hope was finally dashed. The Czechoslovak reply,[4] apart from requesting an extension of the time limits, adhered

[1] Halifax to Newton, 27 September 1938, *DBFP*, 3/II, no. 1136.
[2] *Documents on International Affairs, 1938*, II, 270–1.
[3] Halifax to Newton and Halifax to Henderson, 27 September 1938, *DBFP*, 3/II, nos. 1138, 1140; Laffan, *Crisis over Czechoslovakia*, pp. 412–13.
[4] Newton to Halifax, 29 September 1938, *DBFP*, 3/II, no. 1203; Hubert Ripka, *Munich Before and After* (London, 1939), pp. 199–201; Killanin, *Four Days*, pp. 118–20.

to the earlier and comparatively milder Anglo-French proposals which were to be carried out only after the question of a guarantee had been settled. Should the negotiations conducted on this basis fail, an international conference, naturally with Czechoslovak participation, was to be convened. Alternatively 'the Czechoslovak Government...would willingly agree to arbitration of differences by President Roosevelt'.

Chamberlain was not content to ignore Prague's view. In brusque terms[1] he informed the Czechs that

this (success) can only be achieved if the Czech Government are prepared at this stage to give to Mr Chamberlain a wide discretion and not tie his hands at the outset by making absolute conditions.

In the meantime he, Daladier, Hitler and Mussolini had already agreed to settle the problem which Hitler had so deliberately inflated. They arranged for a conference among themselves at Munich, from which the country immediately affected was to be excluded.

[1] Halifax to Newton, 29 September 1938, *DBFP*, 3/II, no. 1210.

16 MUNICH AND ITS CONSEQUENCES

Between 15 and 20 September 1938 three States decided that a fourth which was not consulted had to give up part of its territory. There was no precedent for this in international relations, and it took place in clear breach of solemn international obligations: the Covenant of the League of Nations in the case of Great Britain and France,[1] and the German–Czechoslovak Arbitration Treaty in the case of Germany. Under extreme pressure the Prague Government had found itself compelled to accept the 'proposals' of territorial sacrifice which it had previously rejected. Even so, it was only prepared to cede the territory on condition that its new frontiers be simultaneously guaranteed. Later the Czechs refused to go beyond the concessions they had made.

Chamberlain had wished to make amends at least for the formal defects of the procedure he had followed, i.e. the complete exclusion from the negotiations of the country most concerned. On the 28th he therefore sent a message to Hitler saying that he was ready 'to come to Berlin myself at once to discuss arrangements for the transfer with you and representatives of the Czech Government, together with representatives of France and Italy, if you (Hitler) so desire'.[2] But this would have been merely a discussion about the details of the transfer; the principle of the matter had already been 'settled' and the four powerful negotiators would merely 'persuade' a helpless fifth not to make any trouble. Even this sad travesty of an international conference did not take place: Hitler was no longer interested and Chamberlain's initiative remained unanswered.

Even at that late hour Prague had not quite abandoned hope of averting the worst. Beneš sent a personal message to Chamberlain

---

[1] Article 10 of the Convenant of the League of Nations: 'The Members of the League undertake to respect and preserve as against external aggression the territorial integrity and existing political independence of all Members of the League.'

[2] Halifax to Henderson, 28 September, *DBFP*, 3/II, no. 1158.

urging him 'to do nothing in Munich which could put Czecho-slovakia in a worse situation than under the Anglo-French proposals ...I beg...that nothing may be done in Munich without Czecho-slovakia being heard.'[1] Jan Masaryk asked the Foreign Office[2] to admit Czechoslovak representatives to the conference, wisely leaving the question open as to the capacity in which they were to attend. A few hours before the conference was due to start, Masaryk announced that Czechoslovakia would not take part but would hold herself in readiness to participate in any other international con-ference attended by both Germany and Czechoslovakia.

If the Czechoslovak Government's official appeals met with little response in the West, those of the Sudeten German Democrats went utterly unheeded. Nonetheless they did win a moral victory over those who short-sightedly believed in Hitler because they wanted to do so. Rarely before can a prophetic warning have been so completely ignored and yet translated into reality so quickly and painfully as the comment on the Munich conference in the Prague German Social Democrats' newspaper.[3]

Germany...wished to occupy the Sudeten German districts and used the Sudeten German population as a means to this end. And she wanted more than our border territories: she wanted the way open to the South-East. Those who are still willing to trust in a declaration of the Third Reich, e.g. that after the settlement of the Sudeten German problem it had no further territorial demands in Europe, will learn the truth, even though it may be too late.

Perhaps the most incredible thing about the Munich conference was that before meeting the two dictators, the two Western Prime Ministers had come to no pre-agreement about joint tactics. Hitler and Mussolini were not at that time the close allies they were to become, but they were united in their determination to outdo the democracies. A document was 'given' to Mussolini – by Ribben-trop, according to one source, by Attolico, the Italian Ambassador in Berlin, according to another – containing the demands Hitler was to put forward in Munich. Weizsäcker, Erich Kordt (Ribben-trop's secretary) and Paul Schmidt (Hitler's interpreter) – all three professional diplomats and none of them Nazis – tried after the

---

[1] Newton to Halifax, 28 September 1938, *DBFP*, 3/II, no. 1194.
[2] Masaryk to Harvey, 28 September 1938, Masaryk to Halifax, 29 September 1938, *DBFP*, 3/II, no. 1198, 1220.
[3] *Sozialdemokrat* (Prague), 29 September 1938.

war to spread the impression that it was actually a 'moderate' programme, compiled by such 'moderates' as Goering, Neurath and Weizsäcker, behind the back of the 'aggressive' Ribbentrop. Unfortunately this theory does not conform with the facts. As Boris Celovsky rightly points out,[1] if Goering and Neurath had deliberately sabotaged extremist plans at Munich, they would surely not have missed the chance of putting this forward in their favour at the Nuremberg trials. Naturally enough, they produced every mitigating circumstance, but the Munich question was not mentioned.

One of the sources[2] explains that Hitler had approved the draft before it was sent to Attolico, while the other[3] insists that Ribbentrop himself handed the document to his colleague Ciano in the special train bringing him to Munich, after Mussolini had asked Hitler what he was going to demand from Czechoslovakia. Whatever the facts, it is not true that there was a successful conspiracy among peace-loving German diplomatists against Hitler's war plans. The two dictators actually agreed on a joint plan of action whereby Mussolini was to assume the task of conveying Hitler's demands to the two unsuspecting Western statesmen as his own mediation proposal.

An international conference without precedent

The first personal contact between Daladier and Chamberlain since their meeting in London on the 26th, three days before, took place in the *Führer* building at Munich.[4] Even then Daladier did not discuss any joint action with Chamberlain. What happened at Munich between midday of 29 and morning of 30 September 1938 was an international conference whose character – irrespective of what was to be negotiated and decided – makes it a unique event in the history of diplomacy. It was convened in an atmosphere of crisis aggravated by Hitler's war threats, and Chamberlain and Daladier had come to save the peace of the world. But there was no

---

[1] Celovsky, *Münchner Abkommen*, p. 462.

[2] Mario Donosti (pseudonym), *Mussolini e L'Europa* (Rome 1945), p. 124, quoted by Laffan, *Crisis over Czechoslovakia*, p. 437.

[3] Filippo Anfuso, *Rome–Berlin im diplomatischen Spiegel* (Munich 1951), pp. 75ff.

[4] Edouard Daladier, 'Je signe sous l'œil bleu et dur d'Hitler', *Candide* (Paris), 21 September 1961.

chairman, no agenda and no rules of procedure. Discussions went on quite informally and at time the meeting split up into several debating groups. There were no arrangements for shorthand minutes and of course tape recordings were not yet available. All we have to go by are the more or less reliable notes made by some of the officials. It may be that the outcome of the conference would have been just as objectionable if it had taken place according to the normal conventions, but the deliberate lack of formality which Daladier and Chamberlain accepted without demur only smoothed the path to their deception.

Hitler began the proceedings with one of his anti-Czech tirades, the patent untruthfulness of which neither Chamberlain nor Daladier corrected. In fact he encountered no fundamental opposition. Chamberlain, with little support from Daladier, did make a few half-hearted attempts to get permission for a Czechoslovak representative to be 'at hand', but Hitler curtly refused and it was eventually agreed that the four participating States bore the sole responsibility. The only clash between Daladier and Hitler has been recounted by Daladier himself.[1] He threatened to leave if Hitler was determined to annihilate Czechoslovakia, but when Hitler repeated that 'he certainly did not want any Czechs', Daladier was quickly soothed.

Mussolini then produced the text of his mediation proposal[2] which was neither his nor in any essential detail different from Hitler's original demands. Neither Chamberlain nor Daladier seems to have realized that the two dictators had been acting in unison, however odd it might appear that Mussolini, usually so prone to impetuosity, had a detailed plan ready. But the Western statesmen were only too glad of a 'compromise proposal' not coming from Hitler and they accepted it at once as the basis for negotiations. A one-and-a-half hour interval followed during which no effort was made to co-ordinate any Anglo-French steps. Mussolini's alleged proposal was then raised to the level of a generally accepted solution and it was on this basis that the Agreement was signed after midnight. A meaningless concession was now mentioned

[1] In *Candide*, 21 September 1961.
[2] *DGFP*, D/ii, no. 669 (The Foreign Ministry's Draft for the Munich Conference).

for the first time: the occupation of the areas to be ceded by Czechoslovakia was not to take place on 1 October but was to be spread
over a period of ten days, beginning on the 1st. An occupation of
the whole area, 24 hours after the Munich Agreement was signed,
would have been impossible anyway. Another such concession was
the setting-up of an International Commission in which Czechoslovakia was to be represented: its task to be the drawing up of
definite frontiers after plebiscites had been arranged in certain
ill-defined areas. (The farce of a plebiscite was later quietly dropped.[1])
When the Commission met in Berlin, the Czechoslovak delegates
found themselves face to face with a united front of the other four
States and all territorial disputes were settled in Germany's favour.

The rest of the conference was taken up with petty arguments
about trifles. The document signed at Munich, made to appear as
a harmless arrangement for carrying out an agreement 'already
accepted in principle regarding the transfer of Sudeten German
territory', obliged Czechoslovakia to evacuate an undefined area in
five stages by 10 October. The first four stages, to be concluded by
4 October, were indicated on a map attached; the extent of the fifth,
which was to be ceded to Germany by the 10th, was to be determined
by the 'International Commission'. In other words, Czechoslovakia
was asked to make a territorial sacrifice the size of which was not
specified. In the end Prague had to submit to the decision of the
Commission which awarded to Germany not only, as the Agreement
put it, 'areas of predominantly German character' but also a purely
Czech district around Domažlice (Taus). It is significant that even
Hans Krebs, a former Nazi deputy in the Czechoslovak Parliament
who had fled to Germany in 1933 and was now acting on a sub-
committee of the International Commission for the German
Ministry of the Interior, wanted to leave a town in this area to
Czechoslovakia, but his intervention was vetoed by the German
War Ministry.[2]

The question of the guarantee

After his return from Munich Chamberlain called a Cabinet meeting

---

[1] *DGFP*, D/IV (Washington 1951), no. 56, Minutes of the Eighth Meeting of
the International Commission held in Berlin on 13 October 1938.
[2] Henderson to Halifax, 7 October 1938, *DBFP*, 3/II, no. 165.

for the evening of 30 September. Only one sentence in his description of events is worth quoting today:[1]

> The guarantee of France and Great Britain entered into operation at once, while
> the guarantees of Germany and Italy come into operation after the Hungarian
> and Polish minorities question had been settled.

Everybody present was enthusiastic about the 'triumph of
diplomacy' which the Prime Minister pretended to have achieved.
Alfred Duff Cooper, however, announced his resignation.

The unpalatable fact that decisions were made at Munich regarding the territory of a State unrepresented at the conference table was
glossed over by explaining that it was after all only the definition
of details resulting from an agreement which had already been
accepted – albeit reluctantly – by the Prague Government. Even
if one ignores the dubious logic which tries to explain away one
act contrary to international law by another of the same kind, the
conclusion itself has no validity: when Prague was first forced to
capitulate, the Government did so only on the express condition
that a guarantee of Czechoslovakia's new frontiers would come into
force at the same time as the surrender of the old ones. This demand
was reiterated on the eve of Munich, but in the event there was
no question of an automatic guarantee of the new borders. In an
appendix to the Munich Agreement Great Britain and France
expressed their readiness to keep to their guarantee offer of 19
September. Germany and Italy, on the other hand, promised a
guarantee to Czechoslovakia, 'as soon as the question of the Polish
and Hungarian minorities in Czechoslovakia is settled'. While the
claims of Poland and Hungary were not invented by Hitler, they
were supported by him and synchronized with his tactical requirements. In the course of November 1938 these questions, too, were
cleared up, but when in December the French Ambassador in
Berlin urged that the guarantee, to which there was no longer any
obstacle, be given, Weizsäcker asked whether 'we could not forget
this affair?'[2] Subsequent reminders were treated evasively by

---

[1] *Cab.* 23/95, Minute 93(38), Meeting of 30 September 1938, Colvin, *The
Chamberlain Government*, pp. 168–70.

[2] Coulondre to Bonnet, 22 December 1938; *Le Livre Jaune Français, Documents
diplomatiques 1938–9* (Paris 1939): no. 35: 'Est-ce que cette affaire, m'a-t-il
dit en souriant, ne pourrait pas être oubliée?'

Berlin.[1] The whole question was kept in abeyance until Hitler had ensured, through the Slovak declaration of independence which he engineered and through the German occupation of what remained of the country immediately afterwards, that there was nothing left to guarantee.

Daladier's splendid word about 'safeguarding the honour' of the Western Powers 'by ensuring the departure of these democrats' who preferred a democratic Czechoslovakia to Nazi Germany dissolved into thin air at Munich. The agreement provided for a 'right of option for transfer into the ceded territories and from them'. All that remained was an Option Treaty[2] which Czechoslovakia, bereft of all freedom of action, was forced to conclude with Germany. This made provision for Czechs living in the areas surrendered to Germany, who could opt for Czechoslovakia and would then have to move there. Analogous provisions existed for non-Jewish Germans who wanted to leave Czechoslovakia for Germany but even this regulation remained largely on paper because Kundt, appointed by Hitler to be a sort of 'trustee' for those Germans left 'unredeemed' despite Munich, issued a command not to opt for Germany.[3] These Germans were needed in the country as Hitler's fifth column. At any rate, they had the theoretical possibility of emigrating to the Reich, while no way existed for Germans in the ceded territories to move to Czechoslovakia. Any German democrat who was unable to move into the interior of the country during the last days of September was delivered to the tender mercies of National Socialism, notwithstanding Hitler's contemptuous assurance to Chamberlain that he did not want such Germans.

Prague's final capitulation

The Munich decision, amounting as it did to a death sentence on a central European democracy, was conveyed to its representatives by Chamberlain and Daladier after 2 a.m. on 30 September 1938, and elucidated by a French diplomat[4] who hinted that no formal

---

[1] See the Note Verbale (composed by Hitler himself) to the French Embassy, *DGFP*, D/IV, no. 175.
[2] German–Czechoslovak Treaty about Nationality and Questions of Option, *Reichsgesetzblatt* (1938), II, 896 (20 November 1938).
[3] Newton to Halifax, 8 December 1938, *DBFP*, 3/II, no. 413.
[4] According to the Czechoslovak diplomat Hubert Masařik's report, quoted by

acceptance by Prague was expected. Everything had been settled. Czechoslovakia was merely required to ensure that its representatives attended the first session of the International Commission which was to meet that same afternoon in Berlin. Nevertheless Chamberlain asked Newton[1] to demand a declaration of acceptance from Beneš forthwith. There was no time for counter-arguments, only an unequivocal 'Yes' was admissible.

In the circumstances Prague had no choice but to submit. The defenders of the Munich Agreement are wont to point out that Hitler did not in fact get everything he had demanded at Godesberg. This is true as far as it goes[2] since there were no plebiscites in the allegedly German towns of Brno, Olomouc and Moravská Ostrava, but it does not go very far because the Munich Agreement cannot be regarded in isolation. It was merely the beginning of the end, a step towards the complete absorption of the country within Germany on 15 March 1939.

In Prague the German Chargé d'Affaires called on Krofta shortly after 6 a.m. on 30 September,[3] handing him the text of the Agreement and inviting Czechoslovak participation in the first session of the International Commission. This was followed by prolonged consultations between the President, the Government and the Czechoslovak political parties: the actual victims, the German democrats, were studiously ignored. Towards midday Krofta informed the British, French and Italian Ministers in Prague of the 'acceptance of the decision taken at Munich without us and against us'.[4] 'I do not know,' the Foreign Minister said, in this *impasse* reduced to prophecies, 'whether this decision... will bring advantages to your country... After us it will be the turn of others.' A Government statement declared 'before the whole world its protest against the decisions which were taken unilaterally and

Celovsky, *Münchner Abkommen*, p. 465; Ripka, *Munich Before and After*, pp. 224–7.

[1] British Delegation, Munich, to Newton, 30 September 1938, *DBFP*, 3/II, no. 1225.

[2] See the comparison between Godesberg and Munich in *Survey of International Affairs, 1938*, III (London 1953), 1–6 (article by R. G. D. Laffan).

[3] Hencke to Krofta, 30 September 1938, *DGFP*, D/IV, no. 1.

[4] Ripka, *Munich Before and After*, p. 231; Laffan, *Crisis over Czechoslovakia*, p. 446.

without our participation'. The whole tragedy of the situation became clear when the decision of the International Commission about the fifth occupation zone, taken against the vote of the Czechoslovak delegate, was published on 7 October: the main traffic arteries of the country were severed and purely Czech places awarded to Germany.

Chamberlain even went so far as to oppose an appeal for help to the immediate victims of the Agreement, the German democratic refugees from the areas to be occupied by Germany. When the Lord Mayor of London announced his intention to open such an appeal, the Prime Minister said to the Cabinet[1] that he was afraid that the 'opening of the Lord Mayor's fund might have a bad effect on public opinion in Germany'. He recognized that it was impossible to advise the Lord Mayor to abstain from his intentions, but 'he should be asked to consider very carefully whether, in the circumstances, it was worth while to open a fund'. The Cabinet entrusted the Foreign Secretary with the task of pointing out to the Lord Mayor 'the disadvantages of opening...a fund'. Nevertheless, he opened his appeal and was able to mitigate much misery.

Quite independently of German–Czechoslovak relations, the Munich Conference has acquired the stigma of capitulation. Whenever and wherever the fear arises that democracy might retreat before the forces of totalitarianism, the ghost of Munich is conjured up as a warning. No special emphasis is needed to explain that the memory of the bitter humiliation the Czechs suffered at Munich is ineradicable: it may well be that the non-involvement of the Soviet Union in the whole business enhanced the chances for Communism among such Western-minded people as the Czechs. But why has Munich become the symbol everywhere of a mean sell-out, a settlement of a kind to be avoided at all costs? Might it not be the case that the Munich settlement is misrepresented, since it did after all lead to the realization of a right to self-determination, denied until then?

A 'right' can only be obtained where the concept of right, in the generally accepted sense of the word, already reigns supreme, and that means in the sphere of democracy alone. No one knows how

[1] *Cab.* 23/95, Minute 48(38), Meeting of 3 October 1938. Colvin, *The Chamberlain Government*, p. 120.

many Sudeten Germans wished to realize their aspirations in the form of an *Anschluss* to Germany and in no other way.[1] But even if a plebiscite, held under every democratic guarantee, had produced a majority for such an annexation, it would still remain debatable whether the decision of a group of people to submit freely to a tyranny must necessarily be respected by the rest of the world, for such a decision would deny the right to self-determination of all those Germans, as well as all Czechs, living in the areas affected who were opposed to Hitler. Nobody can be said to have the 'right' to set his house on fire, if others may be endangered by his action. Hitler would have planned to destroy Czechoslovak independence if she had not had a single German citizen within her borders, because she stood in the way of world domination, and the undeniable shortcomings and faults of her ethnic policy counted as nothing compared with the danger threatening the existence of the last democracy east of the Rhine.

After the Munich Agreement had been signed and imposed on a protesting Czechoslovakia, the German Socialists in the country, the last organized legal force of German democracy, were faced with a tragic decision. The party leadership, meeting in Prague, could not and would not declare that the struggle against National Socialism had to be given up as hopeless. On the other hand nothing must be done which could serve as an excuse for the Nazis to persecute the Social Democrats left behind in the occupied territories. In this deeply tragic dilemma the party published a proclamation freeing its followers from all their obligations:[2]

The Great Powers have decided on the transfer of the Sudeten German districts. We have become the victims of this decision. There is no point in remonstrating against these events which have overwhelmed us with the elemental force of fate. *It may be that this fate will also overtake those who have sacrificed us.* Our conduct and theirs will be judged by history...

With admiration we do homage in this hour to the small Czech nation which has to bear the same blows of fate as we do. May it, when this ordeal is over, go forward to happier days. The task of collaboration between the nationalities will remain vital in Central Europe. From the depths of our hearts we wish that it may yet be crowned by a successful conclusion.

[1] Only a few days after Munich a special correspondent of *The Times* reported consternation among the Sudeten Germans. He was told that 'We never expected this...we thought of autonomy, not of this' (*The Times*, 4 October 1938).   [2] *Sozialdemokrat*, 1 October 1938.

Munich and its consequences

Just as six months earlier, after the annexation of Austria, the Gestapo followed closely on the heels of the invading German troops. The only difference was that the majority of the Jews, amply forewarned by knowledge of what had happened in Austria had fled into the interior of Czechoslovakia in time. For the moment this deprived the Nazis of the opportunity to terrorize and humiliate these unfortunate human beings, but if they were unsuccessful in finding a safer refuge abroad, neither the Jews from the districts surrendered at Munich nor these from the rest of the country escaped the fate the Nazis had in store for them. While the absence of the Jews made it difficult for the Nazis to obey the demands of party doctrine, there were still enough German democrats in the country on whom the sadism of the victors could take its revenge. All those tens of thousands who a few months or weeks earlier had openly demonstrated their willingness to support democracy had not disappeared: only a few thousand of those most endangered had succeeded in fleeing into the interior of Czechoslovakia and from the ranks of those left behind the Gestapo collected innumerable victims. If such people did survive Dachau, Mauthausen and other camps, they came back broken.

A British Quaker who was in the country at that time to organize help for what were later to be known as 'displaced persons' has impressively described the spirit of the German democratic refugees from the areas occupied by Germany after Munich. Vandeleur Robinson[1] reports on his visit to a camp holding 130 German Social Democrats in the town of Kroměříž (Kremsier):

The Foreman of these refugees answered the Red Cross Officer's questions about the numbers and origin of his people, the adequacy of the rations supplied, and of the sanitary arrangements; then his feelings overcame him and he launched into a passionate speech, lasting perhaps about three minutes. I cannot reproduce it all, but the purport of it was this – said in a voice that got louder and louder as he went on:

We are good Republicans. We gave our blood for this Republic. We wanted to defend our homes and our freedom. We had arms in our hands; but we were betrayed and sold. We are still good Republicans, we still want our homes and our freedom, whether England and France want us to have them or not. Freedom – Freedom – Freedom!

[1] The author expresses his gratitude to Mr Vandeleur Robinson for permission to reprint part of this report, intended for internal use.

301

The whole room took up the cry, giving the clenched fist salute and shouting *Freiheit! Freiheit! Freiheit!*

Churchill had always been opposed to the policy which had led to Munich. He would have liked nothing better than to have the Agreement annulled when he came to power in 1940, but in France Daladier and Bonnet, both prominent 'men of Munich', were members of the Government and remained so until the eve of the French collapse in June 1940. Thus the French régime could hardly be expected to repudiate what Daladier had signed. Nevertheless, after 16 March 1939, even French practice continued as if the Munich Agreement had never been made. All those who had been Czechoslovak subjects on 30 September 1938 were still regarded as such on French soil and enjoyed the protection of the Czechoslovak Legation in Paris. When war broke out in September, all Czechoslovak citizens in France – including those who came from the areas incorporated into Germany – were required, in accordance with Czechoslovak laws, to enlist for service in the Czechoslovak Forces abroad.[1] Later the 'Free French National Committee' in London, the precursor of the post-war French Government, formally disassociated itself from Daladier's signature to the Munich Agreement on 29 September 1942.[2] De Gaulle declared on that occasion that the Munich Agreement was 'invalid from the beginning' and expressly committed himself to the restoration of Czechoslovakia within the borders of 30 September 1938.

Great Britain too tried to undo Munich 'informally' while Chamberlain and Halifax were still in office. None of the refugees from Czechoslovakia who had been citizens of that country at the time of Munich were regarded as German unless they expressly opted for that nationality (a course naturally taken by no one). The Czechoslovak Legation in London continued to function

---

[1] Agreement between the Czechoslovak Minister Osuský and Daladier as French Minister of War, of 2 October 1939, regarding the reconstitution of the Czechoslovak Army in France, in *Czechoslovak Yearbook of International Law* (London 1942), pp. 232–4.

[2] Text of De Gaulle's letter of 28 September 1942 in *Czechoslovak Sources and Documents. No. 2: Struggle for Freedom* (New York 1943), p. 63. After his return to French soil, De Gaulle formally renewed this declaration on 22 August 1944; text in Beneš, *Šest let exilu a druhé světové války* (Six years of exile and the Second World War) (London 1945), p. 315.

after the German occupation of Prague and remained responsible for all those exiles living in Britain who had been Czechoslovak subjects and had asked for protection. After the outbreak of the war Czechoslovaks in Britain were at first not called up but voluntary service in the Czechoslovak Army in France was encouraged. A large percentage of these volunteers were of German origin.

On the occasion of the second anniversary of the Munich decision, Churchill stated in a broadcast message that the rulers of Germany had 'destroyed the agreement'.[1] On 5 August 1942 in an exchange of notes with Jan Masaryk, the Foreign Minister of the Czechoslovak Government-in-Exile, Anthony Eden pointed out, basing himself on this declaration, that 'as Germany had deliberately destroyed the arrangements concerning Czechoslovakia in 1938, His Majesty's Government regarded themselves as free from an engagement in this respect'.[2] The Agreement, in other words, was not regarded as void *ab initio* but invalidated by post-Munich events. Eden added that 'At the formal settlement of Czechoslovakia's frontiers to be reached at the end of the war, His Majesty's Government will not be influenced by any changes effected since 1938.'

At that time it was still thought that this war, like all wars before it, would end with a formal peace conference. Eden wanted to affirm in advance that Britain would enter it on the clear understanding that Czechoslovakia was to have the frontiers with Germany she had had before the Munich Conference. Since there was in fact no conventional peace settlement, the various post-war Governments of Britain, France and Italy behaved as if Munich had never occurred:[3] after 1945 full Czechoslovak rule over the areas awarded to Germany on that occasion was never questioned.[4]

---

[1] See *Memoirs of Dr Beneš*, p. 116.

[2] Ibid. p. 208. For the diplomatic negotiations preceding this exchange of notes see *Foreign Office Files* (*Czechoslovakia*), F.O. 371, vol. 30835.

[3] On 26 September 1944 the Italian Government repudiated Mussolini's signature on the Munich decision as invalid 'from the beginning'. See Beneš, *Šest let exilu*, p. 316.

[4] In March 1945 the British Government agreed 'that the Czechoslovak Government should exercise full political authority from the date of the unconditional surrender of Germany throughout the area bounded by the frontiers of Czechoslovakia as these existed before the 31st December, 1937'. Memorandum Eden for the War Cabinet, 20 March 1945, W.P. (45)180, *Cab.* 66/63.

Czechoslovakia before Munich

During a visit to Prague in April 1965, Michael Stewart as Foreign Secretary summed up the views of all British post-Chamberlain administrations. He declared the Munich arrangement to have been 'detestable, unjust and dangerous, as events have shown, for the peace of Europe',[1] adding that

I said that the agreement was completely dead and had been dead for many years ...The mere historical fact that it was once made cannot justify any future claims against Czechoslovakia. When the time comes for a final determination of Germany's frontiers by a peace treaty the treaty discussion would start from the basis that Czechoslovak frontiers were not in question.

The United States had no need to reassess its position: it had not been involved in the events of 1938 and 1939, hence the question of recognizing their consequences did not arise.[2]

The latest formulation of the German Federal Republic's policy was contained in Chancellor Kiesinger's declaration on 13 December 1966.[3]

With the Czechoslovak Republic, too, the German people wishes to come to an understanding. The Federal Government condemns Hitler's policy which was directed towards the destruction of the Czechoslovak State. It agrees that the Munich Agreement which was made under the threat of force is no longer valid.

Czechoslovakia herself considers Munich to have been null and void from the start. There are thus different ways of looking at it, but no doubt exists about the *present* invalidity of the Agreement.

The aftermath of Munich

All evidence which has become available meanwhile points to the conclusion that the British Government worried about Hitler's intention after Munich even less than before. The country was reassured by the Prime Minister at the end of January 1939:[4]

[1] According to the text placed at the author's disposal by the Foreign Office.
[2] 'The United States never did recognize the territorial changes which had been made as a result of the Munich agreement...' (Letter by Dr E. Taylor Parks, Chief Research Guidance and Review Division, Historical Office, Department of State, Washington, to the author, dated 14 October 1964.)
[3] *Das Parlament* (Bonn), 21 December 1966. Chancellor Willy Brandt expressed in his programmatic speech of 18 January 1973 the hope 'to come to an arrangement in the foreseeable future whereby the Munich Agreement will cease to be a strain on the relationship between the two states'.
[4] Speech at Birmingham, 28 January 1939, *Bulletin of International News* (London), 11 February 1939, pp. 101–4.

'I cannot believe that any such challenge [for world domination] is intended.' It is difficult to decide whether the Prime Minister's optimism was caused or only reinforced by the rosy reports coming from the British Ambassador in Berlin, but seldom before was a situation so badly misjudged as by Sir Nevile Henderson whose advice in the middle of February 1939 culminated in the following sentence:[1]

In my opinion...it would be as useful both in press and speeches to stress our full reliance in Herr Hitler's peaceful intentions as it is harmful to show suspicion of them.

At the end of February he wrote that Hitler was fully occupied with a – by now forgotten – quarrel between France and Italy:[2]

It seems that Germany, even if she was so disposed, would find it difficult to embark on a serious venture elsewhere.

The question whether one could trust Hitler's word was answered by him in more than positive terms – after all the broken promises:[3]

Personally, I would not go further than to say that as an individual, he would be as likely to keep it (his word) as any other foreign statesman – under certain conditions probably more so.

Consequently, Henderson was opposed to a British policy based on the assumption that Hitler was seeking world domination. Furthermore Ashton-Gwatkin had gone to Berlin, and Lord Halifax quoted him on 8 March[4] as reporting that

he had gained the impression that *no immediate adventure of any larger type was contemplated*. This, however, did not rule out the possibility of further *pressure* being brought to bear on Czechoslovakia.

This was exactly one week before Hitler occupied Prague. When it became clear than an adventure of a larger type was not only contemplated but prepared in all its details, Henderson's biggest, nay only worry was that Hitler might be irritated by strong words coming from London:[5]

I doubt whether Herr Hitler has yet taken a decision and I consider it therefore

[1] Henderson to Halifax, 18 February 1939, *DBFP*, 3/IV (London 1951), no. 118.
[2] Henderson to Halifax, 28 February 1939, *DBFP*, 3/IV, no. 162.
[3] Henderson to Halifax, 9 March 1939, *DBFP*, 3/IV, no. 195.
[4] *Cab.* 23/97, Minute 10(39), Meeting of 8 March 1939, Colvin, *The Chamberlain Government*, p. 184.
[5] Henderson to Halifax, 11 March 1939, *DBFP*, 3/IV, no. 203.

highly desirable that nothing should be said or published during the weekend which would excite him to precipitate action.

A day after the occupation of Prague Sir Orme Sargent severely criticized Henderson in an internal Foreign Office note and pointed to the disastrous effects of his misguided advice:[1]

This misleading forecast of 18 February was particularly unfortunate if, as I suppose, it was one of the factors which decided the Prime Minister to issue to the press the *mot d'ordre* to the effect that the international position could now be viewed with comfort and optimism.

On 12 March Sir Nevile Henderson still reported[2] that he had 'no evidence that the German Government intend to exploit the present unrest in Czechoslovakia'. A day later he could not deny having evidence of troop movements, but on the 14th, the day before the invasion, he was still optimistic, unless the Czechs proved to be 'recalcitrants':[3]

Herr Hitler may not have taken a final decision... My general impression was that no definite line of action has been decided upon but that the use of force was certainly not excluded if the Prague Government proved recalcitrant.

The course of events is well known and no detailed description is necessary here. Blackmailed by Hitler's threat to hand the Slovaks over to Hungary, Slovak 'independence' was proclaimed on the 14th. On the night of the 14th Hitler and Goering threatened the unfortunate Emil Hácha (elected President of Czechoslovakia after the resignation of Beneš), with the destruction of Prague. He was browbeaten into signing a prepared declaration, putting the fate of his people 'with confidence' into the hand of Hitler who had long ago given orders that the country should be occupied on the 15th.

When Chamberlain rose in the afternoon of the 15th in the House of Commons to give a report on the events in Central Europe, he was more concerned to defend his appeasement policy than to condemn Hitler's unprovoked aggression. After his return from Munich he had had this to say to Parliament:[4]

[1] Minute by Sir Orme Sargent, *Foreign Office Files* (*Czechoslovakia*), F.O. 371 vol. 23896.
[2] Henderson to Halifax, 12 March 1939, *DBFP*, 3/IV, no. 217.
[3] Henderson to Halifax, 13 and 14 March 1939, *DBFP*, 3/IV, nos. 220, 232.
[4] *Parliamentary Debates* (*Hansard*), House of Commons, 3 October 1938, vol. 339, col. 45; 15 March 1939, vol. 345, cols. 345–440.

It is my hope and my belief that under the new system of guarantees the new Czechoslovakia will find a greater security than she has ever enjoyed in the past.

Instead of apologizing for offering the worst advice possible in October 1938, Chamberlain boldly declared on 15 March – few politicians had been ever proved wrong in so short a time – that 'the course we took was right'. What Hitler had done, was a 'shock to confidence', but the Prime Minister's advice was to ignore the lesson: 'do not let us on that account be deflected from our course' – which was meant to be a course of further appeasement. Czechoslovakia had 'disintegrated' and the guarantee, given in order to prevent Hitler from 'disintegrating' her was no longer valid: 'His Majesty's Government cannot accordingly hold themselves any longer bound by this obligation.' The Prime Minister had no more to say in evaluating Hitler's action than this:

Even if it may now be claimed that what has taken place has occurred with the acquiescence of the Czech Government, I cannot regard the manner and the method by which these changes have been brought about as in accord with the spirit of the Munich Agreement.

It might have been unwise at this early hour to publicly express doubts about Hitler's assertion that Hácha had voluntarily invited him to occupy his country, but a few hours before the House of Commons met the Cabinet held a meeting. Not even in the secrecy of 10 Downing Street was any doubt expressed about the way Hitler had got Hácha's signature. Lord Halifax spoke continually about an 'agreement signed early this morning'[1] and nobody questioned that. Not even the mildest protest was contemplated by the Cabinet, and the Foreign Secretary was quick to emphasize 'that there was no possibility of effectively opposing what was taking place or influencing the position'. In the Cabinet meeting even more than later in the House of Commons, Chamberlain denied the government's obligation to fulfil their guarantee. He characterized the steps taken by Hitler as 'moral pressure':

It might, no doubt, be true that the disruption of Czechoslovakia had been largely engineered by Germany, but our guarantee was not a guarantee against the exercise of *moral pressure*. The German action had all been taken under the

[1] *Cab.* 23/97, Minute 11(39), Meeting of 15 March 1939, partly quoted by Colvin, *The Chamberlain Government*, p. 186.

guise of an agreement with the Czech Government. The Germans were, therefore, in a position to give a plausible answer to any representations which were
made.

Finally, Chamberlain said that the 'military occupation was
symbolic, more than appeared at the surface'. This was scarcely
the impression of the immediate victims of this 'symbolic' act, but
in defence of the Prime Ministers' Munich signature nothing was
too ridiculous.

In fairness it must be said that two days later although still
defending the Munich Agreement, Chamberlain entirely changed his
tone. In a speech delivered at Birmingham[1] he now spoke about
Hácha 'confronted with demands which he had no power to resist'.
Against all the evidence he claimed not to have been satisfied with
the results of Munich: 'I have never denied that the terms which I
was able to secure at Munich were not those that I myself would
have desired.' Nevertheless, Chamberlain now said all the obvious
things which he would never have said before:

Does not the question inevitably arise in our minds, if it is so easy to discover
good reasons for ignoring assurances so solemnly and so repeatedly given, what
reliance can be placed upon any other assurances that come from the same
source? Is this, in fact, a step in the direction of an attempt to dominate the
world by force?

These words would also have been justified just a year before,
when ignoring assurances solemnly and repeatedly given, Hitler
had invaded Austria. At the Cabinet meeting a day later[2] Chamberlain admitted that in the beginning he had given 'no proper consideration' to the events of 15 March – but even after this declaration
his colleagues still did not question his ability to remain Prime
Minister. Then he explained why he had spoken so differently at
Birmingham:

The Prime Minister said that he had now come definitely to the conclusion
that Herr Hitler's attitude made it impossible to continue to negotiate on the
old basis with the Nazi régime. This did not mean that negotiations with the
German people were impossible.

The Nazi leaders, he said, did not deserve any reliance, but even

---

[1] *British Blue Book*, Cmd. 6106, no. 9. See *Documents on International Affairs
1939–46*, 1 (London 1951), 66–71.
[2] *Cab.* 23/97, Minute 12(39), Meeting of 18 March 1939, Colvin, *The Chamberlain Government*, p. 188.

now admitting he had been deceived by Hitler, he could not help twisting his admission in his favour.

When he had met Herr Hitler, he had thought that while Herr Hitler might mean what he said, it was always possible that he would find reasons to change his views later.

Chamberlain never stated that Hitler *might* mean what he said. His *ipsissima verba* were that 'the impression left on him was that Herr Hitler meant what he said' (17 September 1938). And there is no reason to believe that Hitler changed his views after having promised something; he never intended to keep a promise longer than was convenient. Chamberlain's declarations from 18 March 1939 were a retreat from an untenable position, but it was not a dignified retreat.

In any event, the day before[1] the British Ambassador in Berlin had at least been instructed to 'protest against the changes effected in Czechoslovakia by German military action', to denounce them as 'devoid of any basis of legality' and to stigmatize them as a 'complete repudiation of the Munich Agreement'.

The British refusal to recognize the changes brought about by Hitler as valid facilitated Beneš' struggle for the restoration of Czechoslovak independence. After he had succeeded in 1945, the bulk of the country's German population, irrespective of guilt or innocence, was driven out. But that is another story.

[1] Text of the protest note in *DGFP*, D/IV (London 1956), no. 26. The day before, Neville Chamberlain had answered a question by the Liberal leader Sir Archibald Sinclair (later Lord Thurso) whether Great Britain had protested against Hitler's aggression with 'No, Sir, we have not done so'. Sinclair's further question whether it was proposed to lodge a protest got the reply 'I could not answer that question without notice' (*Parliamentary Debates* (*Hansard*), House of Commons, 16 March 1939, vol. 345, col. 613).

EPILOGUE

Some concluding words seem apposite after a description of events which unavoidably must often appear bitter and full of recriminations. The author has tried hard to mirror events without prejudice and feels he should not be blamed for the picture the mirror reflects. When after careful research something still seemed to admit of different interpretations, the benefit of the doubt has not been denied to anyone.

While the detailed description of events and the analysis of attitudes in bygone times may seem remote to someone fully absorbed by the pressing problems of the 1970s, there are nevertheless some aspects of great topicality involved in this quarrel in – to quote the words of a British Prime Minister – 'a far away country between people of whom we know nothing'. *Tempora mutantur* – this is no doubt true: in the 1970s peace and stability are threatened by forces quite different from those which shook the world in the 1930s. But is the other half of the Latin proverb *et nos mutamur in illis* likewise true? Do we not still sometimes, because it suits our complacency, tend to believe that words mean the same to us and to those who strive for aims directly opposed to ours? The story of how, out of political expediency, obvious fabrications were uncritically accepted as the truth and acted upon, is presented here as a timely warning.

BIBLIOGRAPHY

NOTE ON SOURCES

Most of what is said in this book about events inside Czechoslovakia is based on the personal experience and recollection of the author. Nevertheless, care has been taken to give a printed source for all statements though these sources might in many cases be hardly accessible to English readers.

Regarding British pre-war policy in matters of Czechoslovakia, the author had, after being able to study the relevant Foreign Office files in the original, the privilege of discussing some problems with Mr Francis Ashton-Gwatkin and Mr Robert Stopford, both members of the Runciman Mission of 1938, and Sir Frank Roberts who in 1938 was dealing with Czechoslovak affairs in the Central Department of the Foreign Office. He is indebted to them for valuable advice, but the opinions the author expresses in the book are entirely his own.

Thanks are further due to the numerous institutions and libraries in Europe and America where the author was able to find many of the sources he has used. Those are:

The British Museum and its Newspaper Library at Colindale.
The Royal Institute of International Affairs (Chatham House).
The School of Slavonic and East European Studies, University of London.
The Wiener Library (Institute of Contemporary History), London.
International Instituut voor Sociale Geschiedenis (International Institute for Social History), Amsterdam.
Rijksinstituut voor Oorlogsdokumentatie (State Institute for War History), Amsterdam.
Bibliothèque de Documentation Internationale Contemporaine, Paris.
The New York Public Library.
The Library of Congress, Washington.
The Masaryk and Beneš Collection, University of California, Berkeley.
Bayerische Staatsbibliothek, Munich.
Institut für Zeitgeschichte (Institute of Contemporary History), Munich.
Österreichisches Institut für Zeitgeschichte, Vienna.
Österreichische Nationalbibliothek, Vienna.
Sozialwissenschaftliche Studienbibliothek, Arbeiterkammer (Sociological Research Library of the Chamber of Labour), Vienna.

The author believes that fresh ground has been broken by his narrative which does not only rest on public sources but also considers for the first time unpublished files of the German Foreign Office, the German diplomatic missions abroad and the Reich Chancellory: in many instances these form indeed the backbone of the story. This also applies to similar files of the Austrian Foreign Ministry relating to the revolution of 1918–19. The author was able to study photostats of German diplomatic documents in the Foreign Office Library and

311

Bibliography

the Public Record Office and original papers in the Political Archive of the Foreign Office in Bonn and the Federal Archive at Coblenz. The Austrian State Archive in Vienna granted him access to the 'New Political Archive'. Thanks are rendered to all these authorities.

Apart from the German diplomatic papers which fell into Allied hands in 1945 and are now generally available for research, it is the corpus of British diplomatic documents which began to be published after the Second World War, followed by parallel U.S. publications, which have proved to be of inestimable value. Up to the time this book went to press, French diplomatic papers were available only for the periods of 1 July 1932 to 13 March 1934 and from 1 January 1936 to 29 September 1937 as well as for the months immediately preceding the outbreak of the war, and here only in a small selection.

In 1967 the period of closure for British State papers was reduced from fifty to thirty years: this made it possible to examine, in the Public Record Office, London, unpublished Foreign Office files and Cabinet papers relating to Czechoslovakia for the years 1935 to 1939 and to utilize this extremely valuable material systematically for the first time in this book.

OFFICIAL AND DOCUMENTARY PUBLICATIONS

I. GREAT BRITAIN

British Blue Book, Cmd. 6106, London 1939.
Documents on British Foreign Policy 1919–1939 (*abbr. DBFP*)
    First Series, vol. I (1 July–15 October 1919), London 1947.
    First Series, vol. II (16 October 1919–21 January 1920), London 1951.
    First Series, vol. VI (1919), London 1956.
    Second Series, vol. II (1931), London 1947.
    Second Series, vol. IV (1932–3), London 1950.
    Second Series, vol. V (1933), London 1956.
    Third Series, vol. I (9 March–23 July 1938), London 1949.
    Third Series, vol. II (23 July–30 September 1938), London 1949.
    Third Series, vol. III (September 1938–January 1939), London 1950.
    Third Series, vol. IV (20 January–3 April 1939), London 1951.
Parliamentary Debates (*Hansard*), *House of Commons*, vols. 338, 339 (July to October 1938), and 345 (March 1939).

2. GERMANY

Die Friedensverhandlungen in Versailles, German Foreign Office Publication, Berlin 1919.
Documents on German Foreign Policy 1918–1945 (abbr. *DGFP*)
    Series C (1933–7):
        vol. I: The Third Reich, First Phase, 30 January 1933–14 October 1933, London 1957.
        vol. II: The Third Reich, First Phase, 15 October 1933–13 June 1934, London 1959.
        vol. III: The Third Reich, First Phase, 14 June 1934–31 March 1935, London 1959.
        vol. IV: The Third Reich, First Phase, 1 April 1935–4 March 1936, London 1962.

vol. v: The Third Reich, First Phase, 3 May–31 October 1936, London 1966.
Series D (1937–45)
   vol. i: From Neurath to Ribbentrop, Washington 1949.
   vol. ii: Germany and Czechoslovakia, Washington 1949.
   vol. iv: The Aftermath of Munich, Washington 1949.
   vol. xi: The War Years, 1 September 1940–31 January 1941, London 1961.
   vol. xiii: The War Years, 23 June 1941–11 December 1941, London 1964.
Documents and Materials relating to the Eve of the Second World War vol. i, Moscow 1948.

3. JUDGMENT OF THE INTERNATIONAL MILITARY TRIBUNAL FOR THE TRIAL OF GERMAN MAJOR WAR CRIMINALS (abbr. *IMT*) (London 1946, Cmd. 6964).
The Trial of German Major War Criminals, Vols. ii, v, ix, x, xvii, xix and xxii (London 1946–50).

4. UNITED STATES

Papers relating to the Foreign Relations of the United States, The Paris Peace Conference, 1919, 13 volumes, Washington 1942–7.
Foreign Relations of the United States, 1938, vol. i, Washington 1955.

5. FRANCE

Documents Diplomatiques Français. 1932–1939
   1ʳᵉ Série (1932–5),
      tome i (1 July–14 November 1932), Paris 1964.
      tome ii (16 November 1932 – 17 March 1933), Paris 1966.
      tome iii (17 March–15 July 1933), Paris 1967.
      tome iv (16 July–12 November 1933), Paris 1968.
      tome v (13 November 1933–13 March 1934), Paris 1970.
   2ᵉ Série (1936–9),
      tome i (1 January–31 March 1936), Paris 1963.
      tome ii (1 April–18 July 1936), Paris 1964.
      tome iii (19 July–19 November 1936), Paris 1966.
      tome iv (20 November 1936–19 February 1937), Paris 1967.
      tome v (20 February–31 March 1937), Paris 1969.
      tome vi (1 June–29 September 1937), Paris 1970.
Le Livre Jaune Français, Documents Diplomatiques 1938–1939, Paris 1939.
Les événements survenus en France de 1933 à 1945, Témoignages et documents recueillis par la Commission d'Enquête parlementaire, Paris 1947–52, tome i; Annexes, tome ix.

6. CZECHOSLOVAKIA

Těsnopisecké zprávy o schůzích Národního Shromáždění Republiky Československé (Stenographic minutes of the sessions of the National Assembly of the Czechoslovak Republic), 14 November 1918–31 December 1938.
Tisky k těsnopiseckým zprávám o schůzích Poslanecké sněmovny (Printed reports to the stenographic minutes of the sessions of the House of Representatives), 1920–38. These contain parliamentary motions and interpellations and the Government's replies.

313

Bibliography

Sammlung der Gesetze und Verordnungen (Collection of Laws and Decrees), 1920. (Official German issue of Czechoslovak laws and decrees.)

Statistisches Jahrbuch der Tschechoslowakei (Statistical Yearbook of Czechoslovakia), 1921, 1925, 1929, 1938 (Prague 1921, 1925, 1929 and 1938).

Statistical Handbook of the Czechoslovak Republic, London 1942.

7. AUSTRIA

Bericht über die Tätigkeit der deutschösterreichischen Friedensdelegation in St Germain-en-Laye (Report about the activity of the Austrian peace delegation at St Germain-en-Laye), 2 vols, Vienna 1919.

BOOKS AND PAMPHLETS

Adler, Victor, *Victor Adlers Aufsätze, Reden und Briefe*, vol. 6 (Vienna 1924), vol. 9 (Vienna 1929).

Almond, Nina and Lutz Ralph Haswell (eds.), *The Treaty of St Germain, A Documentary History*, Stanford (U.S.A.) 1935.

Amery, Leopold, *My Political Life*, vol. 3, London 1955.

Anfuso, Filippo, *Rom–Berlin im diplomatischen Spiegel* (Rome–Berlin in the diplomatic mirror), Munich 1951.

Avon, Earl of, *The Eden Memoirs, Facing the Dictators*, London 1962.

Baker, Ray Stannard, *Woodrow Wilson and the World Settlement*, vol. III, London 1933.

Ball, Margaret M., *Post-War German–Austrian Relations, The Anschluß Movement 1918–1936*, London 1937.

Bauer, Otto, *Die Nationalitätenfrage und die Sozialdemokratie*, Vienna 1907 (reissued 1924).

Die Österreichische Revolution, Vienna 1923 (reissued 1965).

Baynes, Norman H. (ed.), *The Speeches of Adolf Hitler April 1922–August 1939*, 2 vols, London 1942.

Benedikt, Heinrich (ed.), *Geschichte der Republik Österreich*, Vienna 1954.

Beneš, Edvard, *Le problème Autrichien et la Question Tchèque. Études sur les luttes politiques des nationalités slaves en Autriche*, Paris 1908.

Détruisez l'Autriche-Hongrie!, Paris 1916.

Problémy nové Evropy (Problems of the new Europe), Prague 1924.

Světová válka a naše revoluce (The World War and our Revolution) [This is the original version of Beneš' memoirs, translated only in excerpts], 3 vols, Prague 1927–35.

Der Aufstand der Nationen [Shortened German edition of memoirs], Berlin 1928.

My War Memoirs [Shortened English edition of memoirs], London 1928.

Das österreichischedeutsche Abkommen, Prague 1931.

Rede an die Deutschen der Tschechoslowakei, Ústí 1935.

Gedanke und Tat (*Selected Writings and Speeches by E. Beneš*), 3 vols, Prague 1937.

Der Präsident in Südböhmen, Prague 1937.

(under the pseudonym 'An Active and Responsible Czechoslovak Statesman') *Germany and Czechoslovakia*, Prague 1937.

Šest let exilu a druhé světové války (Six years of exile and of the Second World War), London 1945.
The Memoirs of Dr. Beneš, London 1954.
Mnichovské Dny (Days of Munich), Prague 1968.
Beneš, Edouard, *Munich*, Paris 1970 [French edition of *Mnichovské Dny*].
Berber, Friedrich (ed.), *Europäische Politik 1933–1938 im Spiegel der Prager Akten*, Essen 1942.
Birkenhead, Earl of, *Halifax, The Life of Lord Halifax*, London 1965.
Bonnet, Georges, *Défense de la Paix, De Washington au Quai d'Orsay*, Geneva 1946.
Boothby, Robert (Lord Boothby), *I Fight to Live*, London 1947.
Borsody, Stephen, *The Triumph of Tyranny*, London 1960.
Braddick, Henderson B., *Germany, Czechoslovakia and the 'Grand Alliance' in the May Crisis, 1938*, Denver (Colorado) 1969.
Brand, Walter, *Die sudetendeutsche Tragödie*, Nuremberg 1949.
Braunias, Karl, *Die Fortentwicklung des altösterreichischen Nationalitätenrechts nach dem Kriege*, Vienna 1938.
Briggs, Mitchell Pirie, *George D. Herron and the European Settlement*, London 1932.
Brockdorff-Rantzau, Count Ulrich, *Dokumente und Gedanken um Versailles*, Berlin 1925.
Brügel, J. W., *Ludwig Czech, Arbeiterführer und Staatsmann*, Vienna 1960.
Brügel, Ludwig, *Geschichte der österreichischen Sozialdemokratie*, 5 vols, Vienna 1922–5.
Butler, Lord, *The Art of the Possible*, London 1971.
(Cadogan) *The Diaries of Sir Alexander Cadogan* (ed. David Dilks), London 1971.
Celovsky, Boris, *Das Münchner Abkommen von 1938*, Stuttgart 1958.
Charmatz, Richard, *Der demokratisch-nationale Bundesstaat Österreich*, Frankfurt 1904.
Churchill, Winston S., *The Second World War*, vol. 1: *The Gathering Storm*, London 1948.
Colvin, Ian, *Vansittart in Office*, London 1965.
The Chamberlain Government, London 1971.
Coolidge, Archibald C., *Ten Years of War and Peace*, Cambridge (U.S.A.) 1927.
Curtius, Julius, *Bemühung um Österreich*, Heidelberg 1947.
Sechs Jahre Minister der Deutschen Republik, Heidelberg 1948.
Czechoslovak Cabinet Ministers on the Complaints of the Sudeten German Party in the Czechoslovak Parliament, Prague 1937.
Czechoslovak Sources and Documents, No. 2: *Struggle for Freedom*, New York 1943.
Czechoslovak Yearbook of International Law, London 1942.
Dalton, Hugh, *The Fateful Years, Memoirs 1931–1945*, London 1957.
Das größere Reich [Series of lectures arranged by the Academy of Administration, Vienna], Berlin 1943.
Der Lebenswille des Sudetendeutschtums (Report of the Conference of the Sudeten German Party on 23 and 24 April 1938), Karlovy Vary 1938.
Documents on American Foreign Relations, January 1938–June 1939, Boston 1939.
Documents on International Affairs 1936, London 1937.

Bibliography

Documents on International Affairs 1937, London 1939.
Documents on International Affairs 1938, vol. II, London 1943.
Donosti, Mario (pseudonym), *Mussolini e L'Europa*, Rome 1945.
Epstein, Leo (ed.), *Studienausgabe der Verfassungsgesetze der Tschechoslovakischen Republik*, Liberec 1923.
Eubank, Keith, *Munich*, Norman (U.S.A.) 1963.
Feiling, Keith, *The Life of Neville Chamberlain*, London 1946.
Fischer, Josef, Patzak, Václav and Perth, Vincenc, *Ihr Kampf, Die wahren Ziele der SdP*, Karlovy Vary 1937.
Flandin, Pierre-Étienne, *Politique Française 1919–1940*, Paris 1947.
Freissler, Robert, *Vom Zerfall Österreichs bis zum tschechoslowakischen Staat*, Zoppot–Berlin 1921.
Gedye, G. E. R., *Fallen Bastions*, London 1939.
Gehl, Jürgen, *Austria, Germany and the Anschluß 1931–1938*, London 1963.
Germany and Czechoslovakia 1918–1945, Documents on German Politics, Prague 1965.
Gilbert, Martin and Gott, Richard, *The Appeasers*, London 1963.
Glück, Werner, *Sprachenrecht und Sprachenpraxis in der Tschechoslowakischen Republik*, Halle 1939.
Grant Duff, Sheila, *German and Czech, A Threat to European Peace*, London 1937.
Europe and the Czechs, London 1938.
Griffin, Joan and Griffin, Jonathan, *Lost Liberty*, London 1939.
Groscurth, Helmutt, *Tagebücher eines Abwehr-Offiziers 1938–1940*, Stuttgart 1970.
Halifax, Lord, *Fullness of Day*, London 1957.
Hankey, Lord, *The Supreme Control of the Paris Peace Conference 1919*, London 1963.
Hannak, Jacques, *Ka*r*l Renner und seine Zeit*, Vienna 1965.
(Harvey) *The Diplomatic Diaries of Oliver Harvey 1937–1940*, London 1970.
Henderson, Alexander, *Eyewitness in Czechoslovakia*, London 1939.
'Operation without Anaesthetics', in the collection edited by Wilfrid Hindle, *Foreign Correspondent, Personal Adventures abroad in Search of News*, London 1939, pp. 81–106.
Henlein, Konrad, *Konrad Henlein spricht* (Speeches on the political movement of the Sudeten Germans), Karlovy Vary 1937.
Heim ins Reich (Speeches 1937–38), Liberec 1939.
Hildebrandt, Rainer, *Wir sind die Letzten* (From the Life of the Resistance fighter Albrecht Haushofer and his friends), Neuwied 1949.
Hodža, Milan, *Federalism in Central Europe*, London 1942.
Hofbauer, Josef and Strauss Emil, *Josef Seliger, ein Lebensbild*, Prague 1930.
Hofbauer, Josef, *Der große alte Mann*, Prague 1938.
Hořec, Jaromír, *Cesty zrady* (Paths of Treason), Prague 1957.
Hunter Miller, David, *My Diary at the Conference in Paris*, 21 vols, New York 1924–6.
Jaszi, Oscar, *The Dissolution of the Habsburg Monarchy*, Chicago 1929 (reissued 1961).
Johnson, Alex Campbell, *Viscount Halifax, A Biography*, London 1941.
Kann, Robert A., *The Multinational Empire*, 2 vols, New York 1950.

Bibliography

Karlgren, Antoine, *Henlein, Hitler et les Tchèques, La question allemande des Sudètes*, Paris 1939.

Killanin, Michael (ed.), *Four Days*, London 1939.

Kirkpatrick, Ivone, *The Inner Circle*, London 1959.

Klepetar, Harry, *Seit 1918...*, Ostrava 1937.

Kordt, Erich, *Wahn und Wirklichkeit*, Stuttgart 1948.

Nicht aus den Akten..., Stuttgart 1950.

Král, Václav (ed.), *Die Deutschen in der Tschechoslowakei 1933–1947*, Prague 1964.

Kvaček, Robert, *Osudná mise* (Fateful Mission), Prague 1958.

Laffan, R. D. G., *The Crisis over Czechoslovakia, January to September 1938* (*Survey of International Affairs 1938*, vol. II), London 1951.

Lansing, Robert, *The Peace Negotiations, A Personal Narrative*, New York 1921.

La Paix de Versailles, vol. V, Paris 1932, vol. IX, Paris 1939, vol. X, Paris 1932.

Laroche, Jules, *Au Quai d'Orsay avec Briand et Poincaré*, Paris 1957.

(Lipski) *Papers and Memoirs of Józef Lipski, Ambassador of Poland, Diplomat in Berlin 1933–1939*, ed. Waclaw Jedrzejewicz, New York 1968.

Lloyd George, David, *The Truth about the Peace Treaties*, 2 vols, London 1938.

Lodgman, Rudolf, *Reden und Aufsätze*, ed. A. K. Simon, Munich 1954.

Luckau, Alma (ed.), *The German Delegation at the Paris Peace Conference*, New York 1941.

Macleod, Iain, *Neville Chamberlain*, London 1961.

Mamatey, Victor S., *The United States and East Central Europe 1914–1918. A Study in Wilsonian Diplomacy and Propaganda*, Princeton 1957.

Mantoux, Paul (ed.), *Les délibérations du Conseil des Quatre*, 2 vols, Paris 1955.

Masaryk, T. G., *Botschaft des Präsidenten T. G. Masaryk* (President Masaryk's Message, delivered at the ceremonial session of the National Assembly on 28 October 1918), Prague 1919.

The New Europe (*The Slav Standpoint*), London 1918.

The Making of a State, Memoirs and Observations, 1914–18, London 1927.

Cesta demokracie (The Path of Democracy) 2 vols, Prague 1933–4.

Massey, Vincent, *What's Past is Prologue*, London 1963.

Michaelis, Herbert and Schraepke, Ernst (eds), *Ursachen und Folgen*, Vom deutschen Zusammenbruch 1918 und 1945 bis zur staatlichen Neuordnung Deutschlands in der Gegenwart, vol. III, Berlin 1959, vol. VI, Berlin 1961 and vol. VII, Berlin 1963.

Middlemas, Keith, *Diplomacy of Illusion*, London 1972.

Molisch, Paul, *Die sudetendeutsche Freiheitsbewegung in den Jahren 1919–1920*, Vienna 1932.

(ed.), *Briefe zur deutschen Politik in Österreich 1848–1918*, Vienna 1934.

Mommsen, Hans, *Die Sozialdemokratie und die Nationalitätenfrage im Habsburgischen Vielvölkerstaat*, Vienna 1963.

Namier, L. B., *Diplomatic Prelude 1938–1939*, London 1948.

Europe in Decay, London 1950.

In the Nazi Era, London 1952.

Naylor, John F., *Labour's International Policy*, London 1969.

Nicolson, Sir Harold, *Diaries and Letters 1930–1939* (ed. Nigel Nicolson), London 1966.

Peace Making 1919, London 1945.

317

Bibliography

Noguères, Henri, *Munich ou la drôle de paix*, Paris 1963; English edition: *Munich or the Phoney Peace*, London 1965.

Norwich, Viscount, *Old Men Forget, The Autobiography of Duff Cooper*, London 1953.

Oldofredi, Hieronymus, *Zwischen Krieg und Frieden*, Vienna 1925.

Opočenský, Jan, *La fin d'Autriche et la Genèse de l'État tchècoslovaque*, Prague 1928.

Umsturz in Mitteleuropa, Dresden–Hellerau 1932.

Osterbegehrschrift. Forderungen der Deutschen Österreichs zur Neuordnung nach dem Kriege, Basle 1916.

Parteikonferenz der Sudetenländer, of 16 September 1917 at Brünn (Conference of the German Social Democrats in Austria), Brno 1917.

Perman, Dagmar, *The Shaping of the Czechoslovak State*, Leiden 1962.

Peroutka, Ferninand, *Budování státu* (Building the State), 5 vols, Prague 1933–6.

Pfitzner, Josef, *Sudetendeutsche Geschichte*, Liberec 1935.

Pick, F. W., *Searchlight on German Africa*, London 1939.

Popovici, Aurel, *Die vereinigten Staaten von Großösterreich*, Leipzig 1906.

Programm der Tschechoslowakischen sozialdemokratischen Arbeiterpartei, formulated at the Party Conference in Prague on 27 and 29 September 1930.

Rauschning, Hermann, *Hitler Speaks*, London 1939.

Redlich, Josef, *Österreichische Politik und Verwaltung im Weltkriege*, Vienna 1925.

Schicksalsjahre Österreichs 1908–1919, 2 vols, Graz–Cologne 1954.

Renner, Karl, *Österreich von der esrten zur zweiten Republik*, Vienna 1953.

Ripka, Hubert, *Munich Before and After*, London 1939.

Ritter, Gerhard, *The German Resistance*, London 1958.

Rothfels, Hans, *The German Opposition to Hitler*, London 1961.

Schulthess' Europäischer Geschichtskalender, New Issue, 1919, 1925, 1933 and 1938 (Munich 1924, 1926, 1934 and 1939).

Scott, William Evans, *Alliance against Hitler, The origins of the Franco-Soviet Pact*, Durham (U.S.A.) 1962.

Seton-Watson, R. W., *Masaryk in England*, Cambridge 1943.

Seymour, Charles (ed.), *The Intimate Papers of Colonel House*, vol. IV, London 1928.

Singule, Hans, *Der Staat Masaryks*, Berlin 1937.

Strang, Lord, *At Home and Abroad*, London 1956.

Strauss, Emil, *Die Entstehung der tschechoslowakischen Republik*, Prague 1935. *Tschechoslowaaische Außenpolitik*, Prague 1936.

Stresemann, Gustav, *Vermächtnis, Der Nachlaß*, vols II and III, Berlin 1932; Condensed English edition: *Gustav Stresemann, His Diaries, Letters and Papers*, 3 vols, London 1935–40.

Tabouis, Geneviève, *The Life of Jules Cambon*, London 1938.

Taylor, A. J. P., *The Habsburg Monarchy 1809–1918*, London 1948.

Temperley, H. W. V., *A History of the Peace Conference at Paris*, vols IV and V, London 1925.

Templewood, Viscount, *Nine Troubled Years*, London 1954.

The History of the Times, IV, pt II, London 1952.

Thompson, Charles T., *The Peace Conference Day by Day*, New York 1920.
Thompson, Laurence, *The Greatest Betrayal*, New York 1968.
Toynbee, Arnold (ed.), *Survey of International Affairs 1936*, London 1937, *1938*, vols II and III, London 1941 and 1953.
Trampler, Kurt, *Deutschösterreich 1918/19, Ein Kampf um Selbstbestimmung*, Vienna 1920.
Vansittart, Lord, *Lessons of my Life*, London 1943.
Bones of Contention, London 1945.
The Mist Procession, London 1958.
Viefhaus, Erwin, *Die Minderheitenfrage und die Entstehung der Minderheiten-schutzverträge auf der Pariser Friedenskonferenz von 1919*, Würzburg 1960.
Vondraček, Felix John, *The Foreign Policy of Czechoslovakia 1918–35*, New York 1937.
Wandycz, Pyotr S., *France and her Eastern Allies 1919–1925*, Minneapolis 1962.
Wheeler-Bennett, J. W., *Munich, Prologue to Tragedy*, London 1948.
Wiskemann, Elizabeth, *Czechs and Germans*, London 1938 (reissued 1967).
The Rome–Berlin Axis, London 1949.
Wrench, John Evelyn, *Geoffrey Dawson and our Times*, London 1955.

CONTRIBUTIONS TO PERIODICALS

Ashton-Gwatkin, F. T. A., 'The Personal Story of the Runciman Mission', *The Listener*, 21 October 1948.
Brand, Walter, 'Die Idee des Volkstums', *Die junge Front*, no. 1 (1930).
'Heute und Morgen', *Die junge Front*, no. 1 (1932).
Bruegel, J. W., 'Munich Again', *Central European Observer* (London), no. 2 (1947), pp. 21–2.
'German Diplomacy and the Sudeten Question before 1918', *International Affairs* (London), July 1961, pp. 323–31.
Daladier, Edouard, 'Munich', *Le Candide* (Paris), 7, 14 and 21 September 1961.
Gasiorowski, Zygmunt J., 'Czechoslovakia and the Austrian Question 1918–1928', *Südostforschungen* (1957), pp. 87–122.
'Stresemann and Poland before Locarno', *Journal of Central European Affairs* (April 1958), pp. 27–47.
Henlein, Konrad, 'Leibesübungen und ihre volkspolitische Bedeutung', *Die junge Front*, no. 4 (1930).
'Die Erziehung unserer Mannesjugend', *Die junge Front*, 6 (1932), 181–8.
Jaksch, Wenzel, 'Náš bezpečnostní problém' (Our security problem), *Dělnická Osvěta* (Workers' Education), Prague, 6 (1934), 205–7.
Kogan, Arthur G., 'Germany and the Germans of the Habsburg Monarchy on the Eve of the Armistice 1918; Genesis of the Anschluß Problem' *Journal of Central European Affairs* (April 1960), pp. 24–50.
Kolejka, Josef, 'Moravský Pakt z roku 1905' (The Moravian Pact of 1905), *Československý časopis historický* (Czechoslovak Historical Journal), 1956, pp. 598ff.
Konirsh, Suzanne, 'Constitutional Aspects of the Struggle between Germans and Czechs in the Austro-Hungarian Monarchy', *Journal of Modern History* (Chicago), September 1955, pp. 231–62.

319

Bibliography

Kvaček, Robert, 'K historii Henleinovy Sudetoněmecké strany' (On the history of Henlein's Sudeten German Party), *Dějepis v škole* (History in the School), Prague 5 (1957), 193–200; 6 (1957), 241–9.

Československo-německá jednání v roce 1936' (Czechoslovak–German negotiations in 1936), *Historie a Vojenství* (History and Military Affairs), Prague, 5 (1965), 721–54.

Lvová, Míla, 'K otázce tzv objednaného ultimátu' (About the question of the so-called ordered ultimatum), *Československý časopis historický*, 3 (1965), 333–49.

Pachta, Jan and Reimann, Paul, 'O nových dokumentech k otázce Mnichova' (About new documents concerning the question of Munich), *Příspěvky k dějinám KSČ* (Contributions to the history of the Czechoslovak Communist Party), 1 (1957), 104–33.

Spina, Franz, 'Die Politik der deutschen Parteien in der Tschechoslowakei', *Süddeutsche Monatshefte* (Munich), November 1928.

Stambrook, F. C., 'The German–Austrian Customs Union Project of 1931: A Study of German Methods and Motives', *Journal of Central European Affairs* (Boulder, U.S.A.), April 1961, pp. 15–44.

Tardieu, André, 'Les Allemands de Bohême et les Traités de la Paix', *Gringoire* (Paris), 23 September 1938.

Vansittart, Lord, 'A Morally Indefensible Agreement', *The Listener*, 4 November 1948.

Wallace, W. V., 'New Documents on the History of Munich', *International Affairs* (London), October 1959, pp. 447–54.

'The Foreign Policy of President Beneš in the Approach to Munich', *Slavonic and East European Review* (December 1960), pp. 108–36.

'The Making of the May Crisis of 1938', *Slavonic and East European Review* (June 1963), pp. 368–90.

Webster, Sir Charles, 'Munich Reconsidered: A Survey of British Policy', *International Affairs* (April 1961), pp. 137–51.

Weinberg, Gerald L., 'The May Crisis 1938', *Journal of Modern History* (September 1957), pp. 213–25.

'Secret Hitler–Beneš Negotiations in 1936–37', *Journal of Central European Affairs* (January 1960), pp. 360–74.

320

INDEX

Abbreviations used: CzS for Czechoslovak, Czechoslovakia
SdP for Sudeten German Party

Index

Index

Clemenceau, Georges (1841–1929), French Premier, 12, 15, 44, 46

colonies: German loss of, 93; hints on possibility of re-acquiring, 195, 240, 246

Communist Party, CzS, 55, 63, 72, 76, 178; in 1935 election, 123, 124

constitution of CzS: question of German participation in framing, 54–7; liberal nature of, 57–9; created by unrepresentative body, 62

Coolidge, Archibald (1866–1928), member of American delegation at Versailles, 43–4

Cooper, Alfred Duff (Lord Norwich, 1890–1964), First Lord of the Admiralty: opposes Munich policy, 254, 260, 262, 269–70, 274, 284–5, 287; resigns, 296

Corbin, Charles (1881–1970), French Ambassador in London, 211

Curtius, Julius (1877–1948), German Foreign Minister, 98, 177

customs union, proposed between Austria and Germany, 98–100, 101; Beneš suggests extension of, to France, CzS, and if possible Italy, 101

Czech, Ludwig (1870–1942), German Social Democrat member of CzS government, 82, 83, 128, 143, 148, 149, 172

Czech Agrarians, see Agrarians, Czech

Czech Social Democrats, see Social Democrats, Czech

Czechoslovak National Council (in exile), 87

'Czechoslovak National Council' (1935), organization for spreading of Czech influence, 131

Czechoslovak Republic (early years): birth of (28 Oct. 1918), 16; as economic unit, 17, 20–1, 45; suggestions for German intervention against, 24–5, 35; Germans in, 26–30, 34–5; Austrian territorial claims against, 30–4; attitude of Weimar Republic to, 35–7; memoranda from, at Versailles, 39–42; willing to cede territory to Germany, 39–40, 177, 264; decision against rectification of frontiers of, 44–7; minorities in, 48, 58–9; languages in, 49, 50, 59–61; not a 'National State', 61–2, 78, 144, 151

Czechs, in Austria-Hungary, 2–3, 59; proposed union of Slovaks and (1848), 7–8; in Austrian governments, 8; in

Reichsrat (1917), 12; Epiphany Declaration by, 12; in CzS Revolutionary National Assembly, 54, 57; move into positions previously closed to them, 65–6

Daily Telegraph, interviews Henlein, (1935) 133–4, (1937) 153

Daladier, Edouard (1884–1970), French Premier, 183; in London discussions, (Apr. 1938) 208–9, (Sept.) 268–70, 286; and CzS Social Democrats, 249, 266, 267, 268; at Munich, 290, 293, 294, 297, 302; War Minister, 302n; mentioned, 183, 288

Dawson, Geoffrey (1874–1944), editor of *The Times*, 251–2

Delbos, Yvon (1895–1956), French Foreign Minister, 157, 158, 164–6, 167

deportations: of Czechs and Moravians, planned by Hitler, 160; of Germans (1945–6), 263, 309

Dérer, Ivan (b. 1884), Social Democrat member of CzS government, 84

Die Zeit, Henlein's newspaper, financed from Berlin, 132

Disarmament Conference (1931), 98

Dulles, Allen (1893–1969), member of American delegation at Versailles, 44

Eden, Anthony (Earl of Avon, b. 1897), Foreign Secretary, 139; in discussions with French, 157, 158, 166; meets Beneš in Prague (1935), 175; suggests German contribution to general appeasement, 195–7; declares Munich Agreement broken by Hitler (1942), 303

education: for Germans and Czechs in Austria-Hungary, 9–10, 11; in CzS, 49, 59, 66, 77, 136, 149, 182

Eisenlohr, Ernst (1882–1959), German envoy in Prague: supports Czechs rather than Germans in CzS, 70; warnings from, 71, 150, 167–8; reports from, 141, 145; on Beneš, 151, 161–2, 177–8; and Agrarian Party, 169; and Sudeten Germans, 173, 174, 206–7, 216; describes Czech attitude to National Socialism, 178; Neurath's instructions to, 183; in May 1938 crisis, 188, 190–1; to British Minister on idea of 'neutralizing' CzS, 209, 224

elections in CzS: (1919 local), 52, 55; (1920), 63, 67, 68; (1925), 63, 72, 74, 80; (1929), 63, 79, 80–1, 137, 234;

Index

Index

Molisch, Paul, Austrian historian, 32, 34
Moravia (to 1918): Czech majority in, 2; undemocratic Diet of, 9; educational provision for Germans and Czechs in, 9–10; claimed by CzS, 16, 36, 43; Reichsrat and (1918), 22–3; Germans in, during transfer from Austria, 29; Southern, claimed by Austria, 42, 44; Beneš travels in (1935), 145
Moravian Compromise (1905), 8–10
Moravian National Committee (1918), Germans on, 29, 67
Moravská Ostrava, 'incident' at (Sept. 1938), 250
Munich Agreement: area lost to CzS by, 266; CzS not included in making, 290, 291–5; question of guarantee in, 295–7; capitulation of CzS to, 297–302; invalidity of, 302–4; aftermath of, 304–9; *The Times* on (1969), 252
Mussolini, Benito (1883–1945), at Munich, 290, 292, 293, 294

Národni Výbor (National Committee), CzS (1918), 16, 27, 28, 29–30, 67; hands over to Revolutionary National Assembly, 54; Imperial German Consul-General and, 86, 87
National Democratic Party, CzS, 76
National Socialism: Eisenlohr on CzS attitude to, 178; Henlein and *Weltanschauung* of, 206, 215, 220, 221, 226, 237, 239, 248
National Socialist Party, Austria, banned (1933), 105
National Socialist Party, CzS, leftist organization, 80–1
National Socialist Party, German, CzS, 63, 126; ask for subsidy from Germany, 75; gain support from Nationalists, 81, 104, 105, and from Agrarians, 105; dissolved (1933), 106, 113, 239; members of, in SdP, 115, 122, 143
National Socialist Party, Germany: economic crisis and, 82; electoral ascendancy of, 104; effect of self-sufficiency measures of, on German industry in CzS, 105; Henlein denies connections with, 117–18, 119, 133, 134, 135–6, 153, 164
Nationalities Statute, 203, 204, 215, 221, 225–6
Naumann, Friedrich (1860–1919), author of *Mitteleuropa*, 10
Nečas, Jaromír (1885–1945), Czech Social

Democrat member of CzS government, 83, 248, 265–6, 267, 268
Němec, Bohumil (1872–1966), Czech botanist, suggested as President, 130, 131
Neunteufel, Raimund (1862–1937), Styrian member of Austrian Reichsrat, 13
Neurath, Konstantin von (1873–1956), German Foreign Minister (1932–8), 140, 177, 198, 218, 255, 293; trial of, 183–4
Newton, Basil (later Sir Basil, 1889–1965), British Minister in Prague (1937–9): instructions to, 155–6, 220, 221, 222, 230, 253; reports from, 158, 189–90, 204; and SdP, 195, 226; and idea of 'neutralizing' CzS, 204, 209, 224; meets Beneš (Sept. 1938), 244, 245, 264; meets Hodža, 265; conveys British demands to Beneš, 279–80, 289; informed of CzS acceptance, 298
Nichols, Philip (later Sir Philip, 1894–1962), British diplomat, 156
Nicholson, Sir Godfrey (b. 1901), M.P., 214
Nicolson, Sir Harold (1886–1968), M.P., 214–15
non-aggression pacts, proposed 176–7, 180, 181, 284
Norton, Clifford (later Sir Clifford, b. 1891), of Foreign Office, 135

Oldofredi, Hieronymus, member of Austrian delegation at Versailles, 42
Olympic Games, Berlin (1936), 140
Opava (Troppau), temporary capital of 'Sudetenland' (1918), 22, 23, 28; industrialists at, 32
Option Treaty, between CzS and Germany (1938), for exchange of populations, 297
Orlando, Vittorio (1860–1952), Italian Foreign Minister, 44
Osusky, Stefan (b. 1889): CzS envoy in Paris, 220; signs agreement with Daladier, 302n

Pacher, Rafael (1857–1936), German Nationalist member of Austrian Reichsrat, 23
Palacký, František (1798–1876), Czech politician and historian, 7–8
pan-European ideas, 98, 99
pan-Germanism, 41; Henlein on, 117, 133; Koch on, 130; Beneš on, 248

330

Index

Rutha, Heinrich (1897–1937), assistant of Henlein, 158
Ruthenia (formerly Hungarian), in CzS, 41, 48
Ruthenians, in CzS, 50

Saar plebiscite (1935), 136
Saenger, Samuel (1864–1944), German Minister in Prague, 36, 70, 89
Sandys, Duncan (b. 1908), M.P., 214
Sargent, Orme (later Sir Orme, 1884–1962), of Foreign Office, 135, 138, 157, 306
Saxony: and German Nationalists (1918), 24–5, 27, 37; districts of CzS projecting into, 40
Schleicher, Kurt von (1882–1934), Reich Chancellor, 101
Schmidt, Paul (1899–1970), Hitler's interpreter, 292
Schmundt, Hitler's adjutant, 189
Schober, Johann (1874–1932), Austrian Foreign Minister, 98
Schubert, Carl von (1882–1947), of German Foreign Ministry, 64, 95–6, 99
Schuschnigg, Kurt von (b. 1897), Austrian Federal Chancellor, 157, 169, 196, 199
Schwerin-Krosigk, Count Lutz (b. 1887), German Finance Minister (1933–45), 120
Sebekovsky, Wilhelm (b. 1907), assistant to Henlein, 217, 239, 247
Selby, Sir Walford (1881–1965), British diplomat, 213n
self-determination, 16, 30, 31–2; only meaningful if state is economically viable, 17, 20–1, 43; at Versailles, 38–9, 42, 44; for Sudeten Germans, Koch on, 63–4; Henlein aims to deprive Czechs of right to, 163; Chamberlain and Halifax on, 262
Seliger, Josef (1870–1920), leader of German-Bohemian workers, 3; deputy-governor of German-Bohemia, 23, 29–30, 34, 42; leader of German Social Democrats, CzS, 52, 69
Serbs, Czechs and, 10
Seton-Watson, Robert W. (1897–1951), 16
Seyss-Inquart, Arthur (1891–1946), Austrian Nazi politician, 163, 196
Silesia: Czech minority in, 2; claimed by CzS, 16, 36, 43; Reichsrat and (1918), 22–3; industrialists in, 32; merged with Moravia for administration (1927), 78

Simon, Sir John (Viscount Simon, 1873–1954): Foreign Secretary, 103; Chancellor of the Exchequer, 260, 273, 281
Sinclair, Sir Archibald (Lord Thurso, 1890–1970), Liberal leader, 214, 309n
Slovak People's Party, 76, 131
Slovakia (formerly Hungarian), in CzS, 16, 41, 84, 124; educational institutions in, 66, 84
Slovaks: under Hungary, 2, 4, 59; proposed union of Czechs and (1848), 7–8; in Revolutionary National Assembly (1918), 54, 57; Chamberlain and, 271; declare independence (Mar. 1939), 297, 306
Slovenes, 13
Social Democratic (All-Austrian) Party, Austria: Brno Nationalities Programme of (1899), 3–4, 13; force electoral reform (1907), 6
Social Democratic (Czech) Party, Austria, 14
Social Democratic (German) Party, Austria: members of, in Bohemia, Moravia and Silesia, 13, 14, 21
Social Democratic Party (Czech), CzS, 72, 80, 85, 121; and German Social Democrats, 81–2; number of votes for (1935), 124; join with German Social Democrats in appeal to Blum (Sept. 1938), 248–9
Social Democratic Party (German), CzS: in temporary coalition with German Nationalists (1918), 21; demonstrations called by, lead to bloodshed; 34; votes for, 52, 63, 80; in discussions with government, 56; question of place in government for, 67, 68, 85; lose ground in 1925 elections, 72; and Czech Social Democrats, 81–2; actively resist Nazis, 105, 107, 108, 121; Henlein on, 169, 171; assure Beneš of their loyalty (1938), 170, 172; ousted from government by threats from SdP, 172, 195; votes for, in local elections (1938), 223; present memorandum to Runciman (Sept. 1938), 233–4; join with Czech Social Democrats in appeal to Blum, 248–9; urgently appeal to British and French, 279; Chamberlain and, 282–3; Daladier and, 286; comment on Munich in newspaper of, 292; proclamation by (1 Oct. 1938), 300; Gestapo and, 301; as displaced persons, 301–2

332

Index